One Hundred Years
of Psychological Research in America

One Hundred Years
of Psychological Research in America

G. Stanley Hall and
the Johns Hopkins Tradition

EDITED BY

Stewart H. Hulse and Bert F. Green, Jr.

The Johns Hopkins University Press
BALTIMORE AND LONDON

The Johns Hopkins University Press
701 West 40th Street
Baltimore, Maryland 21211
The Johns Hopkins Press Ltd, London

The paper in this book is acid-free and meets the guidelines for permanence and durability of the Committee on Production Guidelines for Book Longevity of the Council on Library Resources.

LIBRARY OF CONGRESS CATALOGING IN PUBLICATION DATA
Main entry under title:
One hundred years of psychological research in America.
  Includes index.
  1. Psychology—Research—United States—History—
Congresses. 2. Hall, G. Stanley (Granville Stanley),
1844–1924—Congresses. 3. Johns Hopkins University.
Dept. of Psychology—History—Congresses. I. Hulse,
Stewart H. II. Green, Bert F. III. Title: 100 years
of psychological research in America.
BF76.5.O54 1985   150'.72073   85–8082
ISBN 0–8018–2606–3 (alk. paper)

Contents

Contributors

Mortimer Herbert Appley, President, Clark University, Worcester, Mass.

William Bevan, The John D. and Catherine T. MacArthur Foundation, Chicago, Ill.

Roger Brown, Department of Psychology and Social Relations, Harvard University, Cambridge, Mass.

Alphonse Chapanis, Department of Psychology, The Johns Hopkins University, Baltimore, Md.

Doris R. Entwisle, Departments of Social Relations and Engineering Science, The Johns Hopkins University, Baltimore, Md.

Wendell R. Garner, Department of Psychology, Yale University, New Haven, Conn.

Bert F. Green, Jr., Department of Psychology, The Johns Hopkins University, Baltimore, Md.

Stewart H. Hulse, Department of Psychology, The Johns Hopkins University, Baltimore, Md.

David G. Lavond, Department of Psychology, Stanford University, Stanford, Calif.

David A. McCormick, Department of Psychology, Stanford University, Stanford, Calif.

George A. Miller, Department of Psychology, Princeton University, Princeton, N.J.

Philip J. Pauly, Department of History, Rutgers, The State University, New Brunswick, N.J.

Pamela B. Sklar, Department of Neuroscience, The Johns Hopkins University School of Medicine, Baltimore, Md.

Solomon H. Snyder, Department of Neuroscience, The Johns Hopkins University School of Medicine, Baltimore, Md.

Philip Teitelbaum, Department of Psychology, University of Florida, Gainesville, Fla.

Richard F. Thompson, Department of Psychology, Stanford University, Stanford, Calif.

Preface

Centennials occur every hundred years, of course, and there is a happy predilection to choose them to commemorate important events. In the general biobehavioral sciences, the centennial (celebrated at the University of Chicago) of the publication of Darwin's *Origin of Species* in 1959 was one. And for experimental psychologists, the centennial in 1976 of Wilhelm Wundt's founding of the field in Leipzig, Germany, was another. Many Americans went to Germany to study with Wundt and brought back the new psychology to American universities, but by 1880 none had established a true laboratory for research and for graduate education in psychology. That task was undertaken at the Johns Hopkins University by Granville Stanley Hall in 1883, and Hall's accomplishment provided, in 1983, the occasion for another important centennial. That recognition of Hall's accomplishment was celebrated at Johns Hopkins by gathering together a group of distinguished scholars for a symposium in the fall of 1983. This book grew from the papers presented at that symposium.

Planning for the centennial began in the Department of Psychology at Johns Hopkins in 1981. At that time, a centennial committee was formed from faculty and graduate students within the department. The committee included Alphonse Chapanis, Jeffrey Cynx, Howard Egeth, William Garvey, Stewart Hulse, Richard Katz, Priscilla Kehoe, Donna Kwilosz, Michael McCloskey, Wilson Shaffer, Susan Spear, and Warren Torgerson. After appropriate discussion within the department, the committee invited a list of speakers and moderators to gather in Baltimore on October 12 and 13, 1983. The remarks of the speakers appear in this volume.

Alphonse Chapanis was invited to give the first G. Stanley Hall Lecture, a series that the department will continue on a regular basis in the years to come. His remarks, which speak not only to his professional interests but also to the more modern history of the department, appear as chapter 3.

Several psychologists who earned their doctorates at Johns Hopkins returned to serve as presiders and moderators at conference activities.

They were Professor Lloyd Bond, of the University of Pittsburgh; Dr. Iris Rotberg, Director of Research at the National Institute of Education; Dr. Herbert Weingartner, of the National Institute of Mental Health; and Dr. Hilda Wing, of the U.S. Army Institute for the Behavioral and Social Sciences.

The conference was particularly honored by the presence of Dr. Mortimer Appley, President of Clark University, where G. Stanley Hall continued to make his mark on psychology after he left Johns Hopkins. Dr. Appley's remarks, which appear as chapter 1, were delivered at the conference banquet on the evening of October 12. They provide great insight into the personality of Hall, the young man, and the early energetic traits that shaped his beginning contributions to psychology and to Johns Hopkins. They also tell much about Hall, the mature man, and the events that shaped his later contributions to Clark University and the psychology of the early 1900s.

Debts of gratitude for the successful organization and management of conference activities are due many people besides those who served on the centennial committee. In particular, Casey Camponeschi, Marianna Davis, Joan Krach, Eileen Kelmartin, Bernice Schlenger, Millie Schwienteck, and Nancy Hulse deserve special thanks for their patience and attention to myriad details before, during, and after the conference.

Finally, we gratefully acknowledge the financial help of the Johns Hopkins University, and, in particular, the time, care, and attention of Ross Jones, Vice President for Public Affairs. Special appreciation goes to all the many alumni and friends (both corporate and individual) of the Department of Psychology who gave unstintingly in amounts large and small to assure that the conference would take place. Their names appear on p. 399. Neither the conference nor this commemorative volume would have happened without their support.

Stewart H. Hulse
Bert F. Green, Jr.

Introduction

This book honors the first one hundred years of psychological research in America. More specifically, it honors the traditions established at the Johns Hopkins University by G. Stanley Hall, who formalized the beginning of the research enterprise in this country by founding the first laboratory of psychology in America at Johns Hopkins in 1883. The laboratory itself, initially, and those around it (including Hall) were to endure only a few years—a mere tick of the historical clock of behavioral science. But, along with others of the time elsewhere, Hall scattered in America the seeds of an experimental approach to the study of the mind—and its courier, human and animal action—which revolutionized behavioral science in the Western world. We are currently at a milestone in the germination of that approach as we uncover major pathways in the search for both the behavioral expression of the mind and its biological substrate. This book reflects not only an image of Hall's contributions to Johns Hopkins and to American psychology set in the framework of history but also the current countenance of some important facets of the science he fostered.

It is, of course, impossible to do justice to one hundred years of any single aspect of psychology, much less several, within the scope of a limited number of essays, and it is inherently difficult to provide an organizing theme for them—beyond that provided by the mere occurrence of the centennial event that occasioned the book in the first place. Nevertheless, some threads run through the collection of essays which draw them together, weaving a broader picture of Hall, Johns Hopkins, and the past, present, and future of American psychology.

First, a certain historical perspective surrounds Hall the man and the events in psychology which began during his period of influence. Some of these events took place during his tenure at Johns Hopkins, while many of them occurred at Johns Hopkins after he left. But they were, in a certain measure, dependent upon scientific traditions in psychology, such as laboratory research, that Hall helped to establish.

Second, the essays are organized into a broad scheme that begins with the molecular and moves to the molar. Psychology and behavioral science are very molecular when they engage in the search for the roots of behavior in the cells and chemistry of the central nervous system. In this regard, psychology shares interests with the most biologically oriented of the neurosciences. Psychology becomes molar when it moves to the study of behavior qua behavior and examines the complexities of memory, perception, and language. Psychology reaches its broadest scope when it examines the behavior of organisms interacting in groups. This molecular-molar distinction is easily discernible as the chapters unfold.

Third, the essays refract the molecular-molar dimension into two major aspects of modern experimental psychology: psychobiology and cognitive psychology. These fields are noteworthy because they represent two active fronts in the study of behavior: the search for the functionally significant units in the physiological substrate underlying behavior on the one hand, and, on the other, the search for the meaningful organizing principles for those units in overt behavior itself. In the long run, such organization must hold not only for individuals but also for individuals acting in groups. Experimental psychology and its sister disciplines are currently struggling with a fresh sense of urgency for a rapprochement between these fields. They must by definition share a most intimate relationship, yet there is a curious void between them as they undergo modern scientific scrutiny. In a real sense, the ancient mind-body problem, in the contemporary guise of the brain-behavior problem, has become reified. The essays of this volume speak, implicitly at least, to these two faces of psychology and, in illuminating them, may foster the rapprochement that must come.

Finally, each essay may be read for its own sake as an up-to-date account of the growth of theory and research on an important, timely topic in biobehavioral science. The authors are all significant and visible contributors to their respective fields. Their accomplishments reflect the state of the art; their ideas should shape much of the future.

Historical Perspective

Hall was a singular figure, a man of great intellect, enormous self-confidence (salted with a touch of egotism), and driving, restless energy. Mortimer Herbert Appley, an experimental psychologist and president of Clark University in 1983—an office first filled by Hall—documents this all so well in his chapter "G. Stanley Hall: Vow on Mount Owen." Mount Owen is a rather small hill in Massachusetts, Appley tells us, but large in significance for Hall and the things he set out to accomplish.

Hall started things. He founded not only the laboratory at Johns Hopkins but also the American Psychological Association, the *Psy-*

chological Review, some other journals, and—perhaps of greater significance with the perspective of a hundred years—the tradition of scientific inquiry that has characterized psychology at Johns Hopkins. Before the 1930s, that tradition included James Baldwin and, most important for psychology as we know it today, John B. Watson. Some would argue, perhaps correctly, that the tradition reflects itself most clearly in the students who received their graduate education at Johns Hopkins and left to found other laboratories and departments. Philip J. Pauly captures all this—and much more—in a history that emphasizes the early years of the department.

After World War II, Clifford T. Morgan was invited to Johns Hopkins to reestablish a department of psychology that had fallen victim to the vicissitudes of academic life at the university in the 1930s. Morgan was a many-sided man; like Hall, he was a founder of things. He had a great gift for identifying talented young people and attracting them to a renaissance of psychology at Johns Hopkins. Many of these people have contributed to the centennial conference—and so to this book. Among them was Alphonse Chapanis, who gives us a historical picture of psychology, especially human factors, as it grew at Johns Hopkins with himself, Morgan, Garner, and others in the 1950s and 1960s.

Hulse and Green, in a brief chapter written for the book, bring the history of the department up-to-date. The legacy of the past is clearly present in psychology at Johns Hopkins as it exists in 1983. There is a strong tradition of research psychology, some of it in the biological and neuropsychological tradition, some in the various facets of human experimental and quantitative psychology, some encompassed by the broader framework of social psychology (and sociology) and personality theory. No doubt, the tradition that Hall helped to establish will shape the history to be written in the hundred years to come.

The Molecular-Molar Dimension in Psychology and Behavioral Science

What are the molecular building blocks, the biologically defined units of mind? Are they central to an adequate scientific description of the behavior of living organisms? On the one hand, there is the conviction that an adequate analysis of behavior rests on the assumption of an undivided, causally related dimension beginning with behavior at its most complex and reducing by stages to the physicochemical structure of the brain. On the other hand, however, there is the conviction that although analysis is appropriate at either of these levels, there is a fundamental discontinuity between them that need not be bridged to provide an adequate account of behavior.

Without doubt, these are hefty issues. They are currently of interest to psychologists and also to philosophers, and their consideration is often undertaken with some heat. The molar-molecular dimension, discontinuous or not, heated or cool, is fundamental and serves to organize the chapters of this book.

Psychobiology and the Units of Behavior

To begin with a cup of coffee (heated to be sure) may seem casual, if not strange indeed, but I have never appreciated my cup of coffee so much until I read Snyder and Sklar's account of caffeine's social history, its chemical relatives, and its putative role in controlling physiological function in the human nervous system. Over the years, the classic investigations of Snyder and his colleagues into the pharmacology of the brain have spoken volumes to the role of chemistry in assuring transmission of information from cell to cell and in defining a general "tone" governing broad aspects of brain function. This chapter adds significantly to that work and illustrates how knowledge grows in this important field.

Snyder and Sklar illustrate the search for the functional chemical substrate of the nervous system. Thompson, McCormick, and Lavond take the next step in showing how careful analysis can isolate a sharply defined locus in the mammalian brain for the functional unit controlling a simple, discrete, learned response: the classically conditioned eyelid reflex in the rabbit. Lashley sought the engram in vain; near the end of his career he despaired that it existed in any form that could be localized spatially. Thompson and his collaborators seem to have found it. Their work constitutes another reaffirmation—along with the results of modern radiographic techniques—for the spatial localization of psychological processes in the brain. Of course, it remains to be seen what the engram is in the physico-chemico-anatomical sense, but at least, for a simple, well-defined system that changes with experience, we now know where to look. Perhaps we shall have the remaining answers shortly.

Philip Teitelbaum and his colleagues have spent many years in a distinguished analysis of the role of the lateral hypothalamus in the control of behavior, especially with regard to the role of this and other thalamic centers in the modulation of food intake. According to his earlier view, recovery of function in this system (adequate appetite and control of food intake) is best characterized as a succession of discrete stages of recovery, each rather independent of its predecessor. Now, he points to evidence showing that recovery is better described as the progressive reemergence of functional behavioral units that are inhibited or otherwise masked following damage to the central nervous system—units that are there, in fact, all the time. His generalization of this principle to other systems is fascinating and provides an important model that will no doubt continue to serve psychology well.

Cognitive Psychology and the Larger Organization of Behavior

The foregoing chapters provide functional neurophysiological footprints along a dimension from neurochemistry, to small units of learned behavior, to the control of larger sensorimotor systems. The remaining chapters illustrate how these footprints must eventually lead toward the highly organized behavior characteristic of human sensory perception, thinking, and language—and to the articulation of those processes in social interaction.

Wendell R. Garner takes the first step toward such organization in his summary of many years of research on structural processes underlying human perception. He places his work within the general framework of critical realism, that branch of epistemology that sees in perception an interaction between the physical stimulus and the experiencing observer. He claims shared ground with Roger Shepard, Julian Hochberg, and James Gibson (though, as Garner acknowledges, the latter might have demurred). Garner then describes two main themes of research that have occupied him and his students for a good part of the last twenty years. The first is the problem of pattern goodness; the second is the issue of how stimulus dimensions interact with each other in perception. The unfolding of the research leading to and developing these concepts is an elegant story from the experience of a major figure in the field. To him we owe, among much else, the application of information-theoretic analysis to Gestalt principles in perception, and the identification of the integral-separable distinction in the interaction of stimulus dimensions. These ideas, and the other facts and concepts surrounding them, will continue to play an important role in further analyses of perceptual organization. What is more, they clearly identify some of the most salient phenomena that psychobiologists will eventually have to account for—perhaps near the beginning of their functional analysis of the central nervous system.

Language is a supreme cognitive achievement of humans. Roger Brown has spent a good part of his career in the study of that achievement, and his contribution to this book deals with some new facts at the interface between language as such and language as an intimate part of the cognitive process. Linguistic relativity, as Brown reminds us, is "the view that the cognitive processes of a human being—perception, memory, inference, deduction—vary with the structural characteristics—lexicon, morphology, syntax—of the language he speaks." Put another way, people sharing a common language also necessarily share a certain way of thinking and expressing ideas that is a direct function of experience unique to their culture. Often called the "Whorfian hypothesis" after one of its originators, this idea has had great intuitive appeal and face validity in analyzing the mistakes and misunderstandings that sometimes occur among those speaking different languages. In its purest form, the hypothesis was laid to rest some time ago by Brown and his students, among others, as illustrated through some of the wonderful experiments described in this chapter. However, the hypothesis has recently reappeared through the work of Alfred Bloom on the counterfactual conditional in English as compared with Chinese. The Chinese, Bloom claimed, were relatively incapable of evaluating the logical consequences implied by statements expressed in a form (highly familiar in English) such as "John was not a psychologist, but if he were, he would have sent Dick to the hospital." In response to the query, "Was Dick sent to the hospital?," for example, Bloom would have found many Chinese agreeing (or at least not disagreeing) that in all probability Dick was sick in bed.

Does linguistic relativity exist in the guise of the counterfactual conditional? Read on and see. The research leading to the new answer is just as marvelous as that leading to the original.

How are cognitive processes to be understood? George A. Miller asks this question in the context of a survey of strategies that have been used to analyze cognitive processes. Because the strategies do not seem to have produced natural, enduring fracture lines, Miller calls them "dismemberments." Dismemberment began with the faculty psychologies, marked associationism and the reflex, and now dwells within the computer. Its methods have included mental chronometry, and more recently, division into modular units, modeled after computer subroutines, that are functionally (and therefore analytically) independent. As a consequence, Miller claims, current cognitive psychology is retracing a path in which initial discoveries or insights that appear from somewhere in whole cloth dissolve (are dismembered) into a series of microprinciples or microsystems that establish little contact with each other or with that final arbiter, the real world. He urges synthesis and the recognition that it is only with an eye to synthesis that analysis makes sense. Theories often grow from collections of facts achieved through analysis or by accidental discovery, but we should recognize that more often the process is reversed—theory (even just a good idea) provides the truly adequate stimulus for the analytic process.

The final point in this book's journey along the molecular-molar dimension in the organization of behavior appears with Doris R. Entwisle's discussion of her recent studies of certain social interactions during the preadolescent years of life. The work is in the best tradition of G. Stanley Hall, who initiated research in child development at Clark University and wrote about it in his book *Adolescence*.

In a sense, Entwisle's own intellectual career is a reflection of the molecular-molar dimension. She began her graduate education with an interest in physiological psychology, she tells us, and moved from there to child development—especially as it is affected by stresses associated with "major life transitions." The stresses in question are those experienced by parents and children as the child first enters school, on the one hand, and, on the other, those occasioned by cesarean delivery. This chapter reports results obtained from studies of the latter problem.

Entwisle's chapter is long and rich and will no doubt provide a fertile source of information for many investigators for a long time to come. It makes sense, for example, that in the event of a cesarean birth, mother and child should be separated for as short a time as the procedure permits. However, it is a little disheartening (but, with hindsight, probably inevitable) to learn that parents' image of themselves as adequate parents declines somewhat after the birth of a child. But it is pleasing to find that this is neither more nor less the case for children who are born normally than for those born by cesarean section. The rigors of parenting are real regardless of how children enter the world!

The Future

We have had several views in historical perspective of the science G. Stanley Hall helped initiate, and we have seen how that science is reflected in today's molecular-molar levels of analysis and organization. If the chapters of this book represent major slices of current research in the behavioral sciences, what of the future?

As William Bevan shows so clearly in his chapter on this topic, psychology has become a vast enterprise measured against the standards of Hall's day. He documents the differences well. Among many other things, they include the enormous growth in the American Psychological Association that Hall founded, the changes in the fields of psychology that psychologists now choose to pursue as careers, the changing demographics of the profession that necessarily follows from all of this, and the revolution in the funding of science with its correlated impact on the very organization of universities. Perhaps most important, there is increasing concern with a metaphysics for the pursuit of inquiry into matters psychological (Bevan echos Miller here). Thus, we have Kuhnian paradigms (in original and modulated forms), and we have foxes and hedgehogs among us (read the chapter to find out who they are). As Bevan rightly observes, there is much to suggest a fractured, ill-organized, rather aimless countenance to modern psychology.

Should we therefore despair? Bevan thinks not. He sees, in the increasing interplay between the pure and the applied in the search for knowledge, for example, great hope for our future. He adds that we may be returning to ever-important "cosmological questions" about science, but with fresh approaches based on evolution, development, and adaptation that will assure a major role for psychology. Finally, he reminds us that as we continue our voyage into the perils and joys of the future, it is, indeed, the journey that is everything.

Would Hall approve of the psychology of today? We will, of course, never know; nor will we know his speculations about the course of events over the next one hundred years. But it is to be hoped that he would be proud of the discipline he fostered as it is reflected in the small sample of modern psychology contained in the chapters of this book.

A Final Word

This book is a testament in a major sense to the past and present contributions that men and women associated with the Johns Hopkins University have made to behavioral science. It would have been truly presumptuous, indeed impossible, to limit Hall's centennial celebration to individuals associated directly with that institution. But perhaps a bit of pride will be forgiven for the extent to which the essays do reflect the accomplishments of people who have spent part or all of their professional careers at Johns Hopkins. No doubt, Hall would have been proud of this aspect of his legacy, too.

Stewart H. Hulse

PART I

Historical Perspective

1. G. Stanley Hall: Vow on Mount Owen

Mortimer Herbert Appley

When Granville Stanley Hall was a young man of fourteen, he climbed 1500-ft. Mount Owen, near his family's farm in Ashfield, Massachusetts, and, during a day of soul searching, "vowed to himself he would not be a farmer, but would amount to something in the world" (Wilson 1914, 23). Among other decisions young Hall made on that mountain was one to go on to college and, finally, that he "would not return [to Mount Owen] until he had made a name for himself in the great world" (ibid. 23). I have chosen this "vow on Mount Owen" as the title of this chapter because Hall himself later solemnized the experience and because it shows how deep the roots of his ambitions went. It is fascinating to note that at the time of Wilson's *Sketch* of Hall, in 1914, when Hall was nearing seventy years of age, was twenty-five years into his Clark University presidency, and had achieved eminence in several areas, he apparently felt that the time had still not come to return to climb Mount Owen.

In fact, very few people can look back at their lives and see as much accomplished as in the full life of G. Stanley Hall. And yet, one wonders as one reviews his life and accomplishments, how much more he might have been able to achieve had men of greater power but lesser vision shared his dreams and supported, rather than contravened, his ambitions.

It was my privilege to be named president of Clark University almost four score and seven years after Hall had inaugurated that post. I am the sixth president of Clark, but the first psychologist to hold that position since Hall. In my Opening Convocation Remarks, in the fall of 1974, I had the temerity to suggest that I would hope to continue—I believe I said complete—the job Hall had begun. Little did I realize at the time the impossibility of recapturing a propitious moment in history which had come and gone, nor did I understand, at the time, the limited power of a university presidency or the subtlety and complexity of the forces arrayed against a president, no matter what he or she seeks to accomplish. Whatever the problems of a modern presidency, however, I doubt that anyone anywhere has faced the obstacles in the way of his admittedly lofty aspirations that Hall did when he became president of the new university being formed in Worcester, Massachusetts, in 1888. But I get ahead of my story.

The Early Years

G. Stanley Hall was born in 1846 on his parents' farm in Ashfield, Massachusetts. A descendant from old New England stock going back to the Mayflower on both sides, his father's lineage was traceable to Elder William Brewster and his mother's to John and Priscilla Alden (Hall 1923; Wilson 1914). Unlike John Alden, however, as we know, G. Stanley would very definitely speak for himself on any number of occasions throughout his life.

The Ashfield Halls have been described as "substantial, hard-working, common sense farmers, without much ambition or much education," though G. Stanley's parents were exceptions to this tradition in that they "were more anxious for an education than other members of their family" (Wilson 1914, 13). Stanley's mother spent two years at Albany Female Seminary, one of the few institutions for women at the time. She is said to have passed on a strong love of learning to her children. Both parents taught school for awhile, and Stanley's father served in the Massachusetts legislature. Their home was alive with much reading, writing, debating, and lively discussion of public men and events. Each member of the family kept a journal, which was read aloud, and familiarity with the gospel (through his mother) and the law and public events (through his father) gave Stanley interests far beyond farming or broom making (his father's trade for awhile, at which Stanley also became proficient).

As a youth, Stanley spent considerable time wandering the fields around Ashfield, hunting rifle in hand, his lively imagination peopling the environment with characters and animals he transposed from the classics and other reading he avidly devoured.

Hall's decision to go to college, part of his vow on Mount Owen, was supported by his mother, who saw it as a means to his entering the ministry. Despite his father's early opposition, Stanley was enrolled in Williston Seminary in Easthampton. Then, after teaching district school in the Ashfield area briefly, he went on to Williams College, graduating in 1867. Hall spent the following year at Union Theological Seminary in New York City.

Limits of time and space do not permit me to explore at any length the personal characteristics already in evidence in the young Hall. He, in his *Life and Confessions* (1923), and his many biographers (cf. Ross 1972) allude to unresolved problems between Stanley and his father and describe Stanley's bullying behavior toward his siblings and toward weaker other

boys, his fascination with sex and worries about onanism, his estrange-
ment from the less intellectual people of his acquaintance in Ashfield
(though not from the natural beauty of the area), his exceedingly strong
desire to rise above the mundane, his near reverence for new ideas and for
the men who develop them, his high level of energy, the amount and
quality of his writing, his speaking and musical skills (even as a youth), and
his insatiable curiosity. Both negative and positive traits were to be influential in shaping his decisions and affecting his interactions throughout his
life.

Hall, Philosophy, and the Ministry

Hall freely indulged his broad interests both at Williams College and in
New York City. He wrote and read poetry, participated in oratory and
drama, studied philosophy avidly, and taught school and tutored to earn
money. In New York he systematically explored the streets, seeing much
of the seedy part of the city, attended theater regularly, listened to lectures
and sermons by famous speakers and preachers, one of whom, Henry
Ward Beecher, befriended him. Recognizing that Hall's interests were
more in philosophy than theology, Beecher convinced Hall to go to Germany to study and obtained a $1,000 loan for him from philanthropist
Henry W. Sage to finance his trip. (It is an interesting measure of Hall's
confidence in his own future that he would, at age twenty-two, accept so
large an interest-bearing loan with no foreseeable means of repaying it.)

In 1868, Hall began the first of what were to be three sojourns in
Germany. He studied the language, walked extensively through the Rhi-
neland and in Switzerland, and studied philosophy under Dorner,
Michelet, Altmann, and von Hartmann. He later served briefly as an
amateur correspondent in the 1870 war, and also wrote articles and stories for American magazines to earn money to keep himself in Germany,
though he was in debt when he finally left in 1871.

Returning to America, Hall accepted an offer to teach logic and ethics at
the University of Minnesota, only to have it withdrawn when he explained
what he had been studying abroad. The Minnesota president believed Hall
was "too Germanized" and was certain that Hall's history of philosophy
would "unsettle men and teach them to hold no opinions" (Hall 1923,
196). As we later know, this was to be only one of many occasions in
which Hall found himself ahead of the *Zeitgeist!*

Apparently lacking reasonable alternatives, Hall returned to Union
Theological Seminary to complete his B.D. degree and, for a ten-week
period, actually became pastor of a church in Cowdersport, Pennsylvania;
he was not satisfied with a career in the ministry and soon left it.

After his death, Sara Carolyn Fisher, one of Hall's doctoral students at

Clark, wrote in the *American Journal of Psychology* in 1925: "Stanley Hall was possessed of a vigor, curiosity and intolerance of restraint which made adjustment to the piety and complacent aridity of the New England of the [18] sixties an impossibility. The obvious opening for the intellectually interested individual of his day—the ministry—became increasingly distasteful, and his study in Europe, with the deep draughts of the higher criticism then taken, led to a widening of the breach which completed his unfitness for a theological career" (2).

And Hall's own awareness of his mismatch with a career in the ministry is nicely illustrated in this vignette he later offered of his experience while at Union Theological Seminary: "After preaching our trial sermon before the institution we visited the president for criticisms. When I entered his study for this purpose, instead of discussing my sermon with me he at once knelt and prayed that I be shown the true light and saved from mortal errors of doctrine, and then excused me without a word" (Hall 1923, 178).

Antioch College

Not a man of means, Hall moved from his ministerial post to succeed his later Johns Hopkins colleague, George S. Morris, as full-time resident tutor in the family of investment banker, Jesse Seligman, in the Gramercy Park section of New York City. In 1872, still in his early twenties, he accepted a teaching post in English at Antioch College in Ohio, where he was to remain for almost four years, serving in a diverse number of roles, both curricular and extracurricular. Of his Antioch experience, Hall wrote: "My chair was a whole settee. I taught English language and literature, German, French, philosophy in all its branches, preached, was impressario for the college theatre, chorister, and conducted the rhetorical exercises, and spread out generally" (Wilson 1914, 58). And in a sidenote, reflecting his sense of history and his veneration of men of learning and of innovative leadership, Hall later wrote that one of his treasured memories of his Antioch days was of the spirit of Horace Mann, the distinguished Massachusetts political leader and educator, who founded the college in Yellow Springs. Hall recalled, with obvious pride, if not derived glory, that in his first year there he slept "in the very room and bed in which [Mann] died" (Wilson 1914, 58).

Hall gave of himself generously while at Antioch, as was his wont. In addition to the "settee" already described, he lectured widely on and off campus and was active in the life of both college and the village. In an interesting example of self-sacrifice, Hall described an episode where the faculty were upset with a local group (called the "Great American Literary Bureau") that sold essays to students and sought to put them out of business. Hall took on the task, saying to his colleagues: "You have your homes here and your families. The one who undertakes this investigation will have to contend with unpopularity and bitterness, and possibly will have to go. I am free, and I will do it" (Wilson 1914, 55). He exposed the culprits, suffered the wrath of the townspeople, and left Antioch shortly thereafter.

Hall and Harvard

Hall's departure from Antioch was the result of other motivations, as well. Restless and ambitious, he did not see a future for himself there. Stimulated by reading Wilhelm Wundt's *Physiological Psychology,* which had just been published, Hall decided that he should return to Germany and left Antioch to do so in 1876. However, he got no farther than Cambridge, Massachusetts, where he stopped on his way abroad. Hall accepted a tutorship in English at Harvard, in the hope that he might be able to transfer into philosophy and psychology. No such invitation was to be forthcoming, even though he worked with William James and got to know him quite well. Hall also did research on the muscular perception of space with H. P. Bowditch at the Harvard Medical School, based on which he was granted a doctorate in psychology (the first degree so identified in America) by Harvard's philosophy department in 1878. James sat on his doctoral committee.

Hall's couple of years at Harvard were not easy ones. He was paid only two-thirds of what he had been earning at Antioch and was burdened with a heavy teaching load, despite which he managed his studies with James, Bowditch, and others. We again see Hall's sense of humor and awareness of his own vanity and aspirations when he wrote that he accepted the relatively unattractive Harvard offer in order to attain "what was then to ambitious young students, at least to those reared near the heart of New England who daily pray with their faces toward the golden statehouse dome, the supreme earthly felicity of a chair, or even a footstool, at Harvard" (quoted by Wilson 1914, 63, from chap. 4 of Hall's *Educational Problems).*

Before proceeding further, let us pause to look at the developing Hall. In his early life and early professional career(s), he was a young man of seemingly boundless energy, of dreams and ambition, of respect for men of learning and of innovative thought and desire to emulate them in the highest; he was clearly willing to give of himself freely, unselfishly, and fully to earn any status or success he might achieve. He had humor and self-insight, but these did not prevent him from being often impatient, sometimes rebellious and intolerant of opposition, and at times devious (in fact, if not in intent) to achieve his ends. These latter traits, somewhat foreshadowed in his early life, became more evident later in his simultaneous careers as psychologist-pedagogue and academic administrator, and both contributed to his successes and limited his full achievements and his satisfaction with them.

Hall's Second German Sojourn

Hall returned to Germany immediately after receiving his doctorate from Harvard. He spent a year working primarily in physiology at Berlin. He then moved to Leipzig to be Wundt's first American student but apparently did no work of his own in Wundt's laboratory. Disappointed with his experience with Wundt (James 1920, 2: 17–18), Hall pursued research on the physiology of muscles and then moved back to Berlin to work with Hermann Helmholz (who, unbeknownst to Hall, had turned his attention from physiology to physics).

While in Berlin, Hall married in September 1879 Cornelia Fisher, a former Antioch acquaintance who was there studying art. Now thirty-three and married but not yet settled into a career, Hall "decided that the way to make a living was to apply psychology to education" (Watson 1968, 371); he spent the next year visiting education centers to study how to prepare himself for such application.

Returning to the United States in the fall of 1880, still without a prospect of a job, the Halls settled near Boston where, to Hall's surprise (and ultimate salvation), President Charles W. Eliot asked him to give a series of Saturday public lectures on education under Harvard sponsorship (though not for Harvard credit), which were so well attended and well received that he was able to successfully repeat them a second year.

The Johns Hopkins University

The turning point in Hall's as yet unsettled life came as a result of his Harvard-sponsored public lecture series. His reputation as a popular lecturer led to an invitation from President Daniel Coit Gilman of the then new Johns Hopkins University to give a similar series in 1881–1882 in Baltimore, which Hall did, again successfully. This, in turn, led Gilman to appoint Hall to a three-year, part-time lectureship in psychology at the university in March 1882 and to provide him an annual grant of $1,000 to build up a psychological laboratory. It was thus at Johns Hopkins where Hall's career as a psychologist and the discipline of experimental psychology in America were both finally to begin.

In her appreciation of Hall, Carolyn Fisher provides an insightful summary of Hall's problems to this point and why he needed a new kind of institution to make use of his peculiar talents:

His spirit of criticism of prevailing trends, his revolt, and his enthusiasm for European institutions aroused the distrust of the type of college president then common [as note his nonappointment at Minnesota, cited earlier and footnoted by Fisher], and so served as a handicap in most of the academic openings of the time. These very qualities, however, rendered him peculiarly adapted to such an institution as the newly founded and for psychology very happily timed Johns Hopkins University, whose first president . . . was suffused with ideals of scientific advancement rather than those of the prevailing propaganda. (Fisher 1925, 2–3)

Despite his lectureship appointment, however, Hall was by no means assured of a permanent post at Johns Hopkins. There was only one chair to be filled, and Gilman continued to seek a prominent philosopher for it. Failing this, he could still choose either of Hall's two colleagues in philosophy, philosophic idealist George S. Morris or philosopher-physicist Charles S. Peirce, over Hall for the post in question.

Already thirty-six, married, and now with two young children, Hall was most anxious to obtain the permanent post at Johns Hopkins, or at any other institution for that matter. As it turned out, several factors worked in his favor. First, Gilman was unable to attract a noncontroversial senior outsider. Then, Peirce was summarily dismissed, early in 1884, as a result of derogatory personal information that was made known to Gilman "from an unidentified source." Third, Morris's quiet manner and modest temper, narrower philosophic interests, and less acceptable theism were no match for Hall's more forceful presence, his more compatible (for Johns Hopkins) scientific and medical orientation, his careful avoidance of confrontation with organized religion (and Hall leaned upon his divinity degree and his nominal church membership for this purpose), or his interest and lecturing skills in pedagogy, all of which Gilman liked. Finally, Hall's friendship with Morris did not prevent him from shading his own views and those of Morris, whenever he could, in favor of his own greater suitability for the post (Ross 1972, 137–47). (Whether he was also involved in Peirce's dismissal is not as clear.)

When Hall wrote Gilman of possible plans to go elsewhere (though he had no firm offer at the time), the president decided to appoint Hall full professor of psychology (and added *pedagogy* to the title, against Hall's preference) in April 1884.

It is interesting to compare Hall's struggle for a secure professional position with the narrower and more direct career path of individuals in academic life today. Hall had taught school, tutored, entered the ministry briefly, and taught English, German, French, and philosophy at the collegiate level before earning his doctorate at age thirty-two; he then struggled for more than six years before he obtained his first secure professional position at age forty.[1] But if status was more difficult to achieve, it was also more highly regarded. Witness Dorothy Ross's description of the newly established professor's obvious pleasure at having "arrived" and his decision to play the role fully:

> Hall thus achieved, at age forty, his first secure professional position. In Baltimore, he visibly expanded to his new eminence. The father now of two small children, Hall bought a substantial house with the ample salary of $4,000 the Hopkins professorship carried. Highly conscious of the social climate of this southern town, he attempted to enter into the life of the local gentry and even rode to hounds in full regalia. (Hall 1923, 244–46, 259). When Hall appeared at the NEA the summer of his appointment, he swelled with pride at his now distinguished status. (*PNEA* 1885, 492–503). Hall's appointment marked for him, as well as his subject of scientific psychology, a coming of age. (Ross 1972, 136)

Hall was to hold his Hopkins chair only four years, but these were to be years of great importance to the new discipline of psychology, which, unlike James and George T. Ladd at the time, Hall took pains to separate from philosophy (Watson 1968, 374). With Gilman's support, Hall developed a psychological laboratory,[2] and began in earnest to promote the "new" psychology, producing graduates imbued with the zeal to investigate problems hitherto considered "insolvable" by philosophers (Fisher 1925, 3–5).

John Dewey, J. McKeen Cattell, and Joseph Jastrow were students at Johns Hopkins when Hall arrived, and William H. Burnham and Edmund C. Sanford (both of whom were to accompany him to Clark) were later among Hall's Johns Hopkins students. Hall threw himself into his new professorship. He lectured on psychology (at both graduate and undergraduate levels), psychological and ethical theories, physiological psychology, and the history of philosophy and education. He worked hard to build a good laboratory, continued to lecture publicly on educational topics, compiled a significant bibliography of education, and published numerous pedagogic and scientific papers in his relatively short tenure at Johns Hopkins (Wilson 1914, 66–67).

At the same time, perhaps out of fear of competition, Hall apparently saw to it that neither Dewey nor Cattell was able to obtain an assistantship at Johns Hopkins, although he led both to believe he was supporting them. This nether side of his personality appeared to surface in good times as well as in bad, it would appear.

Hall's period at Johns Hopkins was one of great accomplishment, and he credited Gilman for setting an atmosphere that made such success possible. In a glowing tribute to Gilman (and indirectly to himself), some thirteen years after Hall had left Johns Hopkins and had himself experienced significant trauma as a founding university president, Hall wrote: "To advance what he has done even a little in the world would satisfy all my ambitions. He has had optimism enough to sustain his own spirit and that of those about him under painful disappointments, and idealism enough to have made a long and painful fight against the materializing tendencies too prevalent here in higher education, and to demonstrate that often the most ideal thing is also the most practical" (Wilson 1914, 30, citing Hall from *Outlook*, August 3, 1901).

He praised Gilman's courage in being unafraid to take on new fields: "The new psychology, for which other institutions had shown only timidity, was here given its first American home. Now the productivity of our fifty American psychic [*sic*] laboratories rivals, if it does not exceed, that of Germany" (Wilson 1914, 69).

While Gilman's interest and encouragement were important, it was Hall's enormous personal and professional ambition and boundless energy and determination that fueled the engine of the new psychology, both at Johns Hopkins and elsewhere.

A gift of $500, mistakenly given to Hall in 1887 with the intention of furthering psychic research (which also used the term "experimental psychology"), enabled him to fulfill another of his desires by beginning the *American Journal of Psychology,* for which he wrote extensively and which he edited for its first thirty-four years. Hall's intense belief in what he was doing led him to invest literally thousands of his own limited dollars in the *Journal* before it could sustain its own costs and eventually turn a profit. Like much of the psychology laboratory equipment, the *Journal* was considered private property, and Hall took both to Clark in 1888.

The Clark Presidency

Hall's decision to leave his quite successful activities at Johns Hopkins for the uncertainty of a new institution can be attributed to a variety of factors, but none so important as his intense personal ambition cited by all his biographers and demonstrated so prophetically in his youthful vow on Mount Owen. In fairness to Hall, it should be noted that the trustees of the newly forming Clark University sought him out to be their first president; Hall made no effort on his own, as far as is known, to leave Johns Hopkins. In fact, Hall reports that he vacillated in his decision after receiving the Clark offer, probing possible greater support from Gilman for his work at Johns Hopkins. But by May 1888, feeling assured that the Clark board would allow him freedom to organize the new university according to his vision of a graduate research center even more focused and selective than Johns Hopkins, he accepted the challenge. A month later, he resigned from Johns Hopkins to begin a nine-month European tour, at Clark's expense, to prepare for his new responsibilities.

Hall heard what he wanted to hear about the wealthy Massachusetts merchant, Jonas Clark, and Clark's plan for a new university. He either ignored what he did not want to hear or believed sufficiently in his own considerable powers of persuasion to expect that he would have Clark's support even though their separate plans clearly conflicted. In his letter of acceptance of the Clark presidency Hall wrote:

> The work of organizing another college of the old New England type, or even the attempt to duplicate those that are best among established institutions old or new, would not induce me to leave [Johns Hopkins]. . . . Believing that, because so much has lately been done in the advancement and diffusion of knowledge among men still further progress is made possible, and animated by the hope that we may together have the wisdom and the strength to take the next step in academic development, I accept the great charge you confide to my hands. (Clark University 1901, 15)

And, in his remarks given at the opening of classes in October 1889, Hall went further in explaining his ideal of a university being made up of a professoriate "of men absorbed in and living only for pure science and high scholarship." He continued, "our plan implies a specialization as imperatively needed for the advanced students, as it would we admit, be unfortunate for students still in the disciplinary collegiate stage" (ibid., 28).

There could be little doubt that Hall and Clark were moving in opposite directions. In his Decennial Address in 1899, after extending cordial greetings to the then ailing and already alienated eighty-four-year-old founder, Hall again reflected on his real agenda in taking on the Clark presidency:

> With a dozen colleges within a radius of one hundred miles doing graduate work, the plainest logic of events suggested at once a policy of transplanting to this new field part of the spirit of the Johns Hopkins University, and taking here the obvious and almost inevitable next step by eliminating college work, although the chief source of income by fees was thereby also sacrificed, and thus avoiding the sometimes bitter competition for students, waiving the test of numbers, and being the first upon the higher plan of purely graduate work, selecting rigorously the best students, seeking to train leaders only, educating professors, and advancing science by new discoveries. (Hall 1899, 48–49).

Yet, Jonas Clark, from the beginning, was undertaking to build literally, as well as figuratively, "a college where boys of limited means—like himself when he was young—could obtain an education at low cost" (Blakeslee 1937, 4). In May 1887, well before Hall was invited to be president, Clark proposed to his fellow trustees that buildings be erected "as may be required for the prosecution of a collegiate course." Only during the four years that the undergraduates would be pursuing such a course would other facilities be readied for those of its graduates who might wish to pursue postgraduate work (Blakeslee 1937, 4). Clark was well on his way toward executing his plan when Hall was hired. He had assembled an eight-acre tract of land in Worcester and was in the process of erecting a main building, of his own design, of some ninety rooms. Even after Hall's appointment, Clark constructed a second building (a chemical laboratory), again of his own rather than Hall's plan, during the period Hall was touring Europe (at Clark's expense and with his blessing), gathering information, including building plans, from educators and leading scientists there.

Hall and Clark had many discussions and had corresponded extensively. Hall lived at Clark's home for several months on arriving in Worcester. They seemed to be getting on famously. But if either thought he had persuaded the other to change his plans, each apparently only persuaded himself that he had. Clark, at age seventy-four when classes began at the new university, was not about to give up his dream of an undergraduate school for poor boys but only to postpone it a few years if he must, to accommodate his new president. And when he allowed Hall to begin with graduate work exclusively, he appeared to have thought that he had Hall's solemn promise to develop a college within three years, which, indeed, he might have had. However, Hall had gone about assembling a graduate research faculty of great distinction, with neither capability for, nor interest in, undergraduate instruction. If a college were to be started it would need a faculty of its own, and considerable additional resources, as Hall saw it. Clark, on the other hand, believed that Hall was being obstinate, if not devious, in pursuing his own dream and not Clark's, and could not understand why the faculty and docents Hall had brought to the university could not teach undergraduates as well as do their own advanced work.

As time went on and neither college plan nor college course appeared, the aging and ailing founder became impatient with Hall. Clark was a quiet, if determined, man who tended to keep his own counsel, and he explained neither to Hall nor to his board what his concerns or intentions were. Instead, he proceeded to reduce and then to completely withdraw his financial support from the new president and from the university that bore his name. Most likely, he came to understand that Hall had begun a unique experiment in higher education that, if successful, would permanently frustrate Clark's dream. Hall's statements give credence to such a likelihood. If Clark's plans were clear, so too, had been Hall's. But Clark, like Hall, may also have heard only what he wanted to hear and, like Hall, was a proud and willful man accustomed to having his way. A successful, self-made man, Jonas Clark may have had even more reason than Hall to believe that his will would dominate. In the end, as it turned out, it was only his posthumous will that did.

In retrospect, it would appear that it was the diametrical opposition in orientation between Clark and Hall which led Clark to withhold and then withdraw his support from the university virtually as soon as it had gotten underway. However, some have suggested that Clark also may have acted as he did because of business reverses and his significant underestimation of the cost of the kind of postgraduate research institution Hall was creating. He was additionally disappointed with the failure of the "good citizens of Worcester" (or elsewhere) to come forward, as he and his trustee colleagues had anticipated, to assist in the university's upkeep. Despite an excellent board of trustees assembled by Clark and despite the promises they and Clark himself gave to the faculty and to the public of generous support for their unique mission, the university suffered almost immediately from financial difficulties that it barely survived. Hall later described the problem most succinctly:

> The key to the history of all the troubles of the early years may, in a sense, be anticipated from the following simple figures. During the first year we spent for salaries and equipment, $135,000; the second year, Mr. Clark contributed $50,000 above the income of the $600,000 that had actually been transferred to the board, making a total income in round numbers, of $92,000; the third year, he gave $26,000, making it $68,000; the fourth year, $12,000, making it $54,000; and the fifth and subsequent years of his life he gave nothing. (Hall 1923, 290–91)

No one knew for certain the size of Clark's fortune or if it would be given to the university he founded. Clark himself declined to share his long-term intentions with anyone, least of all with Hall or the Clark faculty, or even with his able and distinguished fellow trustees. After Clark's funds vanished, Hall consulted with these board members, and, consistent with his own personal style and vanity, decided that it would be best if he did not reveal the desperate financial straits faced by the institution he headed. He, instead, personally absorbed the criticism and anger of his faculty, deliberately shielding Jonas Clark from blame so as not to further alienate the founder and lose the potential of further endowment. As it turned out, he nearly lost his institution as well. "Lack of frankness and lack of funds," wrote Wilson later, in somewhat of an understatement, "brought about strained relations between Founder, President and Faculty which culminated in the resignation of a number of the latter in the summer of 1882" (Wilson 1914, 84).

Indeed, William R. Harper, president of the newly-forming Rockefeller-endowed University of Chicago, arrived in Worcester at the height of faculty dissatisfaction—after only three years of operation of the institution—and offered two-thirds of Hall's faculty twice their salaries and fine new facilities, which they gladly accepted. Hall later wrote of the incident: "When this was done he called on me, inviting me, also, to join the hegira at a salary larger than I was receiving—which, of course, I refused" (Hall 1923, 295). Looking back at this disaster for himself and for his new university, Hall took some perverse pride in the fact that his so carefully assembled and distinguished faculty were assuring the success of a new institution. "Thus Clark had served as a nursery," he reminisced, "for most of our faculty were simply transplanted to a richer financial soil" (ibid. 297).

Hall then "settled in," with only twelve loyal faculty and forty students (having lost approximately twice the number of each) to live on the miniscule endowment-generated annual income of $28,000, which they did until Clark's death in 1900. Poor financially, but "rich in scientific productivity" (Wilson 1914, 84), the group survived the austerity period—not one of the remaining faculty members left for the next twenty-one years; and the record, as we know, was one of considerable achievement, in spite of the dire circumstances.

Clark's death eased the financial pressures on the university, but his earlier wish was incorporated in his will and a collegiate department was finally endowed and begun in 1902. The bitterness and resentment Clark harbored for Hall, and the reasons for his withdrawal of support of the university he founded, were bluntly recorded for posterity in his will, the main body of which was written in 1893 and made public at his death.

He wrote: "I here state that I have no confidence in the future success of [Clark] University under the management of its present President, G. Stanley Hall, and I do not wish nor intend to contribute any more money or property to it, or to its support, until there is a change in that respect." (*Will of Jonas G. Clark,* item 30, paragraph 8). Further, "in case G. Stanley Hall . . . shall resign and cease to have any connection with or relation to that University within one year after the probate of this my will, . . . then and in that case, I hereby give, devise and bequeath to the said University the sum of . . ." (item 31, paragraph 1).

Four years after the will was written, Clark and Hall appear to have reconciled somewhat, though not to the extent of renewal of Clark's direct support to the university. In a codicil to his will, written in 1897, Clark revoked the language requiring that Hall sever his connection with the university as a condition of his bequest, but he explicitly let stand his statement of lack of confidence in Hall. Clark withdrew his ban on Hall, he said, as the latter was now willing to begin a college. His continuing mistrust of Hall was evident, however, as he went on to insist that the trustees "elect a President of the Collegiate Department of the University, *who shall be and remain absolutely independent of the President of the University*" (italics added), as a condition of further support.

Within only three months of the above, Clark added yet another codicil, now rejecting Hall's plans for undergraduate study, which apparently differed from his (though Hall had always denied this), and withdrew his proposed new collegiate endowment until he and the trustees (not Hall) could agree in the matter.

In a final codicil, recorded less than a month later, Clark wrote, with no explanation: "All conditions with reference to the cessation of President Hall's connection with the University wherever set forth or referred to in my said Will and Codicils are hereby revoked, if any doubt remains from the language of the former revocation" (item 4, paragraph 21). He nevertheless then went on to say that when, and only when, Hall left the university could it return to a single presidency "if it seems best" at the time. Thus, in a period of only four months, Clark reversed his partial forgiveness of Hall and then reversed the reversal, leaving Hall's final status as that of a reduced, but not banished, president.

His institution salvaged at last, in a manner of speaking, Hall himself was to continue to be punished by Clark with a voice from the grave, as it were, making the university an offer it could not refuse if it would realize Clark's desire for a collegiate department *and* forever ban Hall from authority over it. Ironically, the final codicil was not found at the reading of the will, and, for several days, Hall later wrote, "I felt that I had saved his bequest from going elsewhere, but at the cost of being dismissed as an unworthy steward myself" (Hall 1923, 306). Hall, despondent but determined, submitted his resignation, over trustee protests that they would prefer to let the will lapse. However, when the final codicil was made public, "withdrawing all [Clark's] animadversions" against him, Hall withdrew his resignation, feeling it his duty to remain "despite the financially more advantageous Chicago [offer] and two offers of presidencies" (Hall 1923, 307).

Clark University, like Johns Hopkins before it, was never to have the full support that would be needed to permit the untrammeled pursuit of pure science both founding presidents desired. But both universities would set remarkable records nevertheless, and both would permanently influence the pattern of advanced higher education then beginning to emerge.

However disappointing to Hall, the extraordinary turn of events at Clark had beneficial side effects. Now head of an impoverished and reduced graduate research institution and with no collegiate department to run, Hall activated his latent post as professor of psychology and sharply increased his efforts as vigorous promoter of the new science. Among other things, he tried, though unsuccessfully, to convince James not to duplicate Clark's work in experimental psychology but to orchestrate the efforts of the two institutions; he organized and became first president of the American Psychological Association; he promoted conferences on pedagogy, lectured widely on psychology, education, and child study, and continued an active personal teaching, editing, and writing program.

Hall's now-famous assemblage of psychologists in 1909, to celebrate the twentieth anniversary of the university's opening, during which Sigmund Freud launched his new and controversial psychoanalysis, was only one of several assemblies Hall managed to convene. Others, in Asian studies and in the natural sciences, were equally successful in gathering eminent international scholars to the small campus in Worcester and equally significant to the respective disciplines involved. With Hall's encouragement, anthropologists, librarians, physicists, and others launched professional and scientific organizations from the Clark campus. He, likewise, continued to promote and be involved in new journals, like the *American Journal of Psychology,* the *Pedagogical Seminary,* the *American Journal of Religious Psychology and Education,* the *Journal of Applied Psychology,* the *Journal of Race Development,* and others.

Hall's Monday night "seminaries" at his home, covering a wide range of topics, are remembered by former colleagues and students as a remarkable stage for a remarkable performer, and Hall himself reflected on them as ideal opportunities for him to display his erudition and synoptic skills. The seminary model and the intimate "elbow teaching" mode of graduate education were innovative concepts that have been widely emulated.

Hall as a Man of Action

Hall, throughout, maintained a schedule few could follow. Wilson, Hall's long-time aide-de-camp during his Clark years, described Hall's typical day as one in which he worked or lectured from 8:00 to 11:00 each morning, had dinner, held conferences until 5:00, took a stiff walk for an hour or more, had a light supper, and returned to his desk from 8:00 until 12:00 or 1:00 A.M. Even when he walked two miles downtown to the theater once a week, he returned to his desk soon after 10:00 P.M. Hall read English, French, and German with equal ease, translated, wrote long reviews, articles, and books, spoke as well as he wrote, was always well prepared, and moved with agility—and frequency—from interest to interest. He did not confine his activities to his academic roles as professor or administrator but spoke to and wrote for the general public, as well; Hall was often controversial, yet he influenced public opinion.

What can we say of a life as full and varied as G. Stanley Hall's? He was a driven man, without a doubt, but one of such enormous energy and ability as to be able to exert a lasting influence on whatever endeavors engaged his attention.

If he left no "Hallians" behind, as some of us in psychology in a later day became Freudians or Lewinians or Hullians, he left legacies probably more significant in the form of both structures and emphases—like the American Psychological Association, the journals, the Johns Hopkins and Clark psychology traditions, the child-study movement, the attention to the developmental process, the beginning of the testing movement, the focus on experimental psychology and experimental pedagogy, the biological and evolutionary emphasis in the study of behavior, the serious study of psychoanalysis, and the ideal of a research university and the study of pure science as an end in itself and as a means to man's salvation.

A sometimes mean, vain, and self-serving man, Hall also could be generous and supportive of others. He seems to have been harder on himself than on anyone else. He was original, highly stimulating, able, energetic, and totally dedicated not only to making his own mark on the world but to bettering that world in ways that would survive him. He accomplished, as we know, an enormous amount in laying the foundation for psychology's acceptance and its future and he furthered Gilman's model of the scientific research university.

What might he had been able to accomplish if Eliot or James had taken him in at Harvard? if Wundt had worked with him more collaboratively? if Helmholz had not already turned to physics when Hall joined him? if Gilman had been able to persuade him to remain at Hopkins? if personal tragedy had not periodically befallen him, such as the loss of his first wife and young daughter in a tragic accident after he had come to Clark, or the loss of his second wife to mental illness? if Jonas Clark had chosen to support Hall's dream of a graduate center devoted to pure science? if Hall had not deceived and lost his faculty only three years after the start of the Clark experiment? if Hall had accepted Harper's invitation and gone to Chicago?

Had he not had the obstacles and tragedies that beset him to overcome, might he have left an even greater legacy for us who follow him? Or was adversity necessary to his achievements? We obviously will never know the answers to these questions. Suffice it to say that the contributions he did make are richer and more numerous than any one person might be expected to make in a single lifetime.

When I came to Clark as president in 1974, I inherited a vastly different institution from the one Hall had created and tried to preserve. The spirit of G. Stanley Hall still pervades the small campus in Worcester, and the ideal of the research university remains to inspire the men who succeeded Hall. But Jonas Clark's spirit also haunts the campus and, in the quiet of the night, one can imagine that one can hear them argue about the potentially intrusive impact "a collegiate department" might have on a graduate research institution dedicated "exclusively to the pure sciences." They are, of course, not the only ones still pursuing the question.

Hall did, finally, revisit Mount Owen before the end of his life. In his *Note on Early Memories,* he recalled vividly his earlier vow to "overcome many real and fancied obstacles and do and be something in the world," observing that this "was an experience that has always stood out so prominently in my memory that I found this revisitation solemn and almost sacramental" (Hall 1920, 328–29). From what we have learned elsewhere it is clear that Hall finally acknowledged that he had, indeed, accomplished something during his life, despite the both "real and fancied obstacles" that he had to overcome.

Notes

1. Hall appears to have "shaved" his age by about two years, apparently having been born in 1844, not 1846, and in February and not in June, as he later claimed—the latter perhaps to distance himself from Jonas Clark.

2. This laboratory is generally considered the first formal laboratory (Fisher [1925, 3] cites 1882 as the founding date while Boring [1963, 162] cites 1883), although James established one of his own at Harvard in 1875.

References

Blakeslee, G. H. An historical sketch of Clark University. In Wallace W. Atwood (Ed.), *The first fifty years: An administrative report.* Worcester, MA: Clark University, 1937, pp. 1–19.

Boring, E. G. *History, psychology, and science: Selected papers.* New York: Wiley, 1963.

Clark University. *Early proceedings of the Board of Trustees: Will of Jonas G. Clark.* Worcester, MA: Clark University Press, 1901.

Fisher, S. C. The psychological and educational work of Granville Stanley Hall. *American Journal of Psychology,* 1925, 36, 1–52.

Hall, G. S. *Decennial address.* Worcester, MA: Clark University, 1899.

Hall, G. S. *Recreations of a psychologist.* New York: D. Appleton & Co., 1920.

Hall, G. S. *Life and confessions of a psychologist.* New York: D. Appleton & Co., 1923.

James, H. *Letters of William James* (Vol. 2). Boston: Atlantic Monthly, 1920.

Proceedings, National Education Association, Washington, D.C., 1885.

Ross, D. G. *Stanley Hall: The psychologist as prophet.* Chicago: University of Chicago Press, 1972.

Watson, R. I. *The great psychologists* (2d ed.). Philadelphia: J. B. Lippincott Co., 1968.

Wilson, L. N. *G. Stanley Hall: A sketch.* New York: G. E. Stechert & Co., 1914.

2. G. Stanley Hall and His Successors: A History of the First Half-Century of Psychology at Johns Hopkins

Philip J. Pauly

In 1880, the thirty-six-year-old G. Stanley Hall was in Leipzig, pursuing postgraduate work in physiology, psychology, and the "logic of science" with Carl Ludwig and Wilhelm Wundt. Hall hoped to return to a professorship in America, and he wrote President Daniel Coit Gilman of the Johns Hopkins University regarding a possible market for his intellectual "wares." He was especially interested in Johns Hopkins because, as he rather awkwardly explained, "Baltimore seems to me the richest virgin soil & I am sure the best of influences might be made to reach and effect the other Universities."[1] It would be another two years before Hall would obtain a lectureship at Johns Hopkins, and two more before he became professor, but he was correct in his estimation that Johns Hopkins was open to new trends and that it was a center that could substantially influence American academic life. The graduate psychology program that he established there, oriented largely around work in the laboratory, was the first of its kind in the United States (Boring 1965; Ross 1972, 242–247). It provided the organizational model and a significant portion of the personnel for American academic psychology in the field's crucial early years.

This chapter describes the creation of Hall's program and the further development of psychology at Johns Hopkins through the 1930s. The two things Hall noted—that Johns Hopkins was not restrained by tradition and that it was a center of influence—can be considered the distinguishing characteristics of the university's psychology department throughout these decades. Influence derived from Johns Hopkins's status as a premier scholarly institution. The continuing lack of tradition, however, was peculiar to that department; and unlike the university's position in American learning, it was not a consciously sought result. Between the founding of the university in 1876 and the end of World War II, two major psychologists—J. Mark Baldwin and John B. Watson—left Johns Hopkins precipitously under clouds of scandal. Even more significantly, the university's financial problems led to two suspensions of the entire program, in

1888 and in 1941. As a result, the department was essentially created anew five times, and the people involved were periodically required to rethink the nature and aims of psychology.

By examining the programs set up by Hall in 1883, by Baldwin in 1903, by Watson in 1909, and by Knight Dunlap in 1920, we can gauge the changing interests and concerns of American psychologists. More particularly, we can see how the meaning and function of Hall's basic creation—the psychology laboratory—changed in ways indicative of broader trends. For Hall, the laboratory was a symbol of psychology's position as a university science. When Baldwin reestablished work in 1903, he brought a specialist to set up experimental work as one part of a broad program within a department of philosophy, psychology, and education. For Watson, the laboratory was the physical and organizational basis for the radical intellectual breakthrough of behaviorism. And for Dunlap, the laboratory became an academic workplace for the "routine" production of research and of doctoral students. While Johns Hopkins was not the leader in all of these developments, its history provides a useful index of the many ways in which American psychology changed from the Gilded Age to the Second World War.

The Origins of Psychology at Johns Hopkins

Two mutually reinforcing myths have long helped to account for the breaks from tradition in both psychology and in educational policy that took place in the early years of Johns Hopkins. Hall's "new psychology" has often been described as an importation from Germany, in particular from Wilhelm Wundt (Boring 1950). And Johns Hopkins, with its emphasis on graduate study and research, has been portrayed as an American version of the nineteenth-century German university. While both claims have considerable factual basis, reliance on such characterizations obscures the more interesting and complex process of innovation within the American context. Before his trip to Leipzig (where he spent much more time with the physiologist Carl Ludwig than with Wundt), Hall had already received (in 1878) a doctorate in psychology from Harvard. Wundt influenced him in only a few—albeit crucial—ways. Furthermore, he was working in a university whose leaders were more concerned with the problems of post-Civil War America than with Germanic scholarship per se. The account that follows necessarily depends largely upon Hugh Hawkins's (1960) and Dorothy Ross's (1972) exhaustive studies of the early years of Johns Hopkins.

At the time of the opening of Johns Hopkins in 1876, there were two different classes of higher educational institutions in America (Veysey 1965). The older Eastern schools such as Harvard, Yale, Princeton, and

Amherst were firmly established and reasonably well funded but were linked closely to small constituencies of alumni and local leaders. A much larger number of small midwestern institutions, including the new land grant colleges, were varied in their aims, but ties to religious denominations and political factions limited their activities. All of these institutions, however, shared one aspiration: they were colleges, with primary emphasis on providing a basic liberal education. Modifications that were beginning at Harvard and at the new Cornell University were still of uncertain scale and significance.

In contrast to this picture, the Baltimore merchant Johns Hopkins established his school *de novo* with the then immense endowment of $3.5 million, and he appointed before his death a board of trustees made up of his fellow Quakers and a few other well-educated Baltimore businessmen. As in other institutions, these trustees were local and sectarian, but they were unusually free to create the kind of institution that seemed to them appropriate. They rejected the obvious paths and chose to establish neither a denominational Quaker school nor an institution designed primarily to provide collegiate training to the Maryland upper classes. Instead, they endorsed the plans of the forty-one-year-old Daniel Coit Gilman, whom they brought from the University of California, to create a new kind of institution in Baltimore. The Johns Hopkins University, while including a college, would educate men beyond that level, primarily to enable them to become the teachers in colleges; allied with that aim would be the mission to advance knowledge through research (Franklin 1910; French 1946; Cordasco 1960; Hawkins 1960; Hannaway 1976).

The motivations of Gilman and the Johns Hopkins board in making this choice were complex. Idealism and the desire to raise American intellectual standards were combined with interest in emulating European—especially German—modes of intellectual activity. In addition to these general considerations, however, there were aims more specific to the situation of Baltimore in the 1870s. In the aftermath of the Civil War, when federal troops still occupied a number of Southern states, Gilman sought reconcilation and reunification. Johns Hopkins, in drawing students from all parts of the country and sending them to staff the many colleges, would be instrumental in creating a single national culture. Beyond this, Gilman sought through Johns Hopkins to spread a new way of thinking in America.[2] From Gilman's standpoint, one of the major banes of American life had been the prevalence of dogmatism. Denominational arguments and religious tests had supplanted the simple religious devotion that had sufficed for American Christians in the early part of the century. Abolitionists and Southern firebrands had incited the Civil War and continued to provoke hostility through Radical Reconstruction and the Ku Klux Klan. Economic dogmatists such as Henry George's "single taxers" had harried Gilman at the University of California and destroyed the spirit of trust between classes and interests he had hoped would underlie the creation of a university in the west. Johns Hopkins and the teachers it would produce would, he hoped, work to replace the spirit of dogmatism with a willingness to listen and compromise in the name of orderly progress.

In this context, one of the notable aspects of the early Johns Hopkins takes on new meaning. Of the six senior professors chosen in the university's first year, four were mathematical and natural scientists. This emphasis resulted partly from the availability of personnel and partly from the common late-nineteenth-century enthusiasm for science. Gilman, however, was not interested primarily in science's results, which had long been presented through texts and lectures in the colleges. Rather, he wanted his university to teach what he saw as scientific attitudes—discipline, self-restraint, and skepticism toward unsupported generalizations. In particular, scientific work would lead students to recognize how much was not known. Within this immensity they would then be able to outline some problem that seemed soluble, and work methodically towards its solution. Like other strong figures of his generation, Gilman perceived that such a form of science could be the sovereign remedy for dogmatic convictions of absolute truth.

The student research laboratory—another Johns Hopkins innovation—provided the basis for teaching such scientific attitudes. It was a controlled environment where students learned, through emulation of the professor and more advanced workers, to restrain their thinking, to formulate soluble problems, and to work methodically toward solutions. The subjects studied and results attained were less valuable than the activity of research itself. The aim was to produce minds with a sense of the attainable. Graduates of the university could explain what they knew, would respect the expertise of others, and would recognize when a question was still open.

This method was applied at Johns Hopkins to both the natural sciences and to the gradually developing work of historians and philologists in their "seminaries." But such a system created difficulties for one field central to university identity in the nineteenth century, namely, philosophy. Gilman recognized from the beginning that selection of faculty in this area would be difficult. To a large part of the surrounding community, the university's scientific emphasis implied a commitment to materialism and atheism. This impression was reinforced when the agnostic evolutionist T. H. Huxley presented the inaugural academic lecture in August 1876 with a conspicuous absence of prayer. To hire a philosopher such as John Fiske, who was a spokesman for Herbert Spencer, would alienate many whose benevolent neutrality was important for the university's long-term success. But the deeper problem was that systematic philosophy of any sort was considered the antithesis of the laboratory spirit. In the traditional curriculum, the college president taught philosophy to all the seniors, presenting them with a comprehensive world view that they could carry through life (Schneider 1963; Kuklick 1977). It would be difficult to harmonize this view of philosophy and its educational function with the other aspects of Johns Hopkins.

It is not surprising that Gilman moved slowly in his search for a philosophy professor. The university could sponsor speculation only on the part of an established figure with impeccable religious ties. Gilman approached a number of European scholars during the university's first years and offered a professorship to the Scottish theologian and moral theorist Robert Flint in 1881, but neither Flint nor anyone else with a sufficiently commanding reputation was willing to come to Baltimore. An alternative path was to develop philosophy as a purely historical discipline open to the same kind of treatment as philology and political history. G. S. Morris of the University of Michigan, known as the translator of Friedrich Ueberweg's classic *Geschichte der Philosophie,* was hired as a half-time professor in 1879 as a way of exploring this avenue. A further possibility was to emphasize those aspects of philosophy that approximated the mathematical sciences in their claims to certainty and methodological rigor. As a result, C. S. Peirce, who worked as a physicist for the U.S. Coast and Geodetic Survey, was given a part-time position to teach logic. Although Peirce had recently published his seminal paper on the pragmatic theory of knowledge, at Johns Hopkins he avoided the bold theorizing that marked his later work. Graduate student John Dewey, for example, was disappointed that Peirce's lectures were designed more for mathematics students than for those interested in philosophy per se (Dykhuisen 1973).

Psychology—long a branch of mental philosophy—was also recognized as a possible approach. English writers such as W. B. Carpenter, Herbert Spencer, and Alexander Bain had promoted the subject in a context that emphasized its ties to the biological sciences. Americans were interested in this approach but were anxious about its controversial materialistic implications. The work of German physiologists such as E. H. Weber, Hermann Helmholtz, and Emil du Bois-Reymond provided a significant contrast, because they demonstrated experimentally the inadequacy of simple deterministic explanations of sensation, perception, and action (Turner 1977; Willey 1978). Their studies promised to lead to more refined understanding of the parameters for epistemological discussion. Wundt's *Grundzüge der physiologischen Psychologie* (1873, 1874) brought together their previously scattered observations and experiments in such a fashion that their implications became clear to a broad academic audience.

William James, an instructor in anatomy and physiology at Harvard, had responded favorably to Wundt's *Grundzüge* and to the movement it represented (Kuklick 1977; Richards 1982). It provided intellectual assistance in his effort to come to terms with Spencer's scientific challenge to human freedom, and it was also useful in his attempt to carve a professional niche in the rather crowded Harvard environment. His course in physiological psychology, begun in 1876, relied extensively on the German works in its extended argument against Spencer's *Principles of Psychology* (1870); and like a number of others who had come to psychology from physiology, James demonstrated standard experiments to his classes. Gilman was open to this psychological side of philosophy. In 1878, he invited James to give ten lectures and then unsuccessfully attempted to hire him on a basis similar to that of Morris and Peirce (Cope 1951). But his interest in psychology was not compelling, either then or in 1881, when James expressed renewed interest in a Johns Hopkins chair; at that time he rejected James's demand for a full professorship, and, on collapse of these negotiations, shifted the search to the ethicist Flint.

G. Stanley Hall, meanwhile, was periodically reminding Gilman of his existence (Hall 1923; Ross 1972). He had emerged from the evangelical environments of western Massachusetts, Williams College, and Union Theological Seminary in the late 1860s to study Hegelian philosophy in Berlin and to teach at the Unitarian Antioch College. Reading Spencer and then Wundt reoriented him toward psychology, and he moved to Harvard to study with James and the physiologist Henry Pickering Bowditch. While he engaged in some experimental work there, his dissertation on the muscular perception of space was primarily observational and theoretical. It was only upon completing his thesis in 1878 that he returned to Germany to study physiology, first with du Bois-Reymond and Hugo Kronecker in Berlin, and then with Carl Ludwig at Leipzig. He also spent some time there with Wundt, attending both his philosophy lectures and psychology seminar and working irregularly in the rudimentary laboratory Wundt had established just a few months earlier (Bringmann and Bringmann 1980). Since he was already quite familiar with Wundt's writings, the lectures did not interest him greatly, and Wundt's experimental program and laboratory techniques were at this time too crude to add much to what Hall already knew (Bringmann, Bringmann, and Ungerer 1980). But the idea that laboratory training in psychology could be part of a university curriculum impressed him enough that he specifically mentioned it to Gilman a few months later. When James bowed out of the running at Johns Hopkins in 1881, Gilman turned to Hall regarding the customary ten lectures. On their completion, Hall was glad to accept a three-year, half-time position to begin the winter of 1883.

The presence of three part-time lecturers—Peirce, Morris, and Hall—in one field on indefinite tenure was unusual at Johns Hopkins, and it was likely that only one would become a full professor. Historians of American philosophy (Fisch and Cope 1952; Hawkins 1960) have wondered— rather disappointedly—why Hall was chosen over Morris and especially over Peirce, universally recognized as one of America's greatest philosophers. In part it was a process of elimination on the basis of personal qualities. Peirce, who was always mistrusted owing to his eccentricities, was terminated suddenly in early 1884 when the astronomer Simon Newcomb brought Gilman unspecified derogatory information regarding his character; while still unknown, these charges may have been related to his divorce and abrupt remarriage the preceding year (Fisch and Cope 1952). Morris, while personally faultless, lacked the forceful presence considered necessary in a Johns Hopkins professor. Hall, in contrast to both, seemed stable, strong, and affable.

Hall also stood out in that he could present his subject to both the university's scientists and to the external theistic community. The strongly religious Morris was at a disadvantage in that he had little to say to the university's dominant natural scientists. Peirce's logical work, on the other hand, lacked apparent relevance to religion; after his notice of nonrenewal he claimed that if retained he would make a special effort to bring the philosophy department "into a state of warm sympathy and friendship with science on the one hand and with Christianity on the other" (Hawkins 1960, 196). Hall was an ordained minister who could claim familiarity with science; and he could also claim—only slightly disingenuously—that his psychological work would lead people away from materialism in order "to flood and transfuse the new and vaster conceptions of the universe and man's place in it . . . with the old Scriptural sense of unity, rationality, and love beneath and above all, with all its wide consequences" (Ross 1972, 140).

But the most important element to Hall's victory was the form of intellectual practice that he brought to the university. From 1879 to 1884, the center of philosophical activity was Peirce's semi-official "Metaphysical Club." Students and faculty from a number of disciplines presented papers that often provoked extended remarks and discussion. Topics varied widely in the first years; but by the fall of 1883 discussions focused on the issue that American scholars worried about most yet sought to defuse—the implications of modern science for religion. In October, Morris presented a paper arguing that religious principles must supplement the concepts of matter and force in order to provide a complete account of the nature of life. At the next meeting, Peirce responded to this seemingly naïve view of the nature of science, and then developed his ideas further the following month in a paper entitled "Materialism, Spiritualism, and the Scientific Spirit." Dewey supported Morris with a paper on the nature of consciousness, and zoology student A. T. Bruce criticized the design argument for the existence of God. Deep convictions about the relations between science and religion, which had up to this time been submerged, were becoming the subject of open argument.[3]

Hall was not in Baltimore that semester. His lecture course on psychology the preceding spring had probably been significant in stimulating these discussions. But his most important commentary on the issues had been through the other activity that he had organized that semester—a course of "practical work in experimental and observational methods of psychological research" (JHU *Circular* 1882, 233). His aim, as he described it to Gilman, had been "to show the kind of work to those interested & indicate, as I hope, problems for the solution of which the technical means & methods at our disposal will prove adequate."[4]

This activity contrasted sharply with that of the Metaphysical Club. In place of such ultimate questions as the nature of consciousness, Hall posed a set of problems chosen on the basis of their solubility. Instead of inconclusive and "dogmatic" argument, Hall gave students training in regular, painstaking work. Experimental psychological studies, in which subject and experimenter were often interchangeable, provided an almost pure form of mental discipline and, as Hall claimed in 1884, "applied logic" (JHU *Circular* 1884, 117). Hall's course demonstrated that philosophy could both avoid dogmatism and provide a valid way of learning to think and act scientifically. Hall became professor because he could offer such a pedagogical promise. It is not surprising that one of Hall's first actions on being appointed professor in 1884 was to "disorganize" the Metaphysical Club.

Hall's Discipline of Psychology

In proposing his course for the spring of 1883, Hall had hoped to attract physiology students already familiar with laboratory work, but in this he was disappointed.[5] Of the four men who signed up—Dewey, E. M. Hartwell, Joseph Jastrow, and James McKeen Cattell—only Hartwell had significant scientific preparation (JHU *Circular* 1883, 93). As a result, there was an even greater pressure than Hall had expected that the laboratory, set up in a house adjacent to the university buildings (possibly 187 Howard Street), would provide basic training in scientific experimentation. Hall proposed a broad range of scientific activities. These included studies of binocular vision, perception of time, coordination of action between the two halves of the body, and the relation between psychological attention and muscular movement. Hall also listed "experimental studies of instinct," "certain psychoprodromae of mental science as testing the theory of devolution as held by H. Jackson, & their relation to medical jurisprudence," and development of work he had recently begun in "taking an inventory of the content of the mind of the average child."[6] Once placed in the laboratory, however, the students focused exclusively on the first four psychophysical subjects, ignoring completely the comparative, psychiatric, and developmental questions.

Like any teacher, Hall had varying degrees of success with his students. Dewey, who had taken no laboratory science as an undergraduate at the University of Vermont, began work on the problem of "the effect attention has in producing involuntary muscular movements" (Dykhuisen 1973). But he soon dropped out of his only organized encounter with learning through experience, and he published no results. Hartwell, who had already completed his doctorate in physiology the preceding year, was an instructor in the biological department. He followed Hall's suggestion to investigate asymmetry in arm movements, in judging distances, and in responding to sounds from different directions. The results were inconclusive, and Hartwell soon gave up research to direct the university physical education program (Ross 1972, 155). Jastrow, son of the one of the principal rabbis of Philadelphia, had graduated from the University of Pennsylvania in 1882. He had begun psychological experiments in his rooms the preceding fall under the general direction of Peirce. With Hall, he took up the time perception problem, examining discrimination between rapidly repeated sounds, differences of direction, and estimation of both silent and noisy time intervals (Ross 1972, 156). Jastrow decided to make psychology his major field, completed his doctorate in 1886, and became professor of psychology at the University of Wisconsin (Jastrow 1930).

The experience of Cattell is the most interesting; and, as a result of the work of Michael Sokal (1981), is available largely in Cattell's own words. Cattell had graduated from Lafayette College in 1880. He then spent two years in Europe, by turns touring, studying philosophy, drinking, dueling, and suffering fits of depression that revolved around religious anxieties and awareness of the lack of meaning in his life. On his parents' urging, he applied successfully for a fellowship at Johns Hopkins in philosophy, but he spent his first semester in a lethargic state that was broken only by periodic "experiments" with the effects of hashish, morphine, ether, caffeine, tobacco, and chocolate. In February 1883, however, he noted in his journal that he had "commenced work this morning in a new physiologico-psychological laboratory" (64). His habits soon became more regular and his intellectual interests more down to earth. In about a month, he developed his own research problem of measuring the time needed to recognize and name letters of the alphabet as an index of the duration of mental processes. At the end of the academic year, Cattell's fellowship in philosophy was not renewed, because Hall was unwilling to press Cattell's superiority over Dewey, and compounded the problem by lying to Cattell that he had recommended him. Cattell raised a storm and left the university. But his semester of laboratory work had put him on a course for Leipzig and Wundt and led him to concentrate for a number of years on the specific problem of measuring "the time it takes to think." On this basis, he set out on a definite career path that culminated in the professorship of psychology at Columbia.

For those who stuck with it, Hall's laboratory thus provided both intellectual and professional discipline. The research topics were an eclectic mixture derived from Hall's dissertation work, his experiences in Germany, and his students' interests. The projects themselves were not terribly significant, but this was to be expected, given the combination of Hall's relative lack of relevant experience, the ad hoc nature of the laboratory, and the explicit intentions in establishing the course.

While the disciplinary value of experimental psychology had been demonstrated, the long-term direction of research remained unclear; and the intellectual vacuum filled only gradually as the laboratory established itself in the university. In January 1884, Hall returned to teach for a second year, and he reestablished his "laboratory of psycho-physiology" on the second floor of the new biology building (JHU *Circular* 1884, 85). When he became professor a few months later, he terminated Dewey's fellowship and gave it to H. H. Donaldson, a physiology student who had assisted him informally in the laboratory from the beginning. Biology students began to work in the lab in significant numbers, and Hall began to acquire charts, models, and apparatus for demonstrations and experiments on such phenomena as hypnotism, binocular vision, and rapid rotation. Requisitions also noted purchase of electrical and chemical supplies, along with "16 frogs, 1 bat, 1 pt. ether."[7] Donaldson began a series of significant researches identifying warm and cold temperature spots on the skin; and after a year in Europe he returned to run the laboratory (now moved to four rooms in the new physics building) in 1886 as associate (assistant professor) in psychology. But most of his work in Europe had been with such neuroanatomists as Bernhard von Gudden and Camilla Golgi, and he began to focus the laboratory increasingly on histology (Donaldson 1888).

Hall made Donaldson autonomous, however, both because he recognized his own limitations in the laboratory and because he was moving into new areas. He expanded his teaching activity to include not only psychology and occasional lectures on pedagogy but also most other aspects of philosophical instruction. But his more important work was in the professionalization of psychology, in particular the creation of a journal. A number of the Johns Hopkins professors had founded scholarly publications, and the university provided support in order to promote scholarship and the university. Hall was unable to get a university subsidy, but still he

announced the *American Journal of Psychology* in 1887, hoping to operate at a profit or attract university funds. The journal provided an outlet
for the work of Hall and his students. But Hall also—through a long
review section—sought to bring together the scattered work he considered
relevant to psychology and to reform the subject through strong criticism
from the standpoint of rigorous science. While Hall's promotional activities unfortunately alienated colleagues such as James, thereby limiting
the journal's significance, he nevertheless succeeded in advertising the
existence of a new psychology within the academic world. And the journal
was not Hall's only professional activity. Beginning in 1884 he studied and
consulted on the management of Baltimore's public insane asylum, and in
1888 he began a general collaboration with Edward Cowles, medical
superintendent of the elite McLean Asylum near Boston. Furthermore, he
shared in the widespread interest of the time in psychic research. When the
American Society for Psychical Research was founded in 1884, he became
one its vice presidents; however, he was skeptical about psychic phenomena and after a few years resigned from the society (Ross 1972, 160–
180).

Hall's effort to build a program in scientific psychology at Johns
Hopkins, while promising, was still unfocused in 1888 when he was offered the presidency of the new Clark University in Worcester, Massachusetts. Uncertain how to proceed, he hinted to Gilman that he would
stay in Baltimore if the university would take over the cost of his journal
and regularize the status and funding of the psychology laboratory. Unfortunately, the university was caught in a financial crisis at this point owing
to the impending bankruptcy of the B&O Railroad, whose stock formed
the basis of the university's endowment. As a result, Gilman was unwilling
to make any commitments. Hall left, and in spite of a student petition that
psychology "forms in our estimation an indispensible part of the full
equipment of a liberal university and should therefore be maintained in its
completeness and entirety," he was not replaced. Elimination of psychology was an easy economy.[8]

Yet, in spite of the university's inability to maintain the program Hall
began, the activities in Baltimore from 1883 to 1888 were crucial to the
creation of a discipline of psychology in America. The students who experienced the Johns Hopkins program—most notably Cattell and Jastrow—
went on to build departments at other major universities. The prestige
Johns Hopkins had lent the field was an important aid to these entrepreneurs. And above all, Hall's use of the laboratory to define the core
of his program became the model for other institutions. This innovation
was recognized even by his most unsympathetic colleagues. In 1895, when
Hall's hopes for Clark University had faded owing to the mistrust he
generated in both the university's founder and its faculty, and when his

predominance in American psychology was being challenged by Cattell's and J. Mark Baldwin's creation of the *Psychological Review,* Hall wrote a grandiose editorial in his journal that implied that essentially all American psychology programs had been founded by his former students. His colleagues indignantly contradicted these arguments; but in all cases, the objectors accepted the principle that the creation of a graduate laboratory was the crucial event in marking when a real program in psychology began to exist (Ross 1972, 242–48). In the 1890s, the concerns of many psychologists—most notably Hall himself—shifted from narrowly physiological experimentation to more broadly naturalistic study of development, and their ties to education programs grew. But the existence of a lab, for teaching and perhaps research, was still what signified that psychology was being done (O'Donnell 1985).

Baldwin: The Integrative Enterprise

There was no graduate psychology program at Johns Hopkins from 1888 to 1903. The university's financial crisis eased by the mid 1890s, but Gilman had no interest in reestablishing a chair. The situation changed when Ira Remsen, the professor of chemistry, became president in 1901. Remsen felt the university needed to reassert its position in American academic life with a number of conspicuous new appointments, and in 1903 he obtained approval for two new chairs—one each in psychology and in philosophy. In August, he wrote to J. Mark Baldwin, professor of psychology at Princeton, regarding recommendations for the new positions. When Baldwin dropped the hint that he himself was considering "a change in [his] base of operations," Remsen leapt to the bait, and negotiations were concluded in a few days with an offer of a professorship of "psychology and philosophy," with a mandate to develop a program second to none.[9]

For reasons that will soon become clear, Baldwin has long been a neglected figure in the history of psychology; his importance in only now being recognized (Cravens and Burnham 1971; Mueller 1976; Broughton and Freeman-Moir 1982). Seventeen years younger than Hall, Baldwin had grown up in a Presbyterian family in Charleston, South Carolina. He studied theology and philosophy at Princeton in the mid 1880s and also spent a few months in 1885 in Leipzig with Wundt and Cattell, familiarizing himself with what had become a much more established organization than Hall had visited five years earlier. After two years of teaching at Lake Forest University, a Presbyterian missionary college near Chicago, he was named professor of psychology at the University of Toronto, where he established a laboratory similar to Hall's. Four years later he returned to

Princeton as professor of psychology, where he set up a similar laboratory (Baldwin 1926).

Just as Baldwin followed Hall's path of using the laboratory to symbolize a new psychology, he also quickly moved beyond the laboratory to the broader concerns that made him a young leader in the field in the 1890s. Like Hall, Baldwin's basic interest at this time was in mental development in the child and the race, as a book of 1894 was entitled. Laboratory work played some role, but was subordinated to naturalistic observation of children, to Darwinian theorizing, and to linkages with sociology and speculative philosophy.

The program Baldwin set up at Johns Hopkins in 1903 reflected these varied intellectual aims. In contrast to Hall's policy of establishing psychology as an independent scientific discipline the meaning of which was sharply restricted, Baldwin coordinated a large department of philosophy, psychology, and (as of 1908) education (JHU *Circular* 1904, 179–80). For a nominal salary, Christine Ladd Franklin, who had studied with Peirce and the mathematician J. J. Sylvester at Johns Hopkins in the late 1870s, lectured on symbolic logic and color perception. C. B. Farrar, a psychiatrist at Sheppard-Pratt Hospital, taught physiological psychology and provided liason with the psychiatric community. When money became available from the state of Maryland, Baldwin hired E. F. Buchner to teach educational psychology and the philosophy of education. He himself covered the areas of developmental psychology and social psychology, along with his increasingly speculative concern with what he called the "genetic theory of reality." Finally, he brought in George Malcolm Stratton from the University of California as associate professor of experimental psychology.

Stratton epitomized experimental psychology at the turn of the century (Bridgman 1958). His reputation was based on a classic study he undertook while a doctoral student in Leipzig in the mid 1890s. In order to resolve the question whether inversion of the optical image on the retina necessarily determined orientation in space, Stratton had devised a set of glasses that produced upright retinal images; he found that in a few days he was able to adapt well to a world "seen" upside down, thereby demonstrating that orientation was the result of central rather than retinal processes. This kind of study, striking in its elegance, simplicity, and *bizarrité*, was the business of experimental psychology. Baldwin was able to lure Stratton to Baltimore with the promise of an assistant (Stratton hired J. W. Baird, a recent Cornell doctoral graduate), a laboratory that occupied half a floor in the biology building, and a $5000 appropriation for new apparatus.[10]

In contrast to the earlier situation, however, Stratton's laboratory did not define the entire field at Johns Hopkins. For Baldwin, experimental psychology was an important element of the larger structure that he was building, one that was essential to the whole, but of no greater significance than a number of the other enterprises. He apparently had little interest in graduate students, and he was not overly concerned with research productivity—Stratton had done little of note after his classic experiment and produced only four short papers in his four years in Baltimore. Rather, Baldwin's emphasis was on creating a community of scholars. In addition to the variety of faculty appointments, he brought such well known Europeans as C. Lloyd Morgan, James Ward, and Pierre Janet to Baltimore for lectures. He sought good relations between his department and biology, supporting the effort to hire H. S. Jennings, author of the highly regarded *Behavior of the Lower Organisms,* as the new professor of zoology in 1906. When Stratton returned to a full professorship at Berkeley in 1908, Baldwin strengthened these links further through appointment of the young comparative psychologist, John B. Watson, instructor at the University of Chicago, in his stead. And he also sought to link the department to the local community, as mentioned above, by adding education to its tasks and increasing his involvement in city affairs by letting it be known that he was available for appointment to the school board. He envisioned a psychology department that would be active on all levels, from protozoa to adolescents.

In the midst of this impressive vision Baldwin was tripped up by a hard nodule of social reality. In the summer of 1908 he was caught in a raid on a "colored house" of prostitution. Initially it seemed merely an embarassing incident. Although reporters recognized him at the police station and relayed the story to university authorities, they were discreet and he was able to get off by giving a false name to the police and arranging through an influential lawyer for charges to be dropped. When the school board nomination came up the next spring, however, it became clear that the episode was not closed. The opponents of Baltimore's mayor saw an opportunity to make political hay; Baldwin's indiscretion was being talked up, and the *Baltimore News* noted sardonically that "unless something unexpected turns up Professor Baldwin of the Johns Hopkins University will be appointed to the School Board. . . . The mayor feels a particular pride in the appointments he has made to the School Board, and is anxious, apparently, to keep up his record by this appointment."[11]

With the guilelessness that so endeared them to their fellow Baltimorean H. L. Mencken, the university trustees now demanded Baldwin's resignation. He agreed that it was necessary to avoid scandal and immediately left the city for Mexico, where he had been an occasional consultant on educational policy. Remsen refused to agree with Baldwin's plea that a long leave of absence would be sufficient to protect the university's good name, and the university received an unconditional resignation on April 17, 1909.[12]

This scandal essentially ended Baldwin's career as a psychologist. He was forced to sell his journals and to resign from the presidency of the International Psychological Congress scheduled to meet in America in 1913. No American university would hire him, and after three years in Mexico he was driven to France by the Revolution. From 1914 to 1917, he was active in promoting American entry into the World War, and after its end he was appointed professor at the Ecole des Hautes Etudes Sociales; but by and large his development as a scholar ended in 1909. With Baldwin's departure from the American scene, his broad developmental views—which recent scholars (Phillips 1977; Broughton and Freeman-Moir 1982) have claimed were a model for Piaget—lost influence in America, so that when he died in 1934, his obituarist (Urban 1935) noted that "the great majority of present day psychologists knew him not."

Watson and the Research Imperative

Baldwin's precipitous departure from Baltimore left hanging the members of his department. They had been collected, supported, and balanced by his considerable intellectual and professional authority; with that gone, their security and status were unclear, both with regard to each other and in the university as a whole. It was at least possible that the events of 1888 would be repeated, and the entire program be eliminated, unless new direction were provided quickly.

John B. Watson, the thirty-one–year–old professor of experimental and comparative psychology, was initially uncertain how to respond. Like Baldwin, Watson grew up in South Carolina; but while Baldwin's parents were well-to-do, transplanted New Englanders, Watson's ne'er-do-well father abandoned his family when John was fourteen (Watson 1936; Cohen 1979; Buckley 1982). In the fervent evangelicalism of upcountry Greenville, his educational opportunities were limited to Furman University, the local Baptist college. In 1900, he followed his undergraduate philosophy teacher's lead in going to the University of Chicago, but once there he rapidly moved out of philosophy to study with the psychologist, J. R. Angell; Hall's former assistant, Donaldson (now Chicago's professor of neurology); and the radical biologist, Jacques Loeb. His doctoral thesis was an examination of the hypothesis that the development of learning ability in the white rat could be correlated with the medulation of the nerve fibers (Watson 1903).

Baldwin was attracted by Watson's concern with the problem of development and by his strong experimental emphasis, and in 1908 he offered Watson a position as associate professor. When Angell countered this,

Baldwin was willing to give him a full professorship. This rank seemed fully justified as the charismatic Watson charmed his Johns Hopkins colleagues and students as much as he had those in Chicago; the 1909 student yearbook, *Hullabaloo,* included a poetic comparison to Sherlock Holmes's companion:

> Another Watson lives with us—I'm sure you all have heard;
> He made a study of a rat, another of a bird,
> He found young gulls afraid of him; that white mice nibbled cheese;
> That brains were made of sawdust, or of anything you please.

Still, Watson's rank meant little as long as Baldwin was present; and after Baldwin's dismissal it was clear that Watson's narrow training and intellectual interests, in addition to his age, were insufficient to enable him to take over his patron's role in the university.

One possibility was for Watson to shift into the biology department. He had established good relations with both the zoologist Jennings and the physiologist W. H. Howell, and he considered such an identification at least as intellectually comfortable as psychology. In late 1909, he was writing R. M. Yerkes of Harvard, his closest intellectual companion, that he was unsure whether he was a psychologist or a physiologist, or some kind of "mongrel."[13] While completely familiar with the Chicago style of psychological functionalism, he had found it of little help in guiding his research into the problems of animal activities that interested him. Yet a shift in professional identification was highly undesirable. Not only was Watson the university's professor of psychology, but in Baldwin's rush to arrange matters during the scandal, he had made Watson the editor of the *Psychological Review,* now America's leading psychology journal.

Watson therefore turned his efforts toward stabilizing his position in the university. In September 1909, he wrote President Remsen: "The affairs of the department are at a crisis, and unless the work at Hopkins is to become a negligible factor we must reorganize." He rejected cooperation with the education professor, E. F. Buchner, on the grounds that he was not "a University man," and he also saw little advantage in maintaining the connection between psychology and philosophy. He sought an independent department of psychology, which would make it "far more easy for me to organize my work and to guide my students." While unwilling to make any immediate changes, Remsen agreed to move gradually in the direction Watson proposed.[14]

Watson's claim that psychology should be an independent science was in many ways similar to that made by Hall twenty-five years earlier. Yet Watson's program differed from Hall's in two fundamental ways. Whereas Hall had seen psychology as the scientific prolegomenon to philosophy, Watson considered the fields completely separate, each valuable in its own place. While Hall had taught philosophy and had resisted other appointments in the field as a form of competition, Watson welcomed A. O. Lovejoy from the University of Missouri to take over a co-equal philosophy program in 1910.[15] But the most important contrast between Watson and Hall was in the sense of what it meant to be a scientific psychologist, a difference epitomized in their relations to the laboratory. For Hall, the laboratory was a symbol devised in the context of advanced pedagogy to demonstrate the nature and status of psychology. But for Watson the lab was the necessary center for creating a future science of psychology. He self-consciously presented himself as a "research man" who would concentrate his efforts as professor on solitary development of an experimental base for psychology through the study of animal behavior.

Johns Hopkins was perhaps the only university where this emphasis was possible. As Watson commented in 1910, "any disadvantages in the place are more than offset by the policy they have here of letting a man alone and in the almost total lack of red tape."[16] In spite of their admiration, Watson was relatively uninvolved with students, and he proposed to continue to study only animals. In other universities, by contrast, there was considerable pressure to teach and also to produce work relevant to philosophy and education. Edward L. Thorndike had abandoned animal work for study of children soon after becoming professor of psychology at Teachers College, and Yerkes was under strong pressure at Harvard to relate his studies of animal problem solving to human situations (O'Donnell 1985).

Watson's famous manifesto of 1913, "Psychology as the Behaviorist Views It," can be seen as an expression of his unique situation. His apologia, that he had "devoted nearly twelve years to experimentation on animals [and] it is natural that such a one should drift into a theoretical position which is in harmony with his experimental work," was not a mere methodological commonplace; rather, it reflected his position as the only full professor of psychology at a major university who devoted himself totally to animal experimentation. His statement that psychology's "theoretical goal is the prediction and control of behavior" expressed the conviction of the laboratory man dedicated to manipulation of the experimental situation. And his general aim in the paper was to elaborate the program of basic research that he had already begun at Johns Hopkins.

In the years from 1913 to 1920, Watson developed and expanded this program. He explored the theoretical implications of behaviorism that led to his theory of thought as subvocal speech (Watson 1913b). He tried (unsuccessfully) to induce the Carnegie Institution to establish a station for the study of animal behavior, and he began agitation for the university to set up a farm to breed research animals, a place where behavioral studies could also be undertaken easily (Cohen 1979, 90). He also began to come to grips with the work of Ivan Pavlov and Vladimir Bechterev, and along with his assistant Karl Lashley he published one of his few experimental studies of human adults, on the possibility of producing conditioned reflexes (Watson and Lashley 1916).

Overall university planning, however, interfered with this development when the long-awaited move from the buildings erected "temporarily" in the 1880s in downtown Baltimore to the new Homewood campus began in 1916 (French 1946). Since only a few buildings had been completed there, space—always in short supply—rose to an even greater premium. Watson had taught occasionally in the medical school and had developed contacts with psychiatrist Adolph Meyer, head of the Phipps Psychiatric Clinic; when the downtown campus closed, Meyer offered Watson space at the clinic to continue and expand his work as he wished. Although he was now over three miles away from the university's academic departments and regular teaching, the administration supported his shift to the medical facilities with no apparent second thoughts regarding his status as professor of psychology.

The medical school, with its established community position and access to human subjects, opened new possibilities for Watson. He did not abandon work with rats—in February 1917 he performed some significant experiments on the influence of timing of rewards on learning (Cohen 1979, 106); but the move to the medical school enabled him to expand and adapt his well-established personal program of intensive experimental practice to humans, with few of the constraints that limited the work of educational psychologists. In late 1916, he began observations and experiments on the grasping and blinking reflexes of infants. With only one or two assistants, Watson undertook the same intensive study of capacities and maturation of abilities that he had undertaken fifteen years earlier with the rat.

World War I interrupted Watson's research from June 1917 to December 1918, but within a few months of his return he had a number of significant projects underway. The observations on babies were picked up where they had been left off, and he found funds to prepare a movie of his experiments. Under the auspices of the federal government's Interdepartmental Social Hygiene Board he undertook a study of the effectiveness of the wartime anti-venereal disease film *Fit to Fight*. And he was hurriedly writing *Psychology from the Standpoint of the Behaviorist* (1919), the most sophisticated presentation of his general views. Genteel pressure on the university enabled him to raise his salary by a third, with a cordial note from President Frank Goodnow: "It would be extremely unfortunate for the University if you were to leave us to accept a call anywhere else."[17] And in spite of his lack of interest in graduate training, a number of promising students were asking to assist him in his experimental work. One was Curt Richter, who would follow in his footsteps in the study of animal behavior; another was Rosalie Rayner, daughter of a prominent Baltimore businessman, who began to assist him with his infant studies. The story of Watson's romance with Rayner and his subsequent dismissal from Johns Hopkins is now largely a matter of public record (Cohen 1979; Buckley 1982). The two fell deeply in love soon after Rayner came to Hopkins from Radcliffe in 1919. After a few months, Watson's wife, Mary, confronted him with love letters she had taken from Rayner's bedroom and demanded that he break off the romance; when Watson persisted in the affair, Mary agreed to a separation. By August, however, Watson was worried that a public scandal would ensue, and he recounted the events at length to Adolph Meyer, admitting that resignation might be the only solution, but hoping to stay on. Asking for "benefit of wise counsel," he authorized Meyer to use his letter as he saw fit (Leys 1984).[18]

Meyer, unfortunately, was not much help. When the university reconvened in late September he informed President Goodnow and argued that unless Watson gave Rayner up immediately, resignation was the only possibility. "Without clear-cut and outspoken principles on these matters, we could not run a co-educational institution, nor could we deserve a position of honor and respect before any kind of public, not even before ourselves." Watson's other close colleague, Arthur Lovejoy, agreed. He had been a moving force behind the founding of the American Association of University Professors in 1913; great pains had been taken in its charter to distinguish academic freedom from "grave moral delinquency." Watson was called to Goodnow's office, pressured to write a one-sentence letter of resignation, and left for New York, where he soon found a new career in advertising.[19] While he continued to write and lecture for some years, his experimental program collapsed, and his ideas hardened in such a way that they were easily shrugged off. He had predicted this accurately—if melodramatically—in his letter to Meyer: "I can find a commercial job. It will not be as bad as raising chickens or cabbages. But I frankly love my work. I feel that my work is important for psychology and that the tiny flame which I have tried to keep burning for the future of psychology will be snuffed out if I go—at least for some time. No man is indispensable. Both psychology and the University can do without me. If I go I shall burn all bridges. I think it is hopeless for the man who has lost to struggle along on the outside with an eye to returning to university work."

Dunlap's Working Department

With Watson's departure, leadership in psychology fell to the junior full professor, Knight Dunlap. Dunlap had graduated from Harvard in 1903 under Hugo Munsterberg and had been brought to Johns Hopkins as an instructor by Baldwin and Stratton (Dunlap 1932; Dorcus 1950). Watson initially had not been enthusiastic about Dunlap's ability but soon decided to support him as a junior colleague who could handle the routine teaching and maintain a presence in human psychology. With the move to Homewood, Dunlap finally became a full professor and began to set up a graduate program on the new campus. But even after the war, as enrollment began to rise, overall control of budget and appointments still lay in Watson's hands.[20]

Within ten days of Watson's resignation, Dunlap submitted a statement of needs for coping in "the present emergency," and three months later presented plans for faculty expansion designed to create a foundation for future development.[21] Dunlap did not claim to be a research genius or intellectual revolutionary. His slow rise through the academic ranks had made him a hard-nosed, even cynical, professional who sought to build a solid institutional structure for his science. The psychologists' activities during the war, primarily in the evaluation of personnel, had boosted the profession's status considerably; it was now considered possible that psychology could be of real social significance in such areas as education, industry, and commerce (Samelson 1977, 1979). Dunlap, like a number of other academic leaders at this time, sought to realize these possibilities by building his department into an efficient academic workshop designed to produce a constant stream of both research and trained professionals. While only twelve doctorates had been granted between 1903 and 1922, in the following decade an average of five were conferred each year, almost half of these to women. Dunlap and the junior faculty he gathered, largely from among his own students, developed an eclectic program that sought to combine training in useful skills, such as testing, with a strong commitment to methodological rigor. He campaigned for the value of solid experimental work and against such "fads" as psychoanalysis (Dunlap 1929).

In this context, the laboratory became a general term describing the department's workspace, constantly changing with the flow of graduate students. And as the number of students grew, availability of research facilities became the most significant factor limiting the department's growth. The theme of correspondence between the psychologists and the university administration, which during Watson's years revolved around salary and research funds, shifted to enrollments and the crying need for room. As Dunlap recalled a few years later, "the laboratory was seldom untenanted between the hours of 8:30 AM and 2:00 the next AM. We had reached, by 1926, a condition of absolute saturation, and it did not seem possible to continue either graduate instruction or research" (Dunlap 1932).

This problem appeared solved in 1926 when psychology moved from the Gilman Hall attic to the Johns Hopkins Hospital's vacant Home for

Crippled and Orphaned Colored Children adjacent to the Homewood campus. The expansion enabled Dunlap to create a new child development institute, and outside grants soon came in, including $2,500 from the National Research Council to study "the effects of copulatory work on learning in the white rat," and $8,900 from Old Gold Cigarettes for research on the psychological effects of smoking. The department's official budget nearly doubled between 1925 and 1931, and the number of faculty increased from four to six.[22]

This period of good fortune, however, did not last. In 1930, the federal government condemned the property on which the psychology building lay in order to expand the adjacent Marine hospital. The university administration initially proposed to build new temporary quarters on the campus; Dunlap agreed, though he warned that activities would be hampered seriously if they were restricted to such a building for more than a few years. But financial problems resulting from the Depression soon led to cancellation of even this plan, and in 1931 the psychology offices were dispersed into various corners of the campus.[23]

With this turn of events, relations between the psychologists and the administration began a long process of deterioration. Dunlap's recommendations for promotion were refused. When he was requested in 1933 to shorten his annual report (to be printed in the university's *Circular*), he replied testily that the only appropriate statement would be that "the activities of the Department of Psychology have been as near to normal as has been possible in its reduced circumstances." In 1935, Dunlap was warned that further reductions were a real possibility, and so the next year he accepted a professorship at the University of California at Los Angeles. A committee to consider the future of psychology did not recommend a replacement. His close associate, Roy Dorcus, followed him west a year later after being given notice of termination, and Buford Johnson, director of the child development institute, retired at age fifty-eight. Two junior faculty lingered until 1941, when President Isaiah Bowman abolished the department completely.[24]

Activity did not begin again until the very different circumstances after World War II. Psychologists had demonstrated their value during the war in areas extending from personnel selection and system design to troop morale and propaganda. Clifford T. Morgan, a former instructor at Harvard who had shifted from rat work to human engineering during the war, was given the task of reestablishing the psychology department in 1946. He drew upon his military contacts to hire a number of assistant professors, including Neil Bartlett, Alphonse Chapanis, Wendell Garner, Eliot Stellar, and Stanley Williams; they were joined by G. Wilson Shaffer, then both dean of the College of Arts and Sciences and professor of physical education. These men (women were not hired and were discouraged from applying to the graduate program) formed the nucleus of the program that has continued to the present day.

Conclusion

The history of psychology at Johns Hopkins exemplifies the rapidity with which the field changed in the half-century between the 1880s and the 1930s. Such change was not merely in the creation of new theories or "schools," nor was it a smooth process of expansion. Rather, the field's scope and relations with both other academic disciplines and with society at large were in flux. The status of the laboratory in the four phases of the Johns Hopkins department exemplifies these transformations. In the 1880s, its primary function was to symbolize a new intellectual attitude toward philosophy that would harmonize with the modern educational goals of Johns Hopkins. Twenty years later, it was one element of a comprehensive intellectual program that linked biology, philosophy, psychology, and education. With Watson it became a center for individual research in the style of "pure science" advocates and with Dunlap the core of an integrated enterprise in graduate training and "normal science." None of these roles was exclusive of the others, and none was completely restricted to one point in time, but they do represent a sampling of the meanings that the laboratory had in the first half-century of American academic psychology.

Johns Hopkins's flexibility kept it at the academic forefront. Given the department's small size, the periodic changeover in personnel put the university in the position more than once to sponsor a new direction psychology. It was able to hire relatively young faculty and provide them a clear field for work; under these circumstances, each professor moved rapidly to realize an independently conceived plan to influence the academic landscape. And psychology as a whole was small enough and open enough that individual effort could make a major difference. The situation at Johns Hopkins thus provided a base for a number of crucial shifts in the field's direction. The openness of that situation, however, came at a tragic personal and professional cost. The intellectual careers of Baldwin and Watson effectively ended with their resignations from the university, and the influence of each was fatally damaged. Furthermore, the process by which psychology progressed through radical changes itself exacted an eventual penalty.

In the mid 1930s, the university presidents Joseph Ames and Isaiah Bowman actively sought to dissolve the department of psychology. The Depression provided the basic incentive for retrenchment, and the department's bad luck in losing its building—essential to the work Dunlap had fostered—made it a particularly obvious target for cutbacks. Sexism was also increasing, and any department that trained large numbers of women was suspect. But administrators were also making a judgment on the history and intellectual status of the field. In 1936, explaining his lack of concern for replacing Dunlap, Bowman recalled that when he had studied psychology at Harvard around 1900, its value had been "through learning factually and in detail that [he] had a mechanism and that [he] might do something with it by conscious effort." He felt that the field had unfortunately failed to realize the "high hopes" of those years.[25] Psychologists, of course, had abandoned such a naïve formulation of their aims long before. Encouraged by institutions such as Johns Hopkins, they had explored a variety of new problems and approaches. But men like Bowman, indoctrinated as students with the ideas Hall and his followers had promoted in the 1880s and 1890s, continued to judge the field by the standards they had learned, and they found it easy to dismiss the achievements of the intervening years. Such a result was not surprising. The irony was that it was Dunlap—of all the Johns Hopkins professors the most committed to solid professional development—who was caught by this survival from the past.

Appendix 2.A   Faculty in Psychology, 1876–1984

G. Stanley Hall   Lecturer—Professor of Psychology and Pedagogy, 1881–1888
Henry H. Donaldson   Instructor—Associate, 1885–1888
Edmund C. Sanford   Instructor, 1888–1889
William H. Burnham   Instructor, 1888–1889
J. Mark Baldwin   Professor of Philosophy and Psychology, 1903–1909
John W. Baird   Assistant, 1904–1906
George M. Stratton   Associate Professor, 1904–1908
Christine Ladd-Franklin   Lecturer in Logic and Psychology, 1904–1909
Knight Dunlap   Instructor—Professor, 1906–1936
Edward F. Buchner   Professor of Education and Philosophy—Professor of Education, 1908–1929
John B. Watson   Professor, 1908–1920
William D. Furry   Instructor, 1909–1910
Karl S. Lashley   Bruce Fellow—Johnston Scholar, 1914–1917
Otto R. Ortmann   Instructor, 1920–1924
Buford Jeanette Johnson   Associate Professor—Professor, 1920–1938
Schachne Isaacs   Instructor—Associate, 1921–1928
Roy M. Dorcus   Associate—Associate Professor, 1925–1937
Henry C. McComas   Lecturer, 1928–1936
Willie May Cook (Mowrer)   Instructor, 1931–1935
Willis C. Beasley   Instructor, 1931–1935
Samuel M. Newhall   Instructor, 1935–1941
John M. Stephens   Associate in Education—Professor of Psychology, 1930–1966

G. Wilson Shaffer   Associate Professor—Professor, 1938–1975; Professor Emeritus, 1975–present
Clifford T. Morgan   Associate Professor—Professor, 1943–1958
William C. H. Prentice   Instructor, 1943–1947
Reginald B. Bromiley   Instructor, 1945–1948
Neil R. Bartlett   Assistant Professor, 1946–1948
Stanley B. Williams   Assistant Professor, 1946–1948
Wendell R. Garner   Instructor—Professor, 1946–1968
Eliot Stellar   Instructor—Assistant Professor, 1946–1954
Alphonse Chapanis   Instructor—Professor Emeritus, 1946–present
Howard D. Baker   Instructor, 1948–1950
Jack W. Gebhard   Assistant Professor, 1948–1950
Richard S. Lazarus   Assistant Professor, 1948–1953
James E. Deese   Assistant Professor—Professor, 1948–1973
Randall M. Hanes   Instructor—Assistant Professor, 1949–1951
Charles W. Eriksen   Instructor—Assistant Professor, 1949–1956
Robert B. Sleight   Assistant Professor, 1950–1951
Lawrence T. Alexander   Instructor, 1950–1951
Hudson J. Bond   Instructor, 1950–1952
Harold W. Hake   Instructor—Assistant Professor, 1950–1955
Ward D. Edwards   Instructor, 1951–1954
Robert S. Lincoln   Research Associate, 1954–1955
Marvin E. Shaw   Research Associate, 1954–1955
Willard F. Day   Research Associate, 1954
Mary S. Ainsworth   Lecturer—Professor, 1956–1975
Clinton B. DeSoto   Instructor—Professor, 1956–present
Leon Otis   Assistant Professor, 1957–1961
Stewart H. Hulse   Instructor—Professor, 1957–present
Leonard Matin   Assistant Professor, 1961–1963
James S. Myer   Assistant Professor—Associate Professor, 1963–1972
Warren Torgerson   Professor, 1965–present
William Bevan   Professor, 1966–1973
Julian C. Stanley   Professor, 1967–present
Howard Egeth   Assistant Professor—Professor, 1965–present
Robert Hogan   Assistant Professor—Professor, 1967–1982
Carnot E. Nelson   Assistant Professor, 1967–1971
William D. Garvey   Professor, 1965–1984
Bert F. Green, Jr.   Professor, 1969–present
Elliott M. Blass   Assistant Professor—Professor, 1969–present
David S. Olton   Assistant Professor—Professor, 1969–present
Roger A. Webb   Assistant Professor, 1971–1974
William S. Stark   Assistant Professor, 1973–1979
Milton E. Strauss   Associate Professor—Professor, 1974–present
Alfonso Caramazza   Assistant Professor—Professor, 1974–present
Stephen M. Kosslyn   Assistant Professor, 1974–1978

James P. Pomerantz   Assistant Professor, 1974–1977
Judith Hall   Assistant Professor, 1976–1980
Michael McCloskey   Assistant Professor—Associate Professor,
   1978–present
Maury Silver   Assistant Professor, 1979–1984
Alan B. Zonderman   Assistant Professor, 1979–1983
Jason Brandt   Assistant Professor, 1981–present
Richard Katz   Assistant Professor, 1981–1984

Appendix 2.B   Doctors of Philosophy, Department of Psychology, 1876–1984

1886   Joseph Jastrow
1888   Edmund C. Sanford
1909   N. Trigant Burrow
1912   Harry Miles Johnson and George Ross Maurice Wells
1913   Gardner Cheney Basset and John Linck Ulrich
1915   Helen Hubbert Caldwell
1916   Mildred Loring Sylvester and Buford Jeanette Johnson
1917   English Bagby and Howard Crosby Warren
1920   David June Carver and Wilbur Harrington Norcross
1921   Curt Paul Richter
1923   Harold Clyde Bingham, Mildred Elizabeth Day, Istar Alida Haupt,
   Stella Agnes McCarty, Carl Allanmore Murchison, Margaret Laura Potter,
   Elizabeth Mattingly Stalnaker, and Gin Hsi Wang
1924   Bertha May Boody, David Brunswick, Helen Elizabeth Eagleson, James
   Quinter Holsopple, Dorothy Wilson Seago, Selden Palmer Spencer, and Isabel
   Clarissa Stewart
1925   Robert Lee Bates, Roy Melvin Dorcus, Abraham Leonard Finesinger,
   Elaine Flitner Kinder, and Edith Totten
1926   Earnest William Atkins, Muriel Whitbeck Brown, Lenoir Henderson
   Burnside, Vivian Ezra Fisher, and Louise Anna Nelson
1927   Robert Morriss Browning, Christian Paul Heinlein, and Louis William
   Max
1928   Evelyn-Wylie Betts, Edith Sibyl Bryan, Elizabeth Duffy, Emily Oothout
   Lamb, George Wilson Shaffer, and Bruce Albion Wentz
1929   Julia Elizabeth Heil Heinlein, Charlotte Rice, and Gregory Schramm
1930   Laurence Armstrong Petran, Magda Voyen Skalet, and Roberta Stevens
   White
1931   Willie Mae Cook, Max Friedrich Eduard Hausmann, Eugenia Ketter
   Linus, Dwight Warren Miles, and Virginia Lafayette Nelson
1932   Elinor Lee Beebe, Pauline O. Eigler, Evelyn Gentry, Robert Clifton
   Lumpkin, Joseph Eugene Morsh, and Orval Hobart Mowrer
1933   Wendell Lavon Gray, Robert Hamilton Peckham, and Vernon Phillip
   Scheidt
1934   Sarah Calista Dunlap and Ruth Taylor Melcher

1935   Martha Elizabeth Thrum
1936   Thomas Willard Harrell, Clarence Daniel Leatherman, Frances Williams
McGehee, Harold Clair Phillips, Carlton Edwards Wilder, and Thornton
Woodward Zeigler
1938   Elwood Ross Harrison and Florence Jennings
1939   Virginia Kagy and Henry Clay Smith
1941   Reuben Albert Baer
1942   Martin Benzyl Macht
1947   Reginald Beswicke Bromley
1948   Eckhard Heinrich Hess, John David Reed, Irving Jackson Saltzman, and
Anchard Frederic Zeller
1949   Joseph Michael Doughty, Frank Loren Smith, and Alex Lewis Sweet
1950   Roland Carl Casperson, Charles Percy Fonda, Randall Melville Hanes,
Jack Roy Strange, and John Peter Zubek
1951   Michael Leyzorek and Robert Altwig McCleary
1953   James Weber Carper, Ray Hyman, Sonia Fellner Osler, and William
Thomas Pollock
1954   Peter Dock Bricker III, Virgil Ruben Carlson, Rita May Halsey, and
Philip Tietelbaum
1955   Peter Michael Lewinsohn and Carroll Vance Truss
1956   Emanuel Averback and Frederick Alexander King
1958   Charles Ray Brown, James Louis Kuethe, Jr., Natalia Potanin, Iris
Comens Rotberg, and John Forrest Strickland
1959   Robert Emmett Murphy, Sheila Murphy Pfafflin, and Richard August
Wunderlich
1960   Daniel Martin Forsyth, Royal Joslin Haskell, Jr., Kenneth Walker Haun,
Leonard Martin Horowitz, and Robert Lee King
1961   Daniel Harris Carson, Elliot Myron Cramer, Miriam Aronstein Safren,
Harry Leroy Snyder, and Maurice Martin Taylor
1962   Winthrop Edward Bacon, John Joseph Bosley, Edmund Benedict
Coleman, Jr., and Insup Kim
1963   Barry Franklin Anderson, Mark Aaron Berkley, Wayne Clement Lee,
Gerald Reubush Miller, and Henry Allen Schwartz
1964   David Eastman Clement, George Ernest MacKinnon, Tapas Kumar Sen,
and Herbert Weingartner
1965   Douglas Gant Pearce and Gregory Roger Lockhead
1966   Louise Poorman Baenninger, Ronald Baenninger, Herbert Horace Clark,
Shiro Imai, Harald Richard Leuba, Marvin London, and Gretchen Schabtach
1967   Gail Messenger Albert, Herbert Haskell Blumberg, Stephen Jesse
Handel, George Christian Jernstedt, and Patrick Leith Ross
1968   William Preas Banks, Stanley Clinton Collyer, Richard Leroy Degerman,
Richard Landolin Gottwald, Bernard Adolph Gropper, Nancy Main Henley,
Michael Geoffrey Johnson, Nancy Rowena Kingsbury, Donald Aaron
Mankin, Lorraine Coogan Scarpa, and Nicholas Zill
1969   Silvia Visscher Bell, Mireille Franke Bertrand, Robert Bruce Horsfall,
Suellen Safir Ruben, and Marilyn Demorest Wang

1970   David John Fruin, Donna Province Grill, Juliet Rapaport Phillips, Steven
Eric Suter, Paul Eugene Van Hemel, Susan Bobbe Van Hemel, and Hilda
Wing
1971   Howard Steven Hock, Robert George Pachella, and Herbert Leon Petri
1972   Ellen Barbara Dickstein, Joel Francis Gordon, Judith Andrea Jacobson,
and Mark Willard Lipsey
1973   Mary Patricia Blehar, Esther Blank Greif, Marion Mayes Jacewitz,
William Marshall Kurtines, and Stephen Robert Snodgrass
1974   Alfonso Caramazza, Matthew Isle Dobrow, Lynn Hussey Fox, Bruce
Wayne Hamill, Daniel Patrick Keating, Mary Louise Biggart Main, Robert
Bruce Ochsman, Robert Neil Parrish, Fred Albert Skellie III, and Jack
Benjamen Yates
1975   Inge Bretherton, Leo David Geoffrion, Grover Cleveland Gilmore,
Richard Jay Haier, Warren Grimes Hall, Frances Ellen Steinberg Harnick,
Craig Thurlow Johnson, Michael John Kelly, Frederick Scott Kraly, Mary
Ellen Phillips Oliveri, Charles Monroe Overbey, Thomas Robert Pentz, and
Gerald Dermot Weeks
1976   Lloyd Bond, Fred Harrison Gage III, David Stanley Goldstein, Gary Don
Gottfredson, Ellen H. Grober, Betty Bosell Hardee, Harry Morton Hersh,
Alicia Fridman Lieberman, Peter Vincent McGinn, Dale McClure Simpson,
and Mary Joyce Cowan Viernstein
1977   Mohammed Bendebba, Rita Sloan Berndt, Stephen D. Gottfredson,
Gerald Peter Krueger, Kathy Charmaine Sanders, Cecilia Helene Solano,
Ralph Brecken Taylor, Martin Hersch Teicher, and Peter John Whitehouse
1978   Hiram Henry Brownell, Catherine Ellen Campbell, Karen Harriet
Heldmeyer, Thomas Grover Land, Carol Jane Mills, Lawrence Cooper Sager,
James Gale Simmons, John Allan Walker, and Ann Leonore Weber
1979   Mark Harold Bradshaw, Stephen Paul Daurio, Karin Gale Hu, Randi
Christine Martin, Paul Roller Michaelis, Diane Mahony Monrad, and Steven
Philip Schwartz
1980   James Thompson Becker, Mark Allan Brecht, John Paul Bruno, Sanford
Jay Cohn, Carl Mark Francolini, Douglas Gordon Hoecker, Peter David
Pagerey, Michael Lewis Stoloff, and Sally Noetzel Wall
1981   Virginia Wise Berninger, Wayne Everett Bohannon, William Randolph
Ford, Barry Gordon, Amy Gene Halberstadt, Gail Ellen Handelmann,
Patricia Elizabeth Pedersen, Jeffrey Lyle Santee, Timothy Allen Satalich, and
Robert Dale Smither
1982   Jonathan Mansfield Cheek, Catherine Patricia Cramer, Stephen Bruce
Fountain, John Anthony Johnson, Mary Anne Johnson, Timothy Hayes
Moran, Karen Angelyn Nolan, Cynthia Sherrill Rand, Joan M. Roemer, and
M. Jeanne Sholl Smith
1983   Catherine Mary Busch, Carol-Ann Marie Emmons, Shalini Gupta, John
Falk Kelley, and David Hugh Schroeder
1984   Margaret Marcus Hale, Margaret May Hamilton, Kathleen Marie
Potosnak, Susan Elise Spear, Robert Anthony Virzi, Maria Soledad Zaragoza,
and Elizabeth Zoltan-Ford

48   *Philip J. Pauly*

Acknowledgments

I would like to thank the staffs of the Ferdinand Hamburger, Jr., Archives, the Alan Mason Chesney Medical Archives, and the Milton S. Eisenhower Library Department of Special Collections, all of the Johns Hopkins University, for their assistance in my search for material. Robert Kargon interested me in the early years of Johns Hopkins when I was a beginning graduate student in the university's history of science program. Michael Sokal was an important stimulus for this project. The following provided support, information, and helpful criticism: John Burnham, Sarah Dunlap Cann, John Higham, Kathryn Jacob, Arthur Norberg, Dorothy Ross, and G. Wilson Shaffer.

Notes

1. G. S. Hall to D. C. Gilman, 3 May 1880, 19 June 1880, Daniel Coit Gilman Papers (hereafter GP), Department of Special Collections, Milton S. Eisenhower Library, Johns Hopkins University.

2. Larry Owens, "Pure and sound government: Laboratories, lecture-halls, and playing-fields in nineteenth century American science," *Isis* (in press).

3. "Records of the metaphysical club: Minutes of proceedings, 1879–1885," Ferdinand Hamburger, Jr., Archives of the Johns Hopkins University (hereafter FHA).

4. Hall to Gilman, 9 October 1882, GP.

5. Hall to Nicholas Murray, 28 May 1882, GP.

6. Hall to Gilman, 9 October 1882, GP.

7. "Cash Book July 1876—August 1887," 14 January 1886, FHA.

8. Hall to Gilman, 13 March 1888, GP; Minutes of the Executive Committee of the Board of Trustees, 15 March 1888, Johns Hopkins University Office of the Secretary, Johns Hopkins University; E. C. Sanford, J. G. Hume, et al. to Gilman, n.d., GP.

9. J. M. Baldwin to I. Remsen, 25 July, 28 July, 29 July, 31 July 1903; Remsen to Baldwin, 27 July, 30 July 1903; Remsen to R. B. Keyser, 22 August 1903, Johns Hopkins University Presidents' Papers (hereafter JHP), FHA.

10. Baldwin to Remsen, 19 February 1904; G. M. Stratton to Remsen, 17 June 1904, JHP.

11. Hugo Munsterberg to Remsen, 8 February 1910; Remsen to Mrs. J. M. Baldwin, 28 December 1910; Henry D. Harlan to Mrs. Baldwin, n.d., not sent, JHP; *Baltimore News*, 6 March 1909; R. J. Richards, *James Mark Baldwin: Evolutionary bio-psychology and the politics of scientific ideas*, unpublished manuscript, 1983.

12. Baldwin to Remsen, 30 March 1909, 17 April 1909; Remsen to Baldwin, 12 April 1909, JHP.

13. J. B. Watson to R. M. Yerkes, 29 October 1909, Robert Mearnes Yerkes Papers, Yale Medical Library, New Haven, Conn.

14. Watson to Remsen, 4 September 1909; Remsen to Watson, 7 September 1909, JHP.

15. Watson to A. O. Lovejoy, 17 April 1910, A. O. Lovejoy Papers, Department of Special Collections, Eisenhower Library, JHU.

16. Ibid.

17. F. J. Goodnow to Watson, 18 March 1920, JHP.

18. Watson to Meyer, 13 August 1920, Adolph Meyer Papers, Alan Mason Chesney Medical Archives, Johns Hopkins University.

19. Meyer to Goodnow, 29 September 1920; Watson to Goodnow, 4 October 1920, JHP.

20. Watson to Remsen, 11 May 1911; Watson to Goodnow, 12 January 1920; Dunlap to Goodnow, 2 February 1920, JHP.

21. Dunlap to Goodnow, 13 October 1920, 3 January 1921, JHP.

22. Dunlap to Goodnow, 12 August 1927; Dunlap to J. S. Ames, 19 January 1929, JHP.

23. Ames to Dunlap, 6 October 1930; Dunlap to Ames, 4 April 1931, JHP.

24. Dunlap to Ames, 25 January 1932, 19 September 1933; Ames to Dunlap, 15 April 1935, JHP; "Report of the committee on psychology," Records of the Johns Hopkins University Academic Council, 8 April 1937, FHA.

25. I. Bowman to E. B. Wilson, 5 March 1936, E. B. Wilson Papers, Harvard University, Cambridge, Mass.

References

Baldwin, J. M. *Mental development in the child and the race: Methods and processes.* New York: Macmillan, 1894.

Baldwin, J. M. *Between two wars, 1861–1921* (2 vols.). Boston: Stratford Co., 1926.

Boring, E. G. A history of experimental psychology (2d ed.). New York: Appleton-Century-Crofts, 1950.

Boring, E. G. On the subjectivity of important historical dates: Leipzig, 1879. *Journal of the History of the Behavioral Sciences,* 1965, *1,* 5–9.

Bridgman, O. George Malcolm Stratton: 1865–1957. *American Journal of Psychology,* 1958, *71,* 460–461.

Bringmann, N. J., & Bringmann, W. G. Wilhelm Wundt and his first American student. In W. G. Bringmann & R. D. Tweney (Eds.), *Wundt studies: A centennial collection.* Toronto: C. J. Hogrefe, 1980.

Bringmann, W. G., Bringmann, N. J., & Ungerer, G. A. The establishment of Wundt's laboratory: An archival and documentary study. In W. G. Bringmann & R. D. Tweney (Eds.), *Wundt studies: A centennial collection.* Toronto: C. J. Hogrefe, 1980.

Broughton, J. M., & Freeman-Moir, J. D. (Eds.). *The cognitive developmental psychology of James Mark Baldwin.* New York: Ablex, 1982.

Buckley, K. W. *Behaviorism and the professionalization of American psychology: A study of John Broadus Watson.* Unpublished doctoral dissertation, University of Massachusetts, 1982.

Cohen, D. *J. B. Watson: The founder of behaviourism.* London: Routledge & Kegan Paul, 1979.

Cope, J. I. Letters of William James to Daniel Coit Gilman. *Journal of the History of Ideas,* 1951, *12,* 609–627.

Cordasco, F. *Daniel Coit Gilman and the Protean Ph.D.* Leiden: E. J. Brill, 1960.

Cravens, H., & Burnham, J. C. Psychology and evolutionary naturalism in American thought, 1890–1940. *American Quarterly,* 1971, *23,* 635–657.

Donaldson, H. H. On the relation of neurology to psychology. *American Journal of Psychology,* 1888, *1,* 209–221.

Dorcus, R. Knight Dunlap: 1875–1949. *American Journal of Psychology,* 1950, *63,* 114–119.

Dunlap, K. The outlook for psychology. *Science,* 1929, *69,* 201–207.

Dunlap, K. Autobiography. In C. A. Murchison (Ed.), *History of psychology in autobiography* (Vol. 2). Worcester, MA: Clark University Press, 1932.

Dykhuisen, G. *The life and mind of John Dewey.* Carbondale: Southern Illinois University Press, 1973.

Fisch, M. H., & Cope, J. I. Peirce at the Johns Hopkins Univeristy. In P. P. Wiener & F. H. Young (Eds.), *Studies in the philosophy of Charles Sanders Peirce.* Cambridge, MA: Harvard University Press, 1952.

Franklin, F. *The life of Daniel Coit Gilman.* New York: Dodd, Mead, & Co., 1910.

French, J. C. *A history of the university founded by Johns Hopkins.* Baltimore: Johns Hopkins Press, 1946.

Hall, G. S. Editorial. *American Journal of Psychology,* 1895, *7,* 3–8.

Hall, G. S. *Life and confessions of a psychologist.* New York: D. Appleton & Co., 1923.

Hannaway, O. The German model of chemical education in America: Ira Remsen at Johns Hopkins (1876–1913). *Ambix,* 1976, *23,* 145–163.

Hawkins, H. *Pioneer: A history of the Johns Hopkins University, 1874–1889.* Ithaca: Cornell University Press, 1960.

Jastrow, J. Autobiography. In C. A. Murchison (Ed.), *History of psychology in autobiography* (Vol.1). Worcester, MA: Clark University Press, 1930.

Johns Hopkins University. *Circulars.* 1878—.

Kuklick, B. *The rise of American philosophy, Cambridge, Massachusetts, 1860–1930.* New Haven: Yale University Press, 1977.

Leys, R. Meyer, Watson, and the dangers of behaviorism. *Journal of the History of the Behaviroal Sciences,* 1984, *20,* 128–151.

Mueller, R. H. A chapter in the history of the relationship between psychology and sociology in America: James Mark Baldwin. *Journal of the History of the Behavioral Sciences,* 1976, *12,* 240–253.

O'Donnell, J. M. *The origins of behaviorism: American psychology, 1870–1920.* New York: New York University Press, 1985.

Pauly, P. J. Psychology at Hopkins: Its rise and fall and rise and fall and. . . . *Johns Hopkins Magazine,* December 1979, *30,* 36–42.

Phillips, S. Psychological antecedents to Piagetian concepts. *Psychologia,* 1977, *20,* 1–14.

Richards, R. J. The personal equation in science: William James's psychological and moral uses of Darwinian theory. *Harvard Library Bulletin,* 1982, *30,* 387–425.

Ross, D. G. *Stanley Hall: The psychologist as prophet.* Chicago: University of Chicago Press, 1972.

Samelson, F. World War I intelligence testing and the development of psychology. *Journal of the History of the Behavioral Sciences,* 1977, *13,* 274–282.

Samelson, F. Putting psychology on the map. In A. R. Buss (Ed.), *Psychology in social context.* New York: Irvington, 1979.

Schneider, H. W. *A history of American philosophy* (2d ed.). New York: Columbia University Press, 1963.

Sokal, M. M. (Ed.). *An education in psychology: James McKeen Cattell's journal and letters from Germany and England, 1880–1888.* Cambridge, MA: MIT Press, 1981.

Spencer, H. *The principles of psychology* (2d ed.). New York: D. Appleton, 1870.

Turner, R. S. Hermann von Helmholtz and the empiricist vision. *Journal of the History of the Behavioral Sciences,* 1977, *13,* 48–58.

Urban, W. W. James Mark Baldwin: Co-editor, *Psychological Review* 1894–1909. *Psychological Review,* 1935, *42,* 303–306.

Veysey, L. R. *The emergence of the American university.* Chicago: University of Chicago Press, 1965.

Watson, J. B. *Animal education.* Chicago: University of Chicago Press, 1903.

Watson, J. B. Psychology as the behaviorist views it. *Psychological Review,* 1913a, *20,* 158–178.

Watson, J. B. Image and affection in behavior. *Journal of Philosophy, Psychology, and Scientific Methods,* 1913b, *10,* 421–428.

Watson, J. B. *Psychology from the standpoint of the behaviorist.* Philadelphia: Lippincott, 1919.

Watson, J. B. Autobiography. In C. A. Murchison (Ed.), *A history of psychology in autobiography* (Vol. 3). Worcester, MA: Clark University Press, 1936.

Watson, J. B., & Lashley, K. S. The conditioned reflex in psychology. *Psychological Review,* 1916, *32,* 89–177.

Willey, T. E. *Back to Kant.* Detroit: Wayne State University Press, 1978.

Wundt, W. *Grundzüge der physiologischen psychologie* (2 vols.). Leipzig: Engelmann, 1873–1874.

3. A Psychology for Our Technological Society; or, A Tale of Two Laboratories
Alphonse Chapanis

One of the germinal events in the history of psychology was the founding by G. Stanley Hall of the first experimental laboratory of psychology in the United States. Hall apparently never foresaw the importance that would later be attached to that event, for in his 623-page autobiography, *Life and Confessions of a Psychologist,* published forty-one years later, he has little to say about it. He does mention it early in his book, but he alludes to it at that point only in introducing another topic, "Since the first laboratory devoted to experimental psychology in this country, which I established in the early eighties at the Johns Hopkins" (7). Much later in the book, he says: "I was given a laboratory, first in the physiological building and then a more generous one in the physics building, and one thousand dollars a year for its equipment. I was enabled to develop not only the first but by far the largest and most productive laboratory of its kind in the country up to the time of my leaving" (277).

Hall also mentioned the laboratory briefly in some reminiscences at the twenty-fifth meeting of the American Psychological Association held in New York in December 1916. On that occasion, he said, " Johns Hopkins, then perhaps almost at the acme of its leadership, decided with great hesitation, as I was afterwards told, to give experimental psychology a try-out, very tentatively however, with an appointment first for six months, then for one year, then three, then five years, with an appropriation of one thousand dollars a year for apparatus" (1917b, 298–299).

Unfortunately, the first American laboratory of psychology had a short life. It was closed in 1888, only five years after its establishment, when Hall accepted the presidency of Clark University, and it was not revived until seventeen years later when J. Mark Baldwin came to Johns Hopkins in 1903 as professor of psychology and philosophy. The inglorious end to his

This chapter is dedicated to my former students who are now my colleagues. They have helped me do what I did and become what I am.

laboratory was evidently a source of some disappointment to Hall for his autobiography has this one final nostalgic note about it: "The Hopkins had already invested considerable money in my department, and had I anticipated that my chair would be left vacant for years and the apparatus of my laboratory distributed among other departments, so that my successor, James Mark Baldwin, would have some special difficulties in reinstalling it years later, I should certainly have hesitated even more than I did about leaving" (259).

Despite its short existence, Hall's laboratory helped to establish an essential feature of psychology as a discipline—its empirical underpinnings. Hall believed that an experimental laboratory should be the core of a program in psychology. That idea spread so quickly that just ten years later at least twenty-four similar laboratories had been founded in the United States.

No less important were the students trained in Hall's laboratory. Hall's own degree, which he received in 1878, was in psychology but his thesis on the muscular perception of space was actually presented to the Department of Philosophy at Harvard and his doctorate came from that department. To Joseph Jastrow, one of Hall's students at Johns Hopkins, goes the distinction of being awarded in 1886 the first true doctorate in psychology in the United States. Jastrow and other students trained in Hall's laboratory—among them James McKeen Cattell, John Dewey, William H. Burnham, and Edmund C. Sanford—also went out to form departments at other major universities. The prestige that Hall and Johns Hopkins bestowed on the field through the education of this small but influential group of graduates undoubtedly contributed to the rapid spread of psychology in America.

Viewed from our contemporary standpoint, the work carried out in Hall's laboratory consisted of a series of minor studies in vision, psychophysics, and psychomotor activity. Although Hall strongly supported and defended experimental psychology throughout his life, he himself did not engage in much laboratory work. His last experimental study, on touch sensitivity, was published in 1887. That notwithstanding, Hall was a prolific writer, and the topics on which he wrote reveal a remarkable breadth of interests. Theology, philosophy, psychic research, color vision, education, child behavior, adolescent behavior, aging, morals, morale, curiosity, animal behavior, music, hygiene, sex education, physical training, and thanatophobia are some of the subjects dealt with in his publications.

Later in life, Hall was greatly affected by World War I, and from 1914 through 1919 he wrote eleven articles touching on some aspect of the war and psychology. He was particularly impressed by the contributions that psychology was able to make to the war. "In the technical sense," he wrote in one article, "this country has set the world a new record in utilizing our science for military efficiency" (1919b, 211), and "I think applied versus pure psychology has abundantly justified itself in this war" (ibid., 212). His views on the relations between pure and applied psychology are congenial to my own. In viewing the "old differentiation between pure and applied psychology," he said in another article, "Must we not . . . realize that research in the latter field may be just as scientific as in any other, and that the immediate utility of our results is at least no longer a brand of scientific inferiority?" (1917a, 12).

Given those statements, I should not have been surprised, I suppose, to find that in an address at the commencement exercises of the Worcester Polytechnic Institute on June 10, 1920, Hall spoke on "the human factors in our modern industrial life." He made a point early in his talk that anticipated by some fifty years what I myself have often said about our technology. "(W)e . . . are beginning to realize," he said, "that it [industry] was made for the betterment of man, and not conversely. It, too, can never be stable until it fits human nature and needs" (1920, 281). So, in a way, Hall was an intellectual father of the field—whose credo is "technology has to be designed to fit man, and not vice versa"—about which I shall talk presently.

Despite those prophetic observations, I can find no evidence in any of Hall's writings that he foresaw the impact that technology would eventually have on society in general and psychology in particular. Although, as I have said, he was greatly impressed by the consequences of World War I, the primary contributions that he saw from psychology during that period applied almost entirely to the area of intelligence testing (1919a). It is easy to understand Hall's perspective on psychology and its future. His psychology and that of his contemporaries was still in its infancy. It had not matured sufficiently to deal with the complex issues we face today. Even more important, perhaps, was that Hall lived at a time when America was undergoing tremendous changes. It is only now that we can look back and appreciate what has happened and what consequences those changes had in store for all of us.

The Evolution of Our Technological Society

We sometimes like to think of ourselves as a young, idealistic nation symbolized by the rugged, self-sufficient individualist. For a long time, and certainly during most of Hall's lifetime, that image was accurate. We had revolted against tyranny and created a structure that allowed everyone to influence his political future. We had conquered a wilderness, taken in millions of immigrants, and developed a standard of living that was once unequaled in the world. We were strong, confident, and self-reliant.

Today, the reality, as the historian Louis Galambos wrote recently (1982), is that America is a middle-aged nation. Our standard of living is no longer the highest in the world. We are no longer self-sufficient; as a nation, we rely on many other distant, and sometimes unstable, countries for our oil, minerals, and even for some of our food. The rapidly expanding economy of the last century has been replaced by a mature corporate economy. What happened to bring us from youth to middle age?

The first change is one in geography. During our country's first two centuries, we continually expanded, encountering new frontiers and opening up new lands with fresh resources—timber, oil, coal, minerals, and agricultural land. When Hall established his laboratory at Johns Hopkins in 1883, ten of our forty-eight continental states had not yet been granted statehood. Hall and his contemporaries were unable to appreciate that there would soon no longer be any new frontiers of that kind to conquer and that the resources with which they were blessed would in some cases be exhausted by the time our generation came into being. Our frontiers today are in the depths of the oceans, in the polar regions, and in the limitless reaches of space. The conquest of these frontiers requires exotic technology that has just recently been developed and that Hall would probably never have been able to visualize.

The second change is demographic. During the early years of our country, the population increased at an astonishing rate. In the eighteenth and nineteenth centuries, the American population doubled in size every 20–25 years. This was due in part to the size of American families that were needed to conquer the land. That natural increase was swelled by waves of immigrants who were pushed out of their homelands and who were attracted by the opportunities of the new country. All that has changed. When Hall established his laboratory in 1883, the population of the United States stood at about 54,000,000, or less than a quarter of our 1983 estimated population of 234,000,000. But in 1924, the year of Hall's death, Congress passed the first law to "limit the immigration of aliens into the United States." What used to be a flood of immigrants dwindled to a trickle. More recently, Americans voluntarily started limiting the size of their families. From 1970 to 1980, our population has increased only about 12 percent, or 1.2 percent per year. This stabilization in population coincides with the end of our geographical expansion. With no more new land to expand into, we have decided, consciously or unconsciously, that we could no longer tolerate an unrestrained growth in population.

The third change is in the American economy. As our land frontiers vanished and our population started to stabilize, our economy had to adjust to those conditions. For most of our history, America was a country blessed with abundant natural resources. Relative to those resources, we were a country chronically short of capital and labor. But we are no longer a young nation filling out an unexplored, unexploited continent. We are, in economic terms, a middle-aged nation trying to learn the best way to use the land and other resources whose limits we can now see. It is hardly an accident that conservation is a relatively recent phenomenon. Throughout most of our history, conservation was unnecessary. We had so many natural resources we felt no need to worry about conserving them. Today we are concerned about our soil, our timber, our oil, our water—nearly all of our resources—and for good reason.

Over the years, the balance between resources, capital, and labor has shifted dramatically. Today, relative to our resources, we are a labor-rich society. Expansion can no longer be achieved through the exploitation of what we have but rather by increases in efficiency. Advances in productivity, technological innovation, and organizational efficiency are now as crucial to our continued success as new resources once were. The search for these elusive goals has penetrated almost every segment of our economy, even into offices where automation is supposed to increase the productivity of what are now called knowledge workers. If Hall were alive today, I am sure he would agree that any applied psychology that tries to stay in touch with our times must recognize the social and economic forces that create the need for such efforts.

The last major change that has brought us to where we are today is technological. It is difficult for us living in 1983 to appreciate what this country was like one hundred years ago when Hall founded his laboratory at Johns Hopkins. Think about it for a minute. In that year, Hall and his contemporaries could travel by rail, but electric streetcars had not yet appeared. The telephone had been invented; in 1883, one hundred years ago, the first directory for the city of Baltimore listed a total of ninety subscribers. City-to-city telephone service was yet to come, although cities were linked by telegraph. There were no electric washing machines, toasters, can openers, dish washers, refrigerators, vacuum cleaners, radios, or television sets. And, of course, there were no automobiles, airplanes, or subways.

In the one hundred years after Hall inaugurated his laboratory, technology advanced at a breathtaking pace. Indeed, most of the technology that we take for granted today has appeared within my own lifetime. In that period there was an event that had special significance for technology and psychology, an event that occurred less than fifty years ago.

World War II

Having seen what Hall had to say about the dramatic effect World War I had on psychology, we can only speculate on what he would have said about the even more profound effects of the Second World War, thirty-five years later. Throughout the 1930s we had been a nation at peace. Our military services were small and neglected because the major energies of the country had been devoted to recovering from the worst depression in the nation's history. Suddenly, in the early 1940s, we were faced with the necessity of selecting, classifying, and training millions of men for war. We had faced these problems in World War I, but the Second World War added new complexities—complexities created by technology. The primitive aircraft of World War I had been replaced with fast, high-performance aircraft that could fly to altitudes where man could not live without life-supporting equipment. The new aircraft could expose a flyer to g-forces that froze his arms and legs to his seat, drained the blood from his head, and even rendered him sightless. And the new aircraft were instrumented to fly at night and through clouds, guided by invisible beacons that made their presence known on instruments of esoteric design.

What had happened to aircraft happened to other machines of war. Radar and sonar changed the nature of air and sea warfare. Ships of war were outfitted with combat information centers. The name is apt, because these centers dealt with a nebulous product—information. A barrage of constantly changing information from radar, sonar, telephone, radio, teletype, and visual reports had to be displayed, assimilated, evaluated, and distributed to battle and weapon stations. The war had suddenly shifted to battling unseen enemies, enemies whose presence was known only through the elaborate and complex creations of technology.

These new machines of war placed great demands on the personnel selection process; they required that operators be chosen for jobs that had never existed before, jobs whose skill requirements had never been studied and catalogued. Training was equally difficult. Then the realization gradually began to form that the best efforts of selection and training specialists were often negated by the way equipment was designed. The realization came slowly because for years everyone had been conditioned to attribute most accidents to "human error." It took a long time for us to discover that "human error" could be caused by or diminished by the way equipment was designed.

Engineers were not quite sure how to design equipment that would prevent or reduce human error, or whether it was even possible to do so. Human behavior seemed so unpredictable—not subject to the same kinds of precise laws with which the engineer worked. Still, some people were perspicacious enough to see that behavioral scientists might be able to contribute to the design process and imaginative enough to try using them that way. That proved to be a focal point for my own eventual career.

When I was commissioned in the army air forces early in 1943, I was first trained as an aviation physiologist. My first permanent duty station was in the Aero Medical Laboratory at the Air Materiel Center, Wright

Field, Dayton, Ohio, an equipment development center. In a manner reminiscent of the circumstances leading up to the establishment of Hall's laboratory, I was assigned to Wright Field on a trial basis. As I learned later, the colonel in charge thought that there might be some psychological problems associated with the air force equipment and that I might possibly be useful in discovering their solutions. I was, I believe, the first psychologist to be so employed, and my primary responsibilities were to do research and make recommendations, not about people but about equipment. That did not mean, as I was to find out, that I had to abandon my skills as a psychologist; rather, I had to learn to exploit them in ways for which I had never been trained.

The Systems Research Field Laboratory at Johns Hopkins

What had happened in the air force was paralleled by developments in the navy. The latter led to the formation of another laboratory at Johns Hopkins—a laboratory that was no less influential than Hall's. This second laboratory helped to create a new kind of psychology—a psychology for our technological society.

That story began in January 1945 when the navy's Bureau of Ships, with the support of other navy organizations, requested the National Defense Research Committee (NDRC) to conduct studies of combat information centers (CICs) and to set up a field laboratory where CICs could be studied under realistic conditions. The request was rated urgent because of the need to get recommendations that could be put into practice as quickly as possible.

One of NDRC's contractors, Harvard University, quickly assembled personnel for this work from existing laboratories and from outside institutions. The group consisted of specialists in applied psychology, motion-and-time engineering, mathematics, physics, sonar, radar, communications, and countermeasures. During the spring of 1945, construction of the systems research field laboratory got under way at the Naval Training Facility at Beavertail Point on Conanicut Island, in Narragansett Bay, Rhode Island. The laboratory was completed in June 1945 and on July 15, 1945, major items of equipment were operational and ready for experimentation.

Hardly had the laboratory been completed when the war came to its sudden end. Personnel quickly scattered to new positions or returned to graduate schools or prewar positions. By the late fall of 1945, the staff of the laboratory had dropped to less than 10 percent of its peak strength.

At the request of the Bureau of Ships and other departments of the navy, the Office of Research and Inventions undertook a continuation of systems research on a peacetime basis. A contract was signed with the Johns

Hopkins University on December 14, 1945, and on January 1, 1946, responsibility for the field laboratory and for those personnel willing to continue the work was transferred to Johns Hopkins.

No long-range or basic research had been attempted under the wartime contract with Harvard University because the emphasis was on making immediate contributions to the war effort. In planning a peacetime program, however, the contract was broader. It provided for "physical, psychological and time-and-motion studies of military information systems and of the various devices for the indication, display, control and transmission of information, which make them up." The objectives of these studies, and I quote from the first progress report of the project, were four in number:

1. To conduct basic research in problems of human perception and performance, out of which will come suggestions and recommendations for the improvement of devices so that they will best suit the capacities of their operators;
2. To investigate the psychological and time-and-motion factors which are important in the most effective use of informational devices;
3. To conduct tests in which the devices are appraised, in the light of man's ability to use them under normal operating conditions, for the kind, amount and accuracy of information which they can handle;
4. To set up and test lay-outs of present or proposed information systems, to measure their performance, and to propose possible methods of improving them.

The systems research project, the first of its kind at a university, had some unique features. First, it was administered by Clifford T. Morgan, newly appointed professor of psychology at Johns Hopkins, but its associate director, Ferdinand Hamburger, Jr., was a professor of electrical engineering at Johns Hopkins. Studies were conducted not only at the field laboratory but in the electrical engineering laboratory and in the psychological laboratory, then in Mergenthaler Hall, in Baltimore. The project also had subcontracts with the industrial engineering laboratory of New York University, and with the time-and-motion laboratory and the applied psychology laboratory at Purdue University. In 1947, another subcontract was set up with the Psychophysical Research Unit of Mount Holyoke College. The subcontract with New York University was terminated in the summer of 1947, and the subcontracts with Purdue ended in 1948. In addition to the academics, the field laboratory had a complement of navy enlisted men under Commander J. S. Wylie, a career naval officer.

This was a rare combination of talent. The Johns Hopkins engineers provided the technical expertise necessary to operate the complicated systems under test. They also devised and constructed devices needed for experimentation. The psychologists and time-and-motion engineers each contributed their brand of expertise to the program. Commander Wylie brought to the work his operational skills and experience, and for subjects we had the navy enlisted men, all of whom had been trained in the use and operation of the devices we tested.

The Systems Research Field Laboratory was unique in other respects. It provided facilities for mocking up and simulating realistically the operation of any CIC, as well as the many ship and fire control stations associated with CICs. A central area of the laboratory, one thousand square feet in size, had movable partitions suspended overhead and removable floor panels that made it possible to reproduce quickly any size or shape of CIC. The mobile floor panels covered cable wells that contained electrical, sound power, interphone, and radio outlets so that any piece of equipment could be quickly relocated and put into operation. Another large room adjoining the central laboratory room contained target generation, control, and recording equipment.

The Systems Research Move to Baltimore

Despite its unique features, the field laboratory suffered from its isolated location. Research was expensive because it required a completely separate plant and facilities far removed from Baltimore. Moreover, keeping the isolated laboratory staffed with competent personnel proved a difficult task. Accordingly, in June 1948, we moved the field laboratory and all its equipment to a large building located at 1315 Saint Paul Street in Baltimore. That building had been taken over for the university's contract research activities under a new administrative entity called the Institute for Cooperative Research (ICR), an organization that has since been replaced by the University Sponsored Projects Office.

The psychological laboratory, as it would now be called, had seven-thousand square feet of floor space and twenty-nine rooms for offices and laboratories. The new laboratory also had at its center an "island" that duplicated the versatile CIC area that had been so successful at the field laboratory. As had been the case in the field laboratory, movable floor panels concealed electrical and other connections, and the interior of the island could be quickly modified as required. Research continued at 1315 Saint Paul Street until December 1954 when all activities were moved to Ames Hall on Homewood Campus.

The research project also underwent several changes in leadership during its existence. When I joined the Systems Research Field Laboratory in August 1946, Clifford T. Morgan was director, a position that he gave up on July 1, 1949, to devote full time to his activities as chairman of the Department of Psychology. Wendell R. Garner assumed the position vacated by Morgan, but when Garner began a year's leave of absence on September 1, 1952, Morgan and I jointly became research contract directors. I resigned on April 6, 1953, to leave for a year at the Bell Laboratories, and Morgan continued as director until Garner's return from his leave of absence on July 1, 1953. At that time, Garner resumed his position as director, and Morgan resigned and had no further role in the project. Garner continued as director until May 1, 1955, at which time I took over until the termination of that contract on October 31, 1958.

The end of the systems research project in 1958 did not mean the end of my research activities. It only meant changes in sponsorship. During the past twenty-five years, my work has been continually supported by various agencies of the government and by industry. About fifteen years ago, that research began to focus on the ways in which interactive human communication was affected by electronic media, areas that are called telecommunicating and teleconferencing. Still more recently, my research has been concerned with communication between users and computers. These research efforts grew so rapidly, were so productive, and attracted so many students that the facilities available in Ames Hall were no longer adequate. That led to the establishment of the Communications Research Laboratory with enlarged, modern facilities that I occupied off-campus.

But that history, the history of the last twenty-five years, is well known and documented. I would prefer to tell you about some other major events that took place in the years from 1946 to 1958, because that part of the history of the department has never been told and because I am one of the only two living psychologists able to report firsthand on what transpired during that period.

The Legacy of Systems Research

Earlier, I spoke of the legacy that Hall's first laboratory bequeathed to Johns Hopkins and to American psychology. Now I would like to tell you about the legacy that the Systems Research Field Laboratory and its successor, the Psychological Laboratory at 1315 St. Paul Street, bequeathed to the present Department of Psychology.

During the late 1940s and early 1950s several of us were considering the design of what were to be the psychology department's new quarters in Ames Hall, the construction of which was to begin shortly. The central laboratory area of the old field laboratory and the "island" area at the St. Paul Street laboratory had proven to be so versatile and useful that we decided to incorporate that same idea into a laboratory area for Ames Hall.

Psychological laboratories, we reasoned, have little need for windows.

Indeed, windows take up valuable wall space that might be used for other purposes. Furthermore, space requirements in a psychological laboratory change, depending on the kind of research that is going on and who is doing it. One investigator might be satisfied with a reasonably small room, another might want a long, narrow space, and still another might want to cut a door or a window through to an adjoining room. With that in mind, we decided to ask for one very large rectangular room with twelve doors, each with an adjoining light switch, temperature control, and ventilation outlet. That room is identified by doors having the even numbers from 216 to 226 and from 244 to 254 on the second floor of Ames Hall. Although there are twelve doors, there may or may not be twelve rooms, because the actual number of rooms depends on the way the interior space has been subdivided at the moment. The large, rectangular room could be quickly and cheaply divided into smaller spaces through the use of plywood partitions.

Although budgetary constraints prevented us from designing into the Ames Hall laboratory area a number of features that we had in the field laboratory and in the ICR laboratory on Saint Paul Street, the basic concept has, I think, been validated over the years. The Ames Hall laboratory area has been modified time and again, and it has provided exactly the kind of flexibility we thought it would.

There are some other legacies from our old systems research laboratories—the coffee room in Ames Hall, now cut in half from its original size, modeled after the navy wardroom in the field laboratory; the heavy machinery still used in the psychology department's shop; the air conditioning system that cools the administrative offices in the department; and a generous assortment of office furniture. Although these transfers of physical arrangements took place before any of the current faculty of the Department of Psychology had joined Johns Hopkins, the present faculty and their students continue to enjoy the benefits of that legacy. The more significant legacy to them, however, rests in the almost entirely unrecognized role that systems research played in the renaissance of psychology at the Homewood campus following World War II.

The Renaissance of Psychology at Homewood

President Isaiah Bowman had completely abolished the Department of Psychology at Johns Hopkins in 1941. To be sure, G. Wilson Shaffer was still a member of the faculty, both as dean of the College of Arts and Sciences and professor of physical education. John M. Stephens, an educational psychologist, was also on the faculty of the School of Education, but the Johns Hopkins catalogs for 1941 and 1942 show no department of psychology and no course listings in the field. Psychology was not really reestablished as a department until 1946 when Clifford T. Morgan, the newly appointed head, set about to revive it. The systems research project that Morgan brought with him played an indispensable role in the renaissance of the department in the years that followed. Of the thirty-two students who received doctorates in psychology from 1947 (there were none in 1946) through 1958, twenty-one had worked as research assistants on the project, and of the twenty-nine faculty members on the department staff from 1946 through 1958, twenty-two, or more than 75 percent, were associated with the project in one way or another and received financial support from it either wholly or in part.

The systems research project also provided a focus for the department's instructional program. A course entitled "Research in Applied Psychophysics" appeared in the catalog for 1946–1947. It was concerned with the application of psychophysical research to instrument and machine design, and was, I believe, the first such course to be taught in any university in the country. In the next year and in the years up to 1958, the psychology department offered courses in industrial psychology, applied psychology, applied experimental psychology, engineering psychology, personnel psychology, and human factors in engineering—a varied set of offerings that quickly earned for Johns Hopkins a worldwide reputation for having one of the best (if not the best) programs in engineering psychology—a reputation that lasted until my retirement from teaching at Johns Hopkins in June 1982, when the program was abandoned.

The Department of Psychology was in a very material sense a creation of systems research and it was and still is indebted to that project not only for the financial aid it provided to both students and staff but also for the focal point it provided for most of the research that was done at Johns Hopkins during that period. In his historical review, Parsons says about the system research project, "The Johns Hopkins program was indeed prolific" (1972, 112). And so it was. In the roughly thirteen years of its existence, 221 reports had been prepared under the auspices of the project, of which 143, or nearly two-thirds, were published in the open periodical literature. Many of these reports are classics, and they have provided the basic data for the human factors design guides that are the current bibles of the profession. Even more important, perhaps, are the graduates of the program who have moved out into the world to take active and important roles in the rapidly expanding technological developments of these times.

The Shaping of a Profession

However important systems research was for the revitalization and growth of psychology at Johns Hopkins, it played an even more significant role in helping to shape a kind of psychology that today is indispensable to our technological society. Late in 1946, Morgan was invited by the Naval Postgraduate School in Annapolis to give a series of lectures on human engineering to the postgraduate engineering students at the school. He, Garner, and I wrote ten lectures, and we engaged Fillmore H. Sanford, then an assistant professor of psychology at the University of Maryland, to convert our technical jargon into easily readable prose. The lectures, given during the spring of 1947, were such a success that we were encouraged to put them out as a report. A 246-page version of the lectures was published in 1947 (Chapanis, Garner, Morgan, and Sanford 1947), just six weeks after the last lecture had been given in Annapolis.

In his preface to the work, Commander Wylie wrote in part:

These lectures, the first coherent public discussion of their subject, show the work which has been done and, even more vividly, the work which still needs doing. The physiological psychologists, whose study is normal man (as opposed to the study of the more highly publicized abnormal), are now beginning to discover this needed basic knowledge—knowledge to be applied by mechanical and electrical and industrial engineers in their problems of design and installation.

The Navy has sponsored this project because the Navy expects to profit from it—profit in terms of machines and systems of machines better designed to fit the men who operate them. But the full value of the work in the years to come will be in civil life, wherever men build tools for other men to work with. (vi)

Wylie's concluding words were indeed prophetic, for the kind of work we described has now spread into almost every facet of our modern technological society.

Although it had been classified "Restricted" (a classification that was canceled in 1963) and so could be distributed only to persons who had the appropriate government clearance, the report was an almost instant success. My recollection is that Morgan had printed first 500, then another 1,000 copies, and our supply of both printings was quickly exhausted. It is interesting to look back at the evidence of our struggle with names. The subtitle of the report is "An Introduction to Human Engineering," but in the lectures themselves we refer to "psychophysical systems research"; in the first lecture (and chapter) we say: "The term human engineering, as we understand it, means essentially the same thing that we mean when we say psychophysical systems research" (Chapanis et al. 1947, 5). This search for a name to call the newly emerging field is also apparent in the names of the courses that were offered in the department from 1946 onward. Recall that the first course we taught was called "Research in Applied Psychophysics." Although the terms "psychophysical systems research" and "applied psychophysics" have now dropped out of usage, the search for an appropriate name for our field has still not been concluded to everyone's satisfaction.

The success of *Lectures on Men and Machines* inspired Garner, Morgan, and me to write a more general textbook, a project on which we embarked almost immediately. Once again, we struggled with the name, because we did not want to alienate psychologists in our effort to convey the full flavor of what we were writing about. The result was a compromise. We called the book *Applied Experimental Psychology* but added the subtitle *Human Factors in Engineering Design*. The book, published in 1949, was the first textbook in the field, and it set the pattern for others that were to follow. I am gratified to recall that when a small group of professionals got together in 1957 to form a new professional society, the name they chose for their organization matched the subtitle of our book. The Human Factors Society is now recognized as the largest and most prestigious society of its kind in the world.

Systems research staff members also played important roles in other influential publications. Stanley B. Williams, Jack W. Gebhard, Eliot Stellar, Wendell R. Garner, and I contributed to a National Research Council book entitled *Human Factors in Undersea Warfare* (Panel on Psychology and Physiology 1949). This work is still regarded as a classic because of the insights it provided on significant research needs and human factors problems in undersea warfare. Two years later, Garner, Gebhard, and I contributed to another document called *Human Engineering for an Effective Air-Navigation and Traffic Control System* (Fitts 1951). That document, prepared under the auspices of the National Research Council's Committee on Aviation Psychology, outlined long-range plans for incorporating human factors into the air traffic control system that was about to be overhauled and redesigned to accommodate the increased air traffic anticipated in the decades to come. That air traffic control system has served us well during the past thirty years, but it is once again becoming overloaded and plans are currently underway to design a completely new system for the future. Needless to say, human factors will again play an important role in those plans.

My book *Research Techniques in Human Engineering* (1959), the first of its kind, was also drafted and largely written under the systems research contract. It is not surprising, therefore, that when the three armed services decided to put together the first comprehensive human engineering guide to equipment design, two of us from the systems research project were its editors (Morgan et al. 1963).

We did not confine our activities to producing the printed word. Although we did not realize it at the time, our other activities were also instrumental in shaping the field of human factors as we know it today:

lecturing professional groups, providing consulting services, and playing host to visitors. Regarding the first, one of us was almost constantly away giving lectures to professional groups too numerous to detail here. Among the more noteworthy of these lectures were revised versions of the talks delivered to the Naval Postgraduate School in Annapolis which we had first given in 1946 and which we repeated in 1950 and 1951, and related lectures delivered to the Naval Postgraduate School in Monterey, California, in 1953. Perhaps the most influential series of lectures were ten that Garner, Gebhard, and I gave in the main auditorium of the Department of Interior Building in Washington, D.C., in the fall of 1950. These lectures were attended by a very large number of persons from government, industry, and the military services, and they helped to spread the word about research in engineering psychology and to demonstrate its importance to our modern technological society.

Regarding the second of our supplementary activities, we engaged in an astonishing amount of consulting to government and industrial organizations. RCA, Bell Laboratories, Dupont, GE, Lockheed, Bendix, Sperry Gyroscope, Glenn L. Martin, Evans Signal Laboratory, Cornell Aeronautical Laboratories, and Westinghouse are some of the industrial groups to which we provided consulting services, generally in support of the design of navy equipment. In a substantial number of instances, these activities opened up new job opportunities for engineering psychologists when the organizations with which we consulted hired their own experts on a full-time basis and sometimes even formed departments of such experts. At the same time, members of our staff went aboard navy ships to observe and report on radar and other installations, and for years we provided continuing consulting services to the Cockpit Development Panel of the navy's Bureau of Aeronautics and to the Systems Coordination Division at the Naval Research Laboratory.

Progress Report Number 18, dated February 1, 1950, was the first to start listing special activities, such as consulting, lectures, and visits to the laboratory. Subsequent progress reports record an almost constant stream of visitors to find out about our research, to see how we had organized the laboratory, and to become familiar with this newly emerging field. The visitors came from industrial laboratories, from other universities in this country, and from foreign countries—Australia, England, Germany, Holland, Italy, Japan, and Sweden. The most noteworthy of these visits was by a group of nine European specialists—from Austria, England, France, Germany, Holland, Italy, and Norway—sponsored by the European Productivity Agency of the International Cooperation Administration. This group came to learn about human factors and its subfield, engineering psychology, to inspect the Johns Hopkins' laboratories, and to find out about education for human engineers and engineering psychologists. Most of these men returned to establish programs for their own and became prominent members of the profession.

In detailing this history, I do not mean to imply that we were the only force contributing to the development of human factors in America. There was, for example, Project Cadillac conducted by New York University, MIT's Lincoln Laboratory, the University of Michigan's Willow Run Laboratories, and the Laboratory of Aviation Psychology at the Ohio State University and at the University of Illinois. But all these university programs were started several years after the one at Johns Hopkins. There were also, of course, a number of government and private laboratories and private consulting organizations, such as Dunlap and Associates and the American Institutes for Research, that played significant roles in this history. Still, I think I can say without exaggeration that the Johns Hopkins program occupies a distinguished place in the early history and development of human factors and its subfield, engineering psychology, in America.

Engineering Psychology after Systems Research

Without in any way minimizing the impact of the work done by systems research, it was essentially concerned with the design of interlinked components, with what is sometimes referred to today (in disparaging tones) as "knobs and dials psychology." That work was and is still important. It was important because it laid the groundwork for later work and because it showed in concrete terms that engineering psychology could contribute materially to machine design. It is important because in their day-to-day work engineering psychologists still have to be concerned with the design of components—with the knobs, dials, video displays, keyboards, switches, chairs, and tables that are invariably associated with our machine systems.

But human factors and engineering psychology have advanced far beyond a concern with components, and in so doing they have added new dimensions to the field. Our concern now is not just with components but with a much broader concept of systems, those organizations or complexes of operators, machines, procedures, tasks, and environments that have to be made efficient, productive, comfortable, and safe. The complicating factor is that all of these elements have to be considered together and that there are, inevitably, trade-offs among them. Selection procedures and standards depend in part on the complexity of machines and procedures and on the training programs associated with various tasks or jobs. The way machines are designed, in turn, depends in part on the kind of people who will be using the machines and how they will be selected and trained. Sometimes it is cheaper, easier, and more effective to place more emphasis on personnel selection procedures, sometimes on training, sometimes on machine design, sometimes on procedures, sometimes on the redesign of the task, and sometimes on the design of the workplace. But our current perspective is that it is always important to consider all these elements and to decide how much development effort should be allocated to each of them to get the best overall result.

Another important change that has occurred over the years is the penetration of human factors into the civilian and industrial / commercial sector. Whereas in the beginning the field was primarily concerned with military systems, by far the majority of human factors professionals today work on nonmilitary products—on such things as washing machines, stoves, recreational equipment, medical equipment, cameras, telephones, computers, automobiles, teleconferencing systems, air and sea traffic control systems, and nuclear power plants. Engineering psychology has broadened its concerns to include virtually all aspects of our technological society. It is also an interesting observation on the nature of research that it knows no artificial boundaries such as those that are sometimes drawn between military and nonmilitary applications. The work we did years ago on CICs has its counterpart in the considerable amount of research and development now going into the design of disaster response organizations, such as those that are called on in emergencies caused by major fires, floods, earthquakes, volcanic eruptions, and nuclear powerplant failures. The basic principles are valid irrespective of their particular applications.

A Psychology for Our Technological Society

For the past several years, all my research has been supported by industry, and all of my teaching since June 1982 has been in and for industry. With regard to the latter, I have been impressed by both the quantity and quality of the educational programs that are conducted by and for some industries. Although we hear a great deal in academic circles about how much industry has to learn from academia, my recent experience leads me to conclude that academia has something to learn from industry.

Relations between industry and academia are currently a topic of great concern; as I was writing this chapter, *The Johns Hopkins Magazine* published a major article by Elise Hancock on this topic. Hancock's article, however, is mostly concerned with industry-sponsored research in medicine and engineering. Psychology is different from medicine and engineering; I do not think we can generalize about psychology from those two fields. Hancock does note, however, that Westinghouse spends about $27 million on in-house education programs for its employees, and she remarks rhetorically that it might have been cheaper and better for Westinghouse to have spent some of that money sending its employees to take appropriate courses at colleges and universities. What Hancock does not seem to recognize is that one reason industry does not send more of its employees to colleges and universities is that most academic institutions do not teach the kinds of courses industry needs.

Our modern technology needs psychologists desperately. But in my experience, psychologists who are poorly trained or who are trained in a pedestrian academic mold may not only do no good but may actually do some harm. The time has come for psychologists to examine their own curricula with an analytic frame of mind and to ask themselves honestly, "Are we preparing the right kinds of psychologists for our technological society?" Fortunately, a few institutions are willing to conduct such self-examinations.

Conclusion

The subtitle of this chapter is "A Tale of Two Laboratories," and most of what I had to say was about two laboratories. Both were at Johns Hopkins, both flourished, and both are now part of history. But both laboratories have indelibly shaped the world of psychology, and I am pleased that I was able to be part of one of them. Even as G. Stanley Hall wrote about his students that "nearly all of them have since attained eminence" (1924, 232), I too take pride in the many students I have trained who have successfully made their places in the world. Now that I have embarked on my second career, I derive great satisfaction in joining them as colleagues to make the world a better and safer place.

References

Chapanis, A. *Research techniques in human engineering*. Baltimore: Johns Hopkins Press, 1959.

Chapanis, A., Garner, W. R., & Morgan, C. T. *Applied experimental psychology: Human factors in engineering design*. New York: Wiley, 1949.

Chapanis, A., Garner, W. R., Morgan, C. T., & Sanford, F. H. *Lectures on men and machines: An introduction to human engineering*. (Special Devices Center Report No. 166-I-19). Baltimore: Systems Research Laboratory, 1947.

Fitts, P. M. (Ed.). *Human engineering for an effective air-navigation and traffic-control system*. Washington, DC: National Research Council, Division of Anthropology and Psychology, Committee on Aviation Psychology, 1951.

Galambos, L. *America at middle age*. New York: McGraw-Hill Book Co., 1982.

Hall, G. S. Practical relations between psychology and the war. *Journal of Applied Psychology*. 1917a, *1*, 9–16.

Hall, G. S. A reminiscence. *American Journal of Psychology*, 1917b, *28*, 297--300.

Hall, G. S. Practical applications of psychology as developed by the war. *Pedagogical Seminary*, 1919a, *26*, 76–89.

Hall, G. S. Some relations between the war and psychology. *American Journal of Psychology,* 1919b, *20,* 211–223.

Hall, G. S. Psychology and industry. *Pedagogical Seminary,* 1920, *27,* 281–293.

Hall, G. S. *Life and confessions of a psychologist.* New York: D. Appleton & Co., 1924.

Hancock, E. Academe meets industry: Charting the bottom line. *Johns Hopkins Magazine,* 1983, *34*(4), I–IX.

Morgan, C. T., Cook, J. S., III, Chapanis, A., & Lund, M. W. *Human engineering guide to equipment design.* New York: McGraw-Hill, 1963.

Panel on Psychology and Physiology. *A survey report on human factors in undersea warfare.* Washington, DC: National Research Council, Committee on Undersea Warfare, 1949.

Parsons, H. M. *Man-machine system experiments.* Baltimore: Johns Hopkins Press, 1972.

4. Psychology in Recent Years at Johns Hopkins
Stewart H. Hulse and Bert F. Green, Jr.

The preceding chapters by Appley, Pauly, and Chapanis provide an overview of the origins and development of the Department of Psychology at Johns Hopkins until the 1950s. Chapanis's chapter, which stresses the post–World War II period, reflects his interests in the origins of the field of human factors, interests that provided both a direct and an indirect focus for much of the department both then and later. But what of the larger, most recent history of the department over the twenty five or thirty years leading to the centennial? Hulse came to Johns Hopkins in 1957 and Green in 1969 so, together, we have experienced the events of that time. We offer some thoughts, observations, and comments.

Clifford T. Morgan, who became professor and chairman of the department (as Chapanis notes) shortly after the war, was a brilliant, many-sided man, not without a certain similarity to G. Stanley Hall. Like Hall, he was energetic and had done significant research as a young psychologist. As his career developed at Johns Hopkins and later, however, he left the laboratory to observe psychology, to write, and to found things. While at Johns Hopkins, for example, he edited the first of many editions of an innovative text in introductory psychology, drawing on the skills of department members to round out coverage of the field. He left Johns Hopkins formally in 1958, after being an inactive member of the department for a year or so, living and writing in Cambridge on the Eastern Shore of Maryland. He then went to the University of Wisconsin, to the University of California at Santa Barbara, and, finally, to the University of Texas at Austin. He died in Austin in 1976. Until his death, he continued to write books, including revisions of the *Introduction to Psychology*, and *Physiological Psychology*, the latter of which he had first written himself and then revised with Eliot Stellar. Perhaps of greatest significance, however, he was a major force behind the formation of the Psychonomic Society, a group of experimental psychologists that organized in 1960 to discuss and promote research in experimental psychology. He served as first chairman and later as the secretary-treasurer of that organization and founded, edited, and published the several journals that the Society itself now owns and publishes.

Morgan had a major impact on Johns Hopkins and its traditions, but his influence was subtle. He capitalized on the nucleus provided by the Systems Research Field Laboratory, as Chapanis notes, to draw an interesting group of people to Johns Hopkins and the newly reorganized Department of Psychology.[1] Some stayed briefly, some stayed a long time, and some, like Chapanis, stayed for their entire academic careers. Most became distinguished psychologists. Morgan had an uncanny sense about talent and promise. He did not always nurture talent well, but if there were to be a department comprised of the people he attracted to Johns Hopkins during the late 1940s and early 1950s, it would be truly renowned. The group included William Prentice, Neil Bartlett, Wendell Garner, Eliot Stellar, Alphonse Chapanis, Richard Lazarus, James Deese, Charles Eriksen, Harold Hake, Ward Edwards, and Marvin Shaw, to name but a few.

Garner succeeded Morgan as chairman in 1955, and the department began a period of relative stability. Mary Ainsworth joined the faculty in 1956. Clinton DeSoto also came from Wisconsin in 1956, and Stewart Hulse (from Brown) and Leon Otis (from Chicago) in 1957. The staff in 1960 consisted of eight people: Ainsworth, Chapanis, Deese, DeSoto, Garner, Hulse, Otis, and G. Wilson Shaffer (whose primary responsibilities were as Dean of the Faculty of Philosophy and, later, of the Homewood schools). That is a surprisingly small number, given the continuing place of the department within the profession.

The traditions that Morgan and his new colleagues established in the 1940s and 1950s continued into the early 1960s and, of course, later. Chief among these was the tradition of research psychology. Needless to say, with a staff of eight, each faculty member was a rugged individualist, a sole representative of his or her own area of research psychology. Shaffer, occupied largely with his responsibilities as dean, taught a popular course in abnormal psychology. Chapanis and Garner, especially the former, maintained the traditions of human factors but also specialized, respectively, in vision, and in scaling, perception, and information theory. Ainsworth specialized in personality theory and, later, in developmental psychology. Deese's interests spanned animal and human learning, developing from there into psycholinguistics. DeSoto specialized in social psychology and social cognition, while Hulse and Otis maintained interests in animal learning and physiological psychology, respectively.

There was some turnover through the 1960s. Otis left for the Stanford Research Institute in 1960, to be replaced by Leonard Matin. Matin stayed until 1963, leaving for Columbia University. He was replaced by James Myer, who had just received his doctorate from Pennsylvania.

Warren Torgerson arrived from MIT's Lincoln Laboratory in 1964 to take Garner's place as chairman. After a year's leave in England, Garner moved to Yale in 1966. Torgerson undertook to expand the department, at a time when higher education was expanding generally. William Garvey joined the department in 1965 as professor and head of the Center for the Study of Scientific Communication. He became a full-time member of the department in 1968 and brought Carnot Nelson to join the center and the department in 1967. William Bevan arrived in 1966, with primary responsibilities as provost of the university but with an appointment as professor of psychology. He had graduate students and actively pursued research in experimental psychology in addition to his administrative responsibilities. Julian Stanley arrived from Wisconsin with a primary appointment in education in 1967. His primary appointment became psychology in 1971. Robert Hogan, from Berkeley, and Howard Egeth, from Michigan, also arrived in 1967. Bert Green came from Carnegie-Mellon in 1969, along with Elliott Blass (from Pennsylvania) and David Olton (from Michigan). The department numbered only nine in 1965; it had expanded to seventeen in 1970.

With the addition of people such as Torgerson, Stanley, and Green, the department added mathematical psychology to its program. Blass and Olton strengthened the fields of animal learning and behavior and physiological psychology, while Hogan, Nelson, and Garvey broadened the scope of personality research and social psychology.

Through the 1950s and 1960s, the department maintained a very active graduate program. From 1950 through the mid-1960s, the number of new doctorates awarded ranged from two in 1951 to four or five for most of the succeeding years. There was growth of the student population to match that of the faculty as the 1970s approached. Seven doctorates were awarded in 1966, for example, while eleven were awarded in 1968.

Torgerson resigned as chairman in 1969 and was succeeded by Deese. The department was now as large as it would ever become, and as diverse. Graduate work was under way in experimental, quantitative, social, and developmental psychology, as well as in psychobiology, personality, and human factors. The education department was disbanded by the university, and Stanley became a full-time member of the psychology department. Roger Webb arrived to strengthen the developmental program; Myer left for Kent State and was replaced by William Stark, from Wisconsin.

President Gordon resigned from the presidency in 1972, in the wake of serious financial problems, and a period of retrenchment set in for Johns

Hopkins. Deese left in 1973 to become chairman of the psychology department at the University of Virginia, and Ainsworth followed him there in 1974. Webb also left in 1974. Bevan left in 1973 to become executive secretary of the American Association for the Advancement of Science. Garvey took over the chair in 1974 and led the department for a decade. Milton Strauss arrived in 1974, to maintain the department's interest in abnormal psychology; Shaffer retired and became emeritus in 1975. Also in 1974, Stephen Kosslyn from Stanford and James Pomerantz from Yale joined the experimental wing of the department, and the department broke a long-standing tradition by hiring one of its own students, Alfonso Caramazza. Judith Hall arrived in 1976; Hall and Kosslyn gave brief life to the developmental program, but Hall identified with social and Kosslyn with experimental, and, when they left no further attempt was made to maintain developmental psychology in the department. When Pomerantz left for Buffalo, Michael McCloskey joined the faculty (from Princeton), and when Stark left for Missouri, Richard Katz joined the department (from Michigan). In 1977, Maury Silver was added in social and Alan Zonderman in quantitative.

By 1980, Caramazza, Olton, and Strauss had become interested in the study of behavioral deficits of neurological origin, and the current focus on cognitive neuropsychology began to take shape. Jason Brandt, from Boston University, was added in this field in 1981.

Garvey instituted a number of special programs. The most viable—it is still in operation—was the BA / MA program for exceptional undergraduates, who might otherwise finish easily in seven semesters. With a few additional courses and an independent masters-level project, these students could earn both a BA and an MA in four years of concentrated work. For especially exceptional undergraduates, the BA-PhD program was instituted, involving, if all went well, a BA, MA, and PhD in six or seven years. A joint MD-PhD program flourished briefly, but very few students had the combination of practical and scientific interests to wear both coats. A joint JD-PhD program with the University of Maryland law school was designed for students interested in psychology and the law, and a joint program with the School of Public Health was designed for students interested in psychology and health. A special program, Focus on Women, was designed for women interested in a second career as a research psychologist. Students in these programs have enriched the graduate program by keeping an applied emphasis along with Johns Hopkins' traditional academic focus.

Chapanis retired in 1982 and Stanley in 1984, though both maintained research programs associated with the university. Garvey began retiring in 1983 by stepping down as chairman in favor of Olton; in 1984 he left to write, paint, and cook in Maine.

Many of our faculty have had interesting hobbies, but none has been as much a part of the university activities as Garvey's cooking. Each January, his course in breadmaking was attended by nearly all the graduate students; he gave demonstrations regularly for the Johns Hopkins Wednesday noon series and for the JHU Alumni Association. The full professors in the department looked forward each winter to a Saturday feast prepared by "Chef Billy Bocuse," and Garvey's retirement gift from the department was a special set of cookware. Johns Hopkins psychology graduates have long had a reputation for empirical rigor and statistical acumen. Garvey added to this tradition the ability to turn out good French bread.

The department has been served by many loyal workers, more than can be noted here. Two stand out; both retired in the mid 1970s, following many years of service: Peg McDonald, department secretary for Garner, Torgerson, and Deese, and Bill Hamilton, instrument maker for the entire research program for several decades.

As the department reaches the mid 1980s, its main fields are psychobiology, experimental, quantitative, cognitive neuropsychology, and personality and social psychology.

Note

1. We have included as members of the faculty of the department only those individuals who held a full-time, primary appointment in psychology (that is also true of appendix 2.A of Pauly's chapter). This method of listing excludes some distinguished individuals, such as John M. Stephens, whose primary appointment was in education, but who also held a joint appointment in psychology. He is listed separately in *University Circulars* of the 1940s, 1950s, and 1960s as both professor of psychology and professor of education. While our procedure omits some individuals who are important and might be included, it also omits, reasonably we think, many people with part-time appointments, with courtesy appointments, and with other relationships to the department that were purely ancillary to a primary appointment or task elsewhere. In any case, we suggest the *University Circulars* as a reference for further information about those who were affiliated with the department in some capacity but who did not meet our criteria for inclusion here.

PART II

Psychology and the Units of Behavior

5. The Lateral Hypothalamic Double-Disconnection Syndrome: A Reappraisal and a New Theory for Recovery of Function

Philip Teitelbaum

One of the favorite maxims of my father [Niels Bohr] was the distinction between the two sorts of truths, profound truths recognized by the fact that the opposite is also a profound truth, in contrast to trivialities where opposites are obviously absurd.

Hans Bohr, 1967

In 1950, when I began my graduate work in physiological psychology at Johns Hopkins, Cliff Morgan and Eliot Stellar were there; their textbook on physiological psychology had just been published and was to guide the field for the next decade. "Tex" Garner, Al Chapanis, Harry Hake, "Eric" Eriksen, Jim Deese, and Dick Lazarus rounded out the department. The new students were supposed to do library research on a topic related to their interests, directed in their first year by Morgan. However, some cynical advice from one of the more senior graduate students filled me with doubt, and I decided to check his perceptions. In our first conference, Morgan asked me what I wanted to work on. I replied that I wanted to work on the brain and behavior, but did not think I knew enough to do anything. He said, "You just have to jump in. What specific problems interest you?" I listed (1) figural aftereffects, supposed by Kohler and Wallach (1944) to be related to lactic acid build-up in brain cells, so it seemed to me that anoxia should potentiate figural aftereffects. Morgan: "Nice idea, but impractical—it might be dangerous to the subjects and would require a physician on hand at all times." (2) Hebb (1949) had suggested that I.Q. loss after frontal lobe damage might be due not to the absence of normal frontal tissue but to epileptic discharges from the remaining scar tissue. Therefore, implant a coil in the frontal lobes of rats and buzz their brains by remote control while they learn a maze; this should impair their learning. Morgan: "Again nice, but technically quite difficult." (3) A trivial extension of the research of one of the current faculty members. Morgan, slowly: "You don't really want to do that, do you?" "No, but that's what they tell me you have to do to get ahead around here." A long silence by Morgan, then: "No—you don't have to do that. There are three major unsolved problems in how the brain functions after damage: (1) Recovery of function—how does behavior, lost after damage, recover with time? (2) Release phenomena—how do you get more of a normal kind of behavior when tissue is destroyed? (3) Delayed appearance of behavior—how come some effects of damage don't show up until months after the tissue is lost? Here are some references on each topic. Go into the library, study, and pick one to write a paper on."

I buried myself in the library. It became clear that I really wanted to work on recovery of function, but all the work seemed to be on monkeys (Bucy 1949), impractical on Homewood campus. Delayed appearance of behavior seemed relatively intangible. So I chose release phenomena, and picked hypothalamic hyperphagia to work on, because it was a big phenomenon; it was first discovered in humans (i.e., Fröhlich's syndrome, 1904), appeared in many species, and therefore must be of general importance; it could be produced in rats, which were easily obtainable; and my reading had convinced me that sensory stimuli were exaggeratedly important in all release phenomena, and therefore the taste and texture of the food, easily varied, should exaggeratedly affect intake, easily measured. This turned out to be so, became my doctoral thesis (1955), and got me into the study of motivated behavior.

Eliot Stellar and Nelson Krause (1954) had just designed a stereotaxic instrument for the rat (now available from Stoelting Co., Chicago) based on a principle of moving the center of a sphere to any desired coordinate in the brain, enabling an electrode to approach a target from any angle. No one had used it yet, so Eliot helped me, working side by side.[1] We failed at first, so we varied our lesion placements. Several animals refused to eat and drink until they died. I attributed it to surgical trauma. Later, we saw Anand and Brobeck's (1951) papers localizing a lateral hypothalamic "feeding center." Our aphagic animals' lesions were always at the coordinates they specified. We felt like kicking ourselves for missing an obviously important finding.

But our failure had a silver lining. Believing the animals merely debilitated, I tried coaxing them to eat. Earlier, while cleaning the department's rat colony (my assistantship), I used to stop, munch chocolate bars, and offer some to the rats. I soon discovered that, shortly before my break, many rats were lined up at the front of each cage, all waiting for their treat. I remembered this later when trying to tempt aphagic rats to eat, and it was thrilling to see a rat (fig. 5.1), being kept alive by tube-feeding, refusing ordinary food and water for two months postoperatively, suddenly gobble up bits of chocolate (Teitelbaum and Stellar 1954; Teitelbaum 1979).

This seemingly trivial observation led to most of my later research. Lateral hypothalamic aphagia was a way to study recovery of function. As my work on it has progressed over the years, I have changed my thinking again and again. Many years elapsed before I understood that in the study of brain function, and in my own work, a complementarity exists: localization of function versus levels of function. Each view offers a coherent way of thinking and experimenting, but they are antithetical to each other; the virtues of one make vices out of the virtues of the other. Instead of being hampered by complementarity, perhaps we can use it constructively by oscillating between each view, as in a reversible figure-ground illusion (Teitelbaum 1982a, 1982b). I will list some of the early ideas and will illustrate how their complementarities changed our work.

1. Regulation versus Motivation

In 1950, food intake was considered mainly as a problem of homeostatic regulation of the internal environment. Motivational phenomena such as appetite were thought of as psychological epiphenomena, representing only trivial perturbations of the basic quantitative reflexive regulation. Psychologists worked on taste preferences, a form of appetite, useful in selecting food but not in determining the overall amount ingested. For regulation, amount, not palatability, seemed relevant, and it was conceived of in terms of reflexive homeostasis, where deficits in the internal environment might be signaled thermally (Brobeck 1960) or humorally (Kennedy 1953, Mayer 1955). The behavior involved in feeding was assumed to reflect passively and faithfully the changes in the internal environment, so behavior could be used indirectly as a measure of the summed action of the autonomic reflexes of digestion and metabolism. Our work showed that a slight change in the palatability of food greatly affected the amount eaten by obese, hyperphagic animals (Teitelbaum 1955; McGinty, Epstein, and Teitelbaum 1965) and could make the difference between life and death in otherwise aphagic animals (Teitelbaum and Stellar 1954). Motivation and appetite therefore played a major role in how much an animal eats (Teitelbaum 1964). This made the problem relevant and challenging for psychologists. Since that time, psychologists have demonstrated other "nonhomeostatic" forms of ingestion such as tail-pinch induced eating (Antelman and Szechtman 1975; Teitelbaum and Wolgin 1975; Szechtman 1980) and "psychogenic" polydipsia (Falk 1971).

Such phenomena illustrate that two domains of nervous action which might better be kept separate for the time being appear to be mixed in current thinking about food intake. One involves the autonomic control of the internal environment: the vegetative reflexes used to digest, metabolize, and excrete food. These go on whether the animal is awake or asleep, conscious or comatose. For such regulations (e.g., blood sugar and blood pH), control theory seems appropriate (Yamamoto and Brobeck 1965). They can be measured directly in a decerebrate immobilized animal, so behavior need not be used indirectly to assess these variables of the internal environment. The other domain includes the skeletal waking behaviors involved in searching for, approaching, and eating food. Activation by taste, pain, and other seemingly unrelated sensory inputs, as well as learning and memory, can greatly increase the frequency of these behaviors and the amount of food or water ingested (Jacquin and Zeigler 1983, Teitelbaum, Schallert, and Whishaw 1983). Such behavioral variables can override the need state of the internal environment. For example, respiration is mostly autonomic; you can hold your breath for a while, but not long enough to disturb the internal environment much, so control theory works well. Feeding and drinking are at the other extreme of this continuum: the more complex laws of waking behavior can override the internal state; for instance, a person can voluntarily starve to death (see also Schallert and Hsiao 1979). As described below, the first stage of the lateral hypothalamic syndrome functionally disconnects these two domains: complex waking acts appear to be disconnected from the internal environment, and the subcomponents of those acts are disconnected from each other. During recovery, the simplified interaction of the two domains (autonomic and behavioral) in the control of intake may continue to be useful in understanding how activation and motivation interact with autonomic regulation.

2. One Locus—One Function

The lateral hypothalamus is a "hunger center." This idea, based on localization of function, guided the work of Anand and Brobeck. Ideal localization requires that lesions be small, affect only one function, and affect it permanently. Localization is so compelling that Anand and Brobeck reported that their lateral hypothalamic-damaged rats and cats stopped eating and died, not that they refused water as well. (They did mention that one cat did not eat and drink for a day postoperatively, and died the next day, but no emphasis was placed on its adipsia.) They knew that the animals were not drinking but assumed that was a consequence of their failure to eat.[2] That only one function was abolished fit the concept of hypothalamic localization of regulatory functions which had been developed in the work of Ranson, Brobeck's mentor.[3] When Stellar and I replicated Anand and Brobeck's work (fig. 5.1), we were struck by the adipsia as much as by the aphagia, perhaps because we focused on the behavioral functions that remained and returned in recovery.

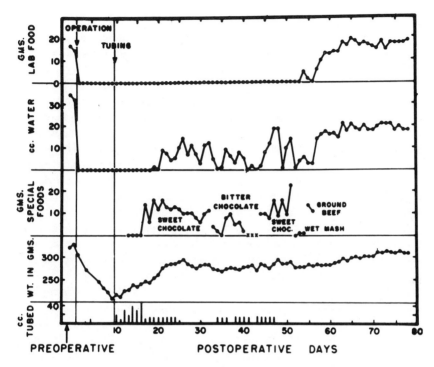

Fig. 5.1. Course of recovery of eating behavior in one rat, following complete refusal to eat and drink produced by hypothalamic damage. The animal loses weight steadily for 10 days, at which time tube-feeding with a liquid diet was begun, to keep it alive. Note that milk chocolate is eaten when the animal will otherwise accept nothing. *Source:* Teitelbaum, P., and Stellar, E. Recovery from the failure to eat produced by hypothalamic lesions. *Science, 1954, 120.* Copyright 1954 by the American Association for the Advancement of Science.

3. One Locus–Two Functions: Hunger and Thirst

From 1954 through 1960, two assumptions stemming from the concept of localization still channeled our thinking: (1) one locus–one function, and (2) a lesion is a one-time event, static and unchanging. Williams and I (1959) found that some lateral hypothalamic-damaged animals regulated their caloric intake adequately on a liquid diet, and, if they also had some medial hypothalamic damage, even overate and became obese, yet refused to eat and drink and died on a diet of dry food and water. They would drink water, but only reluctantly, when forced by operant methods. Anand and Brobeck seemed to be correct in saying that lateral hypothalamic aphagia suppressed hypothalamic hyperphagia, but not on a liquid diet. So puzzling were these findings that Williams and I titled our paper,

"Some Observations on the Starvation Resulting from Lateral Hypothalamic Lesions." Was the deficit solely in thirst, not hunger? But some animals, with larger lesions, also refused the liquid diet and starved to death. Did that mean one locus—two functions?

When Alan Epstein (who also had been a student of Eliot Stellar's at Johns Hopkins) and I began to work together (again under Stellar's auspices) at the Institute of Neurological Sciences of the University of Pennsylvania, we realized that many of the contradictory symptoms presented by an animal after lateral hypothalamic damage could be reconciled by recognizing that the animals were changing continually with each day of recovery. Each puzzling constellation of symptoms seemed to form a qualitatively different stage of recovery (fig. 5.2). First, the animal refuses to eat or drink anything; this is "aphagia and adipsia." Second, it eats palatable foods, but not enough to maintain its weight, and does not drink water; this is "anorexia and adipsia." Third, the animal fails to eat only because it does not drink; this is "adipsia and dehydration-aphagia." Finally, the "recovery" stage appears, in which the animal drinks water, eats dry food, and survives, but depending on the extent of tissue damage, may show residual deficits in eating and drinking. An animal might start in any stage, depending on the size and symmetry of the damage, but it invariably followed the sequence of stages from then on. These qualitatively different stages were formed owing to the fact that hunger

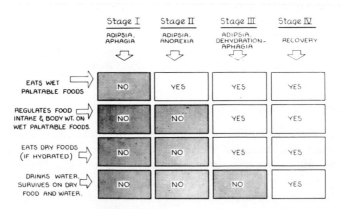

Fig. 5.2. Stages of recovery seen in the lateral hypothalamic syndrome. The critical behavioral events whose presence or absence defines the stages are listed on the left. *Source:* Teitelbaum, P., and Epstein, A. N. The lateral hypothalamic syndrome: Recovery of feeding and drinking after lateral hypothalamic damage. *Psychological Review,* 1962, *69.* Copyright 1962 by the American Psychological Association. Reprinted by permission of the authors.

and thirst were both abolished by the lesions and recovered at different rates. Their out-of-phase recovery showed how, in the third stage, caloric intake could be intact when water regulation was not (hydrational needs were being satisfied as the animal ate rather than drank the liquid diet, while aphagia on dry food was secondary to refusal to ingest water); whereas, in the first and second stage, the counter-experiment of hydrating the animals did not restore eating. Therefore, as far as localization was concerned, we had now arrived at the idea of one locus—two functions (Teitelbaum and Epstein 1962).

4. Levels versus Locus

Stages of recovery seemed to fit the concept of levels of function (Flourens 1824; Jackson 1884), where the earliest stage represented a lower, perhaps decerebrate, level of behavior, and each successive stage illustrated how the behavior was transformed into operant motivated behavior. This meant that localization in the hypothalamus was less important; the system involved ought to be hierarchical, represented and re-represented at every level of integration from spinal cord to cortex (Jackson 1884). Guided by this idea, Cytawa and I (1965, 1967, 1968) observed that spreading cortical depression reinstated the lateral hypothalamic syndrome after recovery, as well as the subcortical syndromes of temperature impairment after preoptic damage and hyperemotionality after septal damage.

Furthermore, the effects of a lateral hypothalamic lesion ought not to be restricted to that point. By diaschisis, a kind of shock (von Monakow 1911), the lesion might de-encephalize the entire hierarchical system, might reduce it to a low level of function, and the process of recovery could then be seen as a gradual re-encephalization. This seemed to resemble the way the system was organized in its development in infancy. Therefore, some parallels ought to exist between development of feeding in infancy and adult recovery of feeding. By slowing down development, Cheng, Rozin, and I (1969, 1971) showed that at weaning, underdeveloped rat pups gained the ability to eat and drink like adults in stages that paralleled recovery after LH damage (fig. 5.3). The recovery process could be viewed as the reintegration of separate controls that added their action to each other to produce levels of function, paralleling such integration in development (Teitelbaum 1971). From this point of view, it becomes heuristically valuable to compare and contrast behavior of normal infants with that of brain-damaged adults. If there are parallels, then unsuspected phenomena present in both development and recovery may emerge. One might also expect animals in the early stages of recovery to show similarities to decerebrates, while those in the later stages should be more

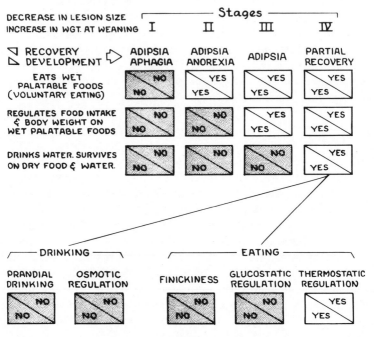

Development of Eating & Drinking
Parallels its Recovery

Fig. 5.3.   Comparison of the development of eating and drinking in infancy and its recovery after lateral hypothalamic lesions in adults. The upper right half of each block represents the recovery of the adult lateral hypothalamic rat, and the lower left the development of the growing infant (thyroidectomized or starvation-stunted to slow down development). Uniform shading in each full block indicates similar responses in recovery and development. *Source:* Teitelbaum, P., Cheng, M.-F., and Rozin, P. Development of feeding parallels its recovery after hypothalamic damage. *Journal of Comparative and Physiological Psychology,* 1969, 67. Copyright 1969 by the American Psychological Association. Reprinted by permission of the authors.

similar to decorticates. The order in which behavioral elements reappear in recovery also becomes noteworthy: the earliest elements to reappear should be more primitive, more infantile, and organized at a more caudal level in the central nervous system. Thus, water intake should be more encephalized than food intake because it recovers later. Support for this conclusion is found in the work of Grill and Miselis (1981) on decerebrate rats, in which food deprivation facilitates nutrient-evoked swallowing, whereas water deprivation does not promote the swallowing of water, suggesting that this component of thirst depends on more rostral mechanisms.

Parallels in development and recovery of the use of the hand had been demonstrated by Twitchell (1951, 1965, 1970). In studying adult hemiplegic patients, he observed that three grasping automatisms described by Seyffarth and Denny-Brown (1948) (the traction response, the true grasp, and the instinctive grasp reaction) could be identified and that they represented sequential stages in recovery of voluntary use of the hand. Similar stages appeared in the development of grasping in normal infants (fig. 5.4). The infant grasp had been studied for many years, but only after the traction response was found in the brain-damaged adult was it recognized in the infant. Thus, the brain-damaged adult highlights some normal characteristics of the infant.

The traction response was a form of grasp that did not depend on touching the palm; indeed, light touch did not elicit it. Merely pulling against the flexors of the arm was sufficient. Vestibular input affects the traction response: when the patient is lying with the paralyzed side down (head also on its side), the traction response is weak and difficult to elicit; conversely, with the paralyzed side up, the grasp is strong and easily elicited. Later in recovery, the fingers flex in response to a distally moving tactile stimulus to the medial palm. This is the true grasp reflex. Eventually, the sight of a stimulus can cause the hand to reach out and grasp it (Twitchell 1951, 1970). With sufficient recovery, true "operant" use of the hand may return.

The sequence of change in the sensory modality that controls the grasp was highly intriguing. If this sensory transformation sequence (kinesthetic-vestibular, tactile, visual, operant) were general (Teitelbaum 1977a), it ought to appear in the recovery and development of feeding after lateral hypothalamic damage. I racked my brains for years but could find no sign of it. Only later did it emerge, in the so-called side effects of lateral hypothalamic damage.

5. One Locus—Many Functions

In 1954, when Stellar and I demonstrated recovery from aphagia and adipsia after lateral hypothalamic damage, the work was criticized on the grounds that the lesions were too small, because the animals should not recover if all the appropriate tissue had been destroyed. We pointed out that if not tube-fed, virtually all the animals died, which was the same criterion of permanence of deficit used by Anand and Brobeck to verify their localization of "feeding centers." This argument had no effect— recovery was bad; it should not occur. So, in later work, we made larger lesions; but if kept alive by tube-feeding, the animals always recovered,

AT BIRTH
TRACTION RESPONSE
Stimulus: Stretch shoulder adductors and flexors
Response: All joints flex

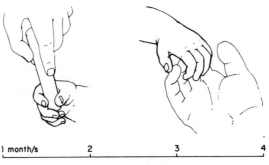

| 1 month/s | 2 | 3 | 4 |

GRASP REFLEX
(INITIAL COMPONENT)   (FULLY FORMED)
S. Contact between thumb and index   S. Distally moving contact medial palm
R. Thumb and index adduct alone   R. All fingers flex

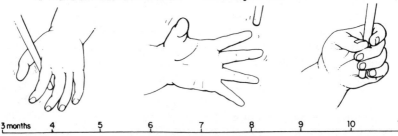

| 3 months | 4 | 5 | 6 | 7 | 8 | 9 | 10 | 1 |

INSTINCTIVE GRASP REACTION
S. Contact radial or ulnar side   S. Contact hand (any part)   S. Contact hand (any part)
R. Hand orients   R. Hand gropes   R. Hand grasps

Fig. 5.4. Evolution of the automatic grasping responses of infants. *Source:* Reprinted with permission from *Neuropsychologia, 3,* Twitchell, T. E., The automatic grasping responses of infants, Copyright 1965, Pergamon Press Ltd.

albeit more slowly and less completely (Teitelbaum and Epstein 1962). However, with larger lesions, unwanted side effects such as somnolence, catalepsy, and akinesia appeared in stage 1, along with the aphagia and adipsia. The localizationists now said the lesions were too large; unrelated systems adjacent to those involved in feeding and drinking were obviously being damaged. But the animals still recovered. So, from the point of view of localization, the lesions were simultaneously too big (side effects occurred) and too small (recovery occurred). A visual illustration of an analogous perceptual paradox is shown in figure 5.5.

It gradually became clear to me that two complementary approaches were possible in the study of the behavioral effects of lateral hypothalamic damage: the localization of missing tissue versus the level of remaining and returning function.[4] As far as I have been able to discover, the concept of localization of function derives from medical anatomy (Morgagni 1769), where, by dissection, distinct organs can be isolated, each in principle having a separate function. One organ, one locus, one function. In the study of the brain, localization of function began to develop in the science of phrenology (Spurzheim 1818). Although phrenology is often held up to ridicule nowadays, some reasonable premises existed for it: in extreme cases of underdevelopment of the brain, a person will be microcephalic as well as mentally retarded. In other words, a small brain leads to a small skull and limited mental capacity. From this, it was not unreasonable for phrenologists to infer that growth of the brain might be reflected in corresponding growth of the skull over it. Further assume that specific mental "organs" are associated with specific parts of the cortex and that highly developed mental faculties should cause overdevelopment of a particular part of the cortex, thus yielding a protuberance in the skull over it. Indeed, recent evidence indicates that specific areas of the cortex do increase in weight and size with specific forms of enriched early experience (Greenough 1975). Why then does phrenology seem ridiculous? One reason is that the skull was being used *indirectly* to make inferences about the

Fig. 5.5. Where the lines converge, the same-length line looks long in comparison with its appearance when not so constrained by those lines.

location of tissue in the brain. Progress in the technology of direct localization of brain structures makes it seem silly to use bumps on the skull to do so.

The modern equivalent of the abandonment of phrenology is happening in neurology, the medical specialty that uses behavioral symptoms indirectly to diagnose where a tumor, a blood clot, or an epileptic focus is located in brain tissue, so that the neurosurgeon can cut it out with as little brain damage as possible. Localization is what is vital here, not an understanding of what the brain does, which is more complex and can wait, as far as medical treatment is concerned. Merely associating a brain region with a behavioral symptom resulting from pathology in that area is sufficient for neurosurgical localization. Like bumps on the skull, behavior is being used indirectly, this time to locate pathological tissue. The tissue is what is really of interest in this approach, not the behavior. Therefore, as soon as a method for direct visual localization of the pathological tissue becomes available (as in the recently developed technique of computerized axial tomography), all that painfully amassed knowledge about behavioral symptoms is no longer needed for localization, becomes irrelevant, and will eventually be ignored and forgotten. Much of current physiological psychology is involved in an indirect use of behavior to infer chemical and anatomical properties of brain tissue. Will such information seem like a waste of time when direct methods of studying the particular tissue become available?

Instead of using behavior indirectly to assess characteristics of brain tissue, a complementary approach is to manipulate brain tissue to help us observe behavior directly. One way is embodied in the study of level of remaining function. It has been fruitful in the past (e.g., Sherrington 1906; Magnus 1926) and is still used successfully (e.g., Jouvet 1967; Villablanca 1971; Grill and Norgren 1978). If all the structures above a certain level are removed or are isolated by complete transection, the caudal nervous system mediates the behavior that remains. If a spinal animal can walk, run, or gallop as a treadmill is moved beneath its feet (Grillner 1975), then the spinal cord alone must be sufficient to organize and execute those gaits. The simplified remainder of the nervous system yields simpler fragments of behavior, revealing the subcomponents that interact to produce normal, more complex, behavior. This is a form of systems analysis: the study of remaining function reveals the subcomponents of the system. The behavior is what is primary here, not the tissue. In computer terminology, it is the software that we are interested in, not the hardware.

Subtotal removal is ambiguous: it can be seen either from the medical-therapeutic view that we need to localize the missing tissue and characterize its anatomy and chemistry, or from the behavioral standpoint where we wish to study the simpler behavior of the remaining system. The work done on the problem will be quite different, depending on which view is taken. In recent years, we have found it useful to view lateral hypothalamic lesions, not primarily in terms of localization but as partial transections. After partial transection, recovery is good; it allows us to study the re-synthesis of behavior. When we treat a lesion in terms of localization, we strive to make it smaller and more selective, so a large lesion is bad. But when we treat it as a partial transection, a large lesion is good—the larger the partial transection, the simpler the behavior that remains. We realized that our labeling of lateral hypothalamic damage in terms only of feeding and drinking had been based on Anand and Brobeck's interest in localiza-tion. With a large enough lateral hypothalamic partial transection, the animal would probably be in a coma for awhile—it could be maintained by tube-feeding, but all motivated behavior would be abolished. In such a state, the vegetative autonomic reflexes of digestion, metabolism, and excretion operate normally enough to keep the animal healthy if intra-gastric meals are provided, but they are disconnected from behavior. A coma is a kind of "zero condition" (Magnus 1926) in which the movement subsystems involved in motivated behavior seem to be inactivated (Teitelbaum 1982a). But recovery can occur. Therefore, instead of being irrelevant and unwanted, the side effects of lateral hypothalamic damage, e.g., somnolence, akinesia, catalepsy, and sensory neglect, become useful signposts of reintegration from coma towards normal motivated behavior (Teitelbaum 1982a). In other words, one locus, many functions.[5]

6. Motivated Behavior: The Animal as a Whole versus Its Parts

Somnolence, akinesia, catalepsy, and sensory neglect are still quite poorly understood. They share several features but have different names because different aspects of a common complex of symptoms have been empha-sized. When viewed as a medical problem, such pathological behavioral states have often been labeled with Greek names. It seems strange for a person or an animal to lie unresponsive, unmoving except for breathing, with eyes closed. If the animal is impossible to arouse, it is said to be in a coma. If it can be aroused, but only by strong stimuli, and the behavior elicited is fragmentary and transient, the animal is said to be stuporous, or, if somewhat more responsive, somnolent. If it appears to be awake (it stands, with eyes open) but remains unmoving, even in awkward postures, it is called akinetic or cataleptic. When it does not orient to sensory stimuli, even though it feels them, it is said to show neglect. With respect to all these states, we tend to view the animal as a whole that is acting strangely and wonder what neural elements have been affected. Medically, we need to treat those neural elements, so the major research emphasis has been to localize the systems whose pathology has precipitated the symptoms and to search for the transmitters involved in order to develop drugs to restore their function. However, we can learn a great deal about these states, and about behavior in general, by studying the behaviors that remain and return. Such fractional forms of behavior are often adaptive, but for a more limited, more reflex function, functionally disconnected from the other subcomponents of normal behavior.

Consider the fully somnolent animal, lying unmoving, 24 hours after extensive bilateral lateral hypothalamic partial transection. It does not right itself, it lacks postural support, and its cortical activity is persistently synchronized, with slow waves of large amplitude. It is not really asleep all the time, but even when it is awake its behavior patterns are so restricted that it gives the illusion of persistent somnolence (Shoham and Teitelbaum 1982). If placed in a tank full of water (33° C), it sinks to the bottom, may actually groom itself underwater, but makes little or no attempt to swim (fig. 5.6). However, in colder water (23° C), it swims vigorously, may climb up on the rim of the tank, leap to the floor, run away, and then

Fig. 5.6.   In warm water, unlike a normal rat which swims to the surface, a rat with bilateral lateral hypothalamic lesions swims little or not at all. A cycle of exhalation under water, as shown in the illustrations is followed by a thrust against the bottom of the tank with the rear leg, propelling the rat to the surface for inhalation. *Source:* Levitt, D. R., and Teitelbaum, P. Somnolence, akinesia and sensory activation of motivated behavior in the lateral hypothalamic syndrome. *Proceedings of the National Academy of Sciences, U.S.A.,* 1975, 72.

become immobile once again (Robinson and Whishaw 1974; Levitt and Teitelbaum 1975). The animal is not paralyzed; the behavior patterns involved in motivated behavior are intact but inaccessible to it. The animal can not spontaneously self-activate them (Teitelbaum, Schallert, and Whishaw 1983). Therefore, lateral hypothalamic damage produces a disconnection syndrome in which some behavioral subcomponents of the whole animal are functionally disconnected from other subcomponents. To understand such an animal, it is helpful to view it in terms of its separate functional parts, not as an intact behaving whole. In the first few days after sufficiently large partial transections, the animal's internal environment appears to be disconnected from those patterns of behavior that are directed outward, toward the external world. The patterns that remain accessible to it are those directed toward the animal's own body— e.g., scratching, grooming, head-shaking, yawning, chewing, swallowing—but orienting, scanning, locomotion, biting, and licking (at external substances or objects) are unavailable to the animal. Strong stimuli such as pain, pressure, and cold can activate them, but stimuli from the animal's internal environment, which are effective in the normal animal and which are the ones we usually focus on when we think of regulation and motivated behavior, do not.

If we pinch the tail of an otherwise completely aphagic cat or rat, it eats vigorously, often enough to keep itself alive (Marshall, Richardson, and Teitelbaum 1974, Antelman, Rowland, and Fisher 1976; Wolgin and Teitelbaum 1978; Rowland, Margues, and Fisher, 1980). Normal rats can also be induced to eat by tail pinch (Antelman and Szechtman 1975; Mufson, Balagura, and Riss 1976; Szechtman 1980; Szechtman and Hall 1980; Fass et al. 1981). Male rats, unresponsive sexually, will mate after painful electric shock (Barfield and Sachs 1968; Caggiula and Eibergen 1969; Barfield and Krieger 1977). Unmaternal female rats lick pups, retrieve them, and keep them in the nest after tail pinch (Szechtman et al. 1977). Performance in a maze for food is facilitated by tail pinch (Koob, Fray, and Iversen 1976). Clearly, the variables that counteract somnolence, catalepsy, and akinesia also promote normal motivated behavior. Since the same variables control them, these seemingly irrelevant, unrelated behaviors are not side effects after all but must be relevant to a common system involved in all motivated behavior. We generally assume that motivational states such as hunger, thirst, or sexual motivation are separate from each other and that they are incompatible with pain and stress. However, the above phenomena suggest that normal motivated behavior requires a background level of tonic general activation, which can be increased by many avenues of stimulation, including stressful ones (also see Marshall, Levitan, and Stricker 1976; Antelman and Caggiula 1978; Wolgin 1982). In the presence of appropriate stimuli that can evoke and direct a particular motivated behavior but which at that instant are not adequate to do so, raising the level of tonic general activation makes the usual stimuli effective once again. This may explain why painful stimuli heighten sexual arousal in some people (Krafft-Ebing 1965; Teitelbaum Schallert, and Whishaw 1983). In the first days after extensive lateral hypothalamic damage, for instance, the animal depends almost completely on external stimuli to make accessible those behavior patterns directed toward the external world. Analogous phenomena are seen in humans with parkinsonism (Martin 1967).

The process of recovery from sufficient large lateral hypothalamic par-

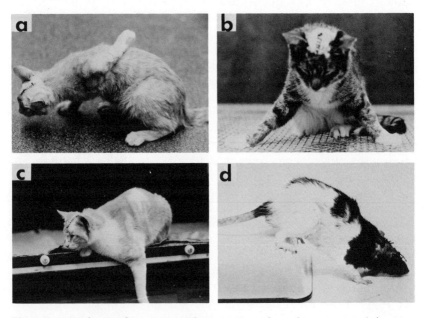

Fig. 5.7.   Cataleptic-akinetic animals maintain awkward postures: *a,* left forelimb of a lateral hypothalamic-damaged cat placed in extreme retroflexion by the experimenter; *b,* extreme abduction of the forelimbs; *c,* one forelimb hangs down off a ledge (Wolgin and Teitelbaum, 1978); *d,* cataleptic posture in a rat treated with 6-hydroxydopamine. *Source:* Figs. *a, b,* and *c* reprinted from Wolgin, D. L., and Teitelbaum, P. Role of activation and sensory stimuli in recovery from lateral hypothalamic damage in the cat. *Journal of Comparative and Physiological Psychology,* 1978, *92,* Copyright 1978 by the American Psychological Association. Reprinted by permission of the authors. Fig. *d* reprinted by permission from *Physiology and Behavior, 21,* Schallert, T., Whishaw, I. Q., De Ryck, M., and Teitelbaum, P., The postures of catecholamine-depletion catalepsy: Their possible adaptive value in thermoregulation. Copyright 1978, Pergamon Press, Ltd.

tial transection allows us to differentiate the remaining and returning behavioral subcomponents involved in the transformation from coma (the complete absence of motivated behavior) to fully integrated normal motivated behavior. Elements of behavior recover at different rates, permitting us to examine them in isolation and then in varying degrees of interaction with other, later recovering, elements.

A major neural system partially transected by lateral hypothalamic damage involves the dopaminergic pathways ascending from the substantia nigra and ventral tegmentum through the lateral hypothalamus to the striatum and other mesencephalic and cortical structures (Ungerstedt 1971; Lindvall et al. 1974). If this were all that were involved in such damage, chemical blockade of dopaminergic receptors in the brain by systemic injection of haloperidol or pimozide ought to mimic the full complex of symptoms produced by LH partial transection. Additional, nondopaminergic systems appear to be affected by lateral hypothalamic partial transection, because the additional symptoms associated with fully developed somnolence (loss of contact-righting, loss of postural support, and loss of cortical activation), though produced by LH damage, are not associated with dopaminergic receptor blockade. However, these non-dopaminergic components appear to recover earliest, because, as recovery progresses, the LH-damaged animal comes to resemble more closely a haloperidol-treated animal, being merely akinetic and cataleptic. Which functions remain in these states, and what factors affect them?

A cataleptic animal will lie unmoving on its back while held in the air in the experimenter's hands. However, if the support is suddenly removed,

Fig. 5.8.   A 6-OHDA-treated rat actively maintains static equilibrium. Here it is shown on all four legs bracing vigorously when its stability is challenged by the experimenter, who is pushing the rat forward and backward (in the direction indicated by the arrows.) *Source:* Schallert, T., De Ryck, M., Whishaw, I. Q., Ramirez, V. D., and Teitelbaum, P. Excessive bracing reactions and their control by atropine and L-DOPA in animal analog of Parkinsonism. *Experimental Neurology,* 1979, 64.

and the cat or rat starts to fall, it instantly rights itself in the air. Similarly, a cataleptic cat will stand on three legs with its left foreleg placed in an awkward position up on its back (fig. 5.7a). If its center of gravity is only slightly displaced by a gentle, lateral push toward the unstably supported left side, the cat instantly replaces the left foreleg on the ground, regaining stable equilibrium and support (Wolgin and Teitelbaum 1978). Any external force that displaces a cataleptic-akinetic animal's center of gravity will be resisted by exaggerated bracing reactions, yielding a form of "negativism" (fig. 5.8). All this can be understood as an isolation and release of a particular multireflex adaptive unit, which we have labeled the postural support subsystem. This subsystem counteracts displacement-produced vestibular and kinesthetic stimuli by righting, bracing, clinging, crouching, and standing, all of which maintain or regain motionless support and equilibrium (Van Harreveld and Kok 1935; De Jong 1945; Schallert et al. 1978a, 1979; De Ryck, Schallert, and Teitelbaum 1980). This state seems bizarre because the subsystem acts in isolation from the other behavioral subsystems, involved in scanning, orienting, locomotion, and ingestion, which are relatively unresponsive to the stimuli that normally activate them (Teitelbaum et al. 1980).

THE EFFECT OF BANDAGING ON POSTURAL SUPPORT

When a cataleptic animal maintains motionless equilibrium and support by clinging to the back of a chair, it keeps its head upright (fig. 5.9, top

Fig. 5.9. (Facing Page) *Top left,* Undrugged adult cat, two days after bilateral lateral hypothalamic damage, clinging cataleptically. *Top right,* bandaging the head and neck produces the backfall reaction (Teitelbaum et al. 1976). *Middle and bottom,* bandage-backfall reaction in a postencephalitic parkinsonism patient. *Middle left,* without the bandage, the patient sits in the wheelchair, holding head and neck erect. *Middle right,* with head and neck bandaged, the patient grasps a wooden bar, which is then raised, and the wheelchair is tilted back. Note that his head has sagged backward. (This does not happen without the bandage; indeed, though not shown here, his head will then tilt forward, keeping head erect, compensating for the backward tilt of the wheelchair). *Bottom left,* the patient's bandaged head remains in the backfall position, even though his arms have been lowered and the wheelchair has been returned to the upright position. *Bottom right,* as soon as the bandage is removed, his head and neck return to the upright position. This reaction does not depend on vision; it occurs even if the eyes are left unbandaged. It depends on pressure on the head and neck. *Source:* Teitelbaum, P. The physiological analysis of motivated behavior. In P. G. Zimbardo and F. L. Ruch (Eds.), *Psychology and life (9th ed.),* Scott, Foresman, 1977.

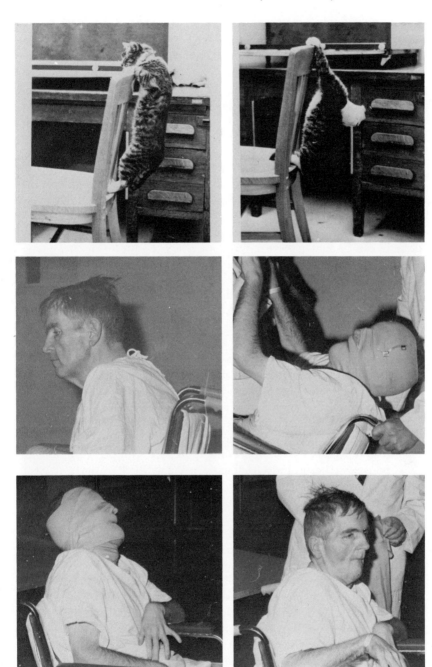

left). If the animal's head and neck are bandaged, the head falls slowly backward, becoming extremely dorsiflexed. The forelimbs extend and the forepaws gradually release their grasp, causing the animal to fall backward off the chair (fig. 5.9, top right) (Van Harreveld and Kok 1935; Van Harreveld and Bogen 1961; Teitelbaum et al. 1976). Lack of vision does not cause the bandage-backfall. If the head and neck are bandaged without covering the eyes, backfall still occurs. However, if the appropriate branches of the trigeminal and the first three cervical nerves are sectioned bilaterally, thus diminishing the effect of pressure on face, scalp, and neck, bandage-backfall does not occur (Van Harreveld and Bogen 1961). Therefore, pressure on the skin of the face, head, and neck seems to inhibit the vestibular and kinesthetic mechanisms that support the head. Does this have adaptive value?

We have seen that many of the seemingly bizarre symptoms of cataleptic akinesia can be understood in terms of reflexive movement subsystems that can act in isolation and that have their own rules, in terms of the specific sense modalities that control them. We can use the simplified animal produced by dopamine-deficiency to study the isolated postural support subsystem. For instance, the cataleptic animal instantly rights in the air when dropped from a supine position but clings or stands unmoving for long periods. If the animal is allowed to cling upside down to a thin but rigid wire frame held in the air, it remains motionless. If the wire frame is dropped, will the rat let go and right itself while falling? As shown in figure 5.10, it remains motionless while falling, clinging to the wire frame all the way, and hits the ground (a soft pillow) on its back (Schallert and Teitelbaum 1981). Clearly, in postural support, clinging is dominant over righting. Clinging to the wire frame signals that the animal has external support so it need not seek support by righting to a prone "readiness-to-land" posture in the air. Indeed, clinging to a matchstick by the front paws alone is sufficient to inhibit righting. In each case, clinging gives a misleading signal of external support and inhibits righting, thus tricking the animal into falling to the ground on its back. The contact stimuli that elicit clinging appear to suppress the vestibular stimulus provided during falling that would otherwise trigger righting.

A similar inhibitory interaction appears to be involved in the bandage-backfall reaction described earlier. The bandage pressure on the head and neck falsely simulates the external support that would be provided if the animal's head were resting on a solid surface. Such external support appears to inhibit the internal vestibular and kinesthetic systems that normally keep the otherwise unsupported head erect, so the bandaged head sags backward. As in the case of clinging versus righting, there is antagonistic interaction of two support signals, external support being domi-

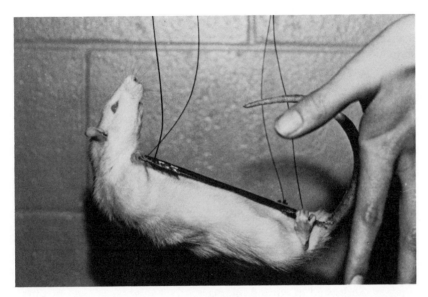

Fig. 5.10.   A haloperidol-treated rat, which otherwise rights normally, fails to right when it is dropped while clinging to four interconnected grid squares. See text for explanation. *Source:* Reprinted with permission from *Physiology* and *Behavior, 27,* Schallert, T., and Teitelbaum, P., Haloperidol, catalepsy, and equilibrating functions in the rat: Antagonistic interaction of clinging and labyrinthine righting reactions. Copyright 1981, Pergamon Press, Ltd.

nant. Several other demonstrations of such inhibitory interactions have been described elsewhere (Teitelbaum, Schallert, and Whishaw 1983).

Do recovery-development parallels also hold for cataleptic-akinesia? A normal newborn kitten clings, holding its head erect (fig. 5.11, top left). When bandaged (fig. 5.11, top right), the head falls backward, the grasp is inhibited, and the kitten will fall backward if allowed. Puppies, baby rabbits, and infant primates (fig. 5.11 middle) also show bandage-backfall. If they are bandaged loosely, backfall does not appear. The pressure of the bandage, not its weight (7–15 g), is essential (Teitelbaum et al. 1976).

Because bandage-backfall appears in primates, one might expect to find it in humans. A normal adult person does not show backfall when the head is bandaged. One of the brain areas affected in lateral hypothalamic damage involves the nigrostriatal pathway, known to be involved in Parkinson's disease. As shown in fig. 5.9, middle and bottom, we were able to demonstrate bandage-backfall in a postencephalitic patient, severely debilitated by parkinsonism. (Several others, less debilitated, perhaps with less wide-spread damage, did not show it). In six normal human infants, ranging from 6 to 11 weeks old, we also demonstrated bandage-backfall (fig. 5.11, bottom). By about three months of age, however, the reaction seemed no longer evident (since excess pressure on the neck can obstruct breathing and might endanger an infant, we always worked with a physician present) (Teitelbaum, Wolgin, Marin, and D'Sousa, unpublished results, described briefly in Teitelbaum 1977b). Therefore, in normal infants or in brain-damaged adults, in whom the support subsystem seems to be more isolated from other movement subsystems than in normal adults, the vestibular and kinesthetic systems involved in support of the head appear to be deactivated by pressure on the skin of the head and neck. Even in normal adult animals, however, pressure on other parts of the torso can have similarly deactivating effects on the support subsystem (Teitelbaum, Schallert, and Whishaw 1983).

In summary, in the isolated, disconnected state of cataleptic-akinesia, postures and actions depend largely on vestibular-kinesthetic and tactile stimuli. (Gastric and thermal stimuli also play a role—see Schallert et al. 1978a). These stimuli are exaggeratedly effective in brain-damaged or drugged adults and in normal infants.

We have seen that the postural support subsystem allows the animal to remain motionless in stable support. Very soon after postural support begins to recover, other subsystems begin to be reactivated, and the animal moves. These subsystems recover separately at different rates, but it is difficult to discern this by ordinary observational methods. We tend to characterize an animal's movements by highlighting a particular feature that seems to make sense and to be adaptive, without distinguishing how their various dimensions have changed in amplitude from one day to the next and how each subcomponent begins to compete with others. Only in circumstances when its behavior seems purposeless or maladaptive do we become alerted to the fact that we do not fully understand it.

For instance, as a lateral-hypothalamic-damaged animal recovers from akinesia, catalepsy, and aphagia, there is a stage in which it walks around

Fig. 5.11.   *Top left,* newborn normal kitten (24 hours old) clings to the experimenter's hand, keeping head and neck erect. *Top right,* the bandage-backfall reaction in the newborn kitten. *Middle left,* a 2-week-old baboon clings to the experimenter's fingers, keeping head and neck erect. *Middle right,* bandage-backfall reaction in the infant baboon (Teitelbaum et al. 1976). *Bottom left,* normal 8-week-old baby girl keeps head and neck up when her body is tilted backward. *Bottom right,* the bandage-backfall reaction in the normal human infant. *Source:* All figs. except *bottom left* and *bottom right* reprinted from Teitelbaum, P., Wolgin, D., De Ryck, M., and Marin, O. S. M. Bandage-backfall reaction: Occurs in infancy, hypothalamic damage, and catalepsy. *Proceedings of the National Academy of Sciences, U.S.A.,* 1976, *73.* *Bottom left* and *bottom right* figs: See Fig. 5.9.

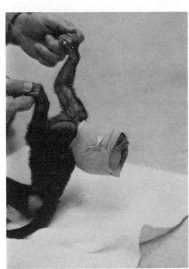

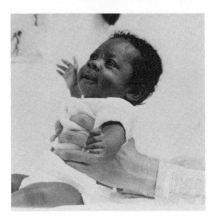

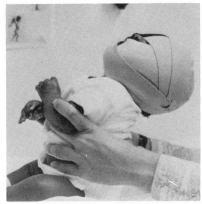

and appears to explore its environment relatively normally. It stops and eats some of the palatable food it encounters, giving the impression that it is engaging in hunger-motivated behavior. However, if it happens to walk into a corner, it is trapped there, sometimes for long periods. A normal animal would simply rear up, turn, and walk away. In contrast, the lateral hypothalamic rat performs a repetitive series of stereotyped, head-scanning movements and stepping patterns (Levitt and Teitelbaum 1975; Golani, Wolgin, and Teitelbaum 1979). It is not that such an animal is normally motivated, merely lacking the motor capacity to make a particular movement. On the contrary, even when the animal is in a blind alley and is walking toward the open end, it seems just as likely to turn back into the dead end as to proceed out of the partial enclosure. At this stage of its recovery, it appears to lack goal-directedness, responding reflexively to each configuration of surfaces it encounters. Such an animal does not seem to be behaving as a whole, achieving a series of goal-directed outcomes. Its snout is reacting to surfaces while its legs engage in support or locomotion. In an open field, these actions of the animal's body parts do not usually oppose each other, and we readily assume that it is acting as a whole. But when the animal walks into a corner, the "whole" seems to behave queerly. Its seemingly goal-directed, holistic behavior makes "mistakes" that trap the animal in the partial enclosure. We realize then that such an animal is merely a collection of parts that are acting independently and may work at cross-purposes.

We therefore used the Eshkol-Wachman movement-notation system (EWMN), which enables the user to see and record the movement of the body parts that compose the whole (Eshkol and Wachman 1958; Eshkol et al. 1973; Golani, Wolgin, and Teitelbaum 1979). It also enabled us to quantify the recruitment of the body segments into each dimension of movement day-by-day. Films were made of the movements of each animal throughout the process of recovery from total akinesia to relatively normal locomotion. These films were analyzed frame by frame, and written "musical scores" of movement sequences were prepared. In this way, it was possible to isolate the dimensions of movement along which recovery occurs. These are illustrated in tracings from representative film frames in figures 5.12 through 5.15. The "natural geometry" of movement (Golani, Wolgin, and Teitelbaum 1979) can also be used to characterize the independent reflexive movement subsystems whose isolated action and interaction can account for the animal's behavior (Teitelbaum et al. 1980).

In the first few days after extensive lateral hypothalamic partial transection, long before forward locomotion appears, static postural antigravity support typically begins to recover cephalocaudally (fig. 5.12), allowing the animal to crouch or stand. At about the same time, small scanning movements of the head appear, along the floor, first laterally (fig. 5.13) and then longitudinally (fig. 5.14). Recovery occurs day by day and is cephalocaudal: i.e., more caudal limb and body segments are recruited into postural support (fig. 5.12) and into larger amplitude scanning movements (fig. 5.13 and fig. 5.14). At first, only the head and then the front legs are recruited, with the hindlegs remaining immobile, rooted to the ground (fig. 5.13*c* and fig. 5.14*a, b, c*). Then the hindlegs join in, allowing the animal to pivot laterally (fig. 5.13 *d*). Somewhat later, forward locomotion returns, but the head scans are under tactile control and are restricted to horizontal surfaces (the floor), so that when a vertical obstruction is encountered, the head does not scan upward (as will occur later in recovery [fig. 5.15]). Thus, the animal can be trapped in corners. Much later in recovery, forward locomotion becomes exaggeratedly dominant and lateral head scans are largely suppressed, so that in an open field the animal

Fig. 5.12. Five phases in cephalocaudal recovery of postural support. In this and in succeeding figures, all line drawings are tracings from individual movie frames. *Source:* Golani, I., Wolgin, D. L. and Teitelbaum, P. A proposed natural geometry of recovery from akinesia in the lateral hypothalamic rat. *Brain Research,* 1979, *164.*

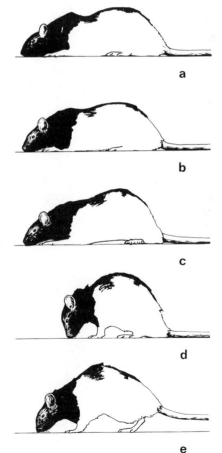

a

b

c

d

e

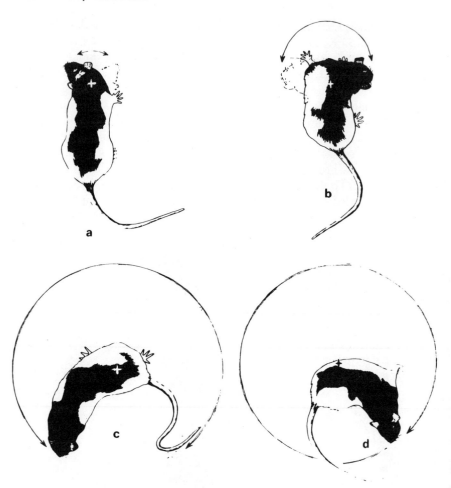

Fig. 5.13. Top view of a rat performing increasingly larger amplitude horizontal lateral movements during four successive phases of recovery. Dashed line and solid line drawings indicate the extreme positions that the rat assumes during each phase. The arrows indicate the amplitude of the movements. The plus sign indicates the root of the movement, beyond which there is practically no recruitment of limb and body segments for movement. During increasingly larger lateral movements (*b, c,* and *d*), the limb and body segments are recruited in a cephalocaudal order. As explained in the text, the exaggerated bending reveals the conflict between postural support and lateral head-scanning. *Source:* See Fig. 5.12.

walks in long, forward trajectories without stopping (Golani, Wolgin, and Teitelbaum 1979).

In the normal animal, these movement subsystems usually work together, so it is difficult to differentiate their individual action. In the brain-damaged animal, however, they are disconnected from each other and recover differentially, so that a tug-of-war goes on between them. For instance, in figures 5.13 and 5.14, as lateral and longitudinal head-scanning movements are repeated with increasing amplitude ("warm-up"), they reach a degree of exaggerated bending (fig. 5.13*b, c*) and stretching (fig. 5.14*a, b, c*) not generally seen in normal animals. This "strait-jacket" phenomenon (Golani, Wolgin, and Teitelbaum 1979) appears to represent the action of two independent subsystems acting at cross-purposes. Thus, when the lateral hypothalamic animal is immobile, its head, body, and legs are used in a coordinated whole-body reaction for maintaining and defending motionless support and equilibrium (Schallert et al. 1978a). As exploratory lateral and longitudinal head-scanning movements appear and grow in amplitude, they have to recruit the front legs and more caudal segments of the body into the scanning action. But the front legs remain rooted to the ground, dominated by the postural support subsystem, so the

Fig. 5.14. Side views of a rat performing increasingly larger amplitude snout movements during three successive phases of recovery. All symbols, and dashed and solid lines as in figure 5.13. As explained in the text, the exaggerated stretching reveals the conflict between postural support and forward head-scanning. *Source:* See Fig. 5.12.

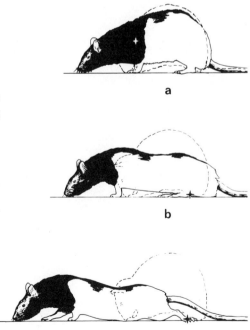

a

b

c

head strains laterally or forward against them in exaggerated movements. Later in recovery, in warm-up from arrest (Golani, Wolgin, and Teitelbaum 1979), the front legs and torso segments are recruited into head-scanning, and the exaggerated bending and stretching shifts to the pelvis as only the hindlegs remain rooted to the ground in postural support, still resisting the scanning actions of the forequarters. Days later, pivoting in circles of 360° or more is seen (fig. 5.13*d*), as the contralateral leg swivels, maintaining "loose contact" (Eshkol and Wachman 1958) and support while the other leg steps backwards in postural adjustment to the head trajectories. Cephalocaudal recruitment of forward movement has also been growing day by day; it is intermingled with and superimposed on the recruitment of lateral scanning and turning. When the hindlegs become recruited into forward stepping, along with the animal's forequarters, the animal is no longer rooted to the ground but can walk forward. A parallel, though slightly complicated warm-up sequence is seen in the initiation of locomotion in an open field by normal infant animals (rats, wild cats, and badgers) (Golani et al. 1981). In the infant rat, forward stretching with snout to the ground during longitudinal trajectories

a

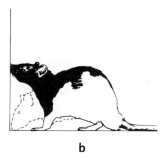

b

Fig. 5.15. Three phases in the recovery of vertical head-scanning. When the animal lacks upward scans along vertical surfaces, it is often trapped in corners. *Source:* See Fig. 5.12.

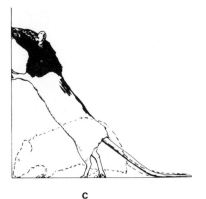

c

is often quite striking, as the hind legs remain rooted to the ground, resisting the "release of contact" (Eshkol and Wachman 1958) that is essential for forward locomotion. Cephalocaudal recruitment had been demonstrated by us in recovery from sensory neglect (Marshall, Turner, and Teitelbaum 1971; Marshall and Teitelbaum 1974). Only now we view it in positive terms, as the cephalocaudal reactivation of head-orienting, a movement subsystem distinct from the others and closely allied with mouthing (biting and licking).

The sensory transformation sequence (kinesthetic-vestibular, tactile, visual, operant) apparent in Twitchell's recovery-development parallel in the use of the hand, missing from the stages of recovery of regulation of food intake, becomes apparent in the recovery of movement. Initially, during cataleptic immobility, kinesthetic and vestibular stimuli dominate the whole-body reactions of the isolated postural support subsystem. Later in recovery, exploratory scanning of the head appears and is controlled by tactile stimulation of the snout; this seems analogous to the tactile control of the exploratory reactions of the fingers in the true grasp and the palpating, supinating, pronating, magnet-following reactions of the instinctive grasp reaction. The traction response makes sense as a powerful whole-hand grasping response that helps the infant primate to cling to its mother's fur, thereby maintaining support, and that is stronger on the side that is up (the hand that should cling most strongly to keep the infant from falling off).

7. Release from Inhibition versus Release of Inhibition

Aphagia, adipsia, and akinesia seem to indicate loss, not release, of normal mechanisms of behavior. But following damage in the nervous system, not only is there release *from* inhibition, there is also a corresponding release *of* inhibition. For instance, a normal rat is made akinetic by 5 or 10 mg / kg haloperidol, which blocks the action of dopamine systems in the brain. If an electrolytic lesion or chemical inactivation by 200 ug GABA is then produced in the nucleus reticularis tegmenti pontis (NRTP), the animal gallops forward (Cheng et al. 1981). The system is flooded with haloperidol, yet the animal is no longer akinetic. Therefore, haloperidol (and presumably LH damage or any other form of dopamine deficiency) appears to produce akinesia by releasing an inhibitory control over movement via a path that includes the NRTP in the ventral pontine tegmentum. Morphine-induced immobility is also abolished by NRTP damage or inactivation (Chesire, Cheng, and Teitelbaum 1983). This pontine system, involved in the inhibition of movement, may be the one described earlier by Klemm (1965, 1969, 1977) in studies of the immobility reflex ("animal hypnosis").

One can selectively disinhibit components of the inhibitory control over movement. Rats become akinetic after intraventricular 6-hydroxydopamine, which damages brain catecholamine systems selectively (Shallert et al. 1978b, 1978c). In this condition, treatment with atropine (a cholinergic blocking agent) releases excessive abnormal walking (Schallert et al. 1978b, 1978c). Their shuffling, short-step gait appears similar in some respects to that seen in some patients suffering from parkinsonism. The locomotion of these rats seems to be controlled by the scanning actions of the head, because light frontal snout or whisker contact inhibits it.

Atropine is ineffective in releasing locomotion in animals made akinetic by large lateral hypothalamic electrolytic partial transections. But when LH-damaged akinetic animals are treated with 45 mg / kg methysergide maleate I.P. (a serotonin receptor blocking agent) as early as 24 hours postoperatively, they crawl forward vigorously (fig. 5.16 *a–f*) (Chesire and Teitelbaum 1982). This is straightline, forward locomotion without support and without head-scanning, head-orienting, or mouthing. It is driven by the hindlegs and is not inhibited by light snout or whisker contact. (Strong snout pressure can shut it down, however.) Therefore, selective neurotransmitter blockade of cholinergic or serotonergic systems appears to release different fractional forms of locomotion, subject to different controls. The deficit phenomenon of akinesia is in part, therefore, a release phenomenon, i.e., a release of excessive inhibition of movement.

8. Behavioral "Acts" versus Continuous Neurological Variables

By using movement-notation analysis to study recovery from lateral hypothalamic cataleptic akinesia, we were able to chart the continuous growth of movement cephalocaudally along vertical, lateral, and longitudinal dimensions. These appeared separately and grew at different rates day by day, indicating that they were being generated by the nervous system during recovery rather than being imposed conceptually by us. Our earlier behavioral observations, without such notation, had led us to a different kind of description, one that was psychologically immediate but not neurologically relevant. We had previously labeled each different "act" as we glimpsed it each day: thus, we would describe crouching, standing, rearing, grooming, pivoting, walking, nosing, orienting, eating, etc. The idea never occurred to us that each particular "act" was simply the composite aggregate of particular values of the amplitudes of movement along a few dimensions. An isolation of continuous neurological movement variables was achieved by Konrad Lorenz (1941) in his ethological analysis of ritualized displays. He used display variation between closely related species of ducks to reveal the dimensions along which evolution operates to

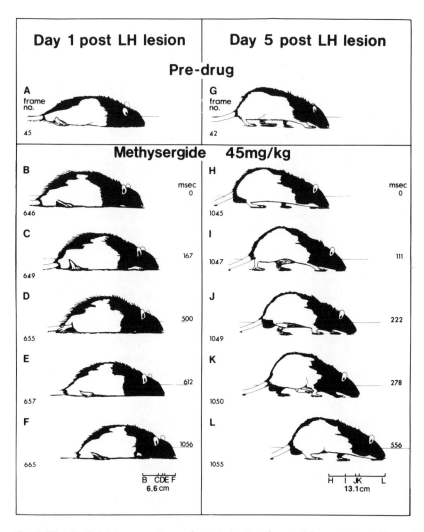

Fig. 5.16.   Preinjection posture and postinjection forward locomotion of lateral hypothalamic rats treated with 45 mg / kg methysergide on postoperative day 1 or 5. Prior to methysergide, the day 1 rat was completely akinetic while the day 5 rat had recovered locomotion. Following the drug, the day 1 rat crawls forward without postural support. The locomotion of the day 5 rat is also significantly increased but is integrated with postural support, which had recovered spontaneously by that time (see text for further details). Drawings are tracings from individual movie frames. *Source:* Reprinted by permission from *Physiology and Behavior, 28,* Chesire, R. M., and Teitelbaum, P., Methysergide releases locomotion without support in lateral hypothalamic akinesia. Copyright 1982, Pergamon Press, Ltd.

exaggerate the movements, and therefore the signal value, in a social display. This is analogous to our use of day-by-day recovery from akinesia to reveal continuous neurological variables in exploratory locomotion.

Golani's (1976, 1982) approach using movement notation to isolate continuous variables in movement is also useful in understanding the stereotyped behaviors induced by dopaminergic agonists. For instance, apomorphine, a dopamine receptor agonist, produces a variety of seemingly unrelated stereotyped acts, such as head-bobbing (Schoenfeld et al. 1975), rearing (Decsi et al. 1979), jumping (Weisman 1971), climbing (Protais et al. 1976), locomotion (Lal and Sourkes 1973), circling (Jerussi and Glick 1976), sniffing, nosing, biting, and licking (Costall and Naylor 1974). To reveal regularities in the drug's action, we simplified the environment to diminish the simultaneous triggering of competing movement subsystems. Rats were injected with apomorphine and placed on a broad glass surface devoid of irregularities or objects that could trigger the mouthing subsystem and without walls that could elicit upward or lateral scanning, which would redirect forward locomotion (Szechtman et al. 1980, 1982, 1985). Instead of waiting long enough after drug injection for a typical behavior to be seen and only then studying it, we followed continuously the effect of the drug from the time of injection throughout the duration of action. The dimensions and trajectories of movement which unfold after apomorphine under these circumstances are lawful and regular. We had earlier described the recovery from the akinesia produced by lateral hypothalamic damage (Golani, Wolgin, and Teitelbaum 1979), which highlights the reactivation of the individual components of the dopaminergic system, damaged by LH lesions, involved in exploratory locomotion. At this dosage, apomorphine, although it is a receptor agonist, appears to produce the opposite effect, a progressive shutdown of the individual components of exploratory locomotion in a regression sequence that is the opposite of lateral hypothalamic recovery. As described earlier, in recovery from lateral akinesia, lateral head trajectories appear first and forward head and body trajectories appear later (figs. 5.13 and 5.14). Lateral head trajectories alone result in pivoting; in combination with forward stepping they produce circling. Eventually, forward locomotion becomes predominant, to the virtual exclusion of turning (Golani, Wolgin, and Teitelbaum 1979). Conversely, in a prototype normal animal under apomorphine on a large, smooth horizontal surface, long, forward locomotion trajectories appear first (fig. 5.17). They then shrink progressively while turning appears and grows in amplitude. Their changing algebraic summation produces the forms of stereotyped exploration (forward walking, circling, pivoting) reported by others. Therefore, in part, the seemingly unrelated diversity of the reported effects of apomorphine

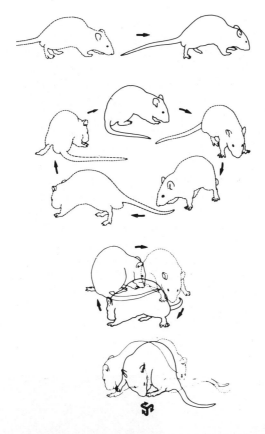

Fig. 5.17. Under the influence of apomorphine (see text for details), dimensions of movement emerge and interact to produce the forms of exploratory locomotion described. In the first few minutes only forward locomotion in long trajectories is seen. Then forward longitudinal movement shrinks as lateral turning movements emerge and grow in amplitude. Their algebraic interaction produces tighter and tighter circling as longitudinal forward locomotion becomes less and less. Pivoting (*bottom*) is turning without any forward locomotion at all. *Source:* Teitelbaum, P., Szechtman, H., Sirkin, D. W., and Golani, I. Dimensions of movement, movement subsystems, and local reflexes in the dopaminergic systems underlying exploratory locomotion. In M. Y. Spiegelstein and A. Levy (Eds.), *Behavioral Models and the Analysis of Drug Action.* Proceedings of the 27th OHOLO Conference, Zichron Ya'acov, Israel, March 28–31, 1982. Amsterdam: Elsevier Biomedical Press, 1982.

on exploratory locomotion is an artifact of focusing on "acts" which appear in different stages of the orderly regression process.

Under apomorphine, as in lateral hypothalamic recovery (figs. 5.13, 5.14, and 5.17), head trajectories are controlled by snout contact (Szechtman et al. 1982; Teitelbaum et al 1982). Therefore, more complex forms of exploration appear as the environment becomes more complex. In a small, high, walled enclosure, for instance, forward locomotion is redirected upward, guided by snout contact along the vertical surfaces, and rearing, climbing, and jumping predominate (fig. 5.18, left half). If a wire mesh floor is present, biting may be evoked, inhibiting locomotion (fig. 5.18, right half) (Szechtman et al. 1982).

One final example should make this point clearer. A few years ago, Alander, Schallert, and I were studying the effects on rat locomotion of large doses of d-amphetamine sulfate (20 mg / kg). About 20 minutes after injection, many of these animals started backing up very rapidly, sometimes right off the table. This seemed the converse of the fact that rats and cats recovering from the dopamine deficiency produced by LH damage walk only forward—they do not back up (Wolgin and Teitelbaum 1978; Golani, Wolgin, and Teitelbaum 1979). So another behavior in dopamine's repertoire was "backing up." In water, the animals swam underwater or dove to the bottom of the tank, never swimming to the

Fig. 5.18. The environment can mold the behavior seen under apomorphine. *Left,* in a small, high-walled enclosure forward locomotion guided by snout contact is redirected upward along the walls, and rearing against walls, climbing, or jumping may predominate. *Right,* alternatively, if a wire mesh floor is present, biting may inhibit locomotion. *Source:* Szechtman, H., Ornstein, K., Teitelbaum, P., and Golani, I. Snout contact fixation, climbing and gnawing during apomorphine stereotypy in rats from two substrains. *European Journal of Pharmacology,* 1982, *80.*

surface as a normal rat would (fig. 5.19). If not plucked from the water in less than a minute, such a rat would drown. Here was still another act to add to amphetamine's list—"sudden drowning death."

Servidio continued the study of these amphetamine-induced behaviors, this time searching for continuous variables. She placed each animal in an open field, away from walls, videotaped it continuously from the onset of drug action, and studied the dimensions of its movement. In the course of the drug's action, several very different "acts" appeared (fig. 5.20). Within a minute or so after injection, exaggerated upward rearing appeared. At 2 minutes, a form of prancing was seen, with the animal walking forward on its hind legs, forelegs in the air. By 3.5 minutes, vigorous forward running appeared. By 10 minutes, lateral head scanning was seen, and by 24 minutes, nosing and sniffing the ground was evident. But it was also clear that the stereotyped "acts" were formed as a composite aggregate of three dimensions of movement, vertical, lateral, and longitudinal, which appeared at different times and waxed and waned separately during the course of the drug's action. One dimension of amphetamine's action is on

Fig. 5.19. Twenty minutes or so after the injection of a large dose of amphetamine, a rat swims underwater or dives to the bottom. It never swims to the surface as a normal rat does; if not plucked from the water within a minute or so, it will drown (Alander, Servidio, Schallert, and Teitelbaum, in preparation).

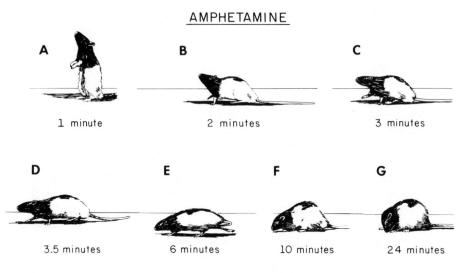

AMPHETAMINE

A   1 minute

B   2 minutes

C   3 minutes

D   3.5 minutes

E   6 minutes

F   10 minutes

G   24 minutes

Time Post Injection

Fig. 5.20.   The continuous monitoring from the time of injection of the effects of amphetamine (20 mg / kg) on the locomotor behavior of a rat in an open field. See text for explanation (Alander, Servidio, Schallert, and Teitelbaum, in preparation).

the head—from vertically up to vertically down. Thus, when placed in water at 20 minutes or so after injection, such animals swam horizontally or dove down—they could not direct their swimming upward at that time, though they could do so in the early minutes of the drug's action (Alander, Servidio, Schallert, and Teitelbaum, in preparation). What about "backing up"? On the ground, as the head is progressively ventroflexed during the action of amphetamine, a point is reached where the snout flexes ventrally toward the body when it contacts the ground. (Forward locomotion has ceased by this time, and the rat is standing in a hunched posture.) When the snout flexes toward the body, it is our impression that it contacts the hindlegs, eliciting a quick two-step backwards. The backwards steps are quickly repeated, yielding "backing up." (This should be analyzed further by filming at high speed.)

9. Differential Cephalocaudal Reactivation of Movement Subsystems versus Stages of Recovery

The above examples suggest that in LH recovery, in development, and during the course of some drugs' action, a behavioral "act" is not an entity, where the whole animal is achieving an outcome, but rather a composite aggregate of independent movement subsystems. The composite form of the act is determined by the particular values of the amplitudes of movement that have differentially developed, recovered, or been induced by the drug. So compelling was our natural human tendency to give an "act" a name that we saw each as separate, discrete, and not connected with other acts. We had fallen into the same perceptual trap when we labeled recovery in terms of stages. A "stage" is like a "level of function" is like an "act." Even though we knew the stages were composite aggregates formed by the differential rate of recovery of eating and drinking, we still thought of them discretely, in terms of stages, because they were such interesting aggregates. It now seems clear that we were studying the aggregate of the movement subsystems involved in approach to food and water (postural support, head-orienting, head-scanning, and forward locomotion) and their interaction with mouthing (biting and licking). Particular values of these (also affected, in later stages, by the need state of the internal environment) yield the four stages of recovery. But the stages are not unitary levels of function once they are recognized as the composite aggregate of particular reactivation magnitudes of a few behavioral subcomponents. These subcomponents appear to be initially disconnected from the internal environment by the lesions. At the same time, they are disconnected from each other and recover independently at different rates, often competing for control of the body and limb segments. Lateral hypothalamic damage therefore produces a double-disconnection syndrome: the reflexes of the internal environment are disconnected from the behavior patterns that operate on the external environment, and these in turn are disconnected from each other. At this point, for me, the emphasis has shifted to the analysis of behavioral subsystems rather than regulation of the internal environment. How the internal environment regains control of these subsystems should add up to the behavioral phenomena of the recovery of regulation of food and water intake. The subsystems seem to be part of all exploratory approaches and interactions with goal objects—perhaps they form intermediate-level building blocks that are relevant to many forms of motivated behavior.

Acknowledgments

This work was supported by funds from the National Institutes of Health grant #R01 NS11671 to Philip Teitelbaum and by a binational United States–Israeli National Science Foundation Grant to Ilan Golani and Philip Teitelbaum. I am grateful to Nancy O'Connell for typing and assistance in compiling the figures. Evelyn Satinoff and Ilan Golani provided helpful criticism. Eckhard H. Hess of the University of Chicago helped me to locate the appropriate reference to the work of Konrad Lorenz. Thanks also to Dr. Esther Sleator and Dr. Bernard D'Sousa, physicians who helped us in studying bandage-backfall in human infants.

Notes

1. Eliot Stellar became my advisor and friend. In 1952, while working on hypothalamic control of food intake as my main interest, Peter Lewinsohn (a fellow graduate student) and I wanted to test Hebb's idea that learning was state-dependent. We would train rats that were under the influence of morphine and test them at a later time either under the influence of the drug or not. If they showed better retention performance when drugged than when undrugged, we would have supported Hebb's idea; otherwise we would have disproved him (or so we thought). Eliot said, "Don't waste your time testing other people's theories." We persisted. So, against his better judgment, Eliot got a drug license and some morphine. The drugged animals seemed in such a blissful state it was difficult to find a reward that would motivate them to learn. In a large room on the fifth floor of Mergenthaler Hall stood a water maze, so we decided to train them to swim a maze to escape from cold water. We carefully designed a counterbalanced experiment that could be done in two separate all-day Saturday sessions, training the rats one day and testing them a week later. The fateful day came, and we swam rats through the maze all morning, recording their performance. At noon we turned off the water flowing through the maze and took a break for lunch. We were proud of being graduate student members of Hopkins Faculty Club, where we could dine graciously and leisurely, with sherbet served between courses. Satisfied, we relaxed in the club by playing billiards. On returning to the experiment, we opened the door, only to find the room flooded with six inches of water. We had turned off the tap at the maze, not at the sink, and the rubber hose connection had burst while we were at lunch. We slammed the door and used buckets to bail the water furiously into the sink. About an hour passed and then came a gentle knock at the door. Eliot opened it, stuck his head in, saw us ankle-deep in water, quietly said "Oh!", and closed the door. His office, 100 feet down the hall, was flooded, and so were the offices on the floor beneath. We waited for the axe to fall, sure that we would be thrown out of graduate school, but no one ever said a word to us. Eliot had obviously explained our accident and had asked the faculty to go easy on us. Jim Deese, whose office was directly beneath our room, could be seen for weeks afterwards ironing his reprints. Needless to say, we never resumed that experiment.

2. When I asked Brobeck about this recently, he wrote, "In the course of learning to use the stereotaxic instrument, Anand attempted to repeat the observations on ventromedial lesions and hyperphagia / obesity. But instead of overeating, his animals failed to eat and soon died. At autopsy his lesions proved to be larger than mine [his fig. 2, p. 125 (in Anand and Brobeck 1951b . . . . P.T)], and we eventually discovered that the milliammeter on the lesion maker had been recently replaced so that Anand's 2 ma. was significantly different from my 2 ma. Anand was astute enough to recognize that the important difference in our operations was in the lateral extent of the lesions, and very shortly he showed that even small lateral lesions (his fig. 5, p. 128) produced aphagia. We knew that the animals were not drinking, but I assumed that was a consequence of the failure to feed, and so we did not mention it in the paper."

3. Brobeck was trained by Stephen Walter Ranson at Northwestern University, in an intellectual line descended from Johns Hopkins University: H. Newell Martin came from England to become the first professor of biology at Johns Hopkins. He

trained H. H. Donaldson, later director of the Wistar Institute in Philadelphia and proponent of the value of rats for laboratory research. Between 1892 and 1906, Donaldson was professor of neurology at the University of Chicago. Ranson, Brobeck's first "chief," received his doctorate from Donaldson's laboratory in 1905. In Brobeck's judgment, in the two decades between 1930 and 1950, Ranson had more influence on the course of neurophysiology than any other person. It came from a single discovery: the utility of the stereotaxic instrument invented by Robert Clarke for use by Victor Horsley, the English neurosurgeon (Brobeck 1974). Ranson had localized the supraoptic nucleus in the hypothalamus, pinpointing its role in diabetes insipidus (Fisher, Ingram, and Ranson 1938). His students were involved in localizing temperature regulation (Magoun et al. 1938), obesity (Hetherington 1940; Hetherington and Ranson 1940), satiety (Brobeck, Tepperman, and Long 1943), and hunger (Anand and Brobeck 1951a, 1951b).

Brobeck also came under the influence of J. F. Fulton, who emphasized levels of function, so Brobeck thought that satiety, the restraint on hunger, was a higher function than hunger itself; it was a distinct surprise to him that they appeared to be localized at the same level, in the medial and lateral hypothalamus, respectively (Brobeck, personal communication).

4. This idea developed from a conversation with Gerald Holton while we were fellows at the Center for Advanced Study in the Behavioral Sciences at Stanford in 1976. His concept of scientific themata (Holton 1973) implied that very basic figure-ground illusions exist in scientific thought just as they do in visual perception. Every idea, being an abstraction, is, by definition, an oversimplification. From a complex array of perceptual elements, we select some fraction as being related. They stand out as a figure, forcing the remaining elements into the background. Where different organizing principles can be found in the same total array, a reversible figure will appear, each representing an alternative "truth" that emerges from the whole. Such partial truths usually form antagonistic pairs, e.g., locus versus level of function.

5. Some years ago, in a beautiful analysis of the concept of setpoint in the central integration of temperature regulation, Satinoff described the progression in her thinking from one setpoint (the prevailing view) to two setpoints (for reflexive versus behavioral thermoregulation) to many setpoints (one for each thermoregulatory response) all working independently yet integrated with each other for the purpose of narrowing the thermoneutral zone, thereby creating the illusion of a single setpoint (Satinoff 1978). In writing the present paper, I realized that my progress from thinking that the lateral hypothalamus was a locus for hunger (one function), to thinking that it involved hunger and thirst (two functions), to finally realizing that what seemed like side effects (catalepsy, akinesia, neglect, somnolence, etc) were not but were all actually related (many functions), represented the same theme she had worked out earlier. So I have used it here.

References

Alander, D., Servidio, S., Schallert, T., & Teitelbaum, P. Amphetamine stereotypy: A regression sequence in which a few continuous biphasic neurological variables interact to generate many stereotyped "acts," in preparation.

Anand, B. K., & Brobeck, J. R. Localization of a "feeding center" in the hypothalamus of the rat. *Proceedings of the Society for Experimental Biology and Medicine,* 1951a, 77, 323–324.

Anand, B. K., & Brobeck, J. R. Hypothalamic control of food intake. *Yale Journal of Biology and Medicine,* 1951b, 24, 123–140.

Antelman, S. M., & Caggiula, A. R. Tails of stress-related behaviors: A neuropharmacological model. In I. Hanin & E. Usdin (Eds.), *Animal models in psychiatry and neurology.* New York: Pergamon Press, 1978.

Antelman, S. M., Rowland, N. E., & Fisher, A. E. Stress related recovery from lateral hypothalamic aphagia. *Brain Research,* 1976, 102, 346–350.

Antelman, S. M., & Szechtman, H. Tail pinch induces eating in sated rats which appears to depend on nigrostriatal dopamine. *Science,* 1975, 189, 731–733.

Barfield, R. J., & Krieger, M. S. Ejaculatory and post-ejaculatory behavior of male and female rats: Effects of sex hormones and electric shock. *Physiology and Behavior,* 1977, 19, 203–208.

Barfield, R. J., & Sachs, B. D. Sexual behavior: Stimulation by painful electric shock to the skin of male rats. *Science,* 1968, 161, 392–394.

Bohr, H. My father. In S. Rozental (Ed.), *Niels Bohr: His life and work as seen by his friends and colleagues.* New York: Wiley, 1967, pp. 325–339.

Brobeck, J. R. Food and temperature. *Recent Progress in Hormone Research,* 1960, 16, 439–466.

Brobeck, J. R. Regulations and integrations. *Canadian Journal of Physiology and Pharmacology,* 1974, 52, 769–779.

Brobeck, J. R., Tepperman, J., & Long, C. N. H. Experimental hypothalamic hyperphagia in the albino rat. *Yale Journal of Biology and Medicine,* 1943, 15, 831–853.

Bucy, P. C. *The precentral cortex.* Urbana: University of Illinois Press, 1949.

Caggiula, A. R., & Eibergen, R. Copulation of virgin male rats evoked by painful peripheral stimulation. *Journal of Comparative and Physiological Psychology,* 1969, 69, 414–419.

Cheng, J.-T., Schallert, T., De Ryck, M., & Teitelbaum, P. Galloping induced by pontine tegmentum damage in rats: A form of "Parkinsonian festination" not blocked by haloperidol. *Proceedings of the National Academy of Sciences, U.S.A.,* 1981, 78, 3279–3283.

Cheng, M.-F., Rozin, P., & Teitelbaum, P. Semi-starvation retards the development of food and water regulations in infant rats. *Journal of Comparative and Physiological Psychology,* 1971, 76, 206–218.

Chesire, R., Cheng, J.-T., & Teitelbaum, P. The inhibition of movement by morphine or haloperidol depends on an intact nucleus reticularis tegmenti pontis. *Physiology and Behavior,* 1983, 30, 809–818.

Chesire, R., & Teitelbaum, P. Methysergide releases locomotion without support in lateral hypothalamic akinesia. *Physiology and Behavior,* 1982, 28, 335–347.

Costall, B., & Naylor, R. J. The role of telencephalic dopaminergic system in the mediation of apomorphine-stereotyped behavior. *European Journal of Pharmacology,* 1974, 24, 8–24.

Cytawa, J., & Teitelbaum, P. Spreading depression and recovery of subcortical functions. *Acta Biologiae Experimentalis (Warsaw),* 1967, 27, 345–353.

Cytawa, J., & Teitelbaum, P. Spreading depression and recovery from septal hyperemotionality. *Folia Biologia*, 1968, *16*, 459–468.

Decsi, L., Gacs, E., Zambo, K., & Nagy, J. Simple device to measure stereotyped rearing of the rat in an objective and quantitative way. *Neuropharmacology*, 1979, *18*, 723–725.

De Jong, H. H. Experimental Catatonia. Baltimore: Williams & Wilkins, 1945.

De Ryck, M., Schallert, T. & Teitelbaum, P. Morphine versus haloperidol catalepsy in the rat: A behavioral analysis of postural support mechanisms. *Brain Research*, 1980, *201*,143–172.

De Ryck, M., & Teitelbaum, P. Neocortical and hippocampal EEG in normal and lateral hypothalamic-damaged rats. *Physiology and Behavior*, 1978, *20*, 403–409.

Eshkol, N., Harries, J., Nul, R., Sapir, T., Seidel, S., Sella, R., & Shoshani, M. *Moving writing reading*. Tel Aviv: Movement Notation Society, 1973.

Eshkol, N., & Wachman, A. *Movement notation*. London: Weidenfeld & Nicolson, 1958.

Falk, J. L. The nature and determinants of adjunctive behavior. *Physiology and Behavior*, 1971, *6*, 577–588.

Fass, B., Strub, H., Greenspon, J. M., Stevens, D. A., & Stein, D. G. A descriptive analysis of tail-pinch elicited eating behavior of rats. *Physiology and Behavior*, 1981, *26*, 355–360.

Fisher, C., Ingram, W. R., & Ranson, S. W. Diabetes insipidus and the neurohormonal control of water balance: A contribution to the structure and function of the hypothalamico-hypophyseal system. Ann Arbor, MI: Edwards Bros., 1938.

Flourens, M. J. P. Recherches experimentales sur les proprietes et les fonctions du systeme nerveux, dans les animaux vertebres. Paris: Crevot, 1824.

Frohlich, A. (1904). Ein fall von tumor der hypophysis cerebri ohne akromegalie. Translated by H. Bruch. *Research Publications of the Association for Research in Nervous and Mental Diseases*, 1940, *20*, XVI–XXVIII.

Golani, I. Homeostatic motor processes in mammalian interactions: A choreography of display. In P. P. G. Bateson & P. H. Klopfer (Eds.), *Perspectives in ethology* (Vol. 2). New York: Plenum Press, 1976, pp. 69–134.

Golani, I. The search for invariants in motor behavior. In K. Immelman, G. W. Barlow, L. Petrinovich, & M. Main (Eds.), *Behavioral development: An interdisciplinary approach*. The Bielefeld Interdisciplinary Conference. London: Cambridge University Press, 1982.

Golani, I., Bronchti, G., Moualem, D., & Teitelbaum, P. "Warm-up" along dimensions of movement in the ontogeny of exploration in rats and other infant mammals. *Proceedings of the National Academy of Sciences, U.S.A.*, 1981, *78*, 7226–7229.

Golani, I., Wolgin, D. L., & Teitelbaum, P. A proposed natural geometry of recovery from akinesia in the lateral hypothalamic rat. *Brain Research*, 1979, *164*, 237–267.

Greenough, W. T. Experimental modification of the developing brain. *American Scientist*, 1975, *63*, 37–46.

Grill, H. J., & Miselis, R. R. Lack of ingestive compensation to osmotic stimuli in chronic decerebrate rats. *American Journal of Physiology*, 1981, *240 (Regulatory Integrative and Comparative Physiology, 9)*, R81–R86.

Grill, H. J., & Norgren, R. Chronically decerebrate rats demonstrate satiation but not bait shyness. *Science*, 1978, *201*, 267–269.

Grillner, S. Locomotion in vertebrates: Central mechanisms and reflex interaction. *Physiological Reviews*, 1975, *55*, 247–304.

Hebb, D. O. *The organization of behavior*. New York: Wiley, 1949.

Hetherington, A. W. Obesity in the rat following the injection of chromic acid into the hypophysis. *Endocrinology*, 1940, *26*, 264–268.

Hetherington, A. W., & Ranson, S. W. Hypothalamic lesions and adiposity in the rat. *Anatomical Record*, 1940, *78*, 149–172.

Holton, G. *Thematic origins of scientific thought: Kepler to Einstein*. Cambridge, MA: Harvard University Press, 1973.

Jackson, J. Hughlings. Croonian lectures on evolution and dissolution of the nervous system. *British Medical Journal*, March 29, 1884, 591–593.

Jacquin, M. F., & Zeigler, H. P. Trigeminal orosensation and ingestive behavior in the rat. *Behavioral Neuroscience*, 1983, *97*, 62–97.

Jerussi, T. P., & Glick, S. D. Drug-induced rotation in rats without lesions: Behavioral and neurochemical indices of a normal asymmetry in nigro-striatal function. *Psychopharmacology*, 1976, *47*, 249–269.

Jouvet, M. Neurophysiology of the states of sleep. *Physiological Reviews*, 1967, *47*, 117–177.

Kennedy, G. C. The role of depot fat in the hypothalamic control of food intake in the rat. *Proceedings of the Royal Society, London, Series B*, 1953, *140*, 578.

Klemm, W. R. Potentiation of animal "hypnosis" with low levels of electric current. *Animal Behavior*, 1965, *13*, 571–574.

Klemm, W. R. Mechanisms of the immobility reflex ("animal hypnosis"). II: EEG and multiple unit correlates in the brain stem. *Communications in Behavioral Biology*, 1969, Part A, *3*, 43–52.

Klemm, W. R. Identity of sensory and motor systems that are critical to the immobility reflex ("animal hypnosis"). *Psychological Record*, 1977, *27*, 145–159.

Kohler, W. & Wallach, H. Figural after-effects: An investigation of visual processes. *Proceedings of the American Philosophical Society*, 1944, *88*(4), 269–357.

Koob, C. F., Fray, P. J., & Iversen, S. D. Tail-pinch stimulation: Sufficient motivation for learning. *Science*, 1976, *194*, 637–639.

Krafft-Ebing, R. von. *Psychopathia sexualis* (translated from the 12th German edition). New York: Stein & Day, 1965.

Lal, S., & Sourkes, T. L. Ontogeny of stereotyped behavior induced by apomorphine and amphetamine in the rat. *Archives Internationales de Pharmacodynamie et de Therapie*, 1973, *101*, 171–182.

Levitt, D. R., & Teitelbaum, P. Somnolence, akinesia and sensory activation of motivated behavior in the lateral hypothalamic syndrome. *Proceedings of the National Academy of Sciences, U.S.A.*, 1975, *72*, 2819–2823.

Lindvall, O., Bjorklund, A., Moore, R. Y., & Stenevi, U. Mesencephalic dopamine neurons projecting to neocortex. *Brain Research*, 1974, *81*, 325–331.

Ljungberg, T., & Ungerstedt, U. Sensory inattention produced by 6-hydroxydopamine induced degeneration of ascending dopamine neurons in the brain. *Experimental Neurology*, 1976, *53*, 585–606.

Lorenz, K. Vergleichende bewegungstudien bei anatiden. *Journal of Ornithology*, 1941, *89*, 194–294. K. Lorenz. *Studies in animal and human behavior*, Vol. 2 (translated by R. Martin). Cambridge, MA: Harvard University Press, 1970.

Magnus, R. Some results of studies in the physiology of posture. *Lancet*, 1926, *211*, 531–536 and 585–588.

Magoun, H. W., Harrison, F., Brobeck, J. R., & Ranson, S. W. Activation of heat loss mechanisms by local heating of the brain. *Journal of Neurophysiology*, 1938, *1*, 101–114.

Marshall, J. F., & Gotthelf, T. Sensory inattention in rats with 6-hydroxydopamine-induced degeneration of ascending dopaminergic neurons: Apomorphine induced reversal of deficits. *Experimental Neurology*, 1979, *65*, 398–411.

Marshall, J. F., Levitan, D., & Stricker, E. Activation-induced restoration of sensorimotor functions in rats with dopamine-depleting brain lesions. *Journal of Comparative and Physiological Psychology*, 1976, *90*, 536–546.

Marshall, J. F., Richardson, J. S., & Teitelbaum, P. Nigrostriatal bundle damage and the lateral hypothalamic syndrome. *Journal of Comparative and Physiological Psychology*, 1974, *87*, 808–830.

Marshall, J. F., & Teitelbaum, P. Further analysis of sensory inattention following lateral hypothalamic damage in rats. *Journal of Comparative and Physiological Psychology*, 1974, *86*, 375–395.

Marshall, J. F., Turner, B. H., & Teitelbaum, P. Sensory neglect produced by lateral hypothalamic damage. *Science*, 1971, *174*, 523–525.

Martin, J. P. *The basal ganglia and posture*. Philadelphia: J. B. Lippincott, 1967.

Mayer, J. Regulation of energy intake and the body weight: The glucostatic theory and the lipostatic hypothesis. *Annals of the New York Academy of Science*, 1955, *63*, 15–43.

McGinty, D. J., Epstein, A. N., & Teitelbaum, P. The contribution of oropharyngeal sensations to hypothalamic hyperphagia. *Animal Behaviour*, 1965, *13*, 413–418.

Monakow, C. V. von. Lokalization der hirnfunktionen. *Journal für Psychologie*, 1911, *17*, 185–200. Reprinted in G. von Bonin (Trans.), *The cerebral cortex*. Springfield, IL: Charles C Thomas, 1960.

Morgagni, G. *The seats and causes of diseases investigated by anatomy*. (3 vols.). (Benjamin Alexander, Trans.). London: printed for A. Millar and T. Cadell, his successor, 1769. (Original work published in Latin in 1761.)

Mufson, E. J., Balagura, S., & Riss, W. Tail pinch-induced arousal and stimulus-bound behavior in rats with lateral hypothalamic lesions. *Brain, Behavior, and Evolution*, 1976, *13*, 154–164.

Peiper, A. *Cerebral function in infancy and childhood*. New York: Consultants Bureau, 1963.

Protais, P., Costentin, J., & Schwartz, J. C. Climbing behavior induced by apomorphine in mice: A simple test for the study of dopamine receptors in striatum. *Psychopharmacology*, 1976, *50*, 1–6.

Robinson, T. E., & Whishaw, I. Q. Effects of posterior hypothalamic lesions on voluntary behavior and hippocampal electroencephalograms in the rat. *Journal of Comparative and Physiological Psychology*, 1974, *86*, 768–786.

Rowland, N. E., Margues, D. M., & Fisher, A. E. Comparison of the effects of brain dopamine-depleting lesions upon oral behaviors elicited by tail pinch and electrical brain stimulation. *Physiology and Behavior*, 1980, *24*, 273–281.

Satinoff, E. Neural organization and evolution of thermal regulation in mammals. *Science*, 1978, *201*, 16–22.

Schallert, T., De Ryck, M., Whishaw, I. Q., Ramirez, V. D., & Teitelbaum, P. Excessive bracing reactions and their control by atropine and L-DOPA in an animal analog of Parkinsonism. *Experimental Neurology*, 1979, *64*, 33–43.

Schallert, T., & Hsiao, S. Homeostasis and life. *Behavioral Brain Science*, 1979, *2*, 118.

Schallert, T., & Teitelbaum, P. Haloperidol, catalepsy, and equilibrating functions in the rat: Antagonistic interaction of clinging and labyrinthine righting reactions. *Physiology and Behavior*, 1981, *27*, 1077–1083.

Schallert, T. Whishaw, I. Q., De Ryck, M., & Teitelbaum, P. The postures of catecholamine-depletion catalepsy: Their possible adaptive value in thermoregulation. *Physiology and Behavior*, 1978a, *21*, 817–820.

Schallert, T., Whishaw, I. Q., Ramirez, V. D., & Teitelbaum, P. Compulsive, abnormal walking caused by anticholinergics in akinetic, 6-hydroxydopamine-treated rats. *Science*, 1978b, *199*, 1461–1463.

Schallert, T., Whishaw, I. Q., Ramirez, V. D., & Teitelbaum, P. 6-Hydroxydopamine and anticholinergic drugs. Reply to Mason and Fibiger. *Science*, 1978c, *202*, 1215–1217.

Schoenfeld, R. J., Neumeyer, J. L., Dafeldecker, W., & Roffler-Tarlov, S. Comparison of structural and stereoisomers of apomorphine on stereotyped sniffing behavior of the rat. *European Journal of Pharmacology*, 1975, *30*, 63–68.

Seyffarth, H., & Denny-Brown, D. The grasp reflex and the instinctive grasp reaction. *Brain*, 1948, *71*, 109–183.

Sherrington, C. S. *The integrative action of the nervous system.* (Issued as a Yale Paperbound, 1961.) Forge Village, MA: Murray Printing Co., 1906.

Shoham, S., & Teitelbaum, P. Subcortical waking and sleep during lateral hypothalamic "somnolence" in rats. *Physiology and Behavior*, 1982, *28*, 323–333.

Spurzheim, G. *Observations sur la phraenologie.* Paris: Treuttel et Wurtz, 1818.

Stellar, E., & Krause, N. P. New stereotaxic instrument for use with the rat. *Science*, 1954, *120*, 664–666.

Szechtman, H. Redirected oral behavior in rats induced by tail pinch and electrical stimulation of the tail. *Physiology and Behavior*, 1980, *24*, 57–64.

Szechtman, H., & Hall, W. G. The ontogeny of oral behavior induced by tail-pinch and electrical stimulation of the tail in rats. *Journal of Comparative and Physiological Psychology*, 1980, *94*, 436–445.

Szechtman, H., Ornstein, K., Hofstein, R., Teitelbaum, P., & Golani, I. Apomorphine induces behavioral regression: A sequence that is the opposite of neurological recovery. In E. Usdin, T. L. Sourkes, & M. B. H. Youdim (Eds.), *Enzymes and neurotransmitters in mental disease.* Chichester, England: Wiley, 1980, pp. 511–517.

Szechtman, H., Ornstein, K., Teitelbaum, P., & Golani, I. Snout contact fixation, climbing, and gnawing during apomorphine stereotypy in rats from two substrains. *European Journal of Pharmacology*, 1982, *80*, 385–392.

Szechtman, H., Ornstein, K., Teitelbaum, P. & Golani, I. The morphogenesis of stereotyped behavior induced by the dopamine receptor agonist apomorphine in the laboratory rat. *Neuroscience*, 1985, *14*, 783–798.

Szechtman, H., Siegel, H. I., Rosenblatt, J. S., & Komisaruk, B. R. Tail pinch facilitates onset of maternal behavior in rats. *Physiology and Behavior*, 1977, *19*, 807–809.

Teitelbaum, P. Sensory control of hypothalamic hyperphagia. *Journal of Comparative and Physiological Psychology*, 1955, *48*, 156–163.

Teitelbaum, P. Appetite. *Proceedings of the American Philosophical Society*, 1964, *108*, 464–472.

Teitelbaum, P. The encephalization of hunger. In E. Stellar & J. M. Sprague (Eds.), *Progress in physiological psychology* (Vol. 4). New York: Academic Press, 1971.

Teitelbaum, P. Levels of integration of the operant. In W. K. Honig & J. E. R. Staddon (Eds.), *Handbook of operant behavior*. Englewood Cliffs, NJ: Prentice-Hall, 1977a, pp. 7–27.

Teitelbaum, P. The physiological analysis of motivated behavior. In P. G. Zimbardo & F. L. Ruch (Eds.), *Psychology and life* (9th ed). Glenview, IL: Scott, Foresman, 1977b.

Teitelbaum, P. Comments on "The lateral hypothalamic syndrome" as a Citation Classic. *Current Contents*, 1979, March 12, vol. 11, 14.

Teitelbaum, P. What is the "zero condition" for motivated behavior? In B. G. Hoebel & D. Novin (Eds.), *The neural basis of feeding and reward*. Brunswick, ME: Haer Institute, 1982a, pp. 7–23.

Teitelbaum, P. Disconnection and antagonistic interaction of movement subsystems in motivated behavior. In A. R. Morrison & P. L. Strick (Eds.), *Changing concepts of the nervous system: Proceedings of the First Institute of Neurological Sciences Symposium in Neurobiology*. New York: Academic Press, 1982b, pp. 467–487.

Teitelbaum, P., Cheng, M.-F., & Rozin, P. Development of feeding parallels its recovery after hypothalamic damage. *Journal of Comparative and Physiological Psychology*, 1969, *67*, 430–441.

Teitelbaum, P., & Cytawa, J. Spreading depression and recovery from lateral hypothalamic damage. *Science*, 1965, *147*, 61–63.

Teitelbaum, P., & Epstein, A. N. The lateral hypothalamic syndrome: Recovery of feeding and drinking after lateral hypothalamic damage. *Psychological Review*, 1962, *69*, 74–90.

Teitelbaum, P., Schallert, T., De Ryck, M., Whishaw, I. Q., & Golani, I. Motor subsystems in motivated behavior. In R. F. Thompson, L. W. Hicks, & V. B. Shvyrkov (Eds.), *Neural mechanisms of goal-directed behavior and learning*. New York: Academic Press, 1980, 127–143.

Teitelbaum, P., Schallert, T., & Whishaw, I. Q. Sources of spontaneity in motivated behavior. In E. Satinoff & P. Teitelbaum (Eds.), *Handbook of behavioral neurobiology: Motivation*. New York: Plenum Press, 1983.

Teitelbaum, P., & Stellar, E. Recovery from the failure to eat produced by hypothalamic lesions. *Science,* 1954, *120,* 894–895.

Teitelbaum, P., Szechtman, H., Sirkin, D. W., & Golani, I. Dimensions of movement, movement subsystems, and local reflexes in the dopaminergic systems underlying exploratory locomotion. In M. Y. Spiegelstein & A. Levy (Eds.), *Behavioral models and the analysis of drug action.* Proceedings of the 27th OHOLO Conference, Zichron Ya'acov, Israel, March 28–31, 1982. Amsterdam: Elsevier Biomedical Press, 1982, pp. 357–385.

Teitelbaum, P., & Wolgin, D. L. Neurotransmitters and the regulation of food intake. *Progress in Brain Research,* 1975, *42,* 235–249.

Teitelbaum, P., Wolgin, D., De Ryck, M., & Marin, 0. S. M. Bandage-backfall reaction: Occurs in infancy, hypothalamic damage, and catalepsy. *Proceedings of the National Academy of Sciences, U.S.A.,* 1976, *73,* 3311–3314.

Twitchell, T. E. The restoration of motor function following hemiplegia in man. *Brain,* 1951, *74,* 443–480.

Twitchell, T. E. The automatic grasping responses of infants. *Neuropsychologia,* 1965, *3,* 247–259.

Twitchell, T. E. Reflex mechanisms and the development of prehension. In K. J. Connolly (Ed.), *Mechanisms of motor skill development.* New York: Academic Press, 1970, pp. 25–45.

Ungerstedt, U. Adipsia and aphagia after 6-hydroxydopamine induced degeneration of the nigrostriatal dopamine system. *Acta Physiologica Scandinavica,* 1971 (Suppl. 367), 95–122.

Van Harreveld, A., & Bogen, J. E. The clinging position of the bulbocapninized cat. *Experimental Neurology,* 1961, *4,* 241–261.

Van Harreveld, A., & Kok, D. J. A propos de la nature de la catalepsie experimentale. *Archives Nederlandaises de Physiologie de l'Homme et des Animaux,* 1935, *20,* 411–429.

Villablanca, J. Specialized lesions: "Cerveau Isole" and "Encephale Isole." In R. D. Myers (Ed.), *Methods in psychobiology: Laboratory techniques in neuropsychology* (Vol. 2). London: Academic Press, 1971, pp. 285–302.

Weisman, A. Cliff jumping in rats after intravenous treatment with apomorphine. *Psychopharmacology,* 1971, *21,* 60–65.

Williams, D. R., & Teitelbaum, P. Some observations on the starvation resulting from lateral hypothalamic lesions. *Journal of Comparative and Physiological Psychology,* 1959, *52,* 458–465.

Wolgin, D. L. Motivation, activation, and behavioral integration. In R. L. Isaacson & N. E. Spear (Eds.), *The expression of knowledge.* New York: Plenum Press, 1982, pp. 243–290.

Wolgin, D. L., & Teitelbaum, P. Role of activation and sensory stimuli in recovery from lateral hypothalamic damage in the cat. *Journal of Comparative and Physiological Psychology,* 1978, *92,* 474–500.

Yamamoto, W. S., & Brobeck, J. R. *Physiological controls and regulations.* Philadelphia and London: W. B. Saunders Co., 1965.

6. Localization of the Essential Memory-Trace System for a Basic Form of Associative Learning in the Mammalian Brain
Richard F. Thompson, David A. McCormick, and David G. Lavond

> In experiments extending over the past 30 years I have been trying to trace conditioned reflex paths through the brain or to find the locus of specific memory traces.
> —K. S. Lashley, "In Search of the Engram"

The overriding problem for analysis of the memory trace in the mammalian brain has been that of localization. In order to analyze neuronal / synaptic mechanisms of memory storage and retrieval, it is first necessary to identify and localize the brain systems, structures, and regions that are critically involved.

Localization of function in the cerebral cortex was a major intellectual issue at the beginning of the twentieth century. The pendulum had swung far away from Gall's phrenology and was now swinging back toward a more reasoned kind of localization. Classic studies in the late nineteenth century using lesions and electrical stimulation had demonstrated localization of the sensory fields and the motor area in mammals, and clinical studies suggested localization of speech areas in humans. From this research it seemed to many a reasonable extrapolation to localize complex phenomena like memory in the association areas of the cerebral cortex. Indeed, Ivan Pavlov was of the opinion that conditioned reflexes were formed and elaborated entirely in the cerebral cortex. To quote Clifford Morgan, former chairman of the psychology department at Johns Hopkins:

Back in 1911, Zeliony, a Russian colleague of Pavlov, first attempted to study conditioning in the totally decorticate dog—a dog deprived of all neocortex. . . . Zeliony failed. His failure caused Pavlov and many others interested in conditioning behavior to believe that conditioning was solely the property of the cerebral cortex. Many years later, in 1930, however, Poltyrew and Zeliony repeated the early attempts. This time they succeeded in obtaining conditioned responses in decorticates (dogs). In fact, in two of the animals a rather sophisticated type of conditioning could be obtained; the animals learned to lift one forepaw (to avoid shock) to the sound of a whistle and the other forepaw to the sound of a knock on wood. These positive results with decorticate conditioning reopened the whole question for American investigators. (Morgan and Stellar 1950, 446.)

Karl Lashley began his search for the engram at the Johns Hopkins University in a collaborative study with Sheppard Franz, who worked at St. Elizabeth's Hospital in Washington, D.C. Franz had studied with Wilhelm Wundt in Leipzig (1896) and took his degree with Cattell in 1898. He developed an extensive research program concerned with recovery of function after brain damage in humans and animals and became skeptical of precise localization of intellectual functions in the cerebral cortex.

At that time Lashley held a somewhat middle position, having also been strongly influenced by his work with John Watson at Johns Hopkins on conditioned reflexes.

In 1914, I think, Watson called attention of his seminar to the French edition of Bechterew and that winter the seminar was devoted to translation and discussion of the book. In the spring I served as a sort of unpaid assistant and we constructed apparatus and planned experiments together. We simply attempted to repeat Bechterew's experiments. We worked with withdrawal reflexes, knee jerk, pupil. Watson took the initiative in all this, but he was also trying to photograph the vocal cords, so I did much of the actual experimental work. I devised drainage tubes for the parotid and submaxillary ducts and planned the salivary work which I published. As we worked with the method I think our enthusiasm for it was somewhat dampened. Watson tried to establish conditioned auditory reflexes in the rat and failed. Our whole program was then disrupted by the move to the lab in Meyer's clinic. There were no adequate animal quarters there. Watson started work with the infants as the next best material available. I tagged along for awhile, but disliked the babies and found me a rat lab in another building. We accumulated a considerable amount of experimental material on the conditioned reflex which has never been published. Watson saw it as a basis for a systematic psychology and was not greatly concerned with the nature of the reaction itself. I got interested in the physiology of the reaction and the attempt to trace conditioned reflex paths through the nervous system started my program of cerebral work. (letter of May 14, 1935, K. S. Lashley to E. R. Hilgard, reproduced with the kind permission of Professor E. R. Hilgard)

One has the feeling that then and throughout his life, Lashley wanted to believe in localization of the memory trace but his own results kept confounding this belief (Lashley 1950).

Lashley and Franz (1917) gave a very balanced and modern treatment of the issues of localization. They considered at length the experimental problems of distinguishing between effects of cortical lesions on memories, per se, or on sensory or motor capabilities. In their experiments, they focused on the frontal cortex of the rat and used a simple maze, which they called a kinesthetic-motor habit, and an inclined plane box. In the latter, the animal had to learn to climb on top of the box, depress the elevated end of an inclined plane, then climb down and go to the food in the now opened box below the inclined plane. (Today, this would be viewed as a rather "cognitive" behavior for a rat). Even very large frontal lesions did not impair learning or memory for the simple maze. The largest bilateral frontal lesions caused loss of the inclined-plane box habit. Interestingly, some of these lesions included much of the hippocampus as well. Smaller lesions had no effect. In their discussion, they raised the notions of mass-action and equipotentiality, though these terms were not used until later (Lashley 1929). Lashley and Franz were greatly struck by the resistance of well-learned habits to cortical insult: "The destruction of cortical tissue has not been extensive enough to prove that learning may take place wholly at the level of the subcortical centers but the evidence at hand is sufficient to justify more extensive experiments upon this point" (Lashley and Franz 1917, 133).

Lashley continued to pursue localization of the memory trace in the cerebral cortex, culminating in his classic 1929 monograph. There he states the extreme cortical localization view, the switchboard theory, and proceeds to demolish it experimentally. He concluded that memory traces were stored in the cerebral cortex but were not localized. He did not consider in any detail the alternative possibility he and Franz had raised earlier that memory traces for certain forms of learning might in fact be localized subcortically. Nonetheless, Lashley continued in search of the cortical engram and in 1950 drew his oft-quoted conclusion: "This series of experiments has yielded a good bit of information about what and where the memory trace is not. It has discovered nothing directly of the real nature of the engram. I sometimes feel, in reviewing the evidence on the localization of the memory trace, that the necessary conclusion is that learning just is not possible. It is difficult to conceive of a mechanism which can satisfy the conditions set for it. Nevertheless, in spite of such evidence against it, learning does sometimes occur" (1950, 477).

The lesion approach to localization of the memory trace poses many problems of interpretation, as noted by Pavlov, Lashley, and many others:

> Notwithstanding the best surgical technic employed by some of these investigators, certain objections are particularly inherent in the method of extirpation. First, the gross mutilation of so fine and complex an organ as the brain is likely to have effects more widespread than simply the absence of the removed part. It is in the words of Pavlov, as if one struck a delicate machine with a sledge hammer and then studied the results. Furthermore, a three-1egged stool falls when any one leg is removed, although that leg is not wholly responsible for holding up the stool—an analogy often used by Adolf Meyer. (Brogden and Gantt 1942, 437).

Electrical stimulation of the brain as a tool for localization of the memory trace was used in a now classic series of studies in the laboratory of W. Horsley Gantt at Johns Hopkins. Gantt, Loucks, W. J. Brogden, and others working in Gantt's laboratory attempted to define "the relation of conditioned reflex function to anatomic pathways" using electrical brain stimulation to elicit the behavioral response to be conditioned, i.e., as an unconditioned stimulus (US). Loucks (1936) showed that a leg flexion elicited by stimulation of the motor area of the cerebral cortex could not be conditioned to a conditioned stimulus (CS).

Brogden (later the first author's major professor in graduate school at the University of Wisconsin) and Gantt completed an extremely important series of experiments using electrical stimulation of the cerebellum as a US (1937, 1942). The results speak for themselves:

> Dog 173—The unconditioned response was variable; most of the time it consisted of flexion of the ipsilateral forelimb, but sometimes flexion of both the ipsilateral hindlimbs occurred. The sound of an electric doorbell was used as the conditioned stimulus. The first conditioned response appeared on the third trial. Conditioning reached 100 percent in the second training session. Continuation of training maintained a high level of conditioning for an additional 5 test periods, whereon the frequency of conditioned responses began to decrease. By the thirteenth test period the conditioned response had disappeared completely, in spite of the fact that the unconditioned stimulus on each trial evoked a clearcut flexion of the ipsilateral forelimb. Four more training sessions failed to reestablish conditioning. No further experiments were performed

with this animal. The conditioned response was more variable than the unconditioned response. Flexion of the ipsilateral forelimb was the prominent characteristic of the conditioned response, although at times it might be accompanied by flexion of the ipsilateral hindlimb or by flexion of the ipsilateral hindlimb and the contralateral forelimb and hindlimb. Cerebellar Lesions: Two small spherical cavities caused by the stimulating electrodes were surrounded by a zone in which there was pronounced mobilization of the microglia and macroglia. The cerebellar cortex overlying these lesions showed degeneration of ganglion cells and proliferation of the microglia in the white matter of the cortical folia. Both lesions were located well within the subcortical white matter. The surrounding subcortical area peripheral to these lesions and the adjacent cerebellar cortex were normal in appearance.

Dog 201—The unconditioned response of this animal was closure of the ipsilateral eyelid. Sometimes the contralateral eyelid also closed in conjunction with the ipsilateral one. The first conditioned response to the bell was observed on the twelfth trial. A score of 15 percent was made in the first test period, 60 percent in the second, 35 percent in the third, 60 percent in the fourth, 85 percent in the fifth and the sixth and 100 percent in the seventh. The conditioned response was almost an exact duplicate of the unconditioned response. It consisted of closure of the ipsilateral eyelid, sometimes accompanied by the contralateral eyelid. Conditioned differentiation was tried, with only slight success. The bell was made the negative conditioned stimulus and a 1000 cycle tone the positive conditioned stimulus. On the eighteenth test period the conditioned response scores were 30 percent for the bell and 100 percent for the tone. No further tests could be made owing to breakage of one of the electrodes.

The locus of the electrodes could not be determined, as no postmortem sutdy was made on this animal.

The outstanding feature of the performances of these animals was the rapidity with which the cerebellar responses became conditioned. In 5 of the 7 animals the frequency of conditioned responses reached the criterion of 100 percent in 40 to 60 trials (2 to 3 test periods). Flexion of the forelimb in the dog, evoked by shock stimulus to the forepaw, was ordinarily conditioned to the sound of a bell in from 240 to 260 trials. Experimental extinction and the conditioning of the response to a second conditioned stimulus occurred with the proper experimental conditions. Conditioned differentiation could be established with approximately the same ease as with other conditioned responses. (Brogden and Gantt 1942, 437–55

There are several important points to be noted in these observations and the others contained in the paper. First, a variety of different movements can be obtained from cerebellar stimulation. Responses as diverse as forelimb flexion and discrete closure of the ipsilateral eyelid conditioned easily, though diffuse body movements owing to contractions of the axial musculature did not. The movements that conditioned well were discrete, adaptive responses that would have avoided noxious stimuli of the sort that would normally have elicited the responses. Second, if a discrete response was elicited by cerebellar stimulation, it conditioned very rapidly to an acoustic or visual CS, significantly more so than if the same response were elicited by an adequate peripheral US. Dog 173 raises another interesting possibility. It appears that a lesion developed in the cerebellum after the animal had learned, possibly from a local infection. If so, could it have abolished the conditioned response by destroying the memory trace?

The fundamental limitation of electrical stimulation of the brain as a tool for localization of the memory trace is of course that the effective action could be remote from the site of stimulation. Indeed, electrical stimulation of virtually any site in the brain can serve as a CS. However, the same is not true when the electrical stimulus serves as a US. Only a limited number of sites can elicit behavior responses and some of these are ineffective for conditioning (e.g., motor cortex). To our knowledge, the cerebellar stimulation effect of Brogden and Gantt is the most impressive in the literature. Even here, the electrical stimulus could be producing its effective action elsewhere than in the cerebellum. Indeed, Brogden and Gantt point to connections via the red nucleus to the thalamus and motor areas of the cerebral cortex as a possibility.

Our Search for the "Engram"

About fifteen years ago, the first author decided to devote the future efforts of his laboratory to an understanding of the neuronal substrates of associative learning and memory in the mammalian brain—to continue Lashley's search for the engram. In earlier years we had focused on more elementary or nonassociative forms of behavioral plasticity—habituation and sensitization—with some degree of success (Thompson and Spencer 1966; Groves and Thompson 1970). In this work, we early made use of what has come to be termed the "model systems" approach to analysis of neuronal substrates of behavioral plasticity or learning, using the flexion reflex of the acute spinal mammal to model the phenomena of habituation and sensitization. Associative learning presents rather more formidable problems—the only completely satisfactory model is an intact, learning mammal, with all the attendant complexities of the mammalian brain.

Pavlov was of course the first to develop and use the model system approach to learning and memory. From the time he discovered the conditioned reflex he saw it as a tool to investigate higher functions of the brain. Lashley, influenced by Pavlov, Bechterev, and Watson, was the first Western scientist to state explicitly the model system approach, namely, to use simple conditioned reflexes as models of associative learning and to localize memory traces by tracking the essential conditioned response circuitry through the brain (see opening quote and his letter to Hilgard).

In recent years, the model system approach to analysis of the neuronal substrates of learning and memory has been valuable and productive. The basic notion is to utilize a preparation showing a clear form of associative learning in which neuronal analysis is possible. When a suitable preparation has been developed, the first issue that must be addressed is that of identifying the neuronal structures and systems that are involved in a given form of learning. Most typically this has been approached using lesions, electrophysiological recording, and anatomical methods. A critical aspect is circuit analysis, tracing the neuronal pathways and systems from the CS channel to the motor neurons. An obvious distinction must be made between the memory-trace system—the necessary structures and pathways from CS receptors to CR effectors—and the memory trace itself, the essential neuronal plasticity that codes the learned response. As the essential structures and pathways are defined, it becomes possible to localize and analyze cellular mechanisms underlying the memory trace (Thompson and Spencer 1966; Kandel and Spencer 1968; Woody et al. 1974; Thompson et al. 1976; Cohen 1980; Tsukahara 1981; Ito 1982; Thompson et al. 1983). One of the many advantages of utilizing a few, well-defined model systems for analysis of brain substrates of learning and memory is that knowledge is cumulative and can be generalized across laboratories.

We adopted a particularly clear-cut and robust form of associative learning in the intact mammal as a model system: classical conditioning of the rabbit nictitating membrane (NM) and eyelid response to an acoustic or visual CS using a corneal airpuff as a US. Classical conditioning of the eyelid response was first done in humans (Cason 1922; Hilgard 1931). Ernest Hilgard was the first to study eyelid conditioning in infrahuman animals in his classical work with Marquis on dogs and monkeys (Hilgard and Marquis 1935, 1936). He and Marquis, then both at Yale, recognized immediately that eyelid conditioning provided an excellent model system for analysis of brain substrates of memory, and they undertook a series of lesion studies with the assistance of John Fulton. They used a visual CS and showed that the visual cortex was not essential for learning of the eyelid CR. Their results pointed to a subcortical memory trace (Marquis and Hilgard 1936, 1937).

Isadore Gormezano, then at Iowa, was the first to publish eyelid conditoning studies in the rabbit and introduced measurement of the nictitating membrane (NM) extension response, both of which have proved advantageous. The rabbit is docile and tolerates restraint well, and the NM response is convenient to measure (Gormezano et al. 1962; Schneiderman, Fuentes, and Gormezano 1962; Deaux and Gormezano 1963). The conditioned NM or eyelid response in the rabbit has been used to very good effect in analysis of basic theoretical issues in learning (e.g., Wagner 1969, 1971, 1981, Gormezano 1972; Donegan and Wagner, in press).

Classical conditioning of the rabbit NM / eyelid response has a number of advantages for anlaysis of brain substrates of learning and memory, which have been detailed elsewhere (Thompson et al. 1976; Disterhoft, Kwan, and Low 1977). Perhaps the greatest single advantage of NM/eyelid conditioning, and classical conditioning paradigms in general, is that the effects of experimental manipulations on learning versus performance can be more easily evaluated than in instrumental procedures. This problem of learning versus performance has plagued the study of brain substrates of learning from the beginning. For example, does a brain lesion or the administration of pharmacological agents impair a learned behavior because it damages the memory trace or because it alters the animal's ability to respond? Or, perhaps, does it alter the animal's motivation to respond? By using Pavlovian procedures, one can estimate the effects of such manipulations on learning and performance by comparing the subject's ability to generate the conditioned response (CR) and unconditioned response (UR) before and after making a lesion or administering a drug. If the CR is affected and the UR is unaffected, one can reasonably assume that the memory-trace system is being affected, as opposed to behavioral performance. Other advantages of the rabbit NM preparation include the absence of alpha conditioning or sensitization, the simple and discrete phasic character of the NM / eyelid response and its ease of measurement, and the fact that use of a corneal airpuff US permits recording of neuronal activity during delivery of the US.

One final advantage of the conditoned NM / eyelid response is the fact that eyelid conditioning has become perhaps the most widely used paradigm for the study of basic properties of classical or Pavlovian conditioning of striated muscle responses in both humans and infrahuman subjects. It displays the same basic laws of learning in humans and in other animals (Hilgard and Marquis 1940). Consequently, it seems highly likely that neuronal mechanisms found to underlie conditioning of the NM / eyelid response in rabbits will hold for all mammals, including humans. We view the conditioned NM / eyelid response as an instance of the general class of conditioned striated muscle responses learned with an aversive US, and we adopt the working assumption that neuronal mechanisms underlying associative learning of the NM / eyelid response will in fact be general for all aversive classical conditioning of discrete striated muscle responses.

NATURE OF THE CONDITIONED RESPONSE

In the rabbit NM-conditioning paradigm, considerably more than just NM extension becomes conditioned. Gormezano and associates first showed that eyelid closure, eyeball retraction, and NM extension all develop during conditioning in essentially the same manner (Gormezano et al. 1962; Schneiderman, Fuentes, and Gormezano 1962; Deaux and Gormezano 1963). The efferent limb thus involves several cranial nerve nuclei. The primary response that produces NM extension is retraction of the eyeball (Cegavske et al. 1976). A major muscle action producing this response is contraction of the retractor bulbus, which in rabbit is innervated by motoneurons of the abducens and accessory abducens nuclei (Gray et al. 1981; Cegavske, Harrison, and Torigoe, in press). However, it appears that most of the extrinsic eye muscles may contract synchronously to some extent with the retractor bulbus (Berthier and Moore 1980). In addition, the external eyelid (which is normally held open in NM conditioning) extends, under control of motoneurons in the seventh nucleus. Finally, there is a variable degree of contraction of facial muscles in the vicinity of the eye. In sum, the total response is a coordinated defense of the eye involving primarily eyeball retraction (NM extension) and eyelid closure with some contraction of periorbital facial musculature (McCormick, Lavond, and Thompson 1982). Simultaneous recordings from one NM and both eyelids during conditioning of the left eye show essentially perfect correlations in both amplitude and latency of the conditioned responses as they develop over the course of training. Although CRs are typically much smaller in the eye opposite to the trained eye and show marked interanimal differences in amplitude, the pattern of response, when clearly present, is on the average highly correlated with those of the eye being trained (McCormick, Lavond, and Thompson 1982).

Recordings of neural activity from the abducens nucleus simultaneously with measurement of NM extension show that the pattern of increased neural unit response precedes and closely parallels the amplitude-time course of the behavioral NM response (fig. 6.1). The cross correlation between the two responses is very high—typically over 0.90 (Cegavske et al. 1976). Eyelid closure shows a similar time course to NM extension, though the onset latency is somewhat shorter. In current work we have found that the patterns of increased neural unit activity in the accessory

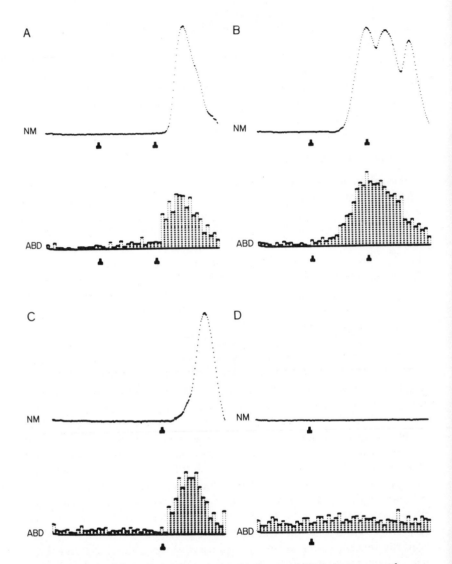

Fig. 6.1. Examples of eight-trial averaged behavioral NM responses and associated multiple unit histograms of abducens nucleus activity (15 msec time bins) for a conditioning animal at the beginning and end of training (A, B) and a control animal at the beginning of training for the airpuff US (C) and the tone CS (D). Note the close correspondence between the histogram of unit activity recorded from the final common path and the temporal form of the behavioral NM response in all cases. *Source:* Cegavske, C. F., Patterson, M. M., & Thompson, R. F. Neuronal unit activity in the abducens nucleus during classical conditioning of the nictitating membrane response in the rabbit *Oryctolagus cuniculus. Journal of Comparative and Physiologial Psychology,* 1979, *93.* Copyright 1979 by the American Psychological Association. Reprinted by permission of the authors.

abducens nucleus and in the seventh cranial nucleus (eyelid control) during performance of the learned response are essentially identical to that seen in the abducens nucleus. In terms of amount of increase in neural unit activity, the response in the seventh nucleus is substantially the largest. The amplitude-time course of the NM extension response mirrors the pattern of increased neuronal unit activity in the relevant motor nuclei with considerable precision on a trial-by-trial basis (except of course for onset latency differences), which is a great convenience. The extension of the NM and / or eyelid across the eye reflects the change in neural unit activity in the final common path—a learned neuronal response that has the same properties in several motor nuclei. We adopted the working hypothesis that the neuronal system responsible for generation of the learned NM / eyelid response will exhibit this same pattern of increased neuronal activity. Something must drive the several motor nuclei in a synchronous fashion.

ROLE OF HIGHER BRAIN STRUCTURES

In this seemingly simple paradigm, higher regions of the brain play important roles (Berger and Thompson 1978a). Indeed, under certain conditions they are critically important (Thompson et al. 1982; Thompson, Berger, and Madden 1983). However, in the standard short delay conditioning paradigm (e.g., CS on for 200 to 500 msec with corneal airpuff or periorbital shock given during the terminal portion of the CS—on period), animals with the cerebral neocortex or hippocampus removed are able to learn (Oakley and Russell 1972; Solomon and Moore 1975), as are animals with all brain tissue above the level of the thalamus or midbrain removed (Enser 1976; Norman, Buchwald, and Villablanca 1977).

Some caution must be exercised in drawing conclusions regarding the locus of the memory trace in the intact animal from results on reduced preparations. The fact that a decerebrate animal can learn the NM / eyelid response does not necessarily mean that the memory trace is normally established in the intact animal below the level of the thalamus, only that the remaining tissue is capable of supporting learning. Oakley and Russell (1977) addressed this issue for the cerebral cortex by first training the animals, then decorticating them, allowing five to ten weeks for recovery and then continuing training. They found a transient depression in conditioned responding but a rapid recovery (marked savings), arguing that a substantial part of the memory trace established in the intact animal is below the level of the cerebral cortex.

A final caveat is warranted. It seems very likely that memory-trace systems develop in higher regions of the brain in classical conditioning, Indeed, evidence to date argues strongly that a memory-trace system develops in the hippocampus very early in training in standard delay classical conditioning of the rabbit NM / eyelid response (Berger and Thompson 1978a, 1978b, 1978c, Berger et al. 1983). However, this presumed hippocampal memory-trace system is not essential for learning or memory of the standard conditioned response, though it does appear to become essential when greater demands are placed on the memory system, as noted above. We focus here on what we term the essential or primary memory-trace system, the neuronal system essential for learning and memory of the standard conditioned response. Throughout, we use "memory trace" to mean this essential memory trace for the standard conditioned NM / eyelid response.

BRAIN SYSTEMS WHERE THE PRIMARY MEMORY TRACE IS NOT LOCATED

We have developed evidence arguing against localization of the memory trace for the NM / eyelid conditioned response to several brain systems. We have detailed these arguments elsewhere (Thompson, Berger, and Madden 1983; Thompson et al. 1983, 1984a, 1984b, 1984c, in press), and will only summarize them here.

The conditioned stimulus channel—the auditory system. During acquisition of the classically conditioned NM / eyelid response to an acoustic CS, there are no changes in evoked neuronal unit activity in the mainline auditory relay nuclei (Thompson et al. 1983). Using a signal detection paradigm with a staircase procedure so that the animal gives learned behavioral NM / eyelid responses 50% of the time to a constant-intensity, threshold-level acoustic stimulus, there are clear evoked neuronal unit responses that are identical on both detection and nondetection trials in the anteroventral cochlear nucleus, the central nucleus of the inferior colliculus, and the ventral division of the medial geniculate body (Kettner et al. 1980; Kettner and Thompson 1982). Because there must be differential activity or activation of the primary memory trace on detection and nondetection trials, the mainline auditory relay nuclei cannot be a part of the essential primary memory-trace system. Some parts of them are obviously essential to convey the information that the CS has occurred, but the memory is not there.

Relfex pathways and motor neurons. The virtually perfect correspondence between the NM and both eyelids and with activity in the relevant motor nuclei (Cegavske, Patterson, and Thompson 1979; McCormick, Lavond, and Thompson 1982 and fig. 1) over the course of learning implies that the primary memory trace is unlikely to develop independently in each motor nucleus. It can most easily be accounted for by assuming a common central system that acts upon the reflex pathways and / or simultaneously on all the relevant motor nuclei (see above). If manipulations of the brain can abolish the conditioned response but have no effect at all on the UR, it is prima facie evidence against the possibility that an essential component of the primary memory trace is in the reflex pathways and / or motor neurons. Morphine has just such an effect on the conditioned NM / eyelid response (Mauk et al. 1982; Mauk, Warren, and Thompson 1982). So do spreading depression of the motor cortex (Papsdorf, Longman, and Gormezano 1965; Megirian and Bures 1969) and lesions of the cerebellum (McCormick et al. 1981, 1982).

The "alpha response" pathway. A sufficiently intense acoustic CS can elicit an alpha eyelid response that has a latency of about 20 msec in the cat (Woody and Brozek 1969). There are thus fairly direct pathways from the primary auditory system to the seventh motor nucleus. However, the minimum onset latency of the conditioned NM / eyelid response is about 80 msec, much too long for the memory trace to be localized to the acoustic alpha response pathway.

   In summary, the essential primary memory trace for standard delay classical conditioning of the NM / eyelid response is below the level of the thalamus and does not appear to be localized in the primary sensory component of the CS channel (here the auditory system), the motor neurons, the reflex pathways, or the acoustic alpha response pathways.

Cerebellum: The Locus of the Memory Trace?

From the above findings, the circuitry that might serve to code the primary memory trace for the NM / eyelid CR in the standard delay paradigm could include much of the midbrain, brain stem, and cerebellum, excluding the primary CS channel (here the auditory relay nuclei), the reflex pathways, and the motor neurons. Because there was no a priori way of determining which of these regions and structures are involved in the memory trace, we undertook, beginning about four years ago, to map the entire midbrain, brain stem, and cerebellum by systematically recording neuronal unit activity (unit cluster recording) in already trained animals (McCormick, Lavond, and Thompson 1983; Thompson et al. 1984). For this purpose, we developed a chronic micromanipulator system that permits mapping of unit activity in a substantial number of neural loci per animal. Increases in unit activity that form a temporal model within a trial of the learned behavioral response were prominent in certain regions of the cerebellum, both in cortex and deep nuclei, the red nucleus, pontine nuclei, and the reticular tegmental nucleus of the pons. Such unit activity is also seen in certain regions of the reticular formation and of course in the

cranial motor nuclei engaged in generation of the behavioral response—
portions of the third, sixth, accessory sixth, and seventh nuclei. The results
to date of the mapping studies point to substantial engagement of the
cerebellar system in the generation of the conditioned response.

NEURAL UNIT RESPONSES

Current studies in which we have recorded neuronal unit activity from the
deep cerebellar nuclei (dentate and interpositus nuclei) over the course of
training have in some locations revealed a striking pattern of learning-
related growth in activity (McCormick et al. 1982; McCormick and

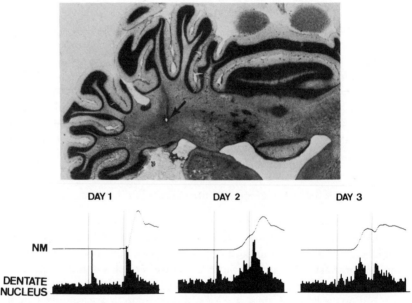

Fig. 6.2.   Histograms of unit cluster recordings obtained from a chronic
electrode in the medial dentate nucleus in an animal during classical
conditioning of NM / eyelid response. The recording site is indicated by the
arrow. Each histogram bar is 9 msec in width and each histogram is summed
over an entire day of training. The first vertical line represents the onset of the
tone and the second vertical line represents the onset of the airpuff. The trace
above each histogram represents the averaged movement of the animal's NM
for the same day, with up being extension of the NM across the cornea. The
total duration of each histogram and trace is 750 msec. The pattern of increased
discharges of cerebellar neurons appears to develop a neuronal "model" of the
amplitude-time course of the learned behavioral response (McCormick, Lavond,
and Thompson 1982).

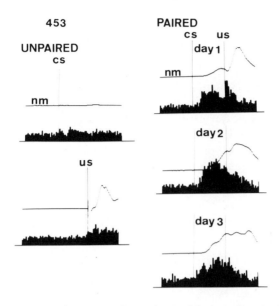

Fig. 6.3. Histograms of unit recordings obtained from a chronic electrode implanted on the border of the dentate / interpositus nuclei in another animal. The animal was first given random, unpaired presentations of the tone and airpuff (104 trials of each stimulus) and then trained with two days of paired training (117 trials each day). Each histogram is an average over the entire day of training indicated. The upper trace represents movement of the NM with up being closure. The first vertical line represents the onset of the conditioning stimulus, while the second line represents the onset of the unconditioned stimulus. Each histogram bar is 9 msec in duration. Notice that these neurons develop a model of the conditioned, but not unconditioned, response during learning and that this neuronal model precedes the learned behavioral response substantiates in time. *Source:* McCormick, D. A., & Thompson, R. F. Neuronal responses of the rabbit cerebellum during acquisition and performance of a classically conditioned nictitating membrane-eyelid response. *Journal of Neuroscience,* 1984, *4(11).* © 1984 *Journal of Neuroscience.*

Thompson, unpublished observations). In the example shown in figure 6.2, the animal did not learn on day 1 of training. Unit activity showed evoked responses to tone and airpuff onsets but no response in association with the reflex NM response, in marked contrast to unit recordings from the cranial motor nuclei. On day 2, the animal began showing CRs, and the unit activity in the medial dentate nucleus developed a "model" of the conditioned response. On day 3, the learned behavioral response and the cerebellar model of the learned response are well developed, but there is still no clear model of the reflex behavioral response.

Another example is shown in figure 6.3. This animal was given unpaired training before acquisition began. Average histograms reveal that the unit activity showed only minimal responses to the tone and airpuff during the unpaired day of training. However, during acquisition, as the animal learned, the unit activity developed a model of the conditioned response. Again, there is no clear model of the unconditioned response. The cerebellar unit model of the learned response precedes the behavioral response significantly in time. A neuronal model of the learned behavioral response appears to develop de novo in the cerebellar deep nuclear region.

The course of development of the conditioned behavioral NM / eyelid response and the concomitant growth in the neuronal unit "model" of the

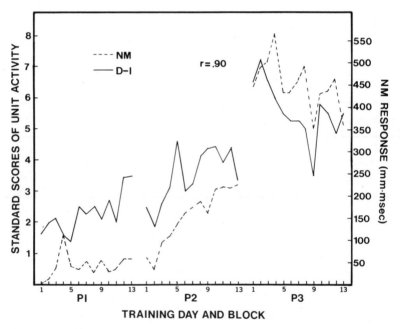

Fig. 6.4. Amplitude of the conditioned response in comparison to the magnitude of the dentate / interpositus neuronal activity in the second half of the conditioned stimulus period over the course of learning. Seven of the recording sites that developed larger type responses were utilized for this figure. Standard scores were calculated by finding the mean number of action potentials counted for the block of training trials in question, subtracting the number of counts in the corresponding half of the Pre-CS period for that block, and dividing by the standard deviation over the entire training session: $(\bar{CS}_{block} - \bar{PCS}_{block})/SD\ PCS_{session})$. The magnitude of the conditioned response was measured as the area under the curve described by the amplitude / time course of the NM response in millimeter milliseconds. *Source:* See Fig. 6.4.

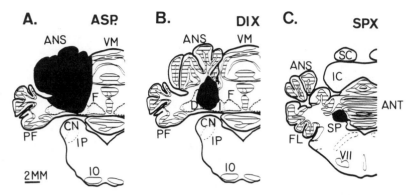

A.   ASP.   B.   DIX   C.   SPX

Fig. 6.5.   Reconstructions of cerebellar lesions effective in abolishing the ipsilateral conditioned NM / eyelid response. *A* is a typical unilateral aspiration of the lateral cerebellum and dentate/interpositus nuclei. *B* represents a unilateral electrolytic lesion of the dentate / interpositus nuclei (*DIX*) in which the overlying cortex is spared. *C* is a localized unilateral lesion of the superior cerebellar peduncle (*SPX*). All reconstructions are through the broadest extent of each lesion. Abbreviations are as follows: *ANS*, ansiform lobe; *CN*, cochlear nucleus; *D*, dentate nucleus; *F*, fastigial nucleus; *ANT*, anterior lobe; *FL*, flocculus; *I*, interpositus nucleus; *IC*, inferior colliculus; *IO*, inferior olive; *IP*, inferior cerebellar peduncle; *PF*, paraflocculus; *SC*, superior colliculus; *SP*, superior cerebellar peduncle; *VM*, vermal lobes; *VII*, seventh nucleus (Thompson et al. 1984a, based on Clark et al. 1982; McCormick et al. 1981; McCormick, Guyer, and Thompson 1982; McCormick, Lavond, and Thompson 1982).

conditioned response in the ipsilateral dentate / interpositus nuclear region are shown for a group of animals in figure 6.4. The correlation between the two measures is +0.90 (McCormick and Thompson, unpublished observations).

ESSENTIAL ROLE OF CEREBELLAR NUCLEI

In current work, we have found that lesions ipsilateral to the trained eye in several locations in the neocerebellum (fig. 6.5)—large ablations of the lateral portion of the hemisphere (fig. 6.6), localized electrolytic lesions of the dentate / interpositus nuclei and surrounding fibers (fig. 6.7), and discrete lesions of the superior cerebellar peduncle (fig. 6.8)—permanently abolish the CR but have no effect on the UR and do not prevent subsequent learning by the contralateral eye (Lavond et al. 1981; McCormick et al. 1981; Clark et al. 1982, 1984; McCormick et al. 1982; McCormick, Guyer, and Thompson 1982; McCormick, Lavond, and Thompson 1982; Thompson 1983). The electrolytic lesion result has recently been repli-

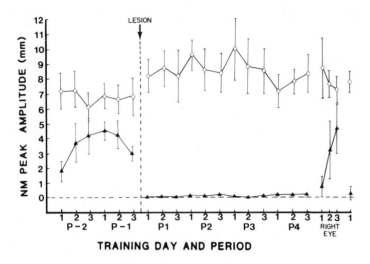

Fig. 6.6.   Effects of ablation of left lateral cerebellum on the learned
NM / eyelid response (six animals). Solid triangles, amplitude of conditioned
response (CR); open diamonds, amplitude of unconditioned response (UCR).
All training was to left eye (ipsilateral to lesion) except where labeled "right
eye." The cerebellar lesion completely and permanently abolished the CR of the
ipsilateral eye but had no effect on the UCR. P_1 and P_2 indicate initial learning
on the two days before the lesion. L_1-L_2 are four days of postoperative training
to the left eye. The right eye was then trained and learned rapidly. The left eye
was again trained and showed no learning, thus controlling for nonspecific
lesion effects. Numbers on abscissa indicate 40 trial periods, except for "right
eye," which are 24 trial periods (McCormick, Lavond, and Thompson 1982).

cated exactly by Yeo et al. (1982) using light as well as tone CSs and a
periorbital shock rather than corneal airpuff UCS. If training is given after
unilateral cerebellar lesion, the ipsilateral eye cannot learn but the contralateral eye learns normally (fig. 6.9) (Lincoln, McCormick, and
Thompson 1982). Lesions in several locations in the ipsilateral pontine
brain stem produce a similar selective abolition of the CR (Desmond and
Moore 1982; Lavond et al. 1981). Although some uncertainty still exists,
the learning-effective lesion sites in the pontine brain stem appear to track
the course of at least a part of the superior cerebellar peduncle.

ROLE OF CEREBELLAR CORTEX

Lesions of the cerebellar cortex do not abolish the basic conditioned
NM / eyelid response (McCormick and Thompson 1983). To date, we
have removed all lobes of the ipsilateral cerebellar cortex except the floc-

culus in different groups of animals (e.g., ansiform lobe; ansiform plus paramedian lobes; paraflocculus; lobule a, nodulus; lobule b, uvula; lobule c, medius medianus and pyramis; and anterior lobe, see fig. 6.11).

However, removal of the ansiform lobe does have a significant effect on the form of the CR. In a normal animal, the NM / eyelid CR tends toward maximum (eyelids closed) at the time of onset of the US (fig. 6.1B). After removal of the ansiform lobe in well-trained animals, the basic CR occurs but the eyelids tend to open somewhat by the time of onset of the US. This CR is less adaptive. Hence, the region of cerebellar cortex that projects to the critical nuclear site does seem to play a role in shaping and timing the

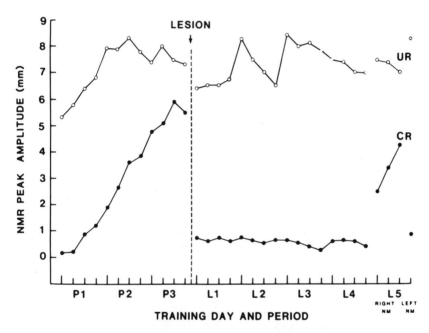

Fig. 6.7. Effects of small unilateral electrolytic lesions of cerebellar nuclei on conditioned and unconditioned NM responses (mean amplitude, $n = 14$). Animals received three days of training (P_{1-3}) on the left eye prior to lesioning. After lesioning (left cerebellar nuclei), animals were trained for four days (L_{1-4}) to test for retention and recovery of the conditioned responses. On the fifth postlesion session (L_5), training was switched to the right (nonlesioned) side, then returned to the left eye ($n = 13$). Results of each training day are represented in four periods of trials, approximately 27 trials per period. Note that CR amplitude was in essence abolished by the lesion, but UR amplitude was unaffected. Note also that the right (nonlesioned) side learned quickly, controlling for nonspecific lesion effects, but that conditioned responding on the left side showed no recovery (Clark et al. 1984).

response. Preliminary evidence suggests that the cortex of the ansiform lobe may also play an important role in initial acquisition of the CR. However, it is not essential for the memory of the basic CR, in contrast to the essential role of the lateral interpositus nucleus.

ELECTRICAL STIMULATION

Electrical stimulation through recording microelectrodes in the medial dentate / lateral interpositus nuclear region elicited a clear NM / eyelid response in eight of nine animals tested in which a neuronal unit "model" of the behavioral learned response was recorded by the electrode (McCormick and Thompson 1983). This response (measurement is of NM extension) has an onset latency from cerebellar nuclear stimulation of approx-

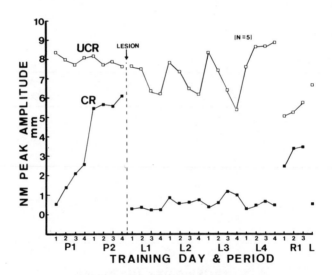

Fig. 6.8.   Effect of very small discrete lesions of the ipsilateral superior cerebellar peduncle (SCP), the major efferent pathway from the lateral cerebellar deep nuclei, on retention and reacquisition of the nictitating membrane (and eyelid) responses, averaged for five animals. Solid squares, amplitude of conditioned response (CR); open squares, amplitude of unconditioned response (UCR). All training was to the left side except where labeled R1. The lesion abolished or severely impaired the ipsilateral CR with no effect upon the UCR. P1-P2 indicate the two days of training before the lesion. L1-L4 indicate the four days of training after the lesion. The contralateral (right) eye was then trained and learned quite rapidly (R1). The left eye was again trained (L) and still showed only very small responses. Numbers on abscissa represent approximately 27 trial blocks (McCormick, Guyer, and Thompson 1982).

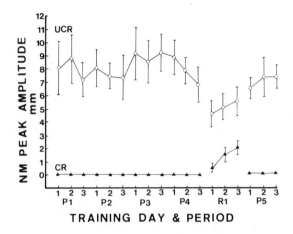

TRAINING DAY & PERIOD

Fig. 6.9.   Effects of ablation of left lateral cerebellum on learning of the nictitating membrane (and eyelid) responses (six animals). Lesions made before any training. Solid triangles, amplitude of conditioned response (CR); open diamonds, amplitude of unconditioned response (UCR). All training was to left eye (ipsilateral to lesion) except where labeled R1. The cerebellar lesion prevented conditioning of the ipsilateral eye but had no effect on the UCR. P1-P4 indicate the four days of postlesion training to the left eye. The right eye was then trained and learned at a rate comparable to that of initial learning of nonlesioned animals. The left eye was again trained (P5) and showed no learning. Numbers on abscissa indicate 40 trial blocks (Lincoln, McCormick, and Thompson 1982).

imately 35 msec (fig. 6.10). This indicates that regions of the deep cerebellar nuclei which develop neuronal responses related to the performance of the learned response contain neuronal elements that when activated, can cause the response to occur. Of nine recording sites that did not yield eyeblinks when stimulated, none of the nine developed neuronal responses related to performance of the conditioned response. Electrolytic lesion of the superior cerebellar peduncle (the major efferent pathway from the deep nuclei) abolishes the ability of deep nuclear stimulation to elicit the NM / eyelid response. This same lesion also abolishes the behavioral conditoned response, as noted earlier.

OVERVIEW

Composite diagrams are shown in figure 6.11, indicating regions of the ipsilateral cerebellar deep nuclei from which the neuronal unit "model" of the learned behavioral response can be recorded (A—solid dots), regions from which electrical stimulation evokes on NM / eyelid response (B—

solid dots), the locus of lesions that permanently abolish the conditioned NM / eyelid response (C), and large cerebellar cortical lesions that do not abolish the conditioned NM / eyelid response (D). Note that the sites of the neuronal model, the sites of effective electrical stimulation, and the effective lesion site are essentially identical, involving the most medial portion of the dentate nucleus and the lateral portion of the interpositus nucleus. Because the efferent fibers from the lateral dentate nucleus course medially as they exit from the dentate, the more medial electrolytic lesion might be interrupting these fibers. However, current work using kainic acid lesions, which are presumed to destroy only cell bodies, appears to localize the effective site to a very small region at the lateral interpositus and possibly the most medial border of the dentate nucleus (Lincoln et al. 1983; Lavond et al. in press) (fig. 6.12). Considering all the lesion results together, the smallest effective lesion appears to be not much more than a cubic millimeter of the deep nuclear tissue.

In the context of the distinction between the essential memory-trace system and the memory trace, our results to date indicate that the ip-

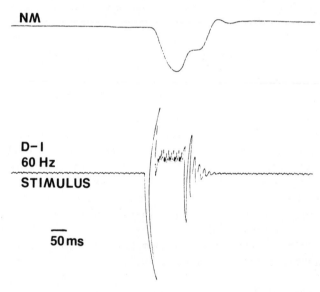

Fig. 6.10.   Example of 60 Hz dentate / interpositus stimulation induced NM extension and eyelid closure response. Stimulus was 60 Hz AC, 150 msec, 75 uA. Each small division represents 0.5 mm of NM movement across the eyeball. Stimulation was from a site from which the neuronal "model" of the behavioral learned response was recorded (see figs. 6.2 and 6.3). The evoked behavioral response here has an onset latency of 35 msec. *Source:* See Fig. 6.3.

silateral medial dentate–lateral interpositus nuclear region is part of the NM / eyelid memory-trace system, almost by definition. The only alternative is that damage to the dentate-interpositus region interferes with the functioning of some other circuitry for which the cerebellum is not normally important. Thus, retrograde degeneration of certain cerebellar afferents might interfere with the functioning of the structure of origin of the afferents, even though the cerebellum is not normally important for the functioning of the structure. However, the fact that lesions of the major cerebellar efferent, the superior cerebellar peduncle, immediately abolish the learned response rules out this possibility. The possibility that unilateral lesions cause asymmetrical imbalance of another system (the Sprague effect—Sprague 1966) is ruled out because bilateral dentateinterpositus lesions abolish the learned response bilaterally (Lavond et al. 1983). Furthermore, the learned response does not recover. Animals with bilateral lesions have been trained repeatedly for as long as three months postlesion and never relearn, even though they are otherwise behaviorally normal (Lavond et al. 1983). Such a long-lasting deficit persisting in otherwise normal animals argues against the possibility that the cerebellar lesions abolish the learned response by removal of tonic activation of neurons outside the cerebellum. We conclude that the medial dentate–lateral interpositus region is an essential part of the memory trace system for the NM / eyelid response.

The Locus of the Memory Trace

In so far as the locus of the memory trace for the learned NM / eyelid response is concerned, there would seem to be three possibilities: (1) structures efferent from the cerebellum for which the cerebellum is a critically important afferent; (2) structures afferent to the cerebellum for which the cerebellum is a mandatory efferent; and (3) the medial dentate and / or lateral interpositus nuclear region of the cerebellum ipsilateral to the trained eye.

Two current findings argue against the first possibility, at least for the NM / eyelid response: the neuronal "model" of the learned behavioral response develops in the medial dentate–lateral interpositus (D-I) region, and electrical stimulation of the D-I nuclei can elicit the behavioral NM / eyelid response, both before and after learning has occurred (Mc-Cormick and Thompson 1983).

At this point, we do not have decisive data to distinguish between the second and third possibilities. In terms of evoked increases in unit activity in the D-I region before training, auditory and somatic sensory information are both present, a necessary requirement for the formation of associations. Detailed somatic-sensory information about the occurrence of

Fig. 6.11.   Summary diagram of the chronic recordings, stimulation, dentate / interpositus lesions, and noneffective lesions of the cerebellar cortex. *A* illustrates the recording sites (●) that developed neuronal responses within the CS period which were greater than two standard scores, as well as the recording sites (○) that did not develop a neuronal response within the CS period. *B* illustrates the sites at which 60 Hz stimulation at 100 uA or the onset of direct current stimulation at 100 uA produces ipsilateral NM extension and eyelid closure. The sites that were ineffective in eliciting eyeblink responses are represented by open circles (○). *C* illustrates a typical stereotaxic lesion of the medial dentate / lateral interpositus nuclear region which abolished the conditioned response. *D* illustrates a composite drawing of aspirations of three animals that were ineffective in abolishing the learned eyeblink response. Note that the medial dentate / lateral interpositus region not only develops neuronal responses related to the performance of the learned response during training but, when stimulated, will elicit an eyeblink response that is dependent, as is the learned response, on the intactness of the superior cerebellar peduncle. Furthermore, lesioning of this region of the deep cerebellar nuclei permanantly abolishes the learned response, while cortical lesions that circumscribe this region do not. Abbreviations are as follows: *ANS*, ansiform lobule (Crus I and Crus II); *ANT*, anterior lobe; *D*, dentate nucleus; *FL*, flocculus; *DCN*, dorsal cochlear nucleus; *F*, fastigial nucleus; *I*, interpositus nucleus; *IO*, inferior olive; *Lob. a*, lobulus A (nodulus); *PF*, paraflocculus; *VN*, vestibular nuclei; *cd*, dorsal crus; *cv*, ventral crus; *g vii*, genu of the tract of the seventh nerve; *icp*, inferior cerebellar peduncle; *vii*, seventh (facial) nucleus; *vii n*, nerve of the seventh nucleus; *viii*, nerve of the eighth nucleus. *Source:* See Fig. 6.3.

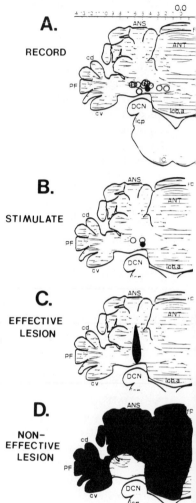

A. RECORD

B. STIMULATE

C. EFFECTIVE LESION

D. NON-EFFECTIVE LESION

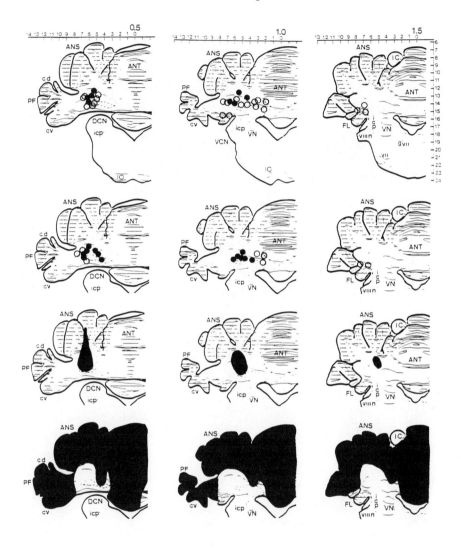

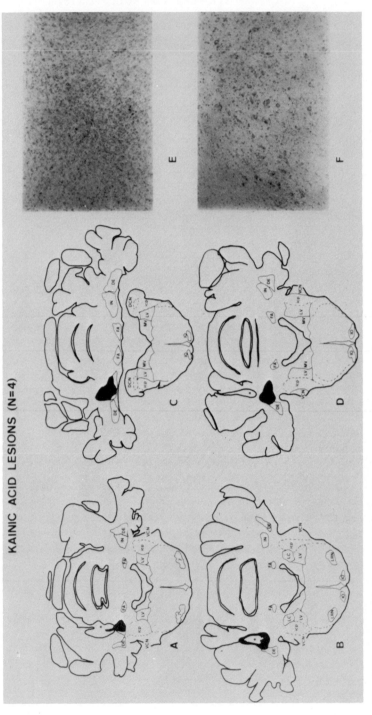

Fig. 6.12. Histological results of the maximum extent of gliosis owing to kainic acid injection in four animals (*A–D*) that completely and permanently abolished memory of the ipsilateral NM / eyelid conditioned response. All animals learned on the eye contralateral to the lesion. *E*, extent of neuron loss and gliosis in left interpositus nucleus in (B); *F*, comparable section from right interpositus in (B); *DE*, dentate nucleus; *IN*, interpositus nucleus (Lavond et al. 1985).

movements, i.e., feedback, is present and is of course a prominent feature of the cerebellar input generally. Response latencies are also consistent. The minimum eyelid conditioned response onset latency is about 80 msec, and the minimum onset latency of unit activity in the D-I that correlates with porduction of the CR can precede this by about 60 msec. The onset latency of tone CS evoked unit activity in the D-I region is 12 msec. This leaves about 8 msec for the auditory input to recruit the neuronal elements in the D-I that generate the learned behavioral response.

If the memory trace is afferent to the cerebellum, it must be in a structure for which the cerebellum is a mandatory efferent, since cerebellar lesions abolish the learned response. There are really only two major structures in the brain that satisfy this requirement: the inferior olive (IO) and the pontine nuclei. Current evidence from our laboratory argues against the IO as the locus of the memory trace (McCormick and Thompson 1983). However, the IO does appear to play a critical role as the system conveying the "reinforcing" aspect of the US to the cerebellum. In current preliminary work, we have found that when lesions are made in the rostromedial portion of the IO (the region receiving nociceptive input from the face via the spinal trigeminal nucleus) in animals previously trained in the NM / eyelid response, the animals show conditioned responses postlesion; but with continued paired training, the conditioned response extinguishes, much as if the US had been omitted and extinction training given (McCormick and Thompson 1983). Lesions of all other portions of the IO do not produce this effect, nor do they abolish the conditioned response.

If these preliminary findings are confirmed, several inferences seem possible. Since the animals show conditioned responding after the effective IO lesion, the memory trace cannot be in the IO. Since the effective IO lesion results in extinction of the conditioned response, the IO must be providing essential input concerning the US/UR to the memory trace. The memory trace must therefore receive major input from the IO. The cerebellum receives just such input, but the pontine nuclei do not. This fact, together with the IO lesion effect, to the extent they hold with further replication, argue that the memory trace is neither in the pontine nuclei nor in the IO. It is either in some other afferent system that must project to the cerebellum or in the interpositus nucleus itself and/or cerebellar cortex.

In terms of the efferent pathway from the memory trace to the behavioral NM / eyelid response, current evidence from our laboratory indicates that it courses out the superior cerebellar peduncle (McCormick, Guyer, and Thompson 1982), crosses to the contralateral side in the peduncle (Lavond et al. 1981), relays in the magnocellular division of the red nucleus (Haley, Lavond, and Thompson 1983; Madden et al. 1983), crosses back to the ipsilateral side, and projects to the lower brain stem as a part of the descending rubral pathway.

A number of investigators have suggested that the cerebellum is involved in the learning, and perhaps storage, of "motor programs" (Brindley 1964; Eccles, Ito, and Szentagothai 1967; Marr 1969; Ito 1970; Albus 1971; Gilbert 1974; Eccles 1977). These authors have indicated that the storage of such information would take place in the cerebellar cortex as a modulation of the parallel fiber synapses of the granule cells onto the Purkinje cells. It is to be noted that most of these theories suggest that the climbing fiber input from the contralateral IO is the "teaching" or reinforcing input Our current IO lesion effect is strikingly consistent with this notion.

Lesions of the cerebellar flocculus have been found to block plasticity of the vestibulo-ocular reflex (VOR) (Ito 1974; Ito, Jastreboff, and Miyashita 1980) and recovery of VOR symmetry after hemilabyrinthectomy (Courjon et al. 1982). Furthermore, recording results from the cerebellar flocculus in the rabbit during adaptive modification of the vestibulo-ocular reflex support this hypothesis (Dufosse et al. 1978), although differing results have been reported in the monkey (Miles and Lisberger 1981).

As noted above, we have failed to find any cortical region that, when removed consistently, abolished the conditioned eyelid response, even though all cortical regions except for the flocculus have been removed. The flocculus itself is most likely not the critical structure involved in the known effective lesions since the lesions track the superior cerebellar peduncle through the brain stem and therefore do not involve the known projection of the floccolus (Dow 1936; Anguate and Brodal 1967). These results imply that if cellular plasticity does occur within the cerebellar cortex during learning of the NM / eyelid response, this plasticity is not essential for the retention of the basic learned motor response. However, as noted above, cerebellar cortex does play an important role in shaping the form of the CR and may play a critical role in initial learning.

Our data to date are most consistent with the hypothesis that the neuronal plasticity that encodes the learned NM / eyelid response is within the critical region of the deep cerebellar nuclei. The interpositus nucleus possesses the neuroanatomical connections that allow it to cause NM / eyelid responses (stimulation results), this nuclear region is also essential for (lesion results) and active during (recording results) learning and retention of the NM / eyelid response. This region contains all of the neuronal connections that would allow it to associate auditory information with the occurrence of the corneal airpuff in order to cause the formation of the "memory trace" for learned NM / eyelid response to the tone.

In terms of putative neuronal / synaptic mechanisms of memory storage, current work in our laboratory by Laura Mamounas and John Madden, in collaboration with Jack Barchas of the psychiatry department, raises the interesting possibility that synaptic inhibitory processes may be critical

(Mamounas et al. 1983). Microinjection of as little as 2 nmol of bicuculline methiodide directly into this same region—medial dentate / lateral interpositus nuclear area—causes a selective and reversible abolition of both the behavioral CR and the neuronal model of the CR (recorded with a microelectrode −.75mm ventral to the tip of the microinfusion cannula) but has no effect on the UR (fig. 6.13). Further, this

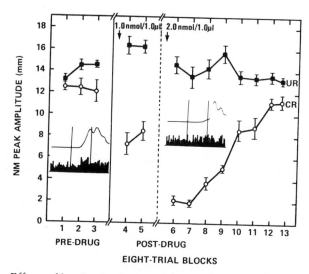

Fig. 6.13. Effects of localized microinjection of bicuculline methiodide into the medial dentate / lateral interpositus region ipsilateral to the trained eye on the well-learned NM / eyelid response. ■ (closed squares) and ○ (open circles) represent the peak amplitude of the unconditioned response (*UR*) and conditioned response (*CR*) respectively. Each training block consists of eight averaged trials with a variable, 30-second intertrial interval. *Left panel:* mean NM response amplitude during three blocks of predrug baseline conditioning. *Center panel:* mean NM response amplitude for two blocks following microinjection of 1 nmol bicuculline methiodide into dentate / interpositus. *Right panel:* mean NM response amplitude for eight blocks following microinjection of 2 nmol of bicuculline methiodide. Note inserts within left and right panels: upper trace in each histogram represents the averaged NM response; lower trace depicts the corresponding dentate / interpositus multiple unit peristimulus histogram. The bin width is 9 msec. The first vertical line in each histogram indicates tone onset; the second vertical line indicates airpuff onset. The predrug histogram is an average of blocks 2 and 3; the postdrug histogram is an average of blocks 6 and 7. Note that local infusion of 2 nmol of bicuculline in the critical medial dentate / interpositus nuclear region (see fig. 6.10) selectively and reversibly abolishes the conditioned response. Infusions in other regions of the cerebellar deep nuclei do not produce this effect. (Mamounas et al., unpublished observations).

selective bicuculline abolition of the learned response is independent of level of training or overtraining. One other drug, picrotoxin, causes the same selective and reversible abolition of the CR. Picrotoxin is believed to block chloride channels associated with GABA inhibition, providing further evidence that GABA inhibitory neurons play a critical role in the memory-trace circuit. Strychnine, believed to block glycine inhibition, does not depress the CR.

The fact that high concentrations of GABA have been localized to these nuclear regions (Okada et al. 1971), coupled with the observations by Chan-Palay (1977, 1978) demonstrating autoradiographic localization of GABA receptors in this region, provides a basis for tentatively postulating that bicuculline produces its selective abolition of the CR in a traditional way—through blockage of inhibitory GABA-ergic transmission. Note that there is no increase in spontaneous unit activity following bicuculline infusion in the recordings shown in figure 6.13—thus, the abolition of both the behavioral and the neuronal learned responses seems not to be due to abnormally increased cellular activity. Instead, it seems more likely to be blocking inhibitory synaptic transmission that is in some way essential for the generation of the learned responses. One calls to mind Eugene Roberts's notion of GABA-ergic processes playing a key role in learning (Roberts 1976, 1980). This result also demonstrates that abolition of the CR by lesions in this region cannot be due to nonspecific persisting effects of the lesion. The bicuculline and picrotoxin abolition of the CR dissipates over time—with CRs retruning to baseline levels by the end of the test session (fig. 6.13), Further, it does not abolish the CR in the eye contralateral to the side of infusion.

GENERALITY OF CEREBELLUM IN LEARNING

How general is our cerebellar result? It is independent of CS modality, holding equally for auditory and visual stimuli, and also independent of the exact nature of the US, holding equally for corneal airpuff and periorbital shock (see above). Because the cerebellum plays an important role in certain reflex movements of the eye, (e.g., the vestibulo-ocular reflex), it could be argued that our results would not generalize to other response systems. However, current work by Nelson Donegan in our laboratory shows that such is not the case—the lateral cerebellum is also essential for classical conditioning of the hindlimb flexion reflex (Donegan, Lowry, and Thompson 1983).

Rabbits were initially trained with a shock UCS to the left hindpaw, using the same conditions otherwise as in NM / eyelid training (i.e., tone CS) and EMG activity recorded from flexor muscles of both hindlimbs. Both hindlimbs developed an equivalent learned flexor response, consistent with the rabbit's normal mode of locomotion. Ablation of the left lateral cerebellum abolishes or markedly reduces this conditioned response in both hindlimbs. Training (i.e., paw shock US) was then given to the right hindlimb and both hindlimbs relearned. When training was then shifted back to the left hindlimb, the learned response in both hindlimbs rapidly extinguished. These results demonstrate that the left cerebellar lesion does not simply prevent the animal from making the learned response in the left hindlimb and support the view that the memory trace for learning of the hindlimb flexion response, like the NM/eyelid learned response, is established unilaterally in the cerebellum. An earlier Soviet report indicates that complete removal of the cerebellum in dogs well trained in leg-flexion conditioning permanently abolished the discrete leg-flexion response (Karamian, Fanaralijian, and Kosareva 1969). Thus, it appears that essential cerebellar involvement in classical conditioning of discrete behavioral responses is not sensory-, species-, or response-specific.

It seems a very reasonable possibility that the memory trace for learning of all classically conditioned discrete, adaptive somatic motor responses occurs in the cerebellum. Perhaps the most prominent feature of such learned responses is their precise timing. At least in aversive learning, the CR is under very strong control by the CS-US interval in terms of onset latency and temporal morphology and is always timed to be at maximum at or shortly before the time when then onset of the US occurs. The cerebellum is very well designed to provide such precise timing (Eccles, Ito, and Szentagothai 1967).

Michael Patterson, a former colleague now at Ohio University, has developed a paradigm for instrumental avoidance conditioning of the eyelid response in the rabbit: whenever the animal extends its NM more than 0.5 mm during the tone CS period, the US does not occur. Comparison with yolked controls indicates that such training does indeed result in instrumental control of the NM response (Patterson, personal communication). In current collaborative work he has found that the same ipsilateral cerebellar lesion of the dentate-interpositus region also abolishes this instrumental avoidance response. Classical conditioning and instrumental avoidance learning of the eyelid response would seem not to be fundamentally different, so far as the brain is concerned. We infer that this result will hold for instrumental avoidance learning of leg flexion and other discrete somatic responses as well.

Summary and a Model

We have developed a hypothetical scheme or model of the neuronal system that could serve as the essential memory-trace circuit for discrete, adaptive learned somatic motor responses. Before we describe the model, it may be helpful to review the salient features of such conditioned responses and our findings on which the model is based. We use eyelid closure and leg flexion learned responses as examples but most data are for the eyelid response.

1. Neutral stimuli that serve as effective CSs—auditory, visual, tactile— do not initially elicit the behavioral responses to be conditioned over a wide range of intensities. "Alpha" responses do not generally occur in the rabbit, nor do sensitization or pseudoconditioning. For eyelid conditioning, both corneal airpuff and periorbital shock can serve as the US but the former is more natural and preferable on several grounds. Backward conditioning does not occur and conditioning does not develop with simultaneous or 50 msec forward training. The most effective CS-US onset interval is from about 200 to 400 msec but conditioning can develop with a CS-US onset interval as long as about 2 sec. Under the conditions of our studies (350 msec, 85 db 1 KHz tone CS; 100 msec, 2.1 N/cm² corneal airpuff US coterminating with CS, intertrial interval 1 min or 30 sec), initial learning of the eyelid closure response requires about 100 trials and the hindlimb flexion response (using paw shock US, 2 mA, other conditions the same as in eyelid training) requires more training. If the left eye is trained and training then shifted to the right eye, the latter learns in just a few trials—there is considerable transfer of training. The onset latency of the well-learned eyelid response is about 80–100 msec following tone CS onset and slightly longer for the hindlimb flexion response.

2. In common with other learned responses, the conditioned eyelid response exhibits a very clear stimulus generalization gradient. Animals trained with a 1 KHz tone will require additional training to a different CS, proportional to the degree of difference. The amount of additional training required to respond equivalently to a 4 KHz tone is less than that required to a 10 KHz tone. If the CS is altered extremely, as from a tone to a light, almost as much training is required to the light as for original learning to the tone. A considerable degree of stimulus specificity is preserved in the memory trace.

3. A high degree of response specificity is characteristic of the learned response. The animal learns to make the most appropriate and specific set of responses possible to deal most effectively with the aversive US—eyelid closure to deal with corneal airpuff and leg flexion to deal with paw shock.

4. Although the tone CS does not elicit the eyelid closure response or other behavioral responses before training, it does elicit relatively short latency but weak and variable evoked unit activity throughout the lateral cerebellar nuclei. This sensory evoked activity seems to be nonspecific but this has not yet been determined at the level of single neuron responses.

5. A neuronal "model"—a pattern of increased frequency of neural unit discharge which precedes and predicts the behavioral learned response for

the eyelid CR (but not the reflex response) can be recorded only in a small region of the lateral interpositus nucleus and nowhere else in the deep nuclei. The neuronal model of the learned response grows over the course of training and is highly correlated with the development of the learned behavioral response.

6. Lesion of this same small region of the interpositus nucleus and nowhere else permanently abolishes the ipsilateral eyelid CR to both tone and light CSs.

7. Electrical stimulation of the same lateral region of interpositus and nowhere else in the deep nuclei elicits the integrated eyelid closure response.

8. Infusion of very small amounts of bicuculline and picrotoxin in this same region and nowhere else in the deep nuclei selectively and reversibly abolishes the eyelid CR but has no effect on the reflex eyelid response to corneal airpuff.

9. Lesion of the more medial interpositus nucleus and nowhere else abolishes the hindlimb flexion CR. (Preliminary observations indicate that electrical stimulation of the more medial interpositus nucleus elicits an integrated hindlimb flexion response.)

10. Anatomical and physiological data (James Houk, personal communication) show that the IO has a clear somatotopic organization that is projected to the interpositus nucleus such that face is most lateral and hindlimb more medial in the interpositus.

11. Preliminary observations indicate that lesion of the rostromedial portion of the contralateral IO results in subsequent extinction of the learned eyelid response. It is as though the animals have been shifted to tone-alone extinction training. CRs are given after the lesion but they gradually extinguish.

12. Lesions of the ipsilateral superior cerebellar peduncle at several locations ranging from its region of exit from the cerebellum to the decussation where it crosses to the contralateral side of the brain permanently abolish the eyelid CR.

13. Lesion or pharmacological inactivation of the contralateral red nucleus (Magnocellular division) abolishes the conditioned eyelid and leg flexion responses.

14. If training is given to the left eye and the left interpositus nucleus then lesioned, the CR is permanently abolished in the left eye but the right eye learns very rapidly—10 to 15 trials compared to about 100 trials for original learning by the left eye. There is extreme transfer of training. If the left interpositus nucleus is first lesioned and training then given to the left eye, it can never learn. However, when training is then shifted to the right eye, it learns in about 100 trials, as though the animal were normal and new to the training situation. There is no transfer of training.

Our hypothetical scheme of the putative memory-trace circuit for simple learned responses—discrete, adaptive somatic motor responses learned to deal with aversive USs—is shown in figure 6.14. Eyelid closure and leg flexion learning are used as the two examples. Interneurons are omitted and the general site of plasticity is assumed to involve the principal neurons shown in the upper left corner (the motor programs) and / or interneurons acting on them. We have drawn these principal neurons as though they were Purkinje cells of the cerebellar cortex, in part to emphasize the similarity of our model with those of Albus, Eccles, Ito, and Marr. However, current lesion data argue that the memory traces for the basic CRs are stored in the interpositus nucleus. On the other hand, our current data suggest that the cerebellar cortex may play an important role in the initial development of the memory trace (see above). For purposes of discussion, assume that they represent the principal cells—the output neurons—of the interpositus nucleus.

In brief, it is assumed that "neutral" stimuli of the sort that are typically used as CSs (tones, lights) activate the principal cells of the critical circuit in a relatively nonspecific manner. Thus, a 1-KHz tone will activate all the principal neurons shown, as will a 4-KHz tone. However, the two tones do

Fig. 6.14. *(facing page)* Scheme of hypothetical memory-trace system for learning of discrete, adaptive, somatic motor responses to deal with aversive unconditioned stimuli. Interneurons are omitted. It is assumed that the site of the memory trace is at the principal neurons shown in the upper left under "motor programs" and / or at associated interneurons. The principal cells are drawn as though they are Purkinje cells of cerebellar cortex to show similarity with theories of cerebellar plasticity (Marr 1969; Albus 1971; Eccles 1977; Ito 1974), but our data suggest that the basic memory trace is stored in the interpositus nucleus, we assume by an analogous circuitry. A given CS (1 KHz) activates a subset of parallel fibers that in turn activate weakly all principal cells. A different tone also activates all principal cells but by a partially different group of "parallel fibers." The US pathway is assumed to be via the IO and "climbing fibers." A given US is assumed to activate only a limited group of principal cells coding the motor program for the defensive response that is specific for the US (eyelid closure, leg flexion). When "parallel fiber" activation occurs at the appropriate time just before "climbing fiber" activation, the "connections" of the parallel fibers to the principal cells activated by the particular US are strengthened. The efferent pathway from principal cells to motor neurons is by way of the superior cerebellar peduncle and red nucleus. This scheme accounts for stimulus specificity, i.e., the fact that CRs show a stimulus generalization gradient, for response specificity of learned responses, transfer, and lesion-transfer effects (i.e., training one eye and then the other before or after cerebellar lesion) and is consistent with all evidence to date. Although hypothetical, each aspect and assumption is amenable to experimental test.

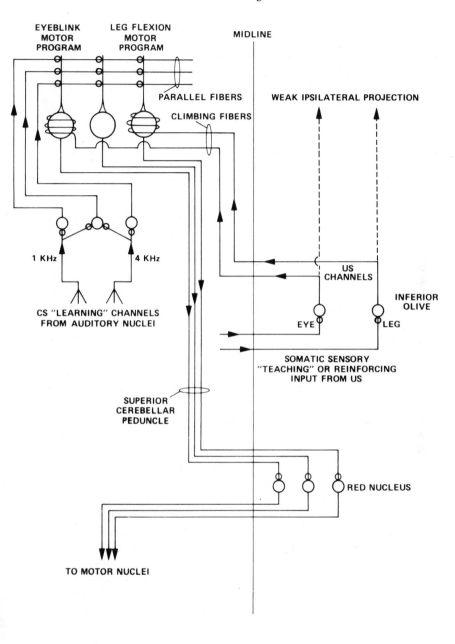

so via overlapping populations of "parallel" fibers. A given tone activates the principal cells nonspecifically and weakly (as we have found) but via a set of fibers that are to some degree different than those for another tone. The more different the two stimuli are, the fewer "parallel" fibers they will activate in common. This scheme permits CS activation of principal neurons to be nonspecific but at the same time preserves stimulus specificity in the "parallel" fiber lines. It thus accounts for the stimulus generalization gradient.

Assume that the training or reinforcing aspect of the US is quite specific and projects via climbing fibers from the IO. In eyelid conditioning, the corneal airpuff US so activates one set of principal neurons, whereas in leg flexion conditioning, the paw shock activates a different set. Assume that these sets are "motor programs" that can generate integrated adaptive responses, eyelid closure or leg flexion, that are appropriate to deal with the particular US. The appropriately timed, nonspecific activation of the principal neurons by the CS and the specific "motor program" set of principal cells activated by the US results in a strengthening of the CS-activated connections to these motor program principal neurons. Thus, in eyelid conditioning, the tone comes to elicit the eyelid closure motor program and in leg flexion conditioning the leg flexion motor program, which exist in different regions of the interpositus nucleus in accordance with its somatotopic motor organization.

The basic assumption is that the memory-trace circuit is "prewired" but the CS activation is "soft-wired" before learning. The connections from any CS to any motor program already exist before training but are too weak to elicit any behavioral responses before training. Activation of this soft-wired CS circuit at the appropriate time before activation of the powerful motor program-specific IO-climbing fiber US input, the teaching or reinforcing input, results in a long-lasting facilitation of the previously weak connections from the CS channel to the specific set of principal neurons, activated by the US via the IO and climbing fibers, most appropriate to deal with the particular US. The response specificity of the learned response is explained by specific activation via the reinforcing US–IO-climbing fiber system.

Our scheme can explain the transfer effects for conditioning of one eye and then the other if we assume a weak input from the IO to ipsilateral cerebellum via axon collaterals of cells projecting to the contralateral cerebellum. If the animal is first trained on the left eye, the memory trace is established in the left cerebellum, and a weaker and variable trace is established in the right cerebellum. Subsequent training on the right eye would then result in rapid learning. Lesion of the left cerebellum after the left eye has learned abolishes the memory trace for the left eyelid response and causes degeneration of the right IO cells. But the weaker right trace has already been established in the right cerebellum. When training is then shifted to the right eye, learning is rapid. However, if the left lesion is made before training, the IO cells degenerate. Training then given to the left eye does not produce learning nor does it establish any plasticity in the right cerebellum because the cells of origin of the weak ipsilateral IO input have degenerated. When training is then shifted to the right eye, the primary trace must be established anew and there is no transfer. A weak pathway interconnecting the lateral deep nuclei of the cerebellar hemispheres could also serve to mediate transfer.

Finally, our scheme assumes that the essential efferent limb of the memory trace-circuit is carried by the superior cerebellar peduncle, which crosses to relay in the magnocellular division of the contralateral red nucleus. From here the rubral pathway crosses back and descends to act on motor nuclei and perhaps also on interneurons of the reflex pathways.

This theoretical scheme is of course tentative and hypothetical but it does account for all of the available data. Each aspect and assumption of the scheme is amenable to experimental test.

A possible type of synaptic arrangement that might be involved in the memory trace is illustrated in figure 6.15, based on Roberts's notion of disinhibition and our pharmacological results. The network is assumed to be in the interpositus nucleus. The key is the GABA inhibitory interneuron, which is assumed to act primarily on another but non-GABA inhibitory interneuron that in turn acts on the principal cell.

Assume that before training the synapses on the GABA interneuron are weak. The CS activates the principal neuron, which in turn activates the non-GABA interneuron, which shuts down the principal neuron, as does the descending Purkinje cell fiber. As a result of training, the synaptic action of the CS channel on the GABA interneuron is strengthened, along with the CS action on the principal cell. This will result in increasing inhibition of the non-GABA inhibitory interneuron, which will allow the strengthened connection from the CS channel to the principal neuron to express itself and yield the CR. Bicuculline and picrotoxin would block the GABA inhibitory interneuron synapse, resulting in greater activation of the non-GABA inhibitory interneuron which could shut down the principal neuron and prevent the CR from being expressed. Note this model implies that synaptic plasticity would develop from the CS "parallel" fiber pathway both onto the principal cell and onto the GABA interneuron. This kind of model implies that blocking of the non-GABA inhibitory interneurons would facilitate the CR.

This example of a possible synaptic model is highly speculative and does not deal adequately with the role of the powerful GABA-ergic inhibition of the descending Purkinje cell axons on neurons of the cerebellar nuclei. Nonetheless, it is at least an example of one synaptic arrangement that

FROM PURKINJE CELL

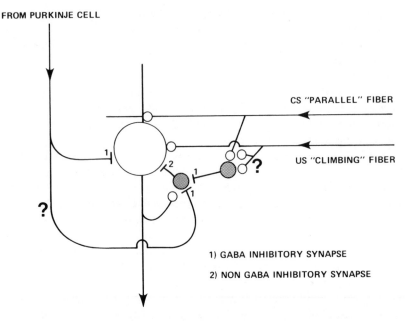

CS "PARALLEL" FIBER

US "CLIMBING" FIBER

1) GABA INHIBITORY SYNAPSE

2) NON GABA INHIBITORY SYNAPSE

Fig. 6.15.   Very hypothetical example of a type of synaptic arrangement in interpositus nucleus which could account for our pharmacological data—the fact that selective application of very small amounts of bicuculline and picrotoxin to the critical site in the interpositus nucleus selectively and reversibly abolishes the CR, but strychnine does not and may even enhance the CR. The basic notion is disinhibition. Over training the "parallel" fiber synapses to the principal cells and to the GABA interneurons are strengthened. As the latter develop they inhibit the normally active non-GABA interneurons, which if active would prevent the principal cells from generating the CR. The action of the Purkinje cells from cerebellar cortex, also GABA-ergic, is assumed to be in some sense parallel to the action of the local GABA-ergic interneurons. The diagram is highly speculative and meant only to show a possible way the memory-trace system might work.

might work. Given what is known about the cerebellum and our pharmacological results to date, there are only a few possible arrangements that could reasonably hold.

We think Lashley would be pleased. Our results to date have localized an essential part of the memory-trace circuit for two conditioned reflexes, eyelid closure and hindlimb flexion, and possibly for the entire class of conditioned reflexes that involve discrete, adaptive behavioral responses with aversive USs. It seems most likely that the memory trace is localized to the lateral deep cerebellar nuclei ipsilateral to the learned response, although this has not yet been proved beyond all doubt. However, because an essential part of the memory-trace circuit has been localized, the entire memory-trace circuit can now be identified and the site or sites of essential neuronal plasticity that code the learned response localized. When this has been done, the cellular neuronal mechanisms that serve to code the memory trace can be analyzed in detail.

Addendum

When we developed the schematic of figure 6.14, we had only very preliminary evidence in favor of the notion that the IO and its climbing fiber input was the "teaching" or reinforcing US-UR pathway for the essential cerebellar memory-trace circuit. Our evidence is now much stronger that it is in fact the essential US teaching input. The IO lesion study in rabbit is now complete (Steinmetz et al. 1984). Destruction of the rostromedial portion of the dorsal accessory olive (DAO), and only this portion of the IO, results in subsequent extinction of the conditioned eyelid response with continued paired tone CS–corneal airpuff US training. In cat, at least, this region of the DAO receives somatic sensory input from the face (Gellman, Houk, and Gibson 1983). Lesion of this region of the DAO before training prevents learning of the conditioned eyelid response, as would be expected. The fact that lesions of this region of the DAO in trained animals do not immediately abolish the CR but instead lead to its eventual extinction argues that the essential memory trace cannot be there.

In current work, we find that electrical microstimulation of the DAO can elicit a variety of discrete behavioral responses, including eyelid closure, the nature of the threshold response being determined by the exact location of the stimulating electrode in the DAO (latency from DAO stimulation ~ 35 msec). If this is now used as the US / UR and paired with a tone CS, the exact response elicited by DAO stimulation is learned to the tone as a CR (Mauk and Thompson 1984). (This result, we think, explains the observations of Brogden and Gantt [1942] on cerebellar stimulation as a US—see above.) Lesion of the critical interpositus region abolishes this 10-established CR, and abolishes the response elicited by IO stimulation (Mauk and Thompson, unpublished observations). This IO stimulation result supports the argument that the cerebellar memory-trace circuit may be the essential circuit for all discrete behavioral responses learned to deal with aversive USs.

Perhaps the most striking result was obtained in animals where the lowest threshold response to DAO stimulation is a discrete response such as eyelid closure which can be measured with a transducer. Having determined the threshold behavioral response, the DAO stimulus intensity was reduced to threshold for the behavioral response, and this US was paired with a tone CS. As a result of this training, the animals learn a well-developed behavioral CR to the tone (a replica of the threshold response to DAO stimulation), even though they give virtually no behavioral responses to the tone CS or the DAO stimulus over training until the behavioral CR develops. This argues against proprioceptive and tactile feedback from the occurrence of the behavioral response to DAO stimulation as an essential component of stimulus input for learning. Activation of the IO-climbing fiber input to the cerebellum would seem to be sufficient to develop the learned response to a tone CS.

The CR established with IO stimulation as the US resembles normal CRs learned to adequate peripheral USs in most ways, e.g., rate of learning, interstimulus interval effect on conditionability (Mauk and Thompson, unpublished observations). However, the animals display no signs of "affect" to the IO stimulus, whereas they of course do to adequate aversive peripheral USs (Mauk and Thompson, unpublished observations). It may be that the "aversive" and "teaching" aspects of effective USs in aversive learning are separable and involve different systems in the brain.

These IO results strengthen the argument that the IO and its climbing fiber input to the interpositus is the essential US teaching input and that the trace is localized to the interpositus. They are also perhaps the first clear empirical evidence supporting the pioneering hypothesis of Albus, Eccles, Ito, Marr, and others that the IO-climbing fiber system is the "teaching" input for learning in the cerebellum.

Acknowledgments

The work reported here was supported in part by research grants from the National Science Foundation (BNS 81-17115), the National Institutes of Health (NS23368), the National Institute of Mental Health (MH26530), the McKnight Foundation, and the Office of Naval Research (N00014-83-K-0238) to R. F. Thompson; Predoctoral Fellowship from the National Institute of Mental Health #5F31 MH08673-02 to D. A. McCormick; Postdoctoral Fellowship from the National Institute of Mental Health #2F32 MH08233-03 to D. G. Lavond. We express deep gratitude to our many associates who collaborated on various aspects of the work reported here: J. Barchas, T. Berger, C. Cegavske, G. Clark, N. Donegan, D. Haley, L. Holt, R. Kettner, J. Lincoln, J. Madden IV, L. Mamounas, M. Mauk, R. Skelton, and J. Thompson.

References

Albus, J. S. A theory of cerebellar function. *Mathematical Bioscience,* 1971, *10,* 25–61.
Anguate, P., & Brodal, A. The projection of the "vestibulo-cerebellum" onto the

vestibular nuclei in the cat. *Archives Italiennes de Biologie*, 1967, *105*, 441–479.

Berger, T. W., Rinaldi, P., Weisz, D. J., & Thompson, R. F. Single unit analysis of different hippocampal cell types during classical conditioning of the rabbit nictitating membrane response. *Journal of Neurophysiology*, 1983, *50*(5), 1197–1219.

Berger, T. W., & Thompson, R. F. Neuronal plasticity in the limbic system during classical conditioning of the rabbit nictitating membrane response. I: The hippocampus. *Brain Research*, 1978a, *145*, 323–46.

Berger, T. W., & Thompson, R. F. Identification of pyramidal cells as the critical elements in hippocampal neuronal plasticity during learning. *Proceedings of the National Academy of Science*, 1978b, *75*, 1572–1576.

Berger, T. W., & Thompson, R. F. Neuronal plasticity in the limbic system during classical conditioning of the rabbit nictitating membrane response. II: Septum and mammillary bodies. *Brain Research*, 1978c, *156*, 293–314.

Berthier, N. E., & Moore, J. W. Role of extraocular muscles in the rabbit (*Oryctolagus cuniculus*) nictitating membrane response. *Physiology and Behavior*, 1980, *2*, 931–937.

Brindley, G. A. The use made by the cerebellum of the information that it receives from sense organs. *International Brain Research Organization Bulletin*, 1964, *3*, 80.

Brogden, W. J., & Gantt, W. H. Cerebellar conditioned reflexes. *American Journal of Physiology*, 1937, *116*, 252–261.

Brogden, W. J., & Gantt, W. H. Interneural conditioning: Cerebellar conditioned reflexes. *Archives of Neurology and Psychiatry*, 1942, *48*, 437–455.

Cason, H. The conditioned eyelid reaction. *Journal of Experimental Psychology*, 1922, *5*, 153–196.

Cegavske, C. F., Harrison, T. A., & Torigoe, Y. Identification of the substrates of the unconditioned response in the classically-conditioned rabbit nictitating-membrane preparation. In I. Gormezano, W. F. Prokasy, & R. F. Thompson (Eds.), *Classical conditioning III: Behavioral, neurophysiological, and neurochemical studies in the rabbit*. Hillsdale, NJ: Lawrence Erlbaum Associates, in press.

Cegavske, C. F., Patterson, M. M., & Thompson, R. F. Neuronal unit activity in the abducens nucleus during classical conditioning of the nictitating membrane response in the rabbit *Oryctolagus cuniculus*. *Journal of Comparative and Physiological Psychology*, 1979, *93*, 595–609.

Cegavske, C. F., Thompson, R. F., Patterson, M. M., & Gormezano, I. Mechanisms of efferent neuronal control of the reflex nictitating membrane response in the rabbit. *Journal of Comparative and Physiological Psychology*, 1976, *90*, 411–423.

Chan-Palay, V. *Cerebellar dentate nucleus, organization, cytology and transmitters*. Berlin: Springer-Verlag, 1977.

Chan-Palay, V. Autoradiographic localization of -aminobutyric acid receptors in the rat central nervous system by using [^{3}H]muscimol. *Proceedings of the National Academy of Science*, 1978, *75*(2), 1024–1028.

Clark, G. A., McCormick, D. A., Lavond, D. G., Baxter, K., Gray, W. J., & Thompson, R. F. Effects of electrolytic lesions of cerebellar nuclei on conditioned behavioral and hippocampal neuronal responses. *Neuroscience Abstracts*, 1982, *8*, 22.

Clark, G. A., McCormick, D. A., Lavond, D. G., & Thompson, R. F. Effects of lesions of cerebellar nuclei on conditioned behavioral and hippocampal neuronal responses. *Brain Research*, 1984, *291*, 125–136.

Cohen, D. H. The functional neuroanatomy of a conditioned response. In R. F. Thompson, L. H. Hicks, & V. B. Shvyrkov (Eds.), *Neural mechanisms of goal-directed behavior and learning*. New York: Academic Press, 1980. pp. 283–302.

Courjon, J. H., Flandrin, J. M., Jeannerod, M., & Schmid, R. The role of the flocculus in vestibular compensation after hemilabyrinthectomy. *Brain Research*, 1982, *239*, 251–257.

Deaux, E. G., & Gormezano, I. Eyeball retraction: Classical conditioning and extinction in the albino rabbit. *Science*, 1963, *141*, 630–631.

Desmond, J. E., & Moore, J. W. A brain stem region essential for classically conditioned but not unconditioned nictitating membrane response. *Physiology and Behavior*, 1982, *28*, 1029–1033.

Disterhoft, J. F., Kwan, H. H., & Low, W. D. Nictitating membrane conditioning to tone in the immobilized albino rabbit. *Brain Research*, 1977, *137*, 127–144.

Donegan, N. H., Lowry, R., & Thompson, R. F. Ipsilateral cerebellar lesions severely impair or abolish retention of classically conditioned leg-flexion responses in the rabbit. *Neuroscience Abstracts*, 1983, *9*, 331.

Donegan, N. H., & Wagner, A. R. Conditioned diminution and facilitation of the UCR: A sometimes-apparent-process interpretation. In I. Gormezano, W. F. Prokasy, & R. F. Thompson (Eds.), *Classical conditioning III: Behavioral, neurophysiological, and neurochemical studies in the rabbit*. Hillsdale, NJ: Lawrence Erlbaum Associates, in press.

Dow, R. S. Fiber connections of the posterior parts of the cerebellum in the cat and rat. *Journal of Comparative Neurology*, 1936, *63*, 527–548.

Dufosse, M., Ito, M., Jastreboff, P. J., & Miyashita, Y. A neuronal correlate in rabbit's cerebellum to adaptive modification of the vestibulo-ocular reflex. *Brain Research*, 1978, *195*, 611–616.

Eccles, J. C. An instruction-selection theory of learning in the cerebellar cortex. *Brain Research*, 1977, *127*, 327–352.

Eccles, J. C., Ito, M., & Szentagothai, J. *The cerebellum as a neuronal machine*. New York: Springer-Verlag, 1967.

Enser, D. Personal communication, July 26, 1976.

Gellman, R., Houk, J. C., & Gibson, A. R. Somatosensory properties of the inferior olive of the cat. *Journal of Comparative Neurology*, 1983, *215*, 278–243.

Gilbert, P. F. C. A theory of memory that explains the function and structure of the cerebellum. *Brain Research*, 1974, *70*, 1–8.

Gormezano, I. Investigations of defense and reward conditioning in the rabbit. In A. H. Black & W. F. Prokasy (Eds.), *Classical conditioning II: Current research and theory*. New York: Appleton-Century-Crofts, 1972, pp. 151–181.

Gormezano, I., Schneiderman, N., Deaux, E., & Fuentes, I. Nictitating membrane:

Classical conditioning and extinction in the albino rabbit. *Science,* 1962, *138,* 33–34.

Gray, T. S., McMaster, S. E., Harvey, J. A., & Gormezano, I. Localization of retractor bulbi motoneurons in the rabbit. *Brain Research,* 1981, *226,* 93–106.

Groves, P. M., & Thompson, R. F. Habituation: A dual-process theory. *Psychological Review,* 1970, *77,* 419–450.

Haley, D. A., Lavond, D. G., & Thompson, R. F. Effects of contralateral red nuclear lesions on retention of the classically conditioned nictitating membrane / eyelid response. *Neuroscience Abstracts,* 1983, *9,* 643.

Hilgard, E. R. Conditioned eyelid reactions to a light stimulus based on the reflex wink to sound. *Psychological Monographics,* 1931, *41*(184), 1–50.

Hilgard, E. R., & Marquis, D. G. Acquisition, extinction, and retention of conditioned lid responses to light in dogs. *Journal of Comparative Psychology,* 1935, *19,* 29–58.

Hilgard, E. R., & Marquis, D. G. Conditioned eyelid responses in monkeys, with a comparison of dog, monkey, and man. *Psychological Monographs,* 1936, *47* (212), 186–198.

Hilgard, E. R., & Marquis, D. G. *Conditioning and learning.* New York: Appleton, 1940.

Ito, M. Neurophysiological aspects of the cerebellar motor control system. *International Journal of Neurology,* 1970, *7,* 162–176.

Ito, M. Control mechanisms of cerebellar motor systems. In F. O. Schmitt & F. G. Worden (Eds.), *The neurosciences, Third study program.* Cambridge, MA: MIT Press, 1974.

Ito, M. Cerebellar control of the vestibulo-ocular reflex: Around the flocculus hypothesis. *Annual Review of Neuroscience,* 1982, *5,* 275–296.

Ito, M., Jastreboff, P. J., & Miyashita, Y. Retrograde influence of surgical and chemical flocculectomy upon dorsal cap neurons of the inferior olive. *Neuroscience Letters,* 1980, *20,* 45–48.

Kandel, E. R., & Spencer, W. A. Cellular neurophysioligical approaches in the study of learning. *Physiological Reviews,* 1968, *48,* 65–134.

Karamian, A. I., Fanaralijian, V. V., & Kosareva, A. A. The functional and morphological evolution of the cerebellum and its role in behavior. In R. Llinas (Ed.), *Neurobiology of cerebellar evolution and development, First international symposium.* Chicago: American Medical Association, 1969.

Kettner, R. E., Shannon, R. V., Nguyen, T. M., & Thompson, R. F. Simultaneous behavioral and neural (cochlear nucleus) measurement during signal detection in the rabbit. *Perception and Psychophysics,* 1980, *28*(6), 504–513.

Kettner, R. E., & Thompson, R. F. Auditory signal detection and decision processes in the nervous system. *Journal of Comparative Physiological Psychology,* 1982, *96,* 328–331.

Lashley, K. S. *Brain mechanism and intelligence.* Chicago: University of Chicago Press, 1929.

Lashley, K. S. In search of the engram. In *Symposia of the Society for Experimental Biology,* No. 4. New York: Cambridge University Press, 1950, p. 454.

Lashley, K. S., & Franz, S. I. The effects of cerebral destruction upon habit-formation and retention in the albino rat. *Psychobiology,* 1917, 71–139.

Lavond, D. G., Hembree, T. L., Lincoln, J. S., & Thompson, R. F. Kainic acid lesion of the cerebellar interpositus nucleus prevents relearning of the NM / eyelid response. *Brain Research*, in press.

Lavond, D. G., Hembree, T. L., & Thompson, R. F. Effect of kainic acid lesions of the cerebellar interpositus nucleus on eyelid conditioning in the rabbit. *Brain Research*, 1985, *326*, 179–182.

Lavond, D. G., Lincoln, J. S., McCormick, D. A., & Thompson, R. F. Effect of bilateral cerebellar lesions on heart-rate and nictitating membrane / eyelid conditioning in the rabbit. *Neuroscience Abstracts*, 1983, *9*, 636.

Lavond, D. G., McCormick, D. A., Clark, G. A., Holmes, D. T., & Thompson, R. F. Effects of ipsilateral rostral pontine reticular lesions on retention of classically conditioned nictitating membrane and eyelid responses. *Physiological Psychology*, 1981, *9*, 335–339.

Lincoln, J. S., Lavond, D. G., Hembree, T. L., Thompson, J. K., & Thompson, R. F. Effect of kainic acid lesions of the cerebellar nuclei on nictitating membrane / eyelid conditioning and an HRP demonstration of cerebellar afferents. *Neuroscience Abstracts*, 1983, *9*, 636.

Lincoln, J. S., McCormick, D. A., & Thompson, R. F. Ipsilateral cerebellar lesions prevent learning of the classically conditioned nictitating membrane / eyelid response. *Brain Research*, 1982, *242*, 190–193.

Loucks, R. B. The experimental delimitation of neural structures essential for learning: The attempt to condition striped muscle responses with faradization of the sigmoid gyri. *Journal of Psychology*, 1936, *1*, 5–44.

Madden, J. IV, Haley, D. A., Barchas, J. D., & Thompson, R. F. Microinfusion of picrotoxin into the caudal red nucleus selectively abolishes the classically conditioned nictitating membrane / eyelid response in the rabbit. *Neuroscience Abstracts*, 1983, *9*, 830.

Mamounas, L. A., Madden, J. IV, Barchas, J. D., & Thompson, R. F. Microinfusion of bicuculline into dentate / interpositus region abolishes classical conditioning of the well-trained rabbit eyelid response. *Neuroscience Abstracts*, 1983, *9*, 830.

Marquis, D. G., & Hilgard, E. R. Conditioned lid responses to light in dogs after removal of the visual cortex. *Journal of Comparative Psychology*, 1936, *22*, 157–178.

Marquis, D. G., & Hilgard, E. R. Conditioned responses to light in monkeys after removal of the occipital lobes. *Brain*, 1937, *60*, 1–12.

Marr, D. A theory of cerebellar cortex. *Journal of Psychology*, 1969, *202*, 437–470.

Mauk, M. D., Madden, J. IV, Barchas, J. D., & Thompson, R. F. Opiates and classical conditioning: Selective abolition of conditioned responses by activation of opiate receptors within the central nervous system. *Proceedings of the National Academy of Science*, 1982, *79*, 7598–7602.

Mauk, M. D., & Thompson, R. F. Classical conditioning using stimulation of the inferior olive as the unconditioned stimulus. *Neuroscience Abstracts*, 1984, *10*, 122.

Mauk, M. D., Warren, J. T., & Thompson, R. F. Selective, naloxone-reversible morphine depression of learned behavioral and hippocampal responses. *Science,* 1982, *216,* 434–435.

McCormick, D. A., Clark, G. A., Lavond, D. G., & Thompson, R. F. Initial localization of the memory trace for a basic form of learning. *Proceedings of the National Academy of Sciences,* 1982, *79*(8), 2731–2742.

McCormick, D. A., Guyer, P. E., & Thompson, R. F. Superior cerebellar peduncle lesions selectively abolish the ipsilateral classically conditioned nictitating membrane / eyelid response of the rabbit. *Brain Research,* 1982, *244,* 347–350.

McCormick, D. A., Lavond, D. G., Clark, G. A., Kettner, R. E. Rising, C. E., & Thompson, R. F. The engram found? Role of the cerebellum in classical conditioning of nictitating membrane and eyelid responses. *Bulletin of the Psychonomic Society,* 1981, *18*(3), 103–105.

McCormick, D. A., Lavond, D. G., & Thompson, R. F. Concomitant classical conditioning of the rabbit nictitating membrane and eyelid responses: Correlations and implications. *Physiology and Behavior,* 1982, *28,* 769–775.

McCormick, D. A., Lavond, D. G., & Thompson, R. F. Neuronal responses of the rabbit brainstem during performance of the classically conditioned nictitating membrane (NM) eyelid response. *Brain Research,* 1983, *271,* 73–88.

McCormick, D. A., & Thompson, R. F. Possible neuronal substrate of classical conditioning within the mammalian CNS: Dentate and interpositus nuclei. *Neuroscience Abstracts,* 1983, *9,* 643.

McCormick, D. A., & Thompson, R. F. Neuronal responses of the rabbit cerebellum during acquisition and performance of a classically conditioned nictitating membrane-eyelid response. *Journal of Neuroscience,* 1984, *4(11),* 2811–2822.

Megirian, D., & Bures, J. Unilateral cortical spreading depression and conditioned eyeblink responses in the rabbit. *Experimental Neurology,* 1969, *27,* 34–45.

Miles, F. A., & Lisberger, S. G. Plasticity in the vestibulo-ocular reflex: A new hypothesis. *Annual Review of Neuroscience,* 1981, *4,* 273–299.

Morgan, C. T., & Stellar, E. *Physiological psychology.* New York: McGraw-Hill, 1950.

Norman, R. J., Buchwald, J. S., & Villablanca, J. R. Classical conditioning with auditory discrimination of the eyeblink in decerebrate cats. *Science,* 1977, *196,* 551–553.

Oakley, D. A., & Russell, I. S. Neocortical lesions and classical conditioning. *Physiology and Behavior,* 1972, *8,* 915–926.

Oakley, D. A., & Russell, I. S. Subcortical storage of Pavlovian conditioning in the rabbit. *Physiology and Behavior,* 1977, *18,* 931–937.

Okada, Y., Nitsch-Hassler, C., Kim, J. S., Bak, I. J., & Hassler, R. Role of gamma-aminobutyric acid (GABA) in the extrapyramidal motor system. I: Regional distribution of GABA in rabbit, rat guinea pig and baboon CNS. *Experimental Brain Research,* 1971, *13,* 514–518.

Papsdorf, J. D., Longman, D., & Gormezano, I. Spreading depression: Effects of applying KC1 to the dura of the rabbit on the conditioned nictitating membrane response. *Psychonomic Science,* 1965, *2,* 125–126.

Roberts, E. Desinhibition as an organizing principle in the nervous system: The role of the GABA system. In E. Roberts, T. N. Chase, and D. B. Tower (Eds.), *GABA in nervous system function.* New York: Raven Press, 1976, pp. 515–539.

Roberts, E. Epilepsy and antiepileptic drugs: A speculative synthesis. In G. H. Glaser, J. K. Penny, and D. M. Woodbury (Eds.), *Antiepileptic drugs: Mechanisms of action.* New York: Raven Press, 1980, pp. 667–713.

Schneiderman, N., Fuentes, I., & Gormezano, I. Acquisition and extinction of the classically conditioned eyelid response in the albino rabbit. *Science,* 1962, *136,* 650–652.

Skelton, R. S., Donegan, N. H., & Thompson, R. F. Superior colliculus lesions disrupt classical conditioning to visual but not auditory stimuli. *Neuroscience Abstracts,* 1984, *10,* 132.

Solomon, P. R., & Moore, J. W. Latent inhibition and stimulus generalization for the classically conditioned nictitating membrane response in rabbits (*Oryctolagus cuniculus*) following dorsal hippocampal ablation. *Journal of Comparative and Physiological Psychology,* 1975, *89,* 1192–1203.

Sprague, J. M. Interaction of cortex and superior colliculus in mediation of visually guided behavior in the cat. *Science,* 1966, *153,* 1544–1547.

Steinmetz, J. E., McCormick, D. A., Baier, C. A., & Thompson, R. F. Involvement of the inferior olive in classical conditioning of the rabbit eyelid. *Neuroscience Abstracts,* 1984, *10,* 122.

Thompson, R. F. Neuronal substrates of simple associative learning: Classical conditioning. *Trends in Neuroscience,* 1983, 6(7), 270–275.

Thompson, R. F., Barchas, J. D., Clark, G. A., Donegan, N., Kettner, R. E., Lavond, D. G., Madden, J. IV, Mauk, M. D., & McCormick, D. A. Neuronal substrates of associative learning in the mammalian brain. In D. L. Alkon & J. Farley (Eds.), *Primary neural substrates of learning and behavioral change.* Cambridge, MA: Cambridge University Press, 1984a, pp. 71–99.

Thompson, R. F., Berger, T. W., Berry, S. D., Clark, G. A., Kettner, R. E., Lavond, D. G., Mauk, M. D., McCormick, D. A., Solomon, P. R., & Weisz, D. J. Neuronal substrates of learning and memory: Hippocampus and other structures. In C. D. Woody (Ed.), *Conditioning: Representation of involved neural functions.* New York: Plenum Press, 1982.

Thompson, R. F., Berger, T. W., Berry, S. D., Hoehler, F. K., Kettner, R. E., & Weisz, D. J. Hippocampal substrate of classical conditioning. *Physiological Psychology,* 1980, 8(2), 262–279.

Thompson, R. F., Berger, T. W., Cegavske, C. F., Patterson, M. M., Roemer, R. A., Teyler, T. J., & Young, R. A. A search for the engram. *American Psychologist,* 1976, *31,* 209–227.

Thompson, R. F., Berger, T. W., & Madden, J. IV. Cellular processes of learning and memory in the mammalian CNS. *Annual Review of Neuroscience,* 1983, 6, 447–491.

Thompson, R. F., Clark, G. A., Donegan, N. H., Lavond, D. G., Lincoln, J. S., Madden, J. IV, Mamounas, L. A., Mauk, M. D., McCormick, D. A., and Thompson, J. K. Neuronal substrates of learning and memory: A "multiple-trace" view. In J. L. McGaugh, G. Lynch, & N. M. Weinberger (Eds.), *Neurobiology of learning and memory.* New York: Guilford Press, 1984b.

Thompson, R. F., Clark, G. A., Donegan, N. H., Lavond, D. G., Madden, J. IV, Mamounas, L. A., Mauk, M. D., & McCormick, D. A. Neuronal substrates of basic associative learning. In L. Squire & N. Butters (Eds.), *Neuropsychology of memory*. New York: Guilford Press, 1984c.

Thompson, R. F., Donegan, N. H., Clark, G. A., Lavond, D. G., Lincoln, J. S., Madden, J. IV, Mamounas, L. A., Mauk, M. D., & McCormick, D. A. Neuronal substrates of discrete, defensive conditioned reflexes, conditioned fear states, and their interactions in the rabbit. In I. Gormezano, W. F. Prokasy & R. F. Thompson, (Eds.), *Classical conditioning III: Behavioral, neurophysiological, and neurochemical studies in the rabbit*. Hillsdale, NJ: Lawrence Erlbaum Associates, in press.

Thompson, R. F., McCormick, D. A., Lavond, D. G., Clark, G. A., Kettner, R. E., & Mauk, M. D. The engram found? Initial localization of the memory trace for a basic form of associative learning. In J. M. Sprague & A. N. Epstein (Eds.), *Progress in psychobiology and physiological psychology*. New York: Academic Press, 1983, pp. 167–196.

Thompson, R. F., & Spencer, W. A. Habituation: A model phenomenon for the study of neuronal substrates of behavior. *Psycholgoical Review*, 1966, *173*, 16–43.

Tsukahara, N. Synaptic plasticity in the mammalian central nervous system. *Annual Review of Neuroscience*, 1981, *4*, 351–379.

Wagner, A. R. Stimulus selection and "modified continuity theory." In G. H. Bower & J. T. Spence (Eds.), *Psychology of learning and motivation* (Vol. 3). New York: Academic Press, 1969.

Wagner, A. R. Elementary associations. In H. H. Kendler & J. T. Spence (Eds.), *Essays in neobehaviorism: A memorial volume to Kenneth W. Spence*. New York: Appleton-Century-Crofts, 1971.

Wagner, A. R. SPO: A model of automatic memory processing in animal behavior. In N. E. Spear & R. R. Miller (Eds.), *Information processing in animals: Memory mechanisms*. Hillsdale, NJ: Lawrence Erlbaum Associates, 1981.

Woody, C. D., & Brozek, G. Changes in evoked responses from facial nucleus of cat with conditioning and extinction of an eye blink. *Journal of Neurophysiology*, 1969, *32*, 717–726.

Woody, C. D., Yarowsky, P., Owens, J., Black-Cleworth, P., & Crow, T. Effect of lesions of coronal motor areas on acquisition of conditioned eye blink in the cat. *Journal of Neurophysiology*, 1974, *37*, 385–394.

Yeo, C. H., Hardiman, M. J., Glickstein, M., & Russell, I. S. Lesions of cerebellar nuclei abolish the classically conditioned nictitating membrane response. *Neuroscience Abstracts*, 1982, *8*, 22.

7. Caffeine: Historical, Behavioral, and Molecular Features
Solomon H. Snyder and Pamela B. Sklar

Caffeine is the most widely used psychoactive substance on earth. Besides being present in coffee, tea, and cocoa, caffeine is contained in a large number of soft drinks as well as in over-the-counter preparations for headache and dieting.

Because of its ubiquity and of its status as a food additive in cola drinks, an understanding of caffeine's behavioral actions is important to clarify any possible adverse behavioral effects, especially in children. Whereas adults derive the majority of their caffeine from coffee, children obtain a major portion from soft drinks. A typical brewed cup of coffee contains about 100 mg of caffeine, whereas a 12-ounce soft drink possesses only about 20 mg. Thus, one would assume that children normally ingest much less caffeine than adults. However, when caffeine is calculated per unit of body weight, several field studies have indicated that preadolescent children consume as much caffeine as adults.

Chemically, caffeine is a methylxanthine, based on the purine structure. Three methylxanthines are widely distributed in food: caffeine, theophylline, and theobromine. The relative amounts of the different methylxanthines vary in foods. Coffee contains caffeine exclusively. Tea contains a good bit of caffeine but also a substantial amount of theophylline, while chocolate has a high concentration of theobromine and much less caffeine. All three of these methylxanthines produce similar effects. However, theobromine is considerably weaker as a central stimulant than caffeine or theophylline, while the latter two have about similar potencies.

Xanthines affect many organs in the body. Because of its bronchodilatory actions, theophylline is the most widely used drug in the treatment of asthma. Xanthines have positive inotropic effects on the heart and have been used as cardiotonics. Xanthines are also diuretics, which underlies their use as diet medications. Thus, understanding thoroughly the basis for the behavioral effects of xanthines may provide insight into the regulation of numerous body organs.

Introduction of Coffee and Tea into Western Civilizations

It is impossible to date with any precision the discovery of the stimulant property of coffee and tea. Tea has been used in China for medical and religious purposes for many centuries. The stimulant effects of tea and coffee are similar, as are their social implications. Coffee generally contains more caffeine than tea and so its stimulant effects are more readily apparent. Accordingly, this historical account will focus mainly on coffee.

Colorful legends abound as to the discovery of the coffee bean's invigorating properties. Dates given vary from 656 A.D. to 1750 A.D., although coffee was probably known in Ethiopia for much longer than that. Certainly by the 1600s, its use had started to spread. One widely cited legend concerns an Arabian herder who noticed that his goats remained awake five or six consecutive nights after eating certain plants. The imam, spiritual leader of the monastery that owned the goats, tried the berries himself. He experienced sweating, tremors, and, most importantly, insomnia. He ordered the berries boiled and the drink served to monks that they might remain awake for midnight religious services.

Since the Muslim religion forbade consumption of wine, coffee also began to fill the role of a nonalcoholic social drink. However, from the earliest times its mildly stimulating effects were not universally appreciated. On the one hand, coffee produced the desired quality of wakefulness; on the other hand, it led to the establishment of coffeehouses in which heated discussions of social, political, and religious topics threatened the general peace and tranquility. The first edict forbidding the use of coffee was not directed against detrimental effects on the body but specifically against the behavioral stimulant nature of the drink. In 1511, the governor of Mecca closed the coffeehouses. Thus, the first recorded interdiction of caffeine stemmed from its tendency to "incline men and women to extravagances prohibited by law" (Ukers 1922). Edicts against coffee proved to be unpopular and usually lasted only a short time.

The introduction of coffee, tea, and cocoa into western Europe proved problematic for the authorities. Of the three, the first to be introduced was cocoa, by Spanish traders in 1528, followed by tea to Holland in 1610, and then coffee obtained in 1615 by Venetian traders. Coffee reached France in the late sixteenth century. Somewhat later it was introduced into England, and still later it spread from southern Germany. Each time coffee entered a new country events similar to those in Mecca prevailed. In late sixteenth-century Rome, coffee worried leading priests, who pronounced it an invention of Satan contrived to replace wine in the holy services. They appealed to Pope Clement VIII for a ban, but, when the pope tasted and liked the drink, he proclaimed it a pity to allow the infidels exclusive access and declared that its use be "baptized" for Christianity.

One interesting feature of the writings in these years is their focus on medicinal aspects of tea and coffee. In analyzing side effects, some French physicians were fairly astute. Jacques Tissot in the later 1600s noted the deleterious effects of the acid in coffee on the stomach and felt that coffee removed the mucous lining of the stomach, causing the underlying nerves to become unduly sensitive.

In seventeenth-century Marseilles, opinions within the medical community were divided. Although tea and coffee first could be had only from a druggist, recreational use soon spread following customs imported from the Turks and the Arabs. A medical thesis at the University of Marseilles determined that coffee "was a vile and worthless foreign novelty; that its claim to be a remedy against distempers was ridiculous, because it was not a bean but the fruit of a tree discovered by goats and camels; that it was hot and not cold, as alleged; that it burned up the blood, and so induced palsies, impotence, and leanness; from all of which we must necessarily conclude that coffee is hurtful to the greater part of the inhabitants of Marseilles" (Jacobs 1904).

On the other hand, the French physician Sylvestre Dufour maintained that coffee was good "for menstrual problems, promoted urine flow, strengthened the heart, relieved dropsy, gravel, gout, hypochondria, and scurvy, strengthened air passages, reduced fever, and relieved migraine" (Jacobs 1904).

In Holland, the physician Cornelius Buntckuh was influenced by Harvey's recent discovery of blood circulation and, reasoning that tea speeds the circulation beneficially, he wrote, "We advise tea for the whole nation and for every nation. We advise men and women to drink tea daily; hour by hour if possible; beginning with ten cups a day- and increasing the dose to the utmost quantity the stomach can contain and the kidneys can eliminate" (Jacobs 1904). It is thought that this emphasis on tea's invigorating the circulation and hence the mind led to the custom of starting the day with a cup of tea.

A Turkish ambassador from Mohammed IV seems to have been responsible for the social use of coffee in Paris. He arrived there in 1669, and legend has it that, in order to obtain information about the plans of Louis XIV, he served coffee to the ladies of the court hoping to make them more talkative. Several years later the first coffeehouse for the public was opened in Paris. Coffee's popularity among nobility and commoners alike then spread quickly.

Although England is regarded as a country of tea drinkers, from 1680 to 1730 London consumed more coffee than any other city. Alcoholism had become rampant at this time of prolonged civil war and political unrest, and coffee gained popularity as a treatment. Nevertheless, coffeehouses, serving coffee, tea, chocolate, and sherbet, soon became enemies of the authorities, as politicians (some threatening the king's power) were habitués. After being closed by edict of Charles II and then reopened following public outcry, coffeehouses gradually faded away and tea became the national drink of the English.

These historical aspects of caffeine-containing beverages shed light on how medicine and society responded to a mildly psychoactive substance. The stimulant effects of caffeine have been hailed by some as a panacea for many physical ailments and as a solution for mental distress. Others have denounced the substances for the same effects that secured praise. Despite our present familiarity with caffeine, some of the same debates have re-emerged as government is asked to rule on the safety of caffeine.

Discovery of the Active Principle

Coffee, tea, and cocoa are not the only drinks with pleasantly stimulating effects. South Americans prepare drinks from maté leaves, yoca, and guarana, while the West Africans chew kola nuts. It was not until the 1800s that the active principles were extracted from all of these beverages and found to be identical. In 1820, Ferdinand Runge first isolated a base from green coffee beans which he named *Kaffebase*. The poet Goethe, a coffee devotee, is thought to have sent him the beans, requesting Runge to perform a chemical analysis of them. In 1825, two French scientists, Robiquet and Pelletier, found a white, crystalline substance with a very high nitrogen content in green coffee beans. This substance became known as caffeine. In 1827, Oudry isolated an alkaloid from tea that he named *thein*, the same chemical. Martius, in 1826, found a substance, guaranin, in guarana paste which somewhat later was shown to be identical with caffeine (Martius 1826 quoted in Ukers 1922). Finally, at a meeting in 1865, the British chemist Bentley could conclude, "It is remarkable that all the most important unfermented beverages in use in different parts of the globe should be prepared from substances containing the same or a closely allied alkaloid." (quoted in Ukers 1922).

Caffeine belongs to a chemical family of compounds, the xanthines. Caffeine is a methylated xanthine, and xanthine is a dioxypurine. Other methylxanthines besides caffeine also possess stimulant properties. The first of these, theobromine, was discovered in cocoa beans in 1842. These three methylxanthines differ from each other in the location of their methyl substituents. Caffeine is 1,3,7-trimethylxanthine, theobromine is 3,7-dimethylxanthine, and theophylline is 1,3,-dimethylxanthine (fig. 7.1).

Early chemical analysis of the methylxanthines proceeded simultaneously with work on other purine derivatives. Emil Fischer deserves credit for analyzing the structures of caffeine and of many other purine

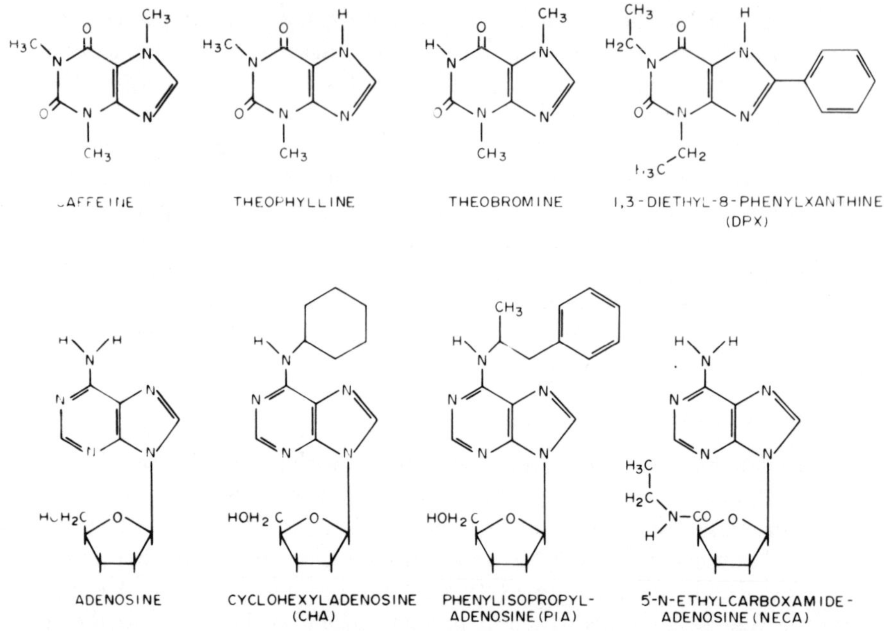

CAFFEINE   THEOPHYLLINE   THEOBROMINE   1,3-DIETHYL-8-PHENYLXANTHINE
                                                                                      (DPX)

ADENOSINE   CYCLOHEXYLADENOSINE   PHENYLISOPROPYL-   5'-N-ETHYLCARBOXAMIDE-
                       (CHA)   ADENOSINE (PIA)   ADENOSINE (NECA)

Fig. 7.1.   Structures of some xanthine and adenosine derivatives. The 1,3-diethyl and the 8-phenyl substituents in DPX result in a thousandfold enhanced potency at adenosine receptors so that ^{3}H-DPX can be used to label adenosine A_1 receptors (Bruns, Daly, and Synder 1980; Murphy and Snyder 1982). The cyclohexyl and phenylisopropyl substituents in CHA and PIA respectively both protect adenosine from degradation by adenosine deaminase and increase affinity for adenosine A_1 receptors. PIA and CHA have much greater affinity for A_1 than A_2 receptors and, when labeled with tritium, are useful tools for binding to adenosine A_1 receptors. NECA, on the other hand, has greater potency at A_2 than A_1 receptors.

derivatives. By 1882, several purines were known including uric acid, xanthine, caffeine, theobromine, hypoxanthine, and guanine. In 1861, Adolph Strecker converted guanine to xanthine and theobromine to caffeine, demonstrating that they were related. He even went so far as to suggest chemical formulas for theobromine and caffeine but was unable to prove that they were correct. In 1882, Fischer converted xanthine into theobromine. It was not until 1895 that he finally synthesized caffeine.

The correct structural formulas for the methylxanthines were suggested by Medicus in 1875. The more influential chemist Fischer proposed different, incorrect structures. In theobromine, he put the methyl group on the correct nitrogen in the imidazole moiety but put the methyl group on the wrong nitrogen in the pyrimidine ring. Fifteen years later, he rigorously obtained four correct structures, and in 1898 he identified purine itself.

In 1906, Ludwig Roselius first decaffeinated coffee beans. Roselius and Wimmer obtained an American patent for a process that used steam and pressure to facilitate extraction of caffeine from the bean, which is usually quite resistant to solvents. The first brand to be sold, Sanka, remains the most popular.

Beverages Containing Caffeine

Coffee usually comes from the beans of *Coffea arabica, Coffea liberica,* or *Coffea robusta* strains. They may vary in caffeine content, and some varieties of the *Coffea* genus have no caffeine, e.g., *Coffea mauritiana* and *Coffea humboltiana.* The caffeine content of the typical commercial beans varies from 0.8% to 1.8% of the dry weight of the bean. Preparation of coffee can also modify its caffeine content. A typical cup of instant coffee has 60 mg to 70 mg of caffeine, while brewed coffee has about 100 mg of caffeine and drip coffee has 150 mg.

Tea derives from the plant *Cammellia sinensis.* Caffeine content differs throughout the shoot, with the bud having the greatest concentration. The caffeine content in a typical cup of tea varies, like that of coffee, with variety and preparation. In general, levels are lower than in coffee. Black tea contains about 40 mg of caffeine per cup and green tea about 35 mg per cup.

The Mayan Indians of Central America used the cocoa bean, and Columbus first brought it to Spain. Cortez introduced cocoa as a hot beverage. Today, cocoa beans are used mainly to produce chocolate, cocoa, and cocoa butter. Caffeine and theobromine content in cocoa beans varies throughout the bean. The portion used for making cocoa has more theobromine than caffeine. A one-ounce bar of chocolate contains 75 mg to 150 mg of methylxanthine, about 90% being theobromine and the rest caffeine.

The other caffeinated beverages, guarana, maté, and yoca, are less well known in North America. Guarana is purported to be the strongest of the caffeine-containing drinks. It is made from seeds of plants of the *Paullinia cupana* and *Paullinia sorbilis,* whose caffeine concentration is about triple that of coffee beans. In the Amazon valley of Brazil, where guarana is most common, the bark of the plant is powdered and mixed with water like cocoa.

Maté, also known as Paraguay tea, comes from the plant *Ilex paraguayensis* and has about the same caffeine concentration as coffee. First used by Peruvian aborigines, maté was brought to Europe by the Spanish. It is prepared by pouring hot water over larger leaf fragments. Yoca derives from the bark of a plant, *Paullinia yoco,* and is the least used of the caffeine drinks, consumed mostly by Indians in southern Colombia, Ecuador, and Peru.

The original method of ingesting caffeine from the kola bean involved chewing the bean itself. All our present-day soft drinks are flavored by kola nuts. Originally, their caffeine content comprised whatever was in the nuts. However, for standardization purposes, exogenous caffeine was added. For product uniformity, the U.S. Food and Drug Administration has required a caffeine content of 0.1% to 0.2% in any beverage designated a "cola." The caffeine added to Coca Cola is "natural," extracted from coffee beans used to prepare decaffeinated coffee. Pepsi Cola utilizes synthetic caffeine.

Behavioral Effects

A popular conception holds that moderate amounts of caffeine enhance psychomotor performance, while high doses result in jitteriness and inefficiency. Experimental psychological studies dating back to the turn of the century in general bear out this view. One of the first systematic investigations of caffeine's behavioral effects in 1907 by Rivers and Webber evaluated the ability of subjects to raise weights on their fingers and contrasted effects of 500 mg of caffeine and a placebo (Rivers and Webber 1907). Caffeine consistently improved work output. In measures of finger tapping, some investigators found caffeine to speed up responses (Hollingsworth 1912; Horst, Buxton, and Robinson 1934; Horst et al. 1934; Thornton, Holck, and Smith 1939; Lehmann and Csank 1957) while others found no effect or a slowing (Flory and Gilbert 1943; Adler et al. 1950). These discrepancies appear to have been due to dose-response variations first detected by Hollingsworth (Hollingsworth 1912). At 60 mg or 120 mg of caffeine, psychomotor performance of subjects required to insert a stylus successively into three holes was improved, while performance deteriorated at 180 mg to 240 mg.

In some tests of learning, caffeine improved performance. At 60 mg to 360 mg, caffeine increased the number of arithmetic problems attempted and decreased the amount of time required to perform them (Hollingsworth 1912; Barmack 1940). In other studies, at 180 mg to 360 mg, caffeine increased the speed of typing and decreased the number of errors (Hollingsworth 1912).

More detailed evaluation of enhanced psychomotor performance with caffeine revealed that improvement compared to placebo was most apparent when subjects were progressively fatigued later in the experiment or when they were forced to cope with a large, exhausting work load (Weiss and Laties 1962). Such a conclusion was born out by extensive studies during World War II evaluating the effects of caffeine and amphetamines on performance of soldiers under stressful and exhausting conditions designed to mimic battlefield situations (Seashore and Ivy 1953). For instance, in some studies subjects participated in 20-mile hikes followed by guard duty from 6:00 P.M. to 4:00 A.M., while in others the subjects would go on training marches long distances uphill carrying a full backpack, drive a truck 18 to 20 hours a day, or operate an army tank 5 hours a day. The studies consistently showed that caffeine is most effective in improving performance that has been deteriorating as a result of excessive stress work or fatigue. In well-rested subjects, it is difficult to demonstrate that caffeine enhances performance.

Concern over adverse behavioral effects of caffeine is more frequent than interest in its performance-enhancing effects. The common public perception is that caffeine interferes with sleep. However, many people seem to sleep well after drinking coffee, while others maintain that with a single cup they "can't sleep a wink." How much caffeine is necessary to interfere with sleep? Do people differ in sensitivity? Studies by Goldstein and colleagues (Goldstein 1964; Goldstein, Kaizer, and Warren 1965; Goldstein, Warren, and Kaizer 1965; Goldstein and Kaizer 1969; Goldstein, Kaizer, and Whitby 1969) have clarified some of these questions. In an initial study, medical students evaluated their sleeping behavior by filling out a questionnaire the day after consuming caffeine or placebo (Goldstein 1964). In doses as small as 150 mg, the amount in a single brewed cup of coffee, caffeine prolonged the time required to fall asleep and interfered with the soundness of sleep. The students who normally drank the most coffee were least affected by caffeine.

To evaluate differences in individual sensitivity to caffeine, Goldstein conducted another study in which each subject received caffeine or placebo on several occasions (Goldstein, Warren, and Kaizer 1965). For certain individuals, caffeine delayed invariably the onset of sleep for an hour or more, while with others caffeine never interfered with sleep. Again, the heavy caffeine consumers were least sensitive to the insomniac effects. However, though these individuals subjectively felt that coffee drinking at night did not interfere with their sleep patterns, in fact they did sleep better on the evenings when they were administered placebo.

The nature of the sleep disturbance elicited by caffeine resembles non-drug related insomnia. After consuming 200 mg to 400 mg of caffeine, Karacan and associates (1976) observed a prolonged latency to the onset of sleep, a shifting of stages 3 and 4 to later in the night, and an earlier onset of REM sleep, all features well known in insomniacs.

Apparent individual variations in sensitivity to caffeine might merely reflect variations in tolerance. On the other hand, heavy caffeine consumers might begin to use the substance in larger amounts, because they are intrinsically less sensitive to its adverse effects, while responding to its positive actions. In one study, Goldstein, Kaizer, and Whitby (1969) compared housewives who were either heavy or low consumers of caffeine. The heavy users maintained that they were not disturbed by drinking coffee at night, were not made nervous by its ingestion in the morning, and "felt a need for it." When the two groups were administered caffeine or placebo, they indeed reacted differently. The abstainers were made jittery and nervous by caffeine administered in the morning. By contrast, the heavy coffee drinkers were irritable following placebo, but felt content, less irritable, and more alert when given caffeine. The heavy consumers thus seem less sensitive to the adverse effects of caffeine, such as nervousness and wakefulness, but are more sensitive to its stimulant effects than caffeine abstainers. These differences are not likely related to variations in caffeine metabolism, since blood levels in heavy and low users were the same (Goldstein, Warren, and Kaizer 1965).

In addition to insomnia, one adverse effect is the headache that some people report following cessation of caffeine ingestion. In 1942, Dreisbach and Pfeiffer described the syndrome of irritability, nervousness, restlessness, less energy, and headache in such individuals, while Goldstein's group (Goldstein and Kaizer 1969) and others have confirmed these findings. Ingestion of caffeine quickly alleviates the headache.

Caffeinism

Powers (1925) described a syndrome associated with heavy coffee drinking including vertigo, headache, nervousness, visual disturbances, and tachycardia. Some 50 years later, Greden (1974) described the same syndrome in a series of patients entering a psychiatric clinic for treatment of anxiety neurosis. Most of his subjects were consuming 750 mg to 1000 mg per day of caffeine. The misdiagnoses are not altogether surprising because the symptoms of anxiety neurosis in the DSM-III tabulation include "dyspnea, palpitations, chest discomfort, dizziness, sensory disturbances and gastrointestinal disturbances."

In a follow up study, Greden et al. (1978) monitored caffeine consumption of hospitalized psychiatric patients and observed higher levels of anxiety, tremulousness, and depression in the high caffeine consumers. Winstead (1976), in a similar study, also observed higher levels of current, "state" anxiety but not of personality related "trait" anxiety in heavy caffeine users. This finding suggests that the higher anxiety levels were elicited by the caffeine, rather than the anxiety causing the patients to drink more coffee. In a questionnaire study in the general population, Gilliland and Andress (1981) observed both more anxiety and depression in high caffeine-consuming groups than in low users.

The studies just reviewed involved adults. What about effects in children? As discussed, when calculated per unit weight, children consume as much caffeine in cola drinks as adults ingest in coffee. Unfortunately, there has been little systematic research into the effects of caffeine in children, in part because of the ethical difficulties in administering large doses of psychoactive substances to children in experimental investigations.

Some insight into children's responses to caffeine has come from investigations of the use of caffeine in treating hyperactive behavior. Initial reports suggested caffeine might be as effective as amphetamine (Schnackenburg 1973). Other investigations have failed to find beneficial effects (Connors 1975; Garfinkel, Webster, and Sloman 1975). Nonetheless, these caffeine trials provided a simple setting to assess whether children are more sensitive to caffeine than adults. None of these studies detected stimulant effects of caffeine greater than typical effects in adults.

Recently, direct experimental studies have compared effects of caffeine and placebo in children as well as in adults. In these studies, adult men and prepubertal boys received identical caffeine doses of 3 or 10 mg/kg (Elkins et al. 1981; Rapoport et al. 1981). There were no marked differences in the psychomotor actions of caffeine in children and adults. Interestingly, adults reported side effects more frequently than the children. These included feeling faint and flushed, headache, nausea, nervousness, and jitteriness. The only side effect reported consistently by children was some tendency to feel nervous. On the other hand, caffeine elicited more walking and talking behavior in children than adults.

One societal concern has to do with the chronic effects of caffeine ingestion in children. Some insight into this question derives from clinical studies in which caffeine has been administered chronically to infants suffering from spontaneous apnea. Several researchers (Aranda et al. 1979; Gunn et al. 1979) administered caffeine to children from close to birth for up to two years or more and carefully monitored growth, neurological, and psychological development. No adverse effects have been detected despite exposure to doses up to 20 mg/kg, several times what an average child would encounter from cola drinks.

Molecular Mechanisms of Xanthine Stimulant Effects

In trying to investigate mechanisms that can account for the behavioral effects of xanthines, we should first bear in mind that these substances influence a wide variety of bodily functions. If xanthines act throughout the body by similar molecular mechanisms, then working out ways in which these influences are mediated in one tissue might shed light on what goes on in other parts of the body. There may also be medical consequences. Potential therapeutic uses of caffeine for its behavioral effects are impaired by side effects such as cardiac stimulation with premature ventricular contractions and occasionally more serious arrhythmias. Cardiac and central stimulant actions are major side effects of theophylline use in asthma. If one could develop xanthines with selectivity for particular tissues, therapeutic applications might be greatly extended. Such possibilities are apparent in reviewing the general pharmacology of xanthines.

Grand mal convulsions can be elicited readily by caffeine and theophylline. Convulsions are a not infrequent adverse effect of theophylline use in asthma. Thus, therapeutic blood levels of theophylline in asthma therapy are about 10 μg / ml. Convulsions occur frequently at blood levels of 40 μg / ml and have been reported even at 25 μg / ml. The stimulant effects of theophylline pose problems even in conventional doses. Minimum adult doses of theophylline for asthmatics are about 250 mg, and most patients with moderate to severe symptoms ingest 750 mg, equivalent to seven cups of coffee a day. Since theophylline is a widely used agent in the treatment of asthma, theophylline derivatives without central nervous system stimulation would clearly be desirable.

Besides their importance as side effects, the cardiac effects of xanthines may also have therapeutic utility. Xanthines have been used to treat congestive heart failure because of their cardiotonic influences. For these purposes, water-soluble derivatives of theophylline such as aminophylline, a salt comprised of theophylline and ethylenediamine, are administered parenterally. They decrease peripheral vascular resistance and increase the force of cardiac contraction, thus enhancing the perfusion of most organs. Theophylline is no longer used much for this purpose. It is conceivable that with more potent and selective xanthines there might be cardiotonic therapeutic application.

Xanthines are diuretics. They increase the production of urine with electrolyte patterns similar to those elicited by thiazide diuretics. There is some enhancement of renal blood flow and glomerular filtration rate, but the major part of their diuretic action involves inhibition of renal tubular reabsorption of sodium. The caffeine content of over-the-counter dieting pills produces weight loss largely by its diuretic actions. In the past, xanthines have been employed therapeutically in cardiovascular conditions for their diuretic effects. Like the cardiotonic actions of xanthines, more potent and tissue-selective xanthines lacking central nervous effects would be clinically useful diuretics.

Effects of Xanthines on Cyclic Nucleotides and Calcium Disposition

In trying to understand the mechanism of action of any therapeutic agent, one attempts to satisfy several criteria. The experimental effect observed should occur at concentrations of the drug that exist in the body after therapeutic doses. Even more important, the relative potencies of agents in a homologous series in eliciting the experimental effects should parallel their relative therapeutic potencies. Blood and brain concentrations of theophylline and caffeine at doses commonly employed are 10 μM to 50 μM. Theophylline and caffeine have similar effects in most systems, while theobromine is substantially less potent. Many synthetic xanthines have been studied so that ample numbers of agents in homologous series exist to test rigorously any proposed mechanism of action (Bruns 1981).

Soon after the isolation of cyclic adenosine monophosphate (AMP) and the identification of phosphodiesterase as a cyclic AMP-degrading enzyme, Sutherland and associates (Sutherland and Rall 1958; Butcher and Sutherland 1962) showed that xanthines including caffeine and theophylline inhibit phosphodiesterase. For many years it had been thought that xanthines exert their stimulant and other pharmacologic effects by inhibiting phosphodiesterase. In this way, xanthines would elevate concentrations of cyclic AMP. The catecholamines norepinephrine and dopamine are the first neurotransmitters whose synaptic actions were known to involve cyclic AMP. Since amphetamines, which act by releasing catecholamines, are stimulants, it was presumed that xanthines, by increasing levels of this presumed second messenger of catecholamines, would also exert stimulant effects.

There are a number of drawbacks to the notion that phosphodiesterase inhibition accounts for the stimulant actions of xanthines. First, substantial inhibition of the enzyme requires millimolar concentrations of caffeine and theophylline, roughly 100 times caffeine levels in the brain after typically ingested doses in man. Further, over the years analogous inhibitors of phosphodiesterase have been synthesized which are up to thousands of times more potent than caffeine or theophylline. More potent inhibition of phosphodiesterase is not associated with increased stimulant potency.

Xanthines can affect the disposition of intracellular calcium, which has also been proposed as a mechanism for some xanthine actions. Caffeine does augment the twitch response of isolated skeletal muscle by releasing calcium from the sarcoplasmic reticulum. However, millimolar concentrations of xanthines are required.

In summary, effects of caffeine on cyclic nucleotides and calcium cannot explain its stimulant actions. Numerous studies suggest a much closer link of adenosine to caffeine. Indeed, it is becoming generally accepted that caffeine causes stimulation by blocking receptors for adenosine.

Adenosine

Adenosine (fig. 7.1) is an intermediary of a wide range of metabolic pathways. It is involved in the formation of adenosine triphosphate (ATP) and nucleic acids. In addition, evidence has accumulated that adenosine can influence many organs including the brain via receptors on the surface of cells. Many effects of adenosine are opposite to those of xanthines, suggesting some type of interaction. Moreover, most of the peripheral effects of adenosine are blocked by xanthines.

Adenosine dilates blood vessels, especially in the coronary and cerebral circulation. Pharmaceutical companies over the years have attempted to develop coronary vasodilators by potentiating actions of adenosine. The widely used coronary vasodilator dipyridamole is a potent inhibitor of adenosine accumulation in cells, though it is not established definitely that this action accounts for its therapeutic effects.

Adenosine inhibits platelet aggregation, suggesting that adenosine-mimicking drugs might be useful in the prophylaxis of myocardial infarction. Adenosine strongly inhibits hormone-induced lipolysis, and adenosine derivatives have been evaluated as agents to lower blood lipid levels.

Adenosine has a variety of actions on central neurons. In most instances adenosine inhibits spontaneous neuronal firing (Phillis and Wu 1981; Stone 1981). The inhibitory actions of adenosine seem in large part to be presynaptic, that is, due to the inhibition of release of excitatory neurotransmitters, though there are also postsynaptic effects (Dunwiddie and Hoffer 1980; Okada and Ozawa 1980). In biochemical investigations monitoring transmitter release directly, adenosine in concentrations of 0.1 μM to 10 μM inhibits the release of almost all neurotransmitters evaluated whether they are inhibitory or excitatory (Jhamandas and Sawynok 1976; Harms, Wardeh, and Mulder 1979; Hollins and Stone 1980).

Although adenosine has clear-cut effects on neuronal functioning, it has not been established whether or not adenosine is a neurotransmitter. Understanding the function of adenosine in the brain would be greatly facilitated by the establishment of whether or not it is contained in specific neuronal populations. The successful study of peptides as neurotransmitters has been based in large part on immunohistochemical mapping of peptide-containing neurons localized to specific regions of the brain. No such techniques are presently available for localizing adenosine. If a neurotransmitter pool of adenosine involves only a small percentage of endogenous brain adenosine, one might have difficulty visualizing putative "adenosinergic" neurons.

One alternative approach has been to visualize the localization of adenosine receptors. As will be discussed later, adenosine receptors can be labeled with a variety of ligands; ^{3}H-cyclohexyladenosine (^{3}H-CHA) is particularly effective and widely used (Bruns, Daly, and Snyder 1980). Applying the technique of in vitro autoradiography (Young and Kuhar 1979), we have been able to map in detail the localization of adenosine receptors in the central nervous system (Goodman and Snyder 1981; Goodman and Snyder 1982). There are marked differences in the concentration of adenosine receptors in different brain areas. Highest densities occur in specific areas such as the molecular layer of the cerebellum, the molecular and polymorphic layers of the hippocampus and dentate gyrus, the medial geniculate body, certain thalamic nuclei, and the lateral septum. Others have detected similar localizations (Lewis et al. 1981).

With other neurotransmitters, such as enkephalin, the localization of receptors reflects fairly well the localization of nerve terminals containing the presumed neurotransmitter (Simantov et al. 1977). Thus, conceivably, there exist neuronal systems associated with adenosine in areas of the brain enriched in adenosine receptors.

The localizations of adenosine receptors can also explain neurophysiologic presynaptic inhibitory actions of adenosine. To localize the adenosine receptors that are highly concentrated in the molecular layer of the cerebellum, we made use of neurologic mutant mice that lack specific nerve types (Goodman et al 1983). We found that "Weaver" mice, which lack cerebellar granule cells, also lack adenosine receptors. On the other hand, mutants such as "Nervous," which lack Purkinje cells but have normal granule cells, have normal patterns of adenosine receptors. In "Reeler" mice whose granule cells are transposed to a different layer, there is a similar transposition of adenosine receptors (Goodman et al. 1983). Accordingly, it is apparent that adenosine receptors in the cerebellum are localized to granule cells, especially their axons and terminals in the molecular layer.

Of the five neuronal subtypes of the cerebellum, only the granule cells are excitatory. Thus, the localization of adenosine receptors to granule cell axons and terminals suggests that a function of adenosine in the cerebellum is to inhibit the release of the granule cell excitatory neurotransmitter, which is thought to be glutamic acid (Young et al. 1974). This effect would explain the presynaptic inhibitory actions of adenosine in this part of the brain. In the superior colliculus we found adenosine receptors localized to axon terminals of excitatory neurons (Goodman et al. 1983). Unilateral removal of the eye in rats produced a depletion of adenosine receptors in the contralateral superior colliculus coincident with the degeneration of the excitatory optic nerves. Thus, presumably in the superior colliculus, adenosine could act by inhibiting release of the excitatory transmitter from optic nerves.

Adenosine Receptors and the Behavioral Stimulant Effects of Xanthines

The first biochemical analysis of adenosine receptor activity derived from the work of Sattin and Rall (1970), who showed that adenosine can stimulate the accumulation of cyclic AMP in brain slices by a mechanism that does not involve conversion of adenosine to cyclic AMP but instead by an action on extracellular receptors. These investigators also showed that the effects of adenosine were blocked by theophylline. Effects of adenosine on the cyclic AMP–synthesizing enzyme adenylate cyclase reveal two distinct subtypes of adenosine receptors (van Calker, Muller, and Hamprecht 1979; Burnstock and Brown 1981; Londos, Wolff, and Cooper 1981). In some systems, adenosine stimulates adenylate cyclase, while in other systems it depresses adenylate cyclase. The stimulatory actions of adenosine on adenylate cyclase occur at micromolar concentrations via receptors designated A_2. At A_1 receptors adenosine at nanomolar concentrations inhibits adenylate cyclase activity. There are other structure-activity differences between A_1 and A_2 receptors. The most striking is the marked stereospecificity in the effects of phenylisopropyladenosine (PIA) at A_1 receptors with L-PIA being much more potent than D-PIA. The two isomers, on the other hand, have relatively similar effects at A_2 receptors. Most xanthines have similar potencies in blocking both A_1 and A_2 receptors.

Understanding receptor mechanisms in the adenosine system, like in the major neurotransmitter systems, has been facilitated greatly by direct binding studies with radiolabeled ligands. We have labeled adenosine receptors with ^{3}H-cyclohexyladenosine (^{3}H-CHA) and with the xanthine derivative 1,3-diethyl-8-phenylxanthine (^{3}H-DPX) (Bruns, Daly, and Snyder 1980). Other adenosine ligands can also be employed (Schwabe and Trost 1980; Williams and Risley 1980; Yeung and Green 1981). In all species studied, ^{3}H-CHA binding displays properties of adenosine A_1 receptors with nanomolar potency for adenosine derivatives and stereospecificity for PIA isomers. In bovine, rabbit, and rat brain, ^{3}H-DPX binding shows a drug specificity essentially the same as that of ^{3}H-CHA, while in guinea pig and human brain ^{3}H-DPX binding has much lower affinity and is inhibited poorly by adenosine derivatives (Bruns, Daly, and Snyder 1980; Murphy and Snyder 1982). In guinea pig and human brain, ^{3}H-DPX binding may be associated in part with A_2 receptors or some other site. There is some evidence that one can label A_2 receptors with the adenosine derivative ^{3}H-5′-N-ethylcarboxamidoadenosine (^{3}H-NECA) (Yeung and Green 1981; R. F. Bruns, personal communication).

Our binding studies suggest heterogeneity of adenosine receptors even beyond the A_1, A_2 dichtomy. There are considerable species differences in ^{3}H-CHA binding (Murphy and Snyder 1982). For instance, DPX is about 250 times more potent in competing for ^{3}H-CHA sites in calf than in guinea pig and human brain. Moreover, PIA and CHA are 20 to 100 times more potent in calf than in rat and rabbit brain. These variations raise the possibility of developing drugs with considerable selectivity for one or another organ.

Once adenosine receptors could be labeled by binding techniques, we were in a position to ask whether behavioral effects of xanthines involve actions at adenosine receptors. To monitor the behavioral actions of xanthines, we measured locomotor activity in mice using sensitive, automated detection devices (Snyder et al. 1981; Katims, Annau, and Snyder 1983). Our initial strategy was to compare the potencies of various xanthine derivatives in affecting locomotor activity and in blocking adenosine receptors.

Xanthines such as caffeine and theophylline occupy 50% of adenosine receptors at concentrations in the micromolar range, comparable to blood and brain levels of these drugs after ingestion of a few cups of coffee in man or treatment with therapeutic doses of theophylline in asthma (table 7.1) (Bruns, Daly, and Snyder 1980). Relative potencies of xanthines in enhancing locomotor activity in general correlate with affinities for adenosine receptors labeled with ^{3}H-CHA (Katims et al. 1983). Specificity of these effects is apparent in comparing these actions to those of xanthines at benzodiazepine receptors. It had been speculated that by blocking the sites at which benzodiazepines elicit anxiety reduction and sedation, xanthines might exert their stimulant and perhaps anxiogenic effects (Skolnick, Paul, and Marangos 1980). However, as with phosphodiesterase activity, millimolar concentrations of xanthines are required to compete for benzodiazepine receptors. Moreover, there is no correlation between potencies of xanthines in competing at benzodiazepine receptors and their behavioral stimulant potencies (Snyder et al. 1981).

These effects in general support the hypothesis that xanthines act behaviorally by blocking adenosine receptors. However, there are certain problems. First, some exceptions exist to the correlation between affinities for adenosine receptors and behavioral stimulant effects. Thus, 3-isobutyl-1-methylxanthine (IBMX) has about the same affinity as caffeine for adenosine receptors but does not display locomotor stimulation at doses up to 100 μmol / kg.

Another problem is the existence of biphasic effects observed with some xanthines. Thus, at lower doses caffeine depresses rodent locomotor activity, while it stimulates activity at higher doses (Snyder et al. 1981). IBMX depresses activity at all doses examined. By contrast, 7-(β-hydroxyethyl)-theophylline stimulates locomotor activity at all doses evaluated. The fact that biphasic behavioral effects of xanthines vary with different substances suggests that the stimulant and depressant effects are mediated by distinct mechanisms. Perhaps xanthines elicit locomotor stimulation by blocking adenosine receptors and produce locomotor depression by some other mechanism. To focus on xanthine actions associated with adenosine effects, we decided to evaluate behavioral actions of adenosine derivatives.

Table 7.1   Xanthines: Behavioral Stimulant Potencies, Effects on Adenosine and Benzodiazepine Receptor Binding and Brain Levels

	Receptor Binding [³H]Flunitrazepam IC_{50} (μM)	[³H]CHA	Locomotor Stimulation Threshold ($\mu mol/kg$)	Threshold for Reversing L-PIA Depression ($\mu mol/kg$)
7(β-Chloroethyl)-theophylline	900	10	2.5	10
Theophylline	2000	20	10	5
1,7-Dimethylxan-thine	2000	30	20	10
3-Isobutyl-1-methylxanthine (IBMX)	~1000	50	N / E	2.5
Caffeine	800	50	25	5
7(β-Hydroxy-ethyl)theophyl-line	2000	100	30	10
Theobromine	>2000	150	250	250
8-Chlorotheo-phylline	>2000	500	N / E	N / E
1,9-Dimethylxan-thine	>2000	>1000	N / E	N / E
Isocaffeine	1000	>1000	N / E	N / E

Source: Adapted from Snyder et al. 1981 and Katims, Annau, and Snyder 1983.

Notes: The effects of intraperitoneally injected xanthines on locomotor activity of mice were evaluated alone or when administered together with L-PIA (0.15 μmol / kg) as described (Snyder et al. 1981). Threshold doses are minimal doses to alter locomotor activity significantly from saline controls (Snyder et al. 1981; Katims, Annau, and Snyder 1983). For each drug, six doses were evaluated with 10 to 20 mice at each dose. N / E indicated no effect with 250 μmol / kg the highest tested dose.

Behavioral Effects of Adenosine Derivatives

Adenosine itself cannot be employed, since it is very rapidly metabolized by adenosine deaminase and only poorly penetrates the blood brain barrier. Accordingly, we administered to mice CHA and PIA, which are metabolically more stable, more lipophilic, and thus more likely to enter the brain (fig. 7.1). These adenosine derivatives have dramatic effects on behavior. In low doses, L-PIA reduces locomotor activity (fig. 7.2). This effect appears to be associated specifically with adenosine A_1 receptors, since L-PIA is substantially more potent than D-PIA.

Certain aspects of L-PIA behavioral effects are striking. With many hypnotics, doses slightly higher than those required to reduce locomotor activity produce sleep. By contrast, despite increasing doses of L-PIA to levels 500 times greater than the minimum required to lower locomotor activity, mice remained awake (Snyder et al. 1981). Even the righting reflex is intact at doses 100 times those which depress locomotor behavior. Another striking feature is the absence of lethal effects with L-PIA in doses as great as 800 μmol / kg, about 10,000 times threshold doses for lowering locomotor activity.

It is difficult to compare this unique behavioral spectrum to that of other psychotropic drugs, since the behavioral repertoire of the mouse is so limited. If anything, the apparently large safety margin and the depression of locomotor activity without hypnotic effects tends to resemble actions of benzodiazepines.

In our initial studies (Snyder et al. 1981), we did not evaluate time points at doses of L-PIA lower than 0.1 μmol / kg. More recently, when we examined a larger range of doses, we were surprised to find that in doses lower than those that depress locomotor activity, substantial enhancement of locomotor activity occurs (fig. 7.2) (Katims, Annau, and Snyder 1983). Direct visual inspection of the mice indicates that these low doses produce a fairly well coordinated increase of movement. Such stimulatory actions are observed with doses as low as 0.1 μmol / kg intraperitoneally, or about 4 μg / kg. To our knowledge, such potency exceeds that of any known psychotropic agent in rodents. This potency is even more impressive when

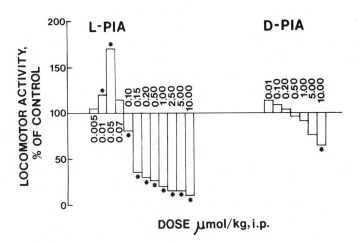

Fig. 7.2.   Effects of L-PIA and D-PIA on locomotor activity of mice. Locomotor activity values are for groups of nine mice at each dose. *p < .05 with Duncans's analysis of significance for individual treatment groups from the saline control group (adapted from Katims, Annau, and Synder 1983).

one considers that L-PIA has substantially less access to the brain than most potent psychotropic agents. Thus, drugs such as amphetamines, neuroleptics, and tricyclic antidepressants are quite lipophilic and attain brain concentrations up to ten times higher than blood levels. By contrast, brain concentrations of L-PIA at behaviorally effective doses are only one-fifth the levels one would predict if the drug distributed equally throughout all body compartments (Katims, Annau, and Snyder 1983).

Since L-PIA is a potent hypotensive agent, one might wonder whether effects on blood pressure or other cardiovascular features account for apparent behavioral actions of L-PIA. However, at behaviorally active doses of L-PIA there are no changes in blood pressure or heart rate (Katims, Annau, and Snyder 1983). We observed some intermittent premature ventricular contractions at these doses with a frequency of one every 10 to 33 minutes. However, the premature ventricular contractions occurred at the same rate with both stimulant and depressant doses of L-PIA and thus show no correlation with the behavioral effects. Also, we found that L-PIA doses producing threshold locomotor stimulation are associated with brain concentrations sufficient to occupy about 50% of adenosine receptors as monitored by ^{3}H-CHA binding (Katims, Annau, and Snyder 1983). Thus, L-PIA's behavioral effects appear to be centrally mediated.

After characterizing effects of L-PIA alone, we wondered whether xanthines might interact with the behavioral effects of L-PIA. When a low, locomotor-depressant dose of caffeine is combined with a locomotor-depressant dose of L-PIA, one sees paradoxically up to a 300% stimulation of locomotor activity. What about other xanthines, such as IBMX, which by itself never produces locomotor stimulation? Combining a locomotor-depressant dose of IBMX with a depressant dose of L-PIA elicits a 250% to 300% stimulation of locomotor activity (table 7.1).

For most of the xanthines, potencies in reversing L-PIA locomotor depression tend to be greater than for stimulating locomotor activity when administered alone. One exception is 7-(β-chlorethyl)theophylline, which is more potent in enhancing locomotor activity alone than in reversing L-PIA depression. The weakest xanthines at adenosine receptors are all either weak or inactive in enhancing locomotor activity or in reversing L-PIA depression. Unlike the complex interactions of caffeine and L-PIA, amphetamine and L-PIA interact in an arithmetic fashion, emphasizing the selectivity of the synergistic interactions of xanthines in L-PIA.

What might account for the paradoxical stimulation that occurs when combining depressant doses of xanthines and L-PIA? Our findings that low doses of L-PIA have stimulant effects may provide an explanation. These actions presumably reflect the existence of sites for which L-PIA has extremely high affinity. Somewhat lower affinity sites, still with rather high affinity, would mediate the depression of locomotor activity by L-PIA. We postulate that xanthines block the lower affinity sites, thus unmasking the stimulant effects of L-PIA at the higher affinity sites. Such a formulation would fit with our own observations that caffeine fails to alter the locomotor enhancement associated with extremely low doses of L-PIA (Katims, Annau, and Snyder 1983).

Taken together, the accumulated evidence suggests strongly that xanthines exert their behavioral stimulant effects by blocking adenosine receptors. Research on adenosine mechanisms may have ramifications beyond simply clarifying why caffeine is a stimulant. The heterogeneity of adenosine receptors in different tissues identified by binding techniques may afford the possibility of designing potent, organ-specific adenosine receptor antagonists. Such agents might have utility as diuretic, cardiac inotropic, or bronchodilating antiasthmatic drugs with reduced side effects. The dramatic behavioral effects of the adenosine derivative L-PIA suggest a therapeutic role for adenosine agonists. Such agents might have utility as sedatives, hypnotics, or antianxiety drugs. Recent electroencephalographic studies indicate that L-PIA in very low doses increases slow wave sleep with no decrease in REM sleep, thus providing a sleep profile potentially preferable to that obtained with current hypnotics (Radulovacki, Miletich, and Green 1982). Additional therapeutic roles for adenosine agonists may derive from their inhibition of platelet aggregation, inhibition of lipolysis, and dilation of coronary arteries.

Acknowledgments

Supported by USPHS grants DA-00266, MH-18501, NS-16375; RSA Award DA-00074 to Dr. Snyder; and grants of the McKnight Foundation and International Life Sciences Institute.

References

Adler, H. F., Burkhardt, W. L., Ivy, A. C., & Atkinson, A. J. Effect of various drugs on psychomotor performance at ground level and simulated altitudes of 18,000 feet in a low pressure chamber. *Journal of Aviation Medicine,* 1950, *21,* 221–236.

Aranda, J. V., Cook, C. E., Gorman, W., Collinge, J. M., Loughman, P. M., Outerbridge, E. W., & Neims, A. H. Pharmacokinetic profile of caffeine in the premature newborn with apnea. *Journal of Pediatrics,* 1979, *94,* 663–668.

Barmack, J. E. The time of administration and some effects of 2 grs. of alkaloid caffeine. *Journal of Experimental Psychology,* 1940, *27,* 690–698.

Bruns, R. F. Adenosine antagonism by purines, pteridines and benzopteridines in human fibroblasts. *Biochemical Pharmacology,* 1981, *30,* 325–333.

Bruns, R. F., Daly, J. W., & Snyder, S. H. Adenosine receptors in brain membranes:

Binding of N⁶-cyclohexyl[³H]adenosine and 1,3-diethyl-8-[³H]-phenyl-xanthine. *Proceedings of the National Academy of Sciences,* 1980, *77,* 5547–5551.

Burnstock, G., & Brown, C. M. An introduction to purinergic receptors. In G. Burnstock (Ed.), *Purinergic Receptors.* London and New York: Chapman & Hall, 1981, pp. 1–45.

Butcher, R. W., & Sutherland, E. W. Adenosine 3',5'-phosphate in biological materials. *Journal of Biological Chemistry,* 1962, *237,* 1244–1250.

Calker, D. van, Muller, M., & Hamprecht, B. Adenosine regulates via two different types of receptors the accumulation of cyclic AMP in cultured brain cells. *Journal of Neurochemistry,* 1979, *33,* 99–1005.

Connors, C. A placebo crossover study of caffeine treatment of hyperkinetic children. *International Journal of Mental Health,* 1975, *4,* 132–143.

Dreisbach, R. H., & Pfeiffer, C. Caffeine withdrawal headache. *Journal of Laboratory and Clinical Medicine,* 1942, *28,* 1212–1219.

Dunwiddie, T. V., & Hoffer, B. J. Adenine nucleotides and synaptic transmission in the *in vitro* rat hippocampus. *British Journal of Pharmacology,* 1980, *69,* 59–68.

Elkins, R. N., Rapoport, J. L., Zahn, T. P., Buchsbaum, M. S., Weingartner, H., Kopin, I. J., Langer, D., & Johnson, C. Acute effects of caffeine in normal prepubertal boys. *American Journal of Psychiatry,* 1981, *138,* 178–183.

Flory, C. D., & Gilbert, J. The effects of benzedrine sulfate and caffeine citrate on the efficiency of college students. *Journal of Applied Psychology,* 1943, *27,* 121–134.

Garfinkel, B. D., Webster, C. D., & Sloman, L. Methylphenidate and caffeine in the treatment of children with minimal brain dysfunction. *American Journal of Psychiatry,* 1975, *132,* 723–728.

Gilliland, K., & Andress, D. Ad lib caffeine consumption symptoms of caffeinism and academic performance. *American Journal of Psychiatry,* 1981, *138,* 512–514.

Goldstein, A. Wakefulness caused by caffeine. *Naunyn-Schmiedebergs Archives Experimental Pathologie und Pharmokologie,* 1964, *248,* 269–278.

Goldstein, A., & Kaizer, S. Psychotropic effects of caffeine in man. III: A questionnaire survey of coffee drinking and its effects in a group of housewives. *Clinical Pharmacology and Therapeutics,* 1969, *10,* 477–488.

Goldstein, A., Kaizer, S., & Warren, R. Psychotropic effects of caffeine in man. II: Alertness, psychomotor coordination and mood. *Journal of Pharmacology and Experimental Therapeutics,* 1965, *150,* 146–151.

Goldstein, A., Kaizer, S., & Whitby, O. Psychotropic effects of caffeine in man. IV: Quantitative and qualitative differences associated with habituation to coffee. *Clinical Pharmacology and Therapeutics,* 1969, *10,* 489–497.

Goldstein, A., Warren, R., & Kaizer, S. Psychotropic effects of caffeine in man. I: Individual differences in sensitivity to caffeine-induced wakefulness. *Journal of Pharmacology and Experimental Therapeutics,* 1965, *14,* 156–159.

Goodman, R. R., Kuhar, M. J., Hester, L., & Snyder, S. H. Adenosine receptors: Autoradiographic evidence for a localization to excitatory neuronal axon terminals. *Science,* 1983, *220,* 967–968.

Goodman, R. R., & Snyder, S. H. The light microscopic *in vitro* autoradiographic localization of adenosine (A₁) receptors. *Neuroscience Abstracts*, 1981, 7, 613.

Goodman, R. R., & Snyder, S. H. Autoradiographic localization of adenosine receptors in rat brain using [³H]cyclohexyladenosine. *Journal of Neuroscience*, 1982, 2, 1230–1241.

Greden, J. F. Anxiety or caffeinism: A diagnostic dilemma. *American Journal of Psychiatry*, 1974, 131, 1089–1092.

Greden, J. F., Fontaine, P. Lubetsky, M., & Chamberlain, K. Anxiety and depression associated with caffeinism among psychiatric inpatients. *American Journal of Psychiatry*, 1978, 135, 963–966.

Gunn, T. R., Metrakos, K., Riley, P., Willis, D., & Aranda, J. V. Sequelae of caffeine treatment in preterm infants with apnea. *Journal of Pediatrics*, 1979, 94, 106–109.

Harms, H. H., Wardeh, G., & Mulder, A. H. Effects of adenosine on depolarization-induced release of various radiolabeled neurotransmitters from rat corpus striatum. *Neuropharmacology*, 1979, 18, 577–580.

Hollingsworth, H. L. The influence of caffeine on mental and motor efficiency. *Archiv für Psychologie*, 1912, 22, 1–166.

Hollins, C., & Stone, T. W. Adenosine inhibition of GABA release from slices of rat cerebral cortex. *British Journal of Pharmacology*, 1980, 69, 107–112.

Horst, K., Buxton, R. E., & Robinson, W. D. The effect of the habitual use of coffee or decaffeinated coffee upon blood pressure, and certain motor reactions of normal young men. *Journal de Pharmacologie*, 1934, 52, 322–337.

Horst, K., Robinson, W. D., Jenkins, W. L., & Bao, D. L. The effect of caffeine, coffee and decaffeinated coffee upon blood pressure, pulse rate and certain motor reactions of normal young men. *Journal de Pharmacologie*, 1934, 52, 307–321.

Jacobs, H. E. *The saga of coffee*. London: Allen & Unwin, 1904.

Jhamandas, K., & Sawynok, J. Methylxanthine antagonism of opiate and purine effects on the release of acetylcholine. In H. W. Kosterlitz (Ed.), *Opiates and endogenous opioid peptides*. Amsterdam: Elsevier North/Holland Biomedical Press, 1976, pp. 161–168.

Karacan, I., Thornby, J. I., Anch, A. M., Booth, G. H., Williams, R. L., & Salis, P. J. Dose-related sleep disturbances induced by coffee and caffeine. *Clinical Pharmacology and Therapeutics*, 1976, 20, 682–689.

Katims, J. J., Annau, Z., & Snyder, S. H. Behavioral interactions between methylxanthines and adenosine derivatives. *Journal of Pharmacology and Experimental Therapeutics*, 1983, 227, 167–178.

Lehmann, H. E. & Csank, J. Differential screening of phrenotropic agents in man. *Journal of Clinical Psychopathology*, 1957, 18, 222–235.

Lewis, M. E., Patel, J., Edley, S. M., & Marangos, P. J. Autoradiographic visualization of rat brain adenosine receptors using N⁶-cyclohexyl[³H]adenosine. *European Journal of Pharmacology*, 1981, 73, 109–110.

Londos, C., Wolff, J., & Cooper, D. M. F. Adenosine as a regulator of adenylate cyclase. In G. Burnstock (Ed.), *Purinergic Receptors*. London and New York: Chapman & Hall, 1981, pp. 287–323.

Murphy, K. M. M., & Snyder, S. H. Heterogeneity of A_1 adenosine receptor binding in brain tissue. *Molecular Pharmacology*, 1982, 22, 250–257.

Okada, Y., & Ozawa, S. Inhibitory action of adenosine on synaptic transmission in the hippocampus of the guinea pig *in vitro*. *European Journal of Pharmacology*, 1980, 68, 483–492.

Phillis, J. W., & Wu, P. H. The role of adenosine and its nucleotides in central synaptic transmission. *Progress in Neurobiology*, 1981, 16, 187–239.

Powers, H. The syndrome of coffee. *Med. J. Record* 1925, 121, 745–747.

Radulovacki, M., Miletich, R. S., & Green, R. D. N^6-(L-phenylisopropyl) adenosine (L-PIA) increases slow-wave sleep (S_2) and decreases wakefulness in rats. *Brain Research*, 1982, 246, 178–180.

Rapoport, J. L., Jensvold, M., Elkins, R., Buchsbaum, M. S., Weingartner, H., Ludlow, C., Zahn, T., & Neims, A. Behavioral and cognitive effects of caffeine in boys and adult males *Journal of Nervous and Mental Disease*, 1981, 169, 726–732.

Rivers, W. H. R., & Webber, H. M. The action of caffeine on the capacity for muscular work. *Journal of Physiology*, 1907, 36, 33–47.

Sattin, A., & Rall, T. W. The effect of adenosine and adenine nucleotides on the adenosine $3',5'$-phosphate content of guinea pig cerebral cortex slices. *Mol. Pharmacol.* 1970, 6, 13–23.

Schnackenburg, R. C. Caffeine as a substitute for Schedule II stimulants in hyperkinetic children. *American Journal of Psychiatry*, 1973, 130, 796–798.

Schwabe, U., & Trost, T. Characterization of adenosine receptors in rat brain by (-)[^{3}H]N^6-phenylisopropyladenosine. *Naunyn-Schmiedebergs Archives of Pharmacology*, 1980, 313, 179–187.

Seashore, R. H., & Ivy, A. C. Effects of analeptic drugs in relieving fatigue. *Psychological Monographs*, 1953, 67, 1–16.

Simantov, R., Kuhar, M. J., Uhl, G. R., & Snyder, S. H. Opioid peptide enkephalin: Immunohistochemical mapping in rat central nervous system. *Proceedings of the National Academy of Sciences*, 1977, 74, 2167–2171.

Skolnick, P., Paul, S. M., & Marangos, P. J. Purines as endogenous ligands of the benzodiazepine receptors. *Federation Proceedings*, 1980, 39, 3050–3055.

Snyder, S. H., Katims, J. J., Annau, Z., Bruns, R. F., & Daly, J. W. Adenosine receptors and behavioral actions of methylxanthines. *Proceedings of the National Academy of Sciences*, 1981, 78, 3260–3264.

Stone, T. W. Physiological roles for adenosine and adenosine $5'$-triphosphate in the nervous system. *Neuroscience*, 1981, 6, 523–555.

Sutherland, E. W., & Rall, T. W. Fractionation and characterization of cyclic adenine ribonucleotide formed by tissue particles. *Journal of Biological Chemistry*, 1958, 232, 1077–1091.

Thornton, G. R., Holck, H. G. O., & Smith, E. L. The effects of benzedrine and caffeine upon performance in certain psychomotor tasks. *Journal of Abnormal Psychology*, 1939, 34, 96–113.

Ukers, W. H. *All about coffee*. New York: Tea & Coffee Trade Journal Co., 1922.

Weiss, B., & Laties, V. G. Enhancement of human performance by caffeine and the amphetamines. *Pharmacological Reviews*, 1962, 14, 1–36.

Williams, M., & Risley, E. A. Biochemical characterization of putative purinergic receptors by using 2-chloro[³H]adenosine, a stable analog of adenosine. *Proceedings of the National Academy of Sciences*, 1980, *77*, 6892–6896.

Winstead, D. K. Coffee consumption among psychiatric inpatients. *American Journal of Psychiatry*, 1976, *133*, 1447–1450.

Yeung, S.-M., & Green, R. D. Binding of 5'-N-ethylcarboxamide ³H-adenosine (³H-NECA) to adenosine receptors in rat striatum. *Pharmacologist*, 1981, *23*, 184.

Young, A. B., Oster-Granite, M. L., Herndon, R. M., & Snyder, S. H. Glutamic acid: Selective depletion by viral induced granule cell loss in hamster cerebellum. *Brain Research*, 1974, *73*, 1–13.

Young, W. S. III, & Kuhar, M. J. A new method for receptor autoradiography: [³H]opioid receptors in rat brain. *Brain Research*, 1979, *179*, 255–270.

PART III

Cognitive and Social Psychology and the Organization of Behavior

8. Interactions of Stimulus and Organism in Perception
Wendell R. Garner

In this chapter, I shall explore some issues concerned with the interactions and relative roles of the stimulus and the organism in perception. By *stimulus* I mean any aspect of the physical world that leads to perception; by *organism* I mean any perceiver of the stimulus. In other words, I am not providing a precise definition of these terms because for present purposes it seems unnecessary to do so.

Epistemology and the Stimulus-Organism Interaction

Since those of us who do research on perception are usually psychologists, we do not ordinarily use the term *epistemology* in our writing on this topic. Epistemology—the study of the nature of knowing—is the philosopher's province; yet the issues I want to discuss are indeed epistemological, since we are concerned with how the organism comes to know the stimulus world. Given this concern, a brief (and of course inadequate) survey of the major epistemological positions will be useful. In this brief description, I follow my colleague at Johns Hopkins for many years, Maurice Mandelbaum (1964).

Subjectivism. In the strong form of subjectivism, idealism denies the existence of an independent physical world. In the weak form, phenomenalism only denies the possibility of knowledge concerning the physical world. In either its strong or weak form, subjectivism is not an epistemological position seriously considered by modern experimental psychologists concerned with perception, and I will not pursue this epistemological position further.

Direct realism. In contrast to the subjectivist position, all perception psychologists I know accept the epistemological position of realism, that there is a real world whose nature we perceive. Basically, there are two forms of realism. The first is direct realism, sometimes called naïve realism. The essential point of direct realism is that the perceived qualities are not different from the actual qualities of the stimulus world. Thus, characteristics that we perceive an object to have actually do belong to that object.

Critical realism. An alternative form of realism is critical realism, a belief that some of the characteristics perceived by organisms actually exist in the physical objects perceived, but that there may be other characteristics, or modified characteristics, that are not independently properties of the physical objects.

STIMULUS AND ORGANISMIC CONCEPTS

I have always considered myself (Garner 1974) to be a critical realist, and I believe that the basic concern of our research is to differentiate the concept of critical realism into its two parts: "realism" as a reflection of the contributions of the real world to perception—the world that is to be perceived; and "critical" as the contribution of the organism that is doing the perceiving. Thus, our basic question is, what is the role of the stimulus in perception and what is the role of the organism?

Psychophysical correlatives. In trying to understand the relative contributions of stimulus and organism to perception, it must be remembered that we, as scientists, are at all times dealing both with a physical world and with a perceiving organism, in other words, with a psychophysical problem. Thus, those stimulus concepts we choose to use are those relevant to perception by an organism, and those organismic concepts we choose to use are those relevant to stimuli to be perceived. Because of this joint interest, there are usually what I shall call psychophysical correlatives, concepts that mutually imply each other, even though we may feel that either the stimulus or the organismic concept is the dominating one. A simple example will illustrate. Consider the concept of visibility. It is that property of light that makes it visible by virtue of having the right wavelengths and intensities. Described this way, visibility is clearly a stimulus property, yet it is a property we would not bother to define if there were not the psychophysical correlative of a seeing organism. Thus, an organism sees what is visible, yet visibility remains a physical or stimulus concept. And in all problems we work on there is this interaction between the two kinds of concept.

Two major issues. If there are always psychophysical correlatives, then how are we to decide whether a particular property or concept is primarily a stimulus concept or an organismic concept, because surely we do try to do that and surely that is the basic question for critical realism. While there are many criteria that enter into our reasoning on this problem, there are two major issues that influence our thinking about it. One of these is the role of experience. Generally speaking, if perception cannot or does not occur unless there is a considerable amount of learning or experience with the objects or stimuli to be perceived, then we are inclined to attribute a large role to the organism, since the organism must be modified for perception to occur. If, on the other hand, perception is direct, immediate, not alterable by experience, then we are more likely to attribute the perception to stimulus properties.

The second issue that enters into the differentiation of stimulus and organismic concepts concerns whether a perceptual process is mandatory or optional. If a percept is mandatory, not alterable by any option of the organism, and is perceived the same by all observers, then we attribute perception to the stimulus. If, on the other hand, the observer can change the percept at will, clearly we are dealing with an organismic process and concept.

Note that the issues of experience and of optionality are not unrelated concepts. If a percept cannot be altered by experience, it is mandatory. Likewise, if all observers perceive an object the same, it is considered mandatory because of the implicit assumption that not all observers would have had the same learning experience. On the other hand, if a perceptual process is optional, almost certainly the process can be modified by experience. Jointly, however, these two issues enter into our thinking about the relation between stimulus and organismic concepts.

SOME CURRENT VIEWS

While not many perception researchers have explicitly stated an epistemological position, a few modern researchers have, and a brief overview of their positions and their contrasting emphases will help clarify the stimulus-organism distinction and facilitate the subsequent discussion.

James Gibson, in a series of three books (1950, 1966, 1979), has stated as formal an epistemological position as any modern researcher on perception. He has declared himself unequivocally a direct realist. However, in arguing that the organism brings relatively little to the perceptual experience, he has made some important conceptual distinctions that are necessary for him to maintain the direct realist position.

One of these distinctions is between the energic and the informational value of a stimulus. Energic variables such as intensity and frequency may contribute to sensations, but they do not convey the kind of information necessary for true perception of objects and spaces. For such visual perceptions an optic array is necessary, and in the optic array are higher-order stimulus variables that he calls invariants. These invariants, things such as energy ratios or texture gradients, and which Gibson places squarely in the stimulus, are what make it possible for Gibson to declare himself a direct realist. The complex information variables are placed in the stimulus, and then the organism directly perceives these complex variables.

Despite Gibson's strong, even polemical, insistence on direct realism, he has the organism playing important roles, roles that have been enhanced in his successive books. For example, in 1966 he emphasized the role of the organism as a seeker of information and distinguished between imposed stimulation that occurs with a passive observer and obtained information that occurs with an active observer. But clearly such information seeking is both optional and crucial, because the nature of the percept is clearly a function of the nature of the information that is sought and found.

In his last book (1979), Gibson further introduced the concept of affordances, properties of objects that give information about what can be done with the object, what it affords the organism. While Gibson maintains that affordances are properties of the objects, nevertheless, "affordances are properties taken with reference to the observer" (1979, 143). Still further, the term *affordance* "implies the complementarity of the animal and the environment" (1979, 127). So while Gibson insists on direct realism and invokes complex stimulus properties to allow a direct realism, the organism seeks information and very specifically seeks information defined in terms of organismic function. These surely are statements of a critical realist.

Julian Hochberg (1978, 1981) has taken a stand as a critical realist and has emphasized the role of the organism in perception, particularly the role of the organism's experience. He is an avowed Helmholtzian, firmly believing in the role of unconscious inference in perception, in strong contrast to Gibson. Hochberg places great emphasis on what he calls Helmholtz's rule, namely, that for any sensory input "the observer perceives the object that would most likely produce the stimulus pattern he is receiving" (1978, 82, but many other places as well). What accounts for likelihood is, of course, experience, and in perceiving any particular object or event, the perceiver engages in a process that, even though unconscious, estimates the likelihood of several possible alternative percepts and chooses that which best fits previous experience.

At the same time that Hochberg places great emphasis on the role of learning and experience, he is also a stimulus theorist, and well understands the necessary role of stimulus properties as well as experiential factors that make organismic concepts so important. He even considers the mandatory-optional distinction as important, especially when based on observer agreement. For example, "whenever observers agree about what they see, . . . there must be some discoverable psychophysical relationship between the objects viewed and the perceptions that result. If there were nothing in the stimulus pattern . . . , there obviously could be no agreement" (1978, 106).

To summarize, Hochberg wants to emphasize the role of experience in perception, but his desire to maintain stimulus concepts keeps him firmly in the camp of the realists. So he also is a critical realist, with a considerable emphasis on the critical part of the term.

Roger Shepard (1981) has recently stated an explicit epistemological position that he calls "psychophysical complementarity." The use of the word *psychophysical* establishes that Shepard is a critical realist in that both organismic (psycho) and stimulus (physical) factors operate in our perceiving the world. His use of the word *complementarity*, however, is meant to clarify how he sees the interrelations between stimulus and organismic concepts. His idea of complementarity is not unrelated to that I expressed earlier with the term "psychophysical correlatives," but by *complementarity* he means something stronger than I do by the use of the word *correlatives*. I mean only to imply that for every stimulus concept there is a related organismic concept, and that the two concepts or properties are necessarily correlated. Shepard's idea is stronger and also therefore more difficult to describe briefly, but as suggested by the term itself, there is an interaction between the stimulus and organism such that the two together provide what neither alone can. Shepard himself uses the analogy of the relation between a lock and a key, in which the two must mesh so that together they perform a needed function. In terms of perception, an internal representation of an object need not be one of simple physical resemblance but may be one of functional interaction.

Of considerable interest for present purposes is the fact that Shepard considers the mandatory-optional distinction to be important. He distinguishes between formational processes as those that produce internal representations that are involuntary, automatic, and efficient, and transformational processes as those that can operate on internal representations such as images.

To contrast the two, many if not most internal representations based upon specific external stimulation are so mandatory that all observers will have the same percept, and no observer can voluntarily change the percept. Such mandatory properties exist even with stimuli that produce illusions. At the other extreme, one can generate internal images and transform (manipulate) them almost at will, enlarging them, changing their orientations, even changing the direction of apparent viewing. Such optional transformational processes lead clearly to organismic concepts, while the mandatory formational processes lead to stimulus concepts. Thus, Shepard too is a critical realist, with both the stimulus and the organism playing important parts in his thinking.

THE COMMON THEMES

Despite the differences in emphases on certain aspects of the perceptual problem, these three writers and I actually agree probably much more than we disagree. All of us (including Gibson, despite his protest) are critical realists and assign a role both to the stimulus and to the organism. Within this framework of critical realism there are at least three themes that are common to all of us.

1. Stimulus and organismic concepts are necessarily correlative in the study of perception. None of us accepts a subjectivist position that would deny the stimulus, and certainly none of us as psychologists rejects the existence of an organism that perceives the world of stimuli. So the study of perception is psychophysical, with concepts that are psychophysically correlative at least, perhaps complementary, and certainly interactive.

2. Perceptual concepts exist on a continuum between organismic and stimulus roles in perception. Experience can play roles in perception that differ in degree; and optionality or mandatoriness also differ in degree. Thus, our concepts can lean toward the stimulus or the organism side of the continuum, but rarely is a particular perceptual concept unequivocally one or the other. We are not dealing in blacks and whites.

3. Stimulus information that leads to perception is complex. For some writers this assumption is perhaps more implicit than explicit, but it is nevertheless very real. Gibson made the assumption very explicit in his distinction between stimulus energy and stimulus information, and the distinction has been explicit in much of my own work. But for all of us, in studying perception we deal with stimulus information, relations between stimuli and stimulus variables. Stimulus energy is not of primary concern in perceptual work.

STRUCTURE OF THE PAPER

After this brief background statement, the rest of this paper will be devoted to an elaboration of two major lines of research with which I have been associated. The perception of pattern goodness is one of these lines, and the perception of interactions between stimulus dimensions is the other. In each case I will show how issues of organism, stimulus, and their interaction are inherently involved in the research. The research on pattern perception will deal primarily with the role of experience and learning in perception, while the research on dimensional interaction will deal primarily with the mandatory-optional issue, but both of these organism-stimulus issues will be involved to some extent with each line of research.

As a parenthetical comment, I should note that this chapter was prepared for the centennial of the opening of the first psychological laboratory in this country, and since this event occurred at the Johns Hopkins University, I have deliberately emphasized research done by people currently or formerly affiliated with this university, either as faculty or as students. I hope my emphasis will seem reasonable.

Stimulus Alternatives and Pattern Goodness

The first research topic I will describe is concerned with the gestalt concept of pattern goodness, a topic that I and my colleagues and students have explored over a twenty-year period. The conceptual issue of persistent concern in this research has been: is pattern goodness primarily a stimulus or an organismic property? We shall see that even though my personal preference is to consider goodness to be a stimulus property, the issue truly involves a number of subissues that need clarification. And the clarification itself requires a little delving into some information-theoretic ideas.

STIMULUS INFORMATION AS ALTERNATIVES

Information theory has left psychology with one very important concept, namely, that the information or meaning contained in an event is not a function of the event itself (or the stimulus, for a perceptual psychologist) but rather is a function of the events or stimuli that could have occurred but did not (see Garner 1962 for more on this topic). This idea that meaning or information of stimuli to an organism requires knowledge or specification of the alternatives requires a distinction between the energic properties of a stimulus, its size, intensity, hue, and so forth, and the informational properties of a stimulus, those that give meaning to the stimulus. As noted earlier, Gibson (1966) made this same distinction between stimulus energy and stimulus information, even though he denied that information theory had much to do with his thinking.

Explicit alternatives. To clarify the role of stimulus alternatives in providing meaning, consider figure 8.1, without for the moment looking ahead to the next figures. This is a stimulus, labeled A, and it is contained within the bounds of a rectangle that is supposed to represent the outline of a card on which the stimulus is drawn. In other words, the rectangular outline is not part of the stimulus. Now describe this stimulus. Since I have used this

Fig. 8.1. Stimulus A (from Garner 1974, with permission).

Fig. 8.2. Stimulus A with stimulus B as an alternative (from Garner 1974, with permission).

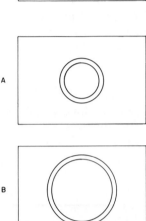

illustration before (Garner 1974), I can expect you to describe it as a circle, possibly as a double circle, maybe even as two concentric circles. Rarely are descriptions other than these used.

Consider this same stimulus A in figure 8.2, where an additional stimulus, B, is provided as context. Once again you are to describe stimulus A. Now almost everybody will include some statement of size in the description of Stimulus A, because the additional stimulus has changed the pertinent descriptors for the stimulus under consideration, A.

Next consider this same stimulus, A, in figure 8.3, where a third stimulus has been added. Now the description of stimulus A will certainly include a statement about location on the card, since stimulus C has a noncentered location.

These are examples of explicit stimulus alternatives, and they demonstrate that the meaning of a stimulus is readily changed by a change in the set of explicit alternatives to a stimulus. These explicit alternatives are certainly stimulus properties, even though they are properties of sets of stimuli, not of individual stimuli. But then that is the whole point: a stimulus cannot be described except by reference to what the alternatives are, and if these alternatives are changed, the meaning of the stimulus is also changed. So information is a function of the alternatives to a stimulus, but information is still a stimulus property.

Inferred alternatives. Does the organism come into this picture at all? The answer is most decidedly yes, and the presumed descriptions of stimulus A will help to clarify the interactive role of the organism. When a set of descriptor terms was used for stimulus A presented alone in figure 8.1, those terms were dictated by the organism's selection of properties of the single stimulus as pertinent. To say that the stimulus is a circle is to say that it is not a square; to say that it has two circles is to say that it could have had one, or possibly three or even more circles. Thus, the viewing organism, by selecting certain properties of a stimulus as pertinent or relevant, infers a set of alternatives, and the inference of a set of alternatives is certainly an organismic property. Or is it? The organism infers what the stimulus implies, and if we were to find that all organisms infer exactly the same stimulus alternatives from a given stimulus, it would appear that the stimulus implication is so strong as to override any real choice or option on the part of the organism. And if a perceptual process is mandatory, it is reasonable to argue that is a result of a stimulus property.

Before moving on to the more specific issue of pattern goodness, it is worth noting now that the idea of stimulus alternatives as providing meaning certainly implicates the organism at least to the extent of there being a required memory system, possibly some learning of alternatives before meaning is clarified, etc. Thus, organismic experience is implicated by an

Fig. 8.3.   Stimulus A with stimuli B and C as alternatives (from Garner 1974, with permission).

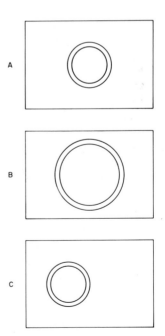

emphasis on stimulus alternatives. Still further, if stimulus alternatives are inferred, the organism is clearly implicated in ways not quite like, but certainly related to, the Helmholtzian unconscious inference that Hochberg (1978, 1981) espouses. Inference is involved, and it need not be conscious. Furthermore, the inference may well be based on prior experience with related materials.

PATTERN GOODNESS AND NUMBER OF ALTERNATIVES

In relating the issue of stimulus alternatives to that of pattern goodness, it is necessary to introduce a further notion of number of alternatives. So far, we have simply noted the role of the particular alternatives in determining the descriptor system. But stimuli may differ from each other in terms of the number of alternatives they have, and once again the number may be explicit or may be inferred.

Rotations and reflections. The first research on this problem of pattern goodness was done by Garner and Clement (1963). Three of the stimuli used are shown in figure 8.4. These dot patterns were generated by placing five dots in the cells of an imaginary 3 × 3 matrix, with the restriction that at least one dot occur in each row and each column. Ninety such patterns

Fig. 8.4. Three of the 5-dot patterns used by Garner and Clement (1963), with rotation and reflection (R&R) equivalence set sizes of 1, 4, and 8.

can be generated, and many more of them are illustrated in Garner (1970a, 1974), but these three are enough to introduce the basic idea of number of alternatives as based upon the physical operations of rotations (in 90° steps) and reflections. To start with the pattern on the right, if the pattern is rotated in 90° steps, or if any of these rotated patterns is reflected to its mirror image, a different pattern is formed. Thus, there are eight equivalent patterns forming a single set of patterns, what we have called R&R (for rotation and reflection) equivalence sets. These eight equivalences exist because the patterns are not symmetrical on the vertical, horizontal, or either diagonal axis. Altogether, there are seven equivalence sets with eight alternatives each.

The pattern in the middle is one pattern from an R&R equivalence set of size four: each of the rotations of this pattern produces a new pattern, but if the pattern shown is reflected about its vertical axis, it simply reproduces itself, and each of the rotated patterns has an axis of reflection about which the pattern reproduces itself. The single axis of symmetry of this pattern is what makes it more restricted than the one on the right. Altogether, there are eight patterns having an equivalence set size of four.

The pattern on the left is symmetrical about its vertical, horizontal, and both diagonal axes, with the result that any rotation or reflection simply reproduces the same pattern, leading to an R&R equivalence set size of one. There are just two such patterns, the one shown and one looking like the + sign.

For an understanding of pattern goodness, the important point is that when these patterns were rated for goodness by experimental subjects, the rated goodness was high for patterns with few alternatives and low for patterns with many alternatives. Thus, as I described this situation in the title of a paper some years ago (Garner 1970a), "good patterns have few alternatives."

Inferred sets. So far, the gestalt concept of pattern goodness seems to be fairly simply related to a physical property of the stimulus, either the physically specifiable number of R&R equivalences or the symmetry relations that lead to these differences in number of equivalences. However, insofar as goodness is related to number of equivalences, the organismic concept of inferred alternatives comes into play, because if perceived goodness is related to number of alternatives, than the organism must infer what the stimulus implies. Since the stimulus implication is sufficient to produce these differences in set size and thus rated goodness, there appears to be no real need for an additional organismic concept.

But the inferred sets of stimuli may not correspond exactly to the implied sets, at least in the simple way illustrated in figure 8.4, and we have evidence that they do not. Handel and Garner (1966) carried out the following experiment: subjects were shown, one at a time, each of the 120 five-dot patterns of the type illustrated in figure 8.4 (120 rather than 90 because the restriction about every row and column being occupied was dropped). They were then requested to draw another pattern that was suggested by, but not identical to, the one they were shown. Any five-dot pattern could be drawn. What happened in this "association" task was that to a very considerable extent the associations were from poor patterns to good ones, but not the converse. A large number of associations, as we might expect, were to other patterns within the same R&R equivalence set; that is, pattern associates were frequently simple rotations or reflections of the given pattern. And a fair number of associations were to patterns of an equal size equivalence set, but beyond that the pattern associates necessarily went to patterns with R&R equivalence set sizes different from that of the given pattern. It is these pattern associates that showed the asymmetry, an example of which is illustrated in figure 8.5.

Fig. 8.5. An example of asymmetric association of patterns showing that good patterns are inferred from poor ones, but poor ones are not inferred from good ones (from Garner 1974, with permission).

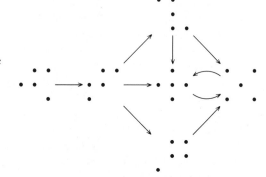

On the left is a pattern with an R&R equivalence set size of eight. When it was the presented pattern, a very common pattern associate was that to its right, as indicated by the arrow, and this pattern comes from an R&R equivalence set of size four. When that pattern was presented, three different patterns were frequently drawn as the pattern associates, those shown to the right again. Two of these (the top and bottom patterns) have the same size of R&R equivalence set (four); thus, these associations were within the same size of equivalence set and therefore general goodness level. The middle pattern, also a frequent associate, is unique, that is, it comes from an R&R equivalence set of size one. The frequent associates of these three patterns are indicated again by the arrows. The top pattern goes to either of the unique R&R patterns, the bottom pattern goes to the "X" pattern, the "+" goes only to the "X," and that pattern in turn produces only the "+" as an association. This general flow of associations means that if the patterns were in fact presented sequentially, then ultimately only the two very good patterns would be used, each producing the other as an associate.

Handel and Garner (1966) described this relation as one of nesting rather than partitioning. The sets of patterns produced by the simple physical operations of rotation and reflection provide a partition of all 120 patterns, with no basic pattern being included within the sets of patterns generated by rotations and reflections of any other basic pattern. But the experimental outcome obtained suggests that good patterns are contained within the sets of poor patterns, though the poor patterns are not contained within the sets of good patterns. Thus, the inferred sets of equivalences are not quite as readily described in terms of physical implications, and we have to assume a more active involvement of the organism in the inference process.

What could produce this relation of nested sets of patterns? Certainly experience and learning may be implicated. It may be that the good patterns occur in an ecologically real world more frequently than do the poor patterns, even though many more poor patterns can exist than good patterns. But the nested relation could also be produced by the organism's selection of stimulus properties. To illustrate, if symmetries are easily perceived properties of stimuli, then the symmetry property may dominate the percept when it is in the presented stimulus but may equally dominate the production process. Or put more simply, people can perceive and imagine symmetric patterns more easily than asymmetric ones.

But once again the interactive relation between the stimulus concept and the organismic concept remains. While it is easy to accept symmetry and even R&R equivalences and sizes as physically specifiable properties, it is less easy to accept the nested inferential process as being based on a physically specifiable property. Bus such a specifiable property does exist; it is simply more complicated and difficult to describe.

STIMULUS SPECIFIC EFFECTS IN PROCESSING

The earliest work on the relation between stimulus alternatives and pattern goodness was concerned primarily with the nature of goodness itself, and that is the work I have been describing. Very soon, however, various researchers began to be interested in the processing consequences of pattern goodness, and almost from the beginning it became clear that there were many processing consequences that were not the result of an explicit set of alternatives. Rather, there seemed to be processing factors that were the result of stimulus-specific properties rather than properties of sets of stimuli. While there are processing outcomes that are the result of such explicit interstimulus properties as similarity, there are also processing outcomes that are relatively independent of such interstimulus factors. Lockhead (e.g., Lockhead and King 1977; King, Crist, and Lockhead 1979) has especially emphasized the role of interstimulus similarity in information processing, and it is clear that such factors have a lot to do with the efficiency of processing. For example, if one pair of stimuli is more dissimilar than another, the time taken to discriminate them is faster, almost regardless of the particular nature of the stimuli. This general factor of interstimulus similarity is, however, not what I shall discuss here since I want to explore the role of the stimulus as having functions not strongly related to sets of alternatives.

Encoding effects. Royer (1966) and Clement and Varnadoe (1967) had done discrimination experiments using reaction time as the measure of performance and found that discrimination time was indeed a function of the goodness of the dot patterns they used (like those I have been describing). I will not describe these experiments in detail but will simply note that the nature of their results strongly suggested that good patterns somehow entered the organism for processing faster than did poor patterns; that is to say, good patterns were encoded faster than poor patterns. This argument was strengthened some years later from the results of an experiment by Bell and Handel (1976), an experiment that used backward masking to determine the efficiency with which various patterns resisted the effects of the masking. Still further, Checkosky and Whitlock (1973) used a memory search paradigm in which one or more dot patterns were held in memory and the experimental subject had to report whether a displayed pattern was in the memory set. While these authors originally felt that their results indicated only a memory effect, a reanalysis of their data by Garner (1974) strongly suggested that there was an encoding effect as well as a memory effect.

These various results that suggested, but did not prove, that good patterns were encoded faster than poor patterns indicated the need for a very straightforward experiment that Garner and Sutliff (1974) carried out. It was a choice reaction time task requiring discrimination between just two stimuli. A total of six dot patterns was used, but the dot patterns in this experiment were nine dots placed in a 5 × 5 matrix, because with nine dots many more patterns are possible. Three of the patterns used were good, coming from R&R equivalence sets of size one, and three of them were poor, coming from R&R equivalence sets of size eight. Two of these patterns, one good and one poor, are shown in figure 8.6.

Fig. 8.6.   One pair of a good and a poor pattern used by Garner and Sutliff (1974) in a discrimination task, with mean reaction time (RT) in milliseconds for each pattern.

The experiment used all 15 pairs of these six-dot patterns in separate discrimination tasks. One stimulus of a pair was presented at a time, and the subject simply gave a different response to each stimulus of the two that could occur. Of the 15 stimulus pairs, 9 of them involved a good and a poor pattern; these pairs were critical to the encoding question, because if good patterns get into the system faster than poor patterns, then in the simple discrimination task the reaction time to the good pattern of the pair should be faster than the reaction time to the poor pattern. Differences in average reaction time between different pairs would occur, of course, as a result of different similarities, but within a single pair there is just one dissimilarity and no reason to expect that one stimulus of the pair should be reacted to faster than the other unless there were some special processing advantage of that particular stimulus. Figure 8.6 shows two patterns that differ in goodness and the average reaction times for the good patterns and the poor patterns for all nine of the pairs involving a good and a poor pattern. The reaction time to the good pattern was 29 msec faster, on the average, than that to the poor pattern, a substantial difference as these experiments go. Furthermore, in each of the nine tasks with both a good and a poor pattern, the good pattern was responded to faster than the poor pattern.

So all processing is not a simple consequence of the nature and number of stimulus alternatives. Something in addition to the properties of the stimulus alternative determines the speed of processing these stimuli. The possibility that is being considered is encoding, which is a rather general term that summarizes all of the factors that are involved in getting a stimulus from out there in the world (e.g., a tachistoscope) into the organism where it can be further processed.

Focusing effects. While the Garner-Sutliff result may be interpreted as an encoding effect, Pomerantz (1977) felt that there was another possible interpretation of the results. Suppose, he argued, that subjects do not carry out the discrimination task by treating both stimulus alternatives on an equal basis. Suppose instead that they choose to focus on one stimulus, keep it in memory, and then carry out a go / no-go decision process. What they would do is decide whether the stimulus presented on a particular trial was the one held in memory, and if it was, press one response key; but if it was not, they would press the other response key, and since the decision to press the other key was a default decision, it would necessarily take slightly longer to make. In other words, all processing is really being done only with respect to the focus stimulus held in memory. Of course, with respect to the Garner-Sutliff result, the assumption is that subjects choose to use the good stimulus as the focus, presumably because it is easier to keep a good stimulus in memory.

One such implication of this idea is that if only one stimulus is being kept in memory and decisions are made only with respect to it, then it should not matter what the alternative stimulus is or even how many alternative stimuli there are. This is the idea that Pomerantz tested. He also used nine-dot patterns so that he, too, had a large supply of good patterns. Then he ran an experiment in which one stimulus always was assigned to one response, while two or four other stimuli were assigned to the other response. He reasoned that subjects in such a task would indeed use a focusing strategy (focusing on the stimulus that had its own response), and his results bore him out.

The actual experiment used either a good or a poor stimulus pattern as the focus; and the nonfocus stimuli, in addition to being either two or four in number, were all good or all poor stimulus patterns. His results are summarized in figure 8.7, where some of the stimulus patterns he actually

Fig. 8.7. Two sets of patterns used by Pomerantz (1977) in a focused classification task, with mean reaction time (RT) in milliseconds for each response with each set of patterns.

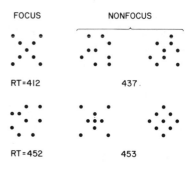

used are also shown. Briefly, it made no difference whether there were two or four nonfocus stimuli; further, it made no difference whether the non-focus stimuli were good or poor patterns. What did make all the difference was the goodness of the focus stimulus, and its effect was so strong that it influenced both the speed of reaction to the focus stimulus as well as to the nonfocus stimuli. Responses to a good focus pattern were very fast—25 msec faster than responses to the nonfocus stimuli, of whatever sort or number. Responses to a poor focus pattern were much slower and were not even faster than responses to the nonfocus stimuli used with the poor focus stimulus. One can easily concur with Pomerantz's conclusion that good stimulus patterns make good focus stimuli, probably because they are easily held in memory. Garner (1978b) later found that other types of stimuli, pairs of parentheses, ((,)),)(, and (), also gave better focusing if the focus stimulus was a good pattern. In this case, when the () stimulus was the focus, performance was much better than if any of the other three stimuli was the focus, and that is the best configuration of the four.

Thus, there are processing consequences of specific stimuli in addition to consequences of the nature and number of stimulus alternatives. While these consequences may involve encoding, they certainly also involve memory factors. Good patterns are easy to hold in memory, regardless of stimulus alternatives.

Sequential same-different task. The focusing task is a procedure in which just one stimulus is held in memory, though the task does not in and of itself require that. When one stimulus is given a special status by making it the only stimulus with its own response, the subject in effect is enticed to use that special stimulus as a focus and then presumably also to use a go / no-go strategy with respect to that one stimulus. The results, of course, show that it apparently happens as planned, especially if the focus stimulus is a good pattern.

There is another common experimental procedure that can bring the role of memory for a particular stimulus under better experimental control, the sequential same-different task. With this task, one stimulus is presented first, followed after a predetermined interval by the second, and the subject's task is to state whether the second stimulus was the same as or different from the first. Clearly with this procedure the first stimulus has to be held in memory in order to compare it with the second stimulus.

Sebrechts and Garner (1981) carried out this experiment with some of the nine-dot patterns used by Pomerantz. In a particular block of trials just two stimuli were used, as in the Garner and Sutliff (1974) discrimination task. Once again the tasks of particular interest are those in which one of the two stimuli was a good pattern and the other was a poor pattern. A particular pair of such stimuli is shown in figure 8.8, along with the reaction times for the two orders of presentation of the stimuli. The reaction times shown, of course, are for responses to different stimuli, since these are the only ones in which the sequence can differ. The results are quite clear: when the good pattern came first, reaction time to say "different" was 33 msec faster than when the poor pattern came first, averaged across all such pairs used.

Fig. 8.8.   A pair of stimuli used in a sequential same-different task by Sebrechts and Garner (1981). The mean different reaction time (RT) in milliseconds is shown for each of the sequential orders of presentation, with the faster RT occurring when the good pattern occurs first.

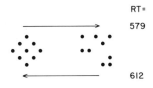

RT=

579

612

This result seems to pin down the interpretation that good patterns are easier to hold in memory. While there may also be encoding factors operating for good patterns as contrasted to poor ones, there can be little doubt that there is a memory advantage for good patterns. In this particular experiment, the second stimulus came on 1.0 sec after the first went off, but Sebrechts (1980) also showed that the memory effect operated over a wide range of times, up to several seconds delay between the first and the second stimulus.

Further evidence of the role of stimulus-specific factors in this result came from responses when the stimuli were the same. "Same" responses to good patterns were considerably faster than to poor patterns, and these faster "same" responses were unaffected by the particular alternative pattern used, either good or poor. So whatever reasonable effects exist as a consequence of the properties of the explicit alternative stimulus, there are processing consequences of the specific stimulus that occur in addition to these.

While the primary topic of this line of research has been pattern goodness, such stimulus-specific effects are not limited to stimuli that can reasonably be considered to differ in goodness. Lasaga and Garner (1983) used four straight lines as stimuli, a vertical, horizontal, and two diagonal lines. There has long been an awareness that diagonal lines provide poorer performance in several information processing tasks than either vertical or horizontal lines, and this research was an attempt to clarify some of the factors operating in this so-called oblique effect. These authors carried out a same-different task much like that done by Sebrechts and Garner (1981), using just two stimuli in a particular block of trials, and in this case having the second stimulus come on immediately after the first. When a diagonal line was paired with a horizontal or vertical line, they found that reaction time was 28 msec faster when the vertical or horizontal line occurred first, thus being the item held in memory. So horizontal and vertical lines have some of the same memory advantage over diagonal lines that good patterns have over poor ones.

Even further, Lasaga and Garner carried out the focusing task that Pomerantz (1977) and Garner (1978b) had used, and found an equivalent result, namely, that when the focus stimulus was a horizontal or vertical line, performance was much better than when a diagonal line was the focus. It would appear that some of these stimulus-specific effects are not the unique province of dot patterns varying in configural goodness.

Thus, the sequential same-different tasks add considerable strength to the argument that good patterns have an advantage over poor patterns when the pattern must be held in memory, even for short periods of time. These experiments do not provide any evidence about encoding advantages, however, and hardly can do so because an encoding advantage would presumably make processing of the second stimulus faster if it is a good pattern. Such an effect could easily be operating, but the memory advantage for the good pattern in the first sequential position would override any evidence of superior encoding for good patterns.

Conclusions about Pattern Goodness

To summarize the research about pattern goodness, a few reasonable conclusions can be stated:

1. Meaning in its informational sense as specified by the stimulus alternatives clearly implicates an organism who knows and understands the nature of the alternatives. So information theory really brought in an organismic concept of meaning; and by de-emphasizing the physical properties of stimuli rightly changed an emphasis on stimulus concepts to one on organismic concepts. And, of course, learning and experience about the alternatives is necessary for the organism to achieve the meaning.

2. If the alternatives to a stimulus are inferred rather than being explicit, it would seem that the organism is implicated still further. Certainly inso-

far as the inference depends on selection of stimulus properties, then the inferred sets of alternatives and the meaning that derives from them are organismic concepts.

3. Nevertheless, I consider pattern goodness to be primarily a stimulus property, even though its understanding requires the concept of inferred sets of stimulus alternatives differing in number. The reason is that the single stimulus so unequivocally implies the nature and number of its alternatives that the inferred set is not under optional control of the perceiving organism.

4. Further evidence of the status of goodness as a stimulus concept comes from the fact that there are many processing consequences of pattern goodness that exist over and above any consequences of explicit stimulus alternatives—and in some cases despite the nature of the alternatives. We must then conclude that the informational concept of meaning in terms of explicit alternatives is not pertinent to an understanding of pattern goodness. A good pattern is a good pattern all by itself, not because of its explicit alternatives.

5. Despite the fact that pattern goodness is a stimulus property, its influences on various types of information processing are distinctly organismic. Such functions as encoding, memory, and memory search are definitely organismic concepts, functions that are influenced by the stimulus property of goodness but that are not themselves stimulus properties or functions.

Before turning to the next line of research on dimensional interactions, let me just note how the optional-mandatory distinction has crept into my argument that pattern goodness is a stimulus property. The interpretation of pattern goodness depends on the concept of inferred sets, but I then argued that the inference was based unequivocally on the set implied by the stimulus. By unequivocally, I mean, of course, that all perceiving organisms select the same stimulus properties upon which to base their inferences, so that there seems to be no option. Thus, when implied alternatives lead to the same inferred alternatives for all perceiving organisms, goodness must be considered as much a stimulus property as the visibility of a light or the audibility of a sound.

Dimensional Interactions

The second research topic I shall describe concerns the nature of dimensional interactions in stimuli of various sorts. I shall not attempt an exact definition of *dimension,* though I have done so elsewhere (Garner 1978a). For present purposes, a dimension will be considered any way in which stimuli can vary, and the topic of dimensional interaction concerns the ways in which two or more dimensions interact in their variation.

INTEGRAL AND SEPARABLE DIMENSIONS

Different measures of dimensional interaction have been used, and these have led to a major distinction between integral and separable dimensional interactions. Other terms for the distinction are unitary or unanalyzable, as contrasted to analyzable. Briefly, the distinction is between those dimensions that interact so that their dimensional status predominates (separable) and those that interact so that the individual nature of the dimensions is lost (integral). A more complete discussion of the many different measures of dimensional interaction can be found in Garner (1974, 1976), but here just enough of the history of the problem will be given to lead us into the issues of organism versus stimulus.

Stimulus similarity. The earliest work on dimensional interaction was done in the context of similarity scaling, in which some measure of confusion or similarity between stimuli is used to describe the nature of the metric relations between stimulus pairs differing on two or more dimensions as a function of their differences on these dimensions singly. The normal expectation is that stimuli differing on two dimensions will show a dissimilarity according to the properties of the Euclidean metric, that is, stimuli differing on two dimensions would differ as the hypotenuse of a right triangle, the two orthogonal sides of the triangle representing the dissimiliarities on the individual dimensions.

Attneave (1950), however, found that stimuli differing in size and form or size and brightness did not give results corresponding to this relatively straightforward expectation based on real-world distance relationships. Rather, he found that the dissimilarity between stimuli differing on two dimensions was more like the sum of the two dissimilarities considered separately. This metric has come to be called the city-block metric because that is how one has to traverse streets in cities: the distance between two corners of a block diagonally apart is the sum of the distances on the two blocks separately.

Torgerson (1958), with the dimensions of brightness and saturation (value and chroma in the Munsell system), obtained results consistent with the Euclidean metric. He suggested that the city-block metric Attneave had obtained might be appropriate when the dimensions are obvious and compelling but that the Euclidean metric would be appropriate otherwise. So here was the beginning of an attempt to distinguish between two types of dimensional interaction.

Other experimenters quickly verified that there were in fact at least two types of dimensional interaction. Shepard (1964) showed that circles varying in size containing a radius varying in angle gave city-block metric. Hyman and Well (1967, 1968) further clarified that there are two different types of dimension by using different types within the same experiment. They confirmed the city-block metric for size and form, as well as for circles with radii in them, but also confirmed the Euclidean metric for value and chroma. In addition, however, they used the value and chroma dimensions in separate chips and found the city-block metric to hold. And lastly, Handel and Imai (1972) showed size and brightness to give a city-block metric while confirming the Euclidean metric for value and chroma.

These early and later studies made clear that the use of similarity measures showed clear evidence of two types of dimensional interaction: the integral interaction that gives the Euclidean metric and the separable interaction that gives the city-block metric. That this distinction was meaningful was quickly shown with other experimental procedures.

Free classification. One experimental procedure to explore the differences between the two types of dimensional interaction is that of free classification. Handel and Imai (1972) used the technique with sets of stimuli like those shown in figure 8.9. In the illustration given, three stimuli are used, but the basic technique can be used with more stimuli. The task for the subject is simply to arrange the three stimuli into two classes. There are three ways in which this can be done with just three stimuli, but the stimuli are chosen to pit two particular types of classification against each other. Stimuli A and B share a common value on dimension X, so if the dimensional structure is important in determining the classification, then the subject would classify stimuli A and B together, with stimulus C being the odd one. However, stimuli A and C are more similar to each other than either is to stimulus B, so if the similarity structure is important in classification, the subject would put stimuli A and C together. Since subjects hardly ever use the classification based on neither dimensions nor similarities, we need not be concerned about the third possible classification.

The results of the experiment can be stated briefly: when the separable dimensions of size and brightness were used, subjects classified by the

Fig. 8.9. Three stimuli differing in two dimensions that can be classified on the basis of dimensional or similarity structure.

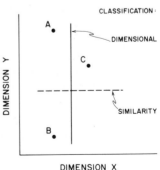

dimensional structure of the stimuli; when the integral dimensions of value and chroma were used, subjects classified by the similarity structure. Thus, integral dimensions are those that have a Euclidean similarity structure and for which subjects use the similarity structure in classification. Separable dimensions, on the other hand, have a city-block similarity structure, but subjects use the dimensional structure as the basis of classification.

Speeded classification. Both similarity measures and free classification are concerned with phenomenal properties of the stimuli, properties that are either reported or readily used as in free classification. At the same time that these research developments were going on, there was another line of research evolving dealing with dimensional interactions but concerning performance measures rather than the phenomenal nature of the interactions. For example, Eriksen and Hake (1955), using an absolute judgment or stimulus identification technique, determined that judgmental accuracy was greater for redundant or correlated visual dimensions than for any of the dimensions used alone. Similar results were obtained by Garner and Creelman (1964) and by Lockhead (1966). None of these experiments was directly concerned with the difference between integral and separable dimensions, though Lockhead had begun to understand the need for such a clarification and first used the term that I have been using, namely, *integral,* for those dimensions that interact to form a new or unitary stimulus.

Speed (or reaction time) was first used as the performance measure with a deliberate attempt to determine the nature of the two main types of dimensional interactions by Garner and Felfoldy (1970, also Garner 1970b). Since their experimental paradigm and its rationale enters into much of what will be discussed later, it will be explained a bit more fully. The stimuli used are generated by the orthogonal combination of two dichotomous dimensions, as illustrated in figure 8.10; to facilitate describing the tasks, the stimuli are labeled A, B, C, and D. The experimental procedure involves using two responses for different types of stimulus set, with time the dependent variable. The original experiments used speed of sorting decks of cards; later experiments have more often used discrete stimulus presentation so that reaction time to each individual stimulus can be measured. There are three types of tasks involving different subsets of these four stimuli, and these produce different dimensional arrangements.

1. One dimension tasks. A pair of stimuli is used and chosen to vary on a single dimension. Thus, if A and B, or C and D, are used, then speed of classification is measured for dimension X. These tasks are really control tasks for single dimensions to serve as the basis of comparison for the other two types of tasks.

Fig. 8.10. A schematic representation of four stimuli generated from orthogonal combinations of dichotomous values on two dimensions.

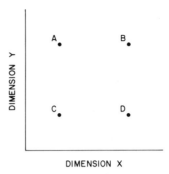

2. Correlated dimension tasks. Two other pairs of stimuli can be used, but in these pairs the two dimensions are correlated. The pairs are, of course, A and D, or B and C. In each of these pairs there is a correlation between the two dimensions. The question to be asked with these tasks is whether classification time is faster when two dimensions are correlated than when the stimuli vary on just one dimension. If there is an improvement, then information from the two dimensions has in some way been integrated. If there is no improvement, then the two dimensions are acting separately. Thus, improvement should go with integral dimensions and no improvement with separable dimensions.

3. Orthogonal dimension tasks. All four stimuli are used in these tasks, with the two dimensions thus being orthogonal or uncorrelated. Classification is required based on one of the two dimensions. With these tasks, then, one dimension is specified as relevant and the other as irrelevant, and the subject must selectively attend to the relevant dimension, ignoring the irrelevant one. The expectation with these tasks is that reaction time will be higher, that is, performance degraded, if the subject cannot ignore the irrelevant dimension, but will be unaffected by the irrelevant dimension if selective attention is possible. That is to say, there should be a decrement in performance with integral dimensions but no effect with separable dimensions.

Experimental results for two pairs of stimulus dimensions used by Garner and Felfoldy (1970) are shown in tables 8.1 and 8.2, and in each case the results are prototypical as described above for an integral and a separable pair of dimensions. Table 8.1 shows the results for the integral dimensions of value and chroma in a single color chip. For classification with each dimension, there is improvement in performance with correlated dimensions and a decrement in performance with orthogonal dimensions.

Table 8.2 shows the prototypical result when these two dimensions are made separable by having each dimension vary in a separate color chip.

Table 8.1   Time (Seconds) to Sort a Deck of 32 Stimulus Cards with 3 Types of Dimensional Arrangement: Integral Dimensions of Value and Chroma in a Single Chip

Relevant Dimension	Dimensional Arrangement		
	One Dimension	Correlated Dimensions	Orthogonal Dimensions
Value	15.1	13.7	18.6
Chroma	14.2	13.2	17.4

Source: Data taken from Garner and Felfody (1970).

There are no significant differences among any of these numbers; in other words, redundant dimensions do not facilitate performance and orthogonal dimensions do not interfere. While too many different dimensional pairs have been investigated to list them all, one of special importance because of its use with children is that of size and brightness. Garner (1977) showed these two dimensions to conform to the prototypical result for separable dimensions.

While the result expected for truly integral dimensions is one of both a redundancy gain and an orthogonal loss, there are other types of dimension in which there is a failure of selective attention but no redundancy gain. The stimuli and dimensions used are geometric in nature, and Garner (1976) has called such dimensional interaction configural. Figure 8.11 shows some stimuli on the left first used by Pomerantz and Garner (1973). The two dimensions are the left and right parentheses, with right and left direction of curvature as the levels on the dimensions. These stimuli show no redundancy gain but also show a complete failure of selective attention to the right or left element. Pomerantz and Garner also demonstrated, however, that if the right element is turned on its side (i.e., rotated 90°), then selective attention is possible. Pomerantz and Schwaitzberg (1975, also Pomerantz 1981) showed that if the two parentheses are placed far enough apart, selective attention is once again possible. And as a last illustration of factors affecting selective attention, if one element is made a bracket instead of a parenthesis, so that the elements are heterogeneous as illustrated on the right in figure 8.11, then selective attention is possible (Garner 1978b). Thus, reaction time can be used to clarify the nature of dimensional interactions and such processes as selective attention.

To summarize at this point, integral dimensions are those that have a Euclidean metric, give free classifications based on similarities, and provide a gain in speeded performance when the dimensions are correlated

Table 8.2   Time (Seconds) to Sort a Deck of 32 Cards with 3 Types of
Dimensional Arrangement: Separable Dimensions of Value and Chroma in
Two Chips

Relevant Dimension	Dimensional Arrangement		
	One Dimension	Correlated Dimensions	Orthogonal Dimensions
Value	15.9	15.7	15.8
Chroma	15.6	15.1	15.1

Source: Data taken from Garner and Felfody (1970).

and interference when one dimension is orthogonally irrelevant. Separable
dimensions are those that have a city-block metric, give free classifications
based on the dimensional structure, and provide no facilitation when the
dimensions are correlated yet no interference when they are orthogonal.
The result with orthogonal dimensions means that selective attention to
dimensions is possible with separable, but not integral, dimensions.

Fig. 8.11.   Two sets of four stimuli formed from   (( )(([ )[
two geometric dimensions. The stimuli on the
left do not allow selective attention to the
elements; those on the right do (after Pomerantz   ())) (])]
and Garner 1973, and Garner 1978b).

Integrality as mandatory. I turn now to the question of organismic versus
stimulus concepts. I have argued consistently (e.g., Garner 1970b, 1974,
1976) that integrality is a stimulus concept. The strongest reason for this
belief lies in the results obtained with speeded classification tasks. If the
very reasonable assumption is made that subjects in these experiments try
to perform as well as they can, then there is a failure to accomplish a
potential facilitation with correlated dimensions if they are separable and
an equally important failure to accomplish selective attention with
orthogonal dimensions if they are integral. If the processing were under
optional control, then subjects could be expected to integrate correlated
information with separable dimensions and to attend selectively to the
relevant dimension when the dimensions are integral. Since they appear
unable to do either of these, the conclusion must be that both integral and
separable dimensions have a mandatory processing consequence in these
tasks; therefore, the property that makes the dimensions integral or separable lies in the stimulus and not in the organism.

Secondary process as optional. As enticing as this simple conclusion is, it cannot, of course, be the whole truth. For example, while similarity relations dominate the perception of integral dimensions, subjects can analyze the dimensions if given enough time to do so. After all, that is how the Munsell color notation system was established. And while dimensional relations and structure dominate the perception of separable dimensions, similarities are perceived, and subjects can make quantitative estimates of similarities. After all, that is how the similarity scaling is accomplished in many experiments.

The way to handle this issue is to consider the mandatory process as primary and the optional processes as secondary (see Garner 1974, 1981). Speeded tasks are those that put the greatest demand on the subject, and that is why the mandatory nature of integrality shows up with the speeded classification tasks. But many other judgment processes are optionally possible, including free classification, serial processing of dimensions, and redefinition of dimensions, in addition to the direct similarity judgments.

Thus, I still consider dimensional integrality to be a stimulus property in that it mandates the nature of the primary process. Other processing consequences or correlates of the integrality-separability continuum, however, are clearly under optional control of the organism, and these properties I would therefore consider organismic. So while it is esthetically pleasing to state that a property is either a stimulus or an organismic concept, the actual psychophysical relations we deal with in the study of perception are simply too complicated for such a simple picture.

While admitting the relatively more complex nature of the stimulus-organism question, the picture obtained from all these experiments done with adult subjects has allowed a moderately clear distinction between integral and separable dimensions. Even this degree of clarity has become somewhat disturbed by more recent research. There are two areas of research I want to discuss that have further complicated but also elaborated and clarified the stimulus-organism issue: developmental studies and variations in task.

DEVELOPMENTAL EFFECTS

Almost any research done in perception, and certainly the research lines reported here, have developmental issues inherent in them. And one general theme in the developmental literature is that perception changes in the course of development from the perception of relatively undifferentiated stimulus perception to a more analytic perception (see Gibson 1969 and Kemler 1982 on this issue). Quite obviously the distinction between integral and separable dimensions should have some special importance for understanding the nature of development, but in understanding the nature of development we can in turn learn more about the integral-separable distinction.

The developmental separability hypothesis. Shepp (1978; also Shepp, Burns, and McDonough 1980) first stated this issue with regard to the nature of the dimensional interactions. Briefly, his developmental separability hypothesis argued that dimensions that are separable for adults start out as integral for children and only with increasing age become separable. Thus, very young children perceive all stimuli in terms of their similarity relations, and only later do they progress to the perception of separable dimensions.

The first evidence for such a developmental change came from an experiment by Shepp and Swartz (1976) using the speeded classification techniques that I argued lead to the concept of integrality as a mandatory and thus stimulus concept. Shepp and Swartz had first and fourth graders sort decks of cards, using the dimensions of color and form (which are separable dimensions for adults). The results of their experiment are displayed in table 8.3, with the three tasks involving one dimension, correlated dimensions, and orthogonal dimensions. While these sorting times are somewhat higher than those obtained with adults, the results were quite clear-cut: first graders showed facilitation with correlated dimensions and interference with orthogonal dimensions. This is, of course, the pattern of data that indicates integral dimensions. The fourth graders, however, in addition to being much faster, also showed no facilitation with correlated dimensions and no interference with orthogonal dimensions, the pattern of data that indicates separable dimensions.

Further evidence for the developmental separability hypothesis comes from studies using the free classification techniques. Smith and Kemler (1977) used the separable (by adult standards) dimensions of size and brightness, with the kind of free classification task illustrated in figure 8.9, in which a similarity and a dimensional classification are pitted against each other with three stimuli. Their subjects were kindergarteners, second graders, and fourth graders, and the average percentage of dimensional classifications rose from 37 to 53 to 67 for the three age groups. Equivalent data were obtained when more complicated classifications of four stimuli were used.

Shepp, Burns, and McDonough (1980) used even younger children, with three age groups of 4, 6–7, and 11–12 years. For classifications of three stimuli with dimensions of size and brightness, their obtained percentages were 18, 53, and 81 for the three age groups respectively. Equivalent results were obtained with the dimensions of size of circle and angle of a radius.

These results, especially those based on speeded classification, certainly

Table 8.3   Time (Seconds) for Children to Sort a Deck of 32 Stimulus Cards with 3 Types of Dimensional Arrangement: Separable Dimensions of Color and Form

Grade	Relevant Dimension	Dimensional Arrangement		
		One Dimension	Correlated Dimensions	Orthogonal Dimensions
First	Color	37.2	34.8	42.5
	Form	38.7	34.6	47.6
Fourth	Color	22.9	23.0	23.1
	Form	23.7	23.1	23.0

Source: Data taken from Shepp and Swartz (1976).

raise a serious issue about integrality and separability being a stimulus property. If it is truly a stimulus property, how can that property change over the developmental stages? Must it not provide for a fixed mode of processing at all age levels? The concept would certainly be cleaner if there were no developmental changes of this sort. Yet it is possible that there really is a mandatory stimulus property that does not change with age of the perceiver, although an optional secondary process does change with age.

Privileged axes. Smith and Kemler (1978) provided evidence that dimensions that are separable for adults are in some way also separable for children. The nature and rationale of their experiment is this: if the dimensional structure predominates in the perception and processing of separable dimensions, then it should not be possible to change the axes of the dimensions without disrupting the processing. Torgerson (1958; see also Garner 1974) made the point that if the Euclidean metric holds, then the dimensional axes can be rotated without any change in the similarity or distance relations between stimuli. If, on the other hand, the city-block metric holds, then a rotation of axes will distort the similarity relations.

So the question raised by Smith and Kemler is this: if brightness and size are truly integral dimensions for children, then one should be able to provide a set of stimuli for classification that is completely equivalent in similarity structure but with the axes defining the "dimensions" being rotated. Figure 8.10 shows a set of four stimuli with the dimensions defined as one ordinarily thinks of them, in this case size and brightness. Figure 8.12 shows a set of four stimuli with exactly the same Euclidean distance relationships but with axes rotated 45° from the original axes. If children perceive stimuli generated from size and brightness dimensions as

Fig. 8.12. The four two-dimensional stimuli of fig. 8.10 with the axes for classification rotated 45° (Smith and Kemler 1978).

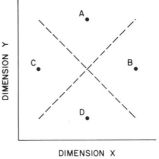

integral, then they should be able to classify a set of stimuli such as that shown in figure 8.12 just as easily as that shown in figure 10.

Smith and Kemler carried out an experiment using speeded classification of two or four stimuli, with stimuli defined by dimensions of size and brightness in the normal way (as in figure 8.10) and also with the new axes (as in figure 8.12). Only the control two-stimulus tasks were used, for example, A versus B or A versus C, but not the tasks with correlated dimensions, A versus D or B versus C. Then both classification tasks were used with all four stimuli, one for each axis of classification. Some of their results for kindergarteners are shown in table 8.4. Note that for the normal axes, there is an increase in classification time from two to four stimuli, indicating the interference effect when orthogonal dimensions are used rather than single dimensions. This is the usual integral effect found with young children. Then note that when two stimuli are used with rotated axes, there is a decrease in sorting time, which is also the effect that should be found with integral dimensions, since with the axes rotated the two original dimensions of size and brightness are correlated. So far the usual result of facilitation with correlated dimensions and interference with orthogonal dimensions has been obtained, indicating that these dimensions are integral for children.

The critical time is that for classifying four stimuli with rotated axes. If integrality holds, that task should be as easy as sorting for stimuli with normal axes; but it clearly does not hold. That task is very difficult for the children, a result that makes clear that the true dimensions of size and brightness are meaningful. Just how meaningful is indicated by the fact that when classification of six stimuli was required, 11 out of 12 children were able to do so with normal axes, but only 1 out of 12 was able to do so with rotated axes. Whatever is happening developmentally, it is clear that dimensions do have a meaningful status for size and brightness even for children who process the dimensions integrally.

Table 8.4   Time (Seconds) to Sort Decks of 24 Cards, with Dimensions of Size and Brightness

	Axes	
Number of Stimuli	Normal	Rotated
2	34.1	32.8
4	38.9	47.1

Source: Data taken from Smith and Kemler (1978).

Notes: Normal axes are as in figure 8.10. Rotated axes are as in figure 8.12. Subjects are kindergarteners.

Mode of processing. Where does this leave integrality as a stimulus concept? I believe that its status as a stimulus concept remains intact even with this more complicated and fascinating developmental evidence. When dimensions are separable, the dimensional structure is important at all age levels, though a more complicated set of experimental operations is necessary to demonstrate its importance with young children. And, of course, integral dimensions are processed according to a similarity structure at all age levels. Thus, it remains necessary to distinguish between two types of dimensional interaction, regardless of age, and with a degree of mandatoriness of processing that implicates stimulus properties as most relevant.

What, then, are the children doing with separable stimuli? They are using as primary that which for adults is secondary, similarity relations. So we are dealing with a difference in mode of processing, not a difference that requires the unreasonable assumption that fundamental stimulus properties are different for children and adults.

There is one very special question that needs to be addressed on this matter. I have argued that integrality is a stimulus concept because with both integral and separable dimensions there is one classification task for which performance would be better if the subjects could use a property they seem unable to use. Specifically, with separable dimensions, they are unable to make use of the redundant information when classifying stimuli with correlated dimensions.

The answer, it seems to me, is that in the child's use of a secondary process, there is a loss of efficiency, overall performance being much poorer. By using the similarity properties of separable dimensions, children are able also to get a gain in performance with correlated dimensions, but they only get this gain because the use of similarity properties of separable dimensions is inefficient. The adult has learned how to be efficient, to use the dimensional structure of separable dimensions. The child, in other words, is not doing something better than the adult except in the sense that by using an inefficient process, some compensation occurs in that the child is able to use the redundant information available with correlated dimensions.

TASK EFFECTS

The second area of research that has complicated the picture of integrality as a stimulus concept comes from more recent research in which different tasks have led to different types of processing, so that we have to consider either that the nature of the dimensional interaction changes with the task or that the organism is able to engage optional processes to a greater extent with some tasks than with others.

Concept learning. The history of research on concept learning is almost a history of research on the role of dimensions in the generation of stimuli and concepts based on subsets of stimuli. Garner (1976) did an analysis of concept learning in line with the integral-separable distinction and suggested that concept learning would be most efficient if the dimensions relevant to the concept were integral while those distinguishing relevant from irrelevant dimensions were separable. Some data were suggestive that this idea had some merit.

Kemler and Smith (1979; see also Kemler 1982) have dealt with the issue of integrality in concept learning very directly. They used an ingenious concept-learning task that required learning of a concept rule involving a relation between a pair of stimuli. The stimuli could differ on different dimensions, and the magnitude of the difference could be large or small. They used two types of concept rule, one based on similarity relations and the other based on dimensional relations.

For the similarity rule, the magnitude of the difference was the relevant factor regardless of the dimension on which the difference occurred. For example, if a pair of stimuli differed by a small amount, it would be classified as a type A pair, while if the pair differed by a large amount, it would be a type B pair.

For the dimensional rule, the dimension on which the difference occurred was the relevant factor regardless of the magnitude of the difference. For example, if a pair of stimuli differed in color, it would be classified as a type A pair, while if the pair differed in size, it would be classified as a type B pair.

Kemler and Smith used two types of stimulus dimensions: value and chroma as integral dimensions, and brightness and size as separable dimensions. In the first experiment, adult subjects were trained on pairs of stimuli in which either the similarity or the dimensional rule could be used because on all trials the two rules were correlated. Then in a test phase the two rules were no longer correlated; thus, the stimuli could be classified by either rule, and the object of the experiment was to discover which rule the subjects had learned in the training phase. The results showed that out of 12 subjects trained with separable dimensions, 11 learned a dimensional rule and the other subject was inconsistent. Of the 12 subjects trained with integral dimensions, only 1 subject learned a dimensional rule, 3 subjects learned a similarity rule, and the other 8 were inconsistent. However, these inconsistent subjects showed a kind of consistency in that they classified most of the pairs with a small difference in line with a similarity rule and most of the pairs with a large difference in line with a dimensional rule.

Thus, while these results overall show differences in line with the expectation that similarity rules would be easy to learn with integral dimensions and dimensional rules would be easy to learn with separable dimensions, they also show that subjects wanted to use a dimensional rule even with the integral dimensions. When the differences between the pairs were large enough, it seemed to make it easier to perceive and then use the dimensions, so subjects used the dimensional rules. Of course, with separable dimensions there was no tendency to use similarity relations at all.

This same kind of asymmetric result was obtained in a second experiment that measured trials to learn either a similarity or a dimensional rule. With separable dimensions, the dimensional rule was learned in 2.1 trials on the average, while 37.5 trials were required to learn the similarity rule. Thus, there is a very great difference between the two types of rules with separable dimensions. With integral dimensions, on the other hand, the similarity rule was learned in 20.5 trials, while the dimensional rule required 41.4 trials. So while the difference expected in favor of easier learning of the similarity rule with integral dimensions was found, the difference in favor of the similarity rule was much less than is the difference in favor of the dimensional rule with separable dimensions. These authors concluded quite reasonably that subjects have a tendency or preference to use dimensional relations in tasks of this sort.

In a similar experiment carried out with children aged five and ten years, Kemler and Smith found that both age groups used dimensional relations (with separable stimuli), thus confirming their earlier findings that even though young children use similarity relations in both speeded and free classification, the dimensional structure of stimuli is available to them and will be used given the appropriate task constraints.

As a contrast to this preference for the use of dimensional relations, Smith (1981) found that adult subjects doing free classifications of stimulus sets varying along four separable dimensions used overall similarity as the basis of classification, even though they used the dimensional structure when the stimuli differed on only two dimensions. And an experiment with children, from kindergarten, second, and fifth grades, showed the usual developmental trend with two-dimensional stimuli but classification on the basis of overall similarity at all ages with four-dimensional stimuli.

These experiments confirm the fact that stimulus sets have both a dimensional and a similarity structure and that what determines primary process is different for integral and separable dimensions. If, however, the task is changed, there can be an optional change to use of the secondary process—dimensional structure for integral stimuli and similarity structure for separable stimuli.

Type of speeded task. The primary basis for my argument that dimensional integrality is a stimulus concept comes from the speeded classification tasks, in which there appears to be a mandatory process operating for both integral and separable dimensions. The classification task, whether used with two or more alternative stimuli, is one in which a single stimulus is presented at a time and the subject assigns it one of two responses. Another speeded task commonly used in information-processing research is the comparison task, in which two stimuli are presented either simultaneously or sequentially, and the subject is required to decide whether the stimuli are the same or different. There is every reason to expect that integral and separable dimensions would show different consequences with this experimental paradigm that would parallel those found with the speeded classification paradigm.

However, this expectation has recently been called into question. Santee and Egeth (1980) used both the speeded classification task and the same-different task (simultaneous and sequential) with the dimensions of form and size, though judgments were always of form; that is, form was always the relevant dimension and size the irrelevant dimension. The data from the speeded classification task showed perfect selective attention for form with irrelevant variation in size. When subjects made judgments of sameness based on the relevant dimension of form, however, the reaction times were higher when the stimulus pair actually differed in size than when the pair was the same in both dimensions. In other words, the "same" response is interfered with if the stimuli are different on the irrelevant dimension, and that is not what one would expect if the subject is efficiently attending to form only. This interference is equivalent to that obtained in the speeded classification task with orthogonal dimensions if they are integral. Thus, these dimensions appear to be integral with the same-different task, even though separable with the speeded classification task.

Yet the results did not show complete integrality with the same-different task. When a pair of stimuli differ, they can differ on just the relevant dimension or on the relevant and the irrelevant dimensions, and with integral stimuli, reaction time should be faster when stimuli differ on two dimensions, as when they differ on two dimensions in speeded classification of correlated dimensions. But Santee and Egeth did not find this facilitation effect.

Some data of my own on this problem are shown in figure 8.13, and these data do show both the interference on the "same" response when the irrelevant dimension differs and also the expected facilitation on the "different" response when the stimuli differ on two dimensions rather than on one. (Hawkins and Shigley 1972 had earlier also shown both interference and facilitation with the dimensions of color, size, and form.) The stimuli used in this experiment were 0, 00, X, XX, differing in form and in length. Both dimensions were used as relevant in the same-different tasks, and the results were equivalent for both dimensions, so the data shown in figure 8.13 are average data for both dimensions. (The data shown are for simultaneous presentation, but equivalent results were obtained with sequential presentation.) The speeded classification task showed these two dimensions to be essentially separable in that there was no facilitation owing to correlated dimensions, and selective attention was possible when classifying by length, though there was slight interference when classifying by form. So here is another experiment demonstrating that a change in experimental task can produce a change in apparent integrality.

The interpretation of these effects is not clear, either to Santee and Egeth or to me. I suspect that we need some more experiments before it will become clear and a better way of determining just how much facilitation and interference is obtained. It may be, for example, that there is simply some response facilitation happening with the same-different procedure, even with separable dimensions, but that the amount of such facilitation is much less than would be obtained with truly integral dimensions.

Fig. 8.13. Reaction times (in milliseconds) for "same" and "different" responses as a function of the number of dimensions on which the two stimuli differ. Average data for the two dimensions of form and length.

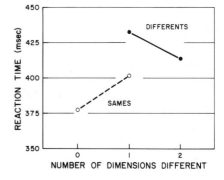

Integrality as a Continuum. A still further issue that enters into an understanding of task-specific effects is that integrality is probably not an all-or-none matter but that different pairs of dimensions differ in the degree of integrality. Garner (1974) made this argument, and more recently Shepp (1982) has made it again, but with some experimental data specific to the issue. Shepp used an experimental procedure that might be called a choice-same technique: one stimulus is presented, followed by a pair of stimuli, and the subject's task is to indicate which of the succeeding pairs is identical to the first stimulus (what Shepp called the cue, and thus the task a cued task). Sameness can be defined, like the same-different tasks, with one dimension as relevant or with two or more as relevant (providing a conjunctive cue and target).

Three pairs of dimensions were used: hue and value, size and brightness, and size of circle with angle of a line within. When one dimension only was relevant, the pattern of results showed complete integrality for hue and value, but an asymmetric form of integrality for both size and brightness and size of circle and angle of line. The asymmetries were attributable to the fact that irrelevant differences in brightness interfered with judgments of size, but not the reverse; and size of circle interfered with judgments of angle of line, but not the reverse. (See Garner 1982 for more on these asymmetries.)

When conjunctive targets were used, the results showed size and brightness to be integral, as well as hue and value, since the divided attention necessary to handle the conjunctive task was very effective. However, size of circle and angle of line were very difficult to use in conjunction, the result that implies separability.

The fact that size and brightness seem to shift from being separable to being at least asymmetrically integral is the major reason for Shepp's argument for integrality as a continuum. It is interesting that size and brightness have so frequently been used in studies of Shepp's developmental separability hypothesis, and that these have been considered separable dimensions for adults. Possibly other dimensions are more firmly separable, and with them even children would not be able to use the similarity structure in free and constrained classification.

These variations in type of performance with different tasks suggest the possibility that there is more option available to the organism than had previously been supposed. Shepp (1982), however, argues that mandatoriness is still more the rule than optionality, because once both the pair of dimensions and the task are specified, there seems to be little option left to the subject's discretion. Yet there must be a gray area in which the subject can shift performance to maximize the satisfaction of task demand.

CONCLUSIONS ABOUT DIMENSIONAL INTERACTION

To summarize the research on dimensional interaction, these conclusions seem reasonable:

1. There is a real difference in how different stimulus dimensions interact, and a major property of this difference is describable as the integrality-separability continuum. A variety of tasks, such as similarity ratings, free classification, and speeded classification, all give a coherent pattern of results displaying the essential differences between integral and separable dimensions. The consistency of these effects across different tasks in itself suggests that integrality is a stimulus property.

2. The most compelling evidence that integrality is a stimulus concept comes from the research with the speeded classification tasks: in the correlated dimension task optimal performance is not obtained with separable dimensions, and in the orthogonal dimension task optimal performance is not obtained with integral dimensions. The mandatory nature of such performance argues strongly that integrality is a stimulus property.

3. With separable dimensions, there is a developmental trend in which younger children process such dimensions as integral. However, further research indicates that even for young children there are clear differences in the perception of integral and separable dimensions. Thus, the developmental trend is best understood as a change in mode of processing.

4. Despite the stimulus nature of the integral-separable distinction, there are many tasks in which subjects do perform in ways more appropriate to a different type of dimensional interaction. For example, subjects can use dimensions in learning concepts with integral dimensions and can classify on the basis of similarity with separable dimensions under the right circumstances. Thus, every set of dimensions can invoke a primary and a secondary process, and option exists because the secondary properties of the stimulus dimensions also exist. What is primary and what is secondary, however, is what distinguishes integral from separable dimensions.

It is no accident, of course, that these conclusions about dimensional interaction have the same general connotation as those about pattern goodness. The argument is that there are properties of stimuli other than their energic properties that truly are stimulus properties, not organismic. Thus, a psychophysics of perception must deal with stimulus concepts more complicated than such things as intensity and frequency of stimulation; structural and informational properties also exist in stimuli.

At the same time, it must be recognized that these stimulus properties influence all kinds of organismic processing. In many cases the processing appears to be mandatory once the stimuli and the tasks are specified. But in other cases option for the organism does exist, and any processing modes that allow option are clearly organismic concepts.

Final Comments

Conclusions about stimulus and organismic concepts have been made within each section. In closing I want to comment briefly on three topics that are parenthetically related to those I have discussed.

THE ROLE OF EVOLUTION

If we ask why there are correlative or complementary properties of the perceiving organism and the perceived physical world, there is no fixed answer. But essentially all writers on these matters have emphasized that the organism is not operating in a vacuum but is necessarily an interacting part of a single world-organism system. Certainly if properties of the organism did not correspond in some realistic way with properties of the world in which the organism exists, the survival possibilities for the organism would be poor, to say the least.

These rather obvious considerations have led some writers to invoke the concept of evolution as an explanation for the complementary nature of the stimulus and organismic properties. Posner (1978), in commenting on various metatheoretical approaches to the study of mind (a broader topic than perception, to be sure) describes both Gibson and me as adopting an evolutionary point of view in our attempts to understand perception. Shepard (1981) is very explicit on this matter, arguing that it is through biological evolution that internal representations of the world have come to mirror the real world.

What provides a distinctive character to this point of view is that if the organism evolutionarily adapts to the environment, then to understand the environment is absolutely crucial in order to understand the organism. So a great deal of psychological research, concerned with understanding organisms, is actually carried out with a primary emphasis on the nature of the stimuli. Certainly this point is clear in the two research themes I have discussed: to understand perceptual processing, one must first understand the nature of the stimulus.

INVERSE EVOLUTION

This argument is that we must understand the nature of the physical world in order to understand the nature of organisms because the physical world has evolutionarily determined the nature of the organism. But there is another reason to study the nature of the physical stimulus, and that requires the idea of an inverse form of evolution, one in which the world has been shaped by the nature of the organism. At least human organisms have had a great deal to say about their physical environment and presumably have adjusted the environment to optimize their own ability to cope with it. To use just one example, a written language has not been imposed on humans, certainly not in its particular form. Humans have created this physical system of communication, and the form it has taken cannot be simply accidental. If we then want to learn something about human organisms, it makes great sense to study a language system that has been evolutionarily developed.

Thus, whether we argue that study of the stimulus will help us understand the organism because the organism has adapted over the millenia to the nature of the environment in which it survives or whether we argue that the organism has to a great extent imposed its characteristics on the environment over these same millenia, psychologists should study the nature of the physical world in order to understand the nature of organisms.

THE PERCEPTION RESEARCHER'S INTEREST IN THE STIMULUS

One last comment has to do with the fact that apparently only people who do perception research seem to be interested in the epistemological issues that pervade this report and more specifically to be interested in the nature of the stimuli used in their research. Why are not these issues and this approach equally important for people studying learning, for example? What is clear is that they have not been.

Shepard comments on this matter by noting that "Hull . . ., as Skinner, treated the stimulus as an unanalyzed entity" (1981, 285). But not just traditional learning theorists have failed to be seriously concerned with the nature of the stimulus. Many psychologists working within an information-processing paradigm have also treated the stimulus with disregard. As I once noted, "For too long we have considered that a stimulus is a stimulus is a stimulus, whose only function is to elicit behavior" (Garner 1970b, 357).

Of course, the answer to the question posed is that learning specialists and some kinds of information-processing specialists have been so concerned with the role of the response as the behavior to be modified that the role of the stimulus in modifying this behavior has been neglected. But we in perception cannot afford to neglect the stimulus, it being more important to us than overt behavior. In fact, if we are trying to understand perception, the role of the response is simply as an indicant to an internal process; the response itself is not the process in which we are interested. It allows communication between the observing subject in our experiments and the experimenter, but the process being studied is truly perception. So we pay less attention to the nature of the response and more to the nature of the stimulus.

And so to conclude, those of us who study perception must try to understand not only the perceiving organism but also the nature of the stimulus world and the interactions between stimuli and organisms.

Acknowledgments

The preparation of this chapter was supported by Grant MH 14229 from the National Institute of Mental Health to Yale University.

References

Attneave, F. Dimensions of similarity. *American Journal of Psychology*, 1950, *63*, 516–556.

Bell, H. H., & Handel, S. The role of pattern goodness in the reproduction of backward masked patterns. *Journal of Experimental Psychology: Human Perception and Performance*, 1976, *2*, 139–150.

Checkosky, S. F., & Whitlock, D. Effects of pattern goodness on recognition time in a memory search task. *Journal of Experimental Psychology*, 1973, *100*, 341–348.

Clement, D. E., & Varnadoe, K. W. Pattern uncertainty and the discrimination of visual patterns. *Perception & Psychophysics*, 1967, *2*, 427–431.

Eriksen, C. W., & Hake, H. W. Multidimensional stimulus differences and accuracy of discrimination. *Journal of Experimental Psychology*, 1955, *50*, 153–160.

Garner, W. R. *Uncertainty and structure as psychological concepts*. New York: Wiley, 1962.

Garner, W. R. Good patterns have few alternatives. *American Scientist*, 1970a, *58*, 34–42.

Garner, W. R. The stimulus in information processing. *American Psychologist*, 1970b, *25*, 350–358.

Garner, W. R. *The processing of information and structure*. Potomac, MD: Lawrence Erlbaum, 1974.

Garner, W. R. Interaction of stimulus dimensions in concept and choice processes. *Cognitive Psychology*, 1976, *8*, 98–123.

Garner, W. R. The effect of absolute size on the separability of the dimensions of size and brightness. *Bulletin of the Psychonomic Society*, 1977, *9*, 380–382.

Garner, W. R. Aspects of a stimulus: Features, dimensions, and configurations. In E. Rosch & B. B. Lloyd (Eds.), *Cognition and categorization*. Hillsdale, NJ: Lawrence Erlbaum, 1978a.

Garner, W. R. Selective attention to attributes and to stimuli. *Journal of Experimental Psychology: General*, 1978b, *107*, 287–308.

Garner, W. R. The analysis of unanalyzed perceptions. In M. Kubovy & J. R. Pomerantz (Eds.), *Perceptual organization*. Hillsdale, NJ: Lawrence Erlbaum, 1981.

Garner, W. R. Asymmetric interactions of stimulus dimensions in perceptual information processing. In T. J. Tighe & B. E. Shepp (Eds.), *Perception, cognition and development: Interactional analyses*. Hillsdale, NJ: Lawrence Erlbaum, 1982.

Garner, W. R., & Clement, D. E. Goodness of pattern and pattern uncertainty. *Journal of Verbal Learning and Verbal Behavior*, 1963, 2, 446–452.

Garner, W. R., & Creelman, C. D. Effect of redundancy and duration on absolute judgments of visual stimuli. *Journal of Experimental Psychology*, 1964, 67, 168–172.

Garner, W. R., & Felfoldy, G. L. Integrality of stimulus dimensions in various types of information processing. *Cognitive Psychology*, 1970, 1, 225–241.

Garner, W. R., & Sutliff, D. The effect of goodness on encoding time in visual pattern discrimination. *Perception & Psychophysics*, 1974, 16, 426–430.

Gibson, E. J. *Principles of perceptual learning and development*. New York: Appleton-Century-Crofts, 1969.

Gibson, J. J. *The perception of the visual world*. Boston: Houghton Mifflin, 1950.

Gibson, J. J. *The senses considered as perceptual systems*. Boston: Houghton Mifflin, 1966.

Gibson, J. J. *The ecological approach to visual perception*. Boston: Houghton Mifflin, 1979.

Handel, S., & Garner, W. R. The structure of visual pattern associates and pattern goodness. *Perception & Psychophysics*, 1966, 1, 33–38.

Handel, S., & Imai, S. The free classification of analyzable and unanalyzable stimuli. *Perception & Psychophysics*, 1972, 12, 108–116.

Hawkins, H. L., & Shigley, R. H. Irrelevant information and processing mode in speeded discrimination. *Journal of Experimental Psychology*, 1972, 96, 389–395.

Hochberg, J. *Perception* (2d ed.). Englewood Cliffs, NJ: Prentice-Hall, 1978.

Hochberg, J. Levels of perceptual organization. In M. Kubovy & J. R. Pomerantz (Eds.), *Perceptual organization*. Hillsdale, NJ: Lawrence Erlbaum, 1981.

Hyman, R., & Well, A. Judgments of similarity and spatial models. *Perception & Psychophysics*, 1967, 2, 233–248.

Hyman, R., & Well, A. Perceptual separability and spatial models. *Perception & Psychophysics*, 1968, 3, 161–165.

Kemler, D. G. Wholistic and analytic modes in perceptual and cognitive development. In T. J. Tighe & B. E. Shepp (Eds.), *Perception, cognition and development: Interactional analyses*. Hillsdale, NJ: Lawrence Erlbaum, 1982.

Kemler, D. G., & Smith, L. B. Accessing similarity and dimensional relations: Effects of integrality and separability on the discovery of complex concepts. *Journal of Experimental Psychology: General*, 1979, 108, 133–150.

King, M. C., Crist, W. B., & Lockhead, G. R. Context and goodness in a focusing task. *Perception & Psychophysics*, 1979, 26, 305–311.

Lasaga, M. I., & Garner, W. R. The effect of line orientation on various information processing tasks. *Journal of Experimental Psychology: Human Perception and Performance*, 1983, 9, 215–225.

Lockhead, G. R. Effects of dimensional redundancy on visual discrimination. *Journal of Experimental Psychology*, 1966, 72, 95–104.

Lockhead, G. R., & King, M. C. Classifying integral stimuli. *Journal of Experimental Psychology: Human Perception and Performance*, 1977, 3, 436–443.

Mandelbaum, M. *Philosophy, science, and sense perception: Historical and critical studies*. Baltimore: Johns Hopkins Press, 1964.

Pomerantz, J. R. Pattern goodness and speed of encoding. *Memory & Cognition*, 1977, 5, 235–241.

Pomerantz, J. R. Perceptual organization in information processing. In M. Kubovy & J. R. Pomerantz (Eds.), *Perceptual organization*. Hillsdale, NJ: Lawrence Erlbaum, 1981.

Pomerantz, J. R., & Garner, W. R. Stimulus configuration in selective attention tasks. *Perception & Psychophysics*, 1973, 14, 565–569.

Pomerantz, J. R., & Schwaitzberg, S. D. Grouping by proximity: Selective attention measures. *Perception & Psychophysics*, 1975, 18, 355–361.

Posner, M. I. *Chronometric explorations of mind*. Hillsdale, NJ: Lawrence Erlbaum, 1978.

Royer, F. L. Figural goodness and internal structure in perceptual discrimination. *Perception & Psychophysics*, 1966, 1, 311–314.

Santee, J.L., & Egeth, H. E. Selective attention in the speeded classification and comparison of multidimensional stimuli. *Perception & Psychophysics*, 1980, 28, 191–204.

Sebrechts, M. M. On the relation between goodness and similarity: Stimulus-specific and context-specific properties. Unpublished doctoral dissertation, Yale University, 1980.

Sebrechts, M. M., & Garner, W. R. Stimulus-specific processing consequences of pattern goodness. *Memory & Cognition*, 1981, 9, 41–49.

Shepard, R. N. Attention and the metric structure of the stimulus space. *Journal of Mathematical Psychology*, 1964, 1, 54–87.

Shepard, R. N. Psychophysical complementarity. In M. Kubovy & J. R. Pomerantz (Eds.), *Perceptual organization*. Hillsdale, NJ: Lawrence Erlbaum, 1981.

Shepp, B. E. From perceived similarity to dimensional structure: A new hypothesis about perceptual development. In E. Rosch & B. B. Lloyd (Eds.), *Cognition and categorization*. Hillsdale, NJ: Lawrence Erlbaum, 1978.

Shepp, B. E. The analyzability of multidimensional stimuli: Some constraints on perceived structure and attention. In T. J. Tighe & B. E. Shepp (Eds.), *Perception, cognition and development: Interactional analyses*. Hillsdale, NJ: Lawrence Erlbaum, 1982.

Shepp, B. E., Burns, B., & McDonough, D. The relation of stimulus structure to perceptual and cognitive development: Further tests of a separability hypothesis. In F. Wilkening & J. Becker (Eds.), *The integration of information by children*. Hillsdale, NJ: Lawrence Erlbaum, 1980.

Shepp, B. E., & Swartz, K. B. Selective attention and the processing of integral and nonintegral dimensions: A developmental study. *Journal of Experimental Child Psychology*, 1976, 22, 73–85.

Smith, L. B. Importance of the overall similarity of objects for adults' and children's classifications. *Journal of Experimental Psychology: Human Perception and Performance*, 1981, *7*, 811–824.

Smith, L. B., & Kemler, D. G. Developmental trends in free classification: Evidence for a new conceptualization of perceptual development. *Journal of Experimental Child Psychology*, 1977, *24*, 279–298.

Smith, L. B., & Kemler, D. G. Levels of experienced dimensionality in children and adults. *Cognitive Psychology*, 1978, *10*, 502–532.

Torgerson, W. S. *Theory and methods of scaling*. New York: Wiley, 1958.

9. Linguistic Relativity
Roger Brown

Linguistic relativity is the view that the cognitive processes of a human being—perception, memory, inference, and deduction—vary with the structural characteristics—lexicon, morphology, and syntax—of the language he or she speaks. It is an ancient view that has been effectively championed in this century by two anthropological linguists: Edward Sapir (1949) and Benjamin Lee Whorf (1956). Linguistic relativity is not an idea that would naturally occur to the person who speaks a single language; the single language will seem to function only as a vehicle of thought, expressing and transmitting but not shaping. To the speaker of two or more structurally unlike languages, such as English and Chinese, it just about always seems evident that one thinks differently in different languages. Edmund Glenn and Maung Gyi, two chief translators for the United Nations, have both said that this is the case and have supported their position with stories of highly consequential misunderstandings. When Khruschev said "We will bury you," he did not mean, as the translation suggested, "in atomic dust" but rather something like "in the dust of our national chariot as we pass you in the economic race."

George Orwell passionately believed that language played an important role in shaping political thought, and in his futuristic *1984* there is a language, Newspeak, that is explicitly designed not simply to provide a medium of expression for the world view of Ingsoc (English Socialism) but to make all other modes of thought impossible. In nonfuturistic 1982 there appeared a book, *Nukespeak,* that argued that the elite who are technically qualified to talk about nuclear war use a lexicon well designed to keep the "unthinkable" unthought, a lexicon of "clean bombs," "preemptive first strikes," and "normal aberrations" (Three Mile Island). The kind of linguistic determinism attributed to Newspeak and to Nukespeak presupposes the truth of linguistic relativity and goes beyond it. The claim is not simply that cognitive structures covary with language structures but that the latter shape and limit the former.

In history, generally, linguistic relativity has more often operated as a presupposition than as an explicit hypothesis, but it has usually figured as a presupposition in revolutionary libertarian thinking rather than in the thinking of established power (Newspeak and Nukespeak). Programs of social reform very often include reforms of language. The most easily accomplished item on the Civil Rights agenda was the displacement of the term *Negro* by the term *Black;* it happened in little more than a year. Not so easy, in fact not yet accomplished and not likely ever to be accomplished, is the displacement of both *Miss* and *Mrs.*, in both writing and speech, by *Ms.* (pronounced /MIZ/), which is favored by some feminists.

It was a part of the program of the French Revolution to extirpate the deferential use of plural *vous* to a single person; Malbec called it a remnant of feudalism. Equality and fraternity called for the use of *tu*, the pronoun of friends and family, in all circumstances, by each person, to each person. Frenchmen made the effort to change their linguistic habits as long as revolutionary fervor lasted, but when it waned, they relapsed into unthinking pronominal acknowledgement of status. Communism in modern Europe had the same pronominal reform program as the French Revolution (against such forms as *vy,* cognate to *vous,* and in favor of *ty*). In China, the traditional honorific *Nin* was the target of attack. In seventeenth-century England, the Society of Friends (Quakers), an equalitarian reformist movement, tried to eliminate deferential *ye* in favor of universal *thou* and *thee.* The fact that these changes were thought to be essential for a revolutionary consciousness seems to imply belief in linguistic relativity and indeed determinism. The fact that none of these reforms has endured tells us something about the inertia of certain aspects of language and also something about the inertia of some aspects of social structure. It may also tell us something about linguistic relativity and determinism.

Only in the present decade, in the psychologically self-conscious United States, has the link between Whorfian relativity and language reform been explicitly recognized. In the effort to win full equality for women, "sexist" language has been attacked on the ground that it embodies and transmits from generation to generation sexist thought. These attacks have come from linguists (Bodine 1975; Lakoff 1973) and psycholinguists (Henley 1977) as well as from laypersons, and Whorf's name has been invoked. It is a pronoun once again that most offends, but this time not a pronoun of address. In English we have the third person masculine *he* as a generic substitute for nouns of indefinite gender such as *somebody, person, reader,* and *child.* Bodine (1975) contends that this usage reflects and helps to maintain an "androcentric" view of the world, and socially alert speakers, writers, and publishers are attempting to eliminate generic *he.* An increasingly common expedient in textbooks is to alternate *he* and *she* as replacements for *child* or *person* in a more or less random manner. The reader experiences an initial vertiginous incohesion, but it wears off.

What is completely new about the present-day attack on *he* is the recognition by some that the existence of the linguistic form alone, which would have satisfied Whorf as evidence of the related sexist thought, is not evidence enough. When *he* is used as anaphor for *child* or *somebody*, it may suggest a person of masculine gender, but it need not since all words are understood not as isolated entities but in context, and, in fact, it is an answerable empirical question whether *he* in the generic sense conjures up a masculine image. There is some psycholinguistic research aimed at answering this question (MacKay 1980; MacKay and Fulkerson 1979), but the answer is not yet unequivocal.

The general hypothesis of linguistic relativity, especially as set forth in Whorf's essays, has stimulated a large amount of discussion in psychology and also a small amount of research. In three kinds of research on relativity, I have felt strongly involved—because of studies of my own and studies done by psychologists who once worked with me. The first kind of research is on the cognitive level of perception and memory and on the linguistic level of the lexicon; it concerns color names. The second is on the cognitive level of logic and on the linguistic level of syntax; it concerns counterfactual conditionals. The third is on the cognitive level of unconscious inference and on the linguistic level of morphology; it concerns implicit causality. These three are the research stories to be told here. The order of their telling is the order in which they were begun. The first two were launched with expectations of relativity but have ended, if they can be said to have ended, with conclusions of cognitive universality. The third—still far from ended—began with expectations of universality and so, if this paper were to follow the current vogue for snappy subtitles, that subtitle would be, "Twice Bitten, Third Time Shy."

Colors and Lexicons

The statement of Whorf's position that is perhaps most general, explicit, and challenging is this one:

The categories and types that we isolate from the world of phenomena we do not find there because they stare every observer in the face; on the contrary the world is presented in a kaleidoscopic flux of impressions which has to be organized in our minds—and that means largely by the linguistic system in our minds. We cut nature up, organize it into concepts, and ascribe significances as we do, largely because we are partners to an agreement to organize it in this way—an agreement that holds throughout our speech community and is codified in the patterns of our language. (Whorf 1956, 213)

There is a recurrent metaphor in Whorf's papers: nature is a formless mass that each language with its grammatical categories and its lexicon "cuts up" or "dissects" in some arbitrary way. In actual fact, his most striking examples all involve inter-language comparisons of grammatical categories, but he did also provide some lexical examples. The most famous of these is: "We have the same word for falling snow, snow on the ground, snow packed hard like ice, slushy snow, wind-driven flying snow—whatever the situation may be. To an Eskimo, this all-inclusive word would be almost unthinkable; he would say that falling snow, slushy snow, and so on, are sensously and operationally different, different things to contend with; he uses different words for them and for other kinds of snow" (Whorf 1956, 216). The notion of language as a categorical system laid like an arbitrary grid upon an unformed reality would seem to fit particularly well the domain of color because, as has long been known, the languages of the world do not all make the same number of lexical cuts and place those they make at widely diverse points. Comparisons of the type pictured in figure 9.1 used to be routinely used by anthropologists to illustrate the arbitrariness of the English (and indeed Standard Average European) color lexicon.

Although figure 9.1 represents linguistic (lexical) facts only, it has cognitive implications that Whorf would not have hesitated to treat as conclusions. Perhaps, for instance, color discrimination is sharper on either side of a lexical boundary than it is within a single lexical domain and so the speaker of English would be better able to distinguish a yellow on one side of his lexical cut from an orange on the other side than would a speaker of either Shona or Bassa for whom no cuts are found in this region. The existence of a physical metric underlying hue would make possible a particularly elegant experiment with pairs of monochromatic lights falling on opposite sides of lexical lines for subjects who speak one language and on the same side of the nearest line for subjects who speak another.

Or there might be differences of recognition memory. A speaker of English shown a blue light or color chip and later asked to identify it in a large and varied array might confuse the blue seen with other blues but should not, as a speaker of Shona might, confuse it with any green and certainly should not confuse it with a purple, as a Bassa might. The prediction of differential recognition derives from the idea that a test color shown and then removed would probably be encoded linguistically and a blue would be more "codable" in English than in either Bassa or Shona. The particular blue could, of course, be named or encoded in all three

English:

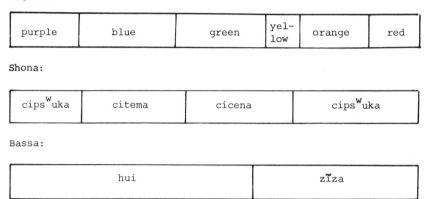

Shona:

Bassa:

Fig. 9.1. Lexical mappings of the color spectrum in three languages (from Gleason 1961, 4).

languages but for speakers of English it would be maximally "codable" in the sense that the name would be simple (monolexemic), would be quickly supplied (short reaction time), would be the same for all speakers and the same for one speaker from occasion to occasion.

In 1954, Brown and Lenneberg did an experiment to test the proposed general relation between linguistic codability and color recognition. They arrived at their prediction that codability and recognition would be positively correlated by a line of thought somewhat less modern and also somewhat less clear than that described above and yet in essentials the same. What must seem strange, however, in view of the fact that the experiment was inspired by differences between languages and by the general thesis of linguistic relativity is the fact that it involved native speakers of English only. Figure 9.1 invites us to compare the codabilities in different languages of the same colors, e.g., a yellow and an orange in English where they are in distinct lexical categories and in Shona or Bassa where they are in the same category. Brown and Lenneberg guessed that it should be possible to study the relationship between codability and recognition with speakers of one language by using different colors—some highly codable in that language (English) such as a good central blue or green and some less codable such as a marginal blue-green that might be called *bluish-green* or *greenish-blue* (not monolexemic names) with a longer temporal delay than would be involved with a good central blue or green, and with less variation across persons and occasions in names supplied. The relation between codability and recognition ought, Brown and Lenneberg reasoned, to be completely general with the same colors differentially codable across languages and different colors not differentially codable in the same language.

Twenty-four Munsell color chips were used for naming and for recognition of which 8 were selected as "best" examples of red, orange, yellow, green, purple, pink, and brown and 16 were selected so as to sample the full spectrum in a systematic way. It was implicit in the thinking of these investigators that the eight best examples, the eight most codable colors in English, surely would not be the best and most codable examples for human beings generally.

There were two procedures with distinct groups of Harvard and Radcliffe students. To get codability scores the colors were shown one at a time and subjects were to name them as rapidly as possible. The eight "best" tended to elicit the familiar monolexemic color words (*blue, green, red*, etc.) from all subjects and with little delay. The remaining 16 elicited a variety of qualified terms (*light green, blue-green*), object-based terms (*lime, avocado, plum*), and special-interest terms (*turquoise, aqua, puce*) varying from subject to subject and produced only after an interval. The several indices of codability were all highly correlated but consensus across speakers was in some ways best and served as the basis for the codability score assigned each chip. In the second procedure, the recognition task, subjects first saw one or more chips and then, after an interval, were asked to identify it (or them) in a systematic array of 120 colors. There were four recognition conditions designed to vary the difficulty of the retention task. In the easiest, only one color was exposed and recognition was tested after just seven seconds. In the most difficult case, four colors had to be retained for three minutes during which the subject was occupied with an unrelated task. In all four conditions codability was positively related to recognition accuracy and the relationship was significant in all but the simplest condition.

Brown and Lenneberg demonstrated that a linguistic variable (codability) rooted in the color lexicon was correlated with a cognitive variable—recognition accuracy. They thought they had, more generally, demonstrated, and are more often credited with having demonstrated, linguistic relativity in the domain of color recogition. And there the matter—not completely, but more or less—rested until 1972 when Eleanor Rosch Heider, who took her doctorate at Harvard where she had worked with Brown among others, exactly reversed the interpretation of the 1954 findings.

Heider determined the codability of the 24 test colors for speakers of, not English only, but for speakers of 23 different languages divided among seven language families, and it turned out that the eight best colors that had been most codable in English were also most codable in all languages studied. Heider also studied recognition in a particularly instructive case: the Dugum Dani, a Stone Age people of New Guinea. The Dani have just two color terms and with these they partition the entire color space: *mili* for dark and "cold" hues, centering on black; *mola* for the complementary set of bright and "warm" hues, centering on white. There were, there could be, no variation in codability scores for the Dani; every chip was either *mili* or *mola,* and so it was interesting to ask whether the 24 test colors would all also be equally recognizable. They were not. The eight best colors, no more codable than any others, were nonetheless most accurately recognized.

The effect of Heider's two results was to transform relativity into universality. The English lexicon, which had been assumed to be one arbitrary dissection of the spectrum among many possible dissections, now seemed to be one lexicon among very many that were organized around the same set of best colors. The best colors, most codable in 25 languages, were also the most accurately recognized colors by speakers of a language (Dani) that had only a minimally differentiated lexicon and no variation of codability across colors. Therefore, it was not relative codability that accounted for relative accuracy of recognition. Rather, it seemed to be the case that certain colors had a universal salience in recognition which also served as anchoring points in the organization of color lexicons—most lexicons, anyway, but not that of the Dani which was a simple dichotomy. The Dani seem to be like the rest of the species as far as color recognition is concerned but oddly unlike everybody else with respect to color lexicon. They do, that is, until one enlarges the sample of lexicons.

Anthropologists Berlin and Kay (1969) studied color lexicons from 98 genetically diverse languages. They also studied the mappings of these lexicons on color space, and a beautiful regularity appeared. The eight common English terms for which Brown and Lenneberg had obtained best colors were: *red, orange, yellow, green, blue, purple, brown,* and *pink.* If we add the achromatic terms *black, gray,* and *white,* we have 11, and 11, Berlin and Kay discovered, is the largest number of basic color terms (defined by strict linguistic criteria) found in any language. The smallest number is, as with the Dani, two. But there are lexicons intermediate in differentiation with three terms, four, five, etc. The Dani lexicon, therefore, is from a world perspective simply the least differentiated end of a continuum that is maximally differentiated in English (and many other languages). This is a generalization but not a particularly beautiful one. The beauty derives from the discovery that when there are 11 terms or 2 terms or 3 or 5, it is always just the same 11, 2, 3, or 5. The same not in the exact location of these margins but rather in the best colors around which they are organized. And now it is time to change terminology and call these best colors by the name they have been known by, since Berlin and Kay christened them and found them to be cognitive universals: the focal colors.

The color terms in the languages constitute a partially ordered cumulative scale and are pictured as such in figure 9.2. One reads the scale from left to right, and the English words are to be understood as that term in whatever language that has the same focal color as does the corresponding English word. As a cumulative scale, figure 9.2 simply tells us that if a language has just two terms, they will center on focal white and black (Dani does); if three, the third will center on focal red; if four, either green or yellow; and if five, whichever of the two remains, etc. Berlin and Kay propose an interpretation of this scale that seems very natural: priority from left to right is to be understood as priority in time and so the scale, from left to right, is taken to represent an order of cultural evolution, evolution of color terms, and it is posited to be invariant or universal. There is reason to believe, Berlin and Kay tell us, that the temporally ordered stages of lexical development are positively correlated with general cultural and / or technological evolution. In 1979, Friedl reported an actual advance in lexicon differentiation made in modern times by a semi-nomadic tribe in southwest Iran, and that step was the step predicted by the evolutionary order.

In the domain of color, linguistic relativity (recognition as a function of arbitrary codability values) has given way to cognitive universality: 11 focal colors the same for all human beings are the most codable in all maximally evolved languages, but whether or not most codable, they are always most recognizable. The evidence of Heider (1972) and of Berlin and Kay (1969) is only the most decisive on this point; there is much more that supports the universalistic view that cognition shapes language. Heider and Olivier (1972) actually carried out the elegant experiment on color discrimination, anticipated for English, Bassa, and Shona, with pairs of hues on either side of a lexical cut for some subjects and the same pairs on the same side of a cut for other subjects. Heider and Olivier did the experiment comparing speakers of English and of Dani and found that lexical cuts do not determine acuity of discrimination. Bornstein, Kessen, and Weiskopf (1976) did a quite similar experiment using a habituation

Fig. 9.2.   The Berlin and Kay proposed universal order of evolution of color terms.

paradigm with four-month-old infants (definitely prelingual) and showed that there is some tendency to perceive color categorically, not in terms of the lexical cuts of a particular language but in terms of the organization of categories around the universal focal hues. Finally, DeValois and DeValois (1975) have identified classes of cells along the retinogeniculostriate pathway that are differentially sensitive to wavelengths in the blue-green-yellow and red appearing regions of the spectrum. And Bornstein (1975) has shown how this neurological model of color vision might account for the universal focals.

In the studies of color naming and color recognition (Bornstein 1976; Brown and Lenneberg 1954; Heider 1972; Heider and Olivier 1972; Lantz and Stefflre 1964; Stefflre, Vales, and Morley (1966), there are certain findings that suggest a residual role for language. In a recognition task, one or more colors is exposed and then removed for an interval after which it is to be identified in some large array of colors. Probably, as Bornstein has suggested (1976) the color(s) can be encoded over the interval in physical (image) form or in verbal form or in both. For the range of conditions studied (one color or four colors; retention intervals from five seconds to three minutes) the hypothesis that best fits the facts is that the two forms of encoding occur together but that the relative importance of the two changes with the complexity of the memory problem: imaginal encoding becoming less important as complexity increases and verbal encoding more important.

The simplest task is the one that has been most often used: one color is to be recognized after a few seconds. The full pattern of evidence suggests that in this case both kinds of encoding occur. The best evidence for physical coding is the fact that focal colors are better recognized than nonfocal colors by both speakers of English (Brown and Lenneberg 1954) and the Dani (Heider 1972; Heider and Olivier 1972), though the former group could use differential verbal encoding whereas the latter group presumably could not. Evidence for verbal encoding, in the simplest case and with the Brown-Lenneberg index of codability, is actually equivocal. The Brown-Lenneberg correlation between recognition accuracy and codability was +.248, positive but not significant, and the correlation for the same measures obtained by Lantz and Stefflre (1964) was actually −.02.

However, Bornstein, using a different but equally simple recognition task, did find a clear encoding effect. He first identified for each subject a monochromatic light somewhere between blue and green that was the point of subjective equality (PSE). He then used that light as a standard to be held in memory and asked whether or not it was the same as each of four lights on the blue side of equality and also each of four on the green side. Bornstein's variable was the name he assigned the PSE; he called it *bluish* half the time and *greenish* half the time. He found that a single light at the psychophysical PSE was equated with greener lights when called *greenish* and bluer when called *bluish*. He concluded, "Here is confirmation of Brown and Lenneberg's (1954) observation that labels for categories serve to stabilize mental images" (Bornstein 1976, 275).

Bornstein's is not the only experiment finding evidence of verbal encoding in the simplest recognition task. Stefflre and his associates (Lantz and Stefflre 1964; Stefflre, Vales, and Morley 1966) found a very strong verbal encoding effect when they characterized the Brown-Lenneberg colors in terms of "communication accuracy" rather than codability. To get communication accuracy scores, some 10 to 20 speakers of a language are, as in the Brown-Lenneberg procedure, asked individually to name each color. In a second step, the names given each particular color are offered, one at a time, to new subjects, decoders, who are asked to try to retrieve from a large array the particular chip that had inspired the name. Each color chip gets a communication accuracy score based on the average error associated with the set of names assigned it. The idea is that verbal encoding for retention is a find of intrapersonal communication and that an index of interpersonal communication accuracy for members of one language community can serve as an approximation of the memory process. When Lantz and Stefflre correlated communication accuracy with simplest-case recognition scores, they obtained a significant value of .51 and so evidence of verbal encoding.

The reason for thinking that verbal encoding grows more important as the complexity of the retention task increases derives from a set of variations in complexity carried out with codability and communication accuracy. Brown and Lenneberg (1954) increased complexity in four steps from one color to be retained for seven seconds to four colors to be retained for three minutes, and the size of the codability–recognition accuracy correlation rose with each increment of complexity: from .248 to .523. Lantz and Stefflre carried out a very similar series with communication accuracy, and their correlations rose from .51 to .78. Communication accuracy always suggests a larger role for verbal encoding than does codability, but with either index the evidence is that verbal encoding becomes more important as the memory task is made more difficult.

The evidence that verbal encoding plays a role in color recognition is quite consistent, but verbal encoding does not necessarily imply linguistic relativity. Since the color lexicons of the world's languages are all fitted to just the same set of focal hues, probably determined by the neurology of color vision, it is reasonable to expect that recognition accuracy scores will prove to be correlated with, for example, communication accuracy scores in every language but also that communication accuracy scores in any one language will be highly, perhaps perfectly, correlated with such scores in any other language. Thus would cognition in the form of the universal focals be the ultimate determinant. There is actually a relevant study, neither recent nor well known. It was done by Stefflre, Vales, and Morley (1966) in Merida with speakers of Spanish and with speakers of Mayan Yucatec. Communication accuracy scores significantly predicted recognition accuracy for each group: Spanish speakers .588; Yucatec speakers .448. The communication accuracy scores for the two languages were positively related (.113), but not significantly so.

The Spanish-Yucatec comparison looks like evidence for linguistic relativity, but it is difficult to say just how strong the evidence is because communication accuracy, a behavioral index, is not a fact about the comparative structures of the languages in question. It is an index that must certainly be affected by the color lexicon but not by the lexicon alone. Imagine the problem of trying to communicate to a speaker of your language a particular shade of green—not focal. The existence or not of a term *green* that includes the focal will be one factor affecting the accuracy with which you can do the job, but probably more important will be the location of the margins of the green category, and Berlin and Kay found much variation in hue margins in the languages they studied, enough to suggest that such variation probably helps keep the Spanish-Yucatec correlation low, a kind of linguistic relativity. Another factor affecting precise color naming must be the resources available in a language for qualifying (*dark* or *bright green*) and compounding (*green-blue*), and this factor also would be a kind of linguistic relativity. Finally, however, color names also depend on the nonlinguistic world. If there is a certain nonprecious stone of just the required shade of green, say malachite, then the encoding problem is solved and accuracy guaranteed for members of one community but not necessarily for members of the other, and the reason for the difference is not linguistic. The probability is, then, that the Spanish-Yucatec study does offer evidence of a degree of linguistic relativity, but what sort of evidence and how much is well hidden in the omnibus index called "communication accuracy."

Counterfactual Conditionals in English and Chinese

In 1972–1973, a young Harvard psychologist named Alfred Bloom was in Hong Kong administering a questionnaire designed to investigate political thinking. He asked the following question in his interviews: "If the government had passed a law requiring that all citizens born outside of Hong Kong make weekly reports of their activities to the police, how would you have reacted?" Since he was interviewing speakers of Chinese, it was not this question he asked but rather its Chinese (Cantonese) equivalent. Bloom is himself bilingual in Chinese and English, and he made his own translations. This particular Chinese translation, however, regularly elicited a surprising answer. One Chinese-speaking interviewee after another, upon being asked how he would have reacted if the Hong Kong government had passed a certain law, answered: "It hasn't."

Bloom's experience with his questionnaire was the starting point of a program of research that eventuated in his 1981 book, *The Linguistic Shaping of Thought: A Study in the Impact of Language on Thinking in China and the West.* In 1983, the *Journal of Asian Studies* published an extremely enthusiastic review of Bloom's book by Benjamin A. Elman of Kyoto University: "It is clear that we can no longer be armchair linguists pontificating about the 'Chinese mind' or the 'Western mind.' Bloom has demonstrated that what we have long suspected to be the case can be evaluated and measured with a great deal of precision" (1983, 613).

Bloom's work is the only empirical study of linguistic relativity that is on the level of generality, imaginativeness, and consequentiality of Whorf's essays. The studies of the counterfactual conditional that developed out of the experience with the questionnaire involve language on the level of syntax and thought on the level of logic. These are levels more representative of Whorf's speculation than are the color lexicon and color recognition, and yet they are only a part of Bloom's book which considers other complex constructions and ultimately Western and Chinese world views. The work on the counterfactuals seems at this writing to have been disconfirmed by Terry Kit-fong Au (1983), but that should not detract from our recognition of Bloom's achievement in finding ways to put some fascinating questions to empirical test.

The questionnaire sentence about the Hong Kong government carries a counterfactual conditional meaning. It states a premise (or condition or supposition) and asks about a conclusion; that is the conditional part. At the same time, the sentence negates the premise or condition; that is the counterfactual part. In English, the counterfactual meaning and the conditional meaning are not expressed in sequentially distinct clauses or sentences but are simultaneously expressed with "if . . . then" and the verbs in what is (loosely) called the subjunctive mode. The linguistic mechanism can be more effectively dissected if we use simple declarative sentences as examples rather than the question about Hong Kong.

A simple conditional $(p \supset q)$ is expressed in English by starting the suppositional clause with *If* and the main clause with *then*, though *then* is optional and often omitted, and putting the verb in the appropriate tense: "If interest rates go down, (then) housing will recover." Suppose one asks, "Have interest rates gone down" or "Will interest rates go down?" The appropriate answer, given only the conditional sentence, is "I have no idea." Let us say instead, "If interest rates were to go down, (then) housing would recover" or, alternatively, "If interest rates had gone down, then housing would have recovered." Suppose now one asks, "Have interest rates at this time gone down?" The appropriate answer is "No, they have not." The subjunctive verb forms ("were . . . would;" "had . . . would have") signal the contrary-to-fact status of the supposition. This construction asks us to entertain implications of premises not now true. In English it is a simple, compact construction. Bloom's study of Chinese grammar lead him to believe that things are otherwise arranged in that language.

In Chinese, the form *ru guo* identifies a supposition, and *jiu* is the word for *then*. This form is used in implicational sentences which imply nothing about truth value, and it is also used in counterfactual cases. One might hear the equivalent of *"ru guo* President Carter had not admitted the Shah of Iran into the United States, *jiu* Carter would have been re-elected" with the contrary-to-fact premise not marked linguistically. The speaker might, nevertheless, expect a listener to arrive at a counterfactual reading because the listener might reasonably be expected to know the facts. When the listener or reader cannot be expected to know the facts, Chinese does mark the supposition as contrary to fact but does so not with a verb form but in an independent statement. Thus: "James not speak Chinese. *Ru guo* James speak Chinese, *jiu* James get a good job in American Embassy, Hong Kong." Very like: "~ p; p ⊃ q."

In Hong Kong and in Taiwan, Bloom formed the impression that while the Chinese language, of course, provides a construction for the explicit expression of counterfactual conditionals, the construction is rarely used. He reports making a content analysis of a Taiwan newspaper over a period of three weeks and finding only a single instance of the construction, and that instance was in a translation of a speech made by Henry Kissinger. His Chinese informants, many of them scholars, told him that there was something "un-Chinese" about counterfactual reasoning. Certainly there is nothing "un-American" about such reasoning. We do it all the time. For instance, any major unhappy event on the national level (an election lost, an assassination attempted) or on the personal level (an illness, an accident, a quarrel) elicits a flow of counterfactuals of the post mortem type: "If it were not for the hostages. . . ." "If Senator Kennedy had just declared sooner. . . ." "If I had put on the snow tires yesterday. . . ." We positively go in for working out the implications of contrary-to-fact suppositions, and Bloom's impression was that the Chinese considered this to be a rather bootless business. He speculated that the compact English construction used for counterfactuals somehow encouraged the creation of an integrated, easily triggered schema for counterfactual thought in a way that the separate sequential clauses in Chinese did not.

To test his hypothesis, Bloom made up certain story problems in both English and Chinese. Something was first established as not the case. Then, from that contrary-to-fact something, a series of implications were drawn.

Finally, with the story in front of them, readers read the implications and were to mark those that were factually true or else to indicate that none of them could be said to be true and to explain why this was so. They ought to have said none were true since all were marked as counterfactual. Here is one story in English and also the questions that followed it:

Bier was an Eighteenth Century European philosopher who wanted very much to investigate the principles of the universe and the laws of nature. Because there was some contact between China and the West at that time, works of Chinese philosophy could be found in Europe, but very few had been translated. Bier could not read Chinese, but if he had been able to read Chinese, he would have discovered that those Chinese philosophical works were relevant to his own investigations. What would have most influenced him would have been the fact that Chinese philosophers, in describing natural phenomena, generally focused on the interrelationships between such phenomena, while Western philosophers by contrast generally focused on the description of such phenomena as distinct individual entities. Once influenced by that Chinese perspective, Bier would then have synthesized Western and Chinese views and created a new philosophical theory which focuses on natural phenomena both in terms of their mutual interrelationships and as individual entities. He would have overcome a weakness in Western philosophical thought of that Century and, moreover, deeply influenced German, French and Dutch philosophers, encouraging Western philosophy to take a step forward and at the same time approach more closely to science.

Please indicate, by choosing *one or more* of the following answers what contribution or contributions Bier made to the West, according to the paragraph above:

1. Bier led Western philosophy to pay attention to natural phenomena as individual entities.
2. He led Western philosophy to pay attention to the mutual interrelationships among natural phenomena.
3. He led European philosophy closer to science.
4. He led Western philosophy one step closer to Chinese philosophy.
5. None of these answers are appropriate. (Please explain your own opinion briefly.)

In the story about the philosopher Bier, in the sentence beginning "Bier could not read Chinese, but if he had been able to read Chinese, he would have . . ." we have the signals of the counterfactual condition:

"if . . . had + *past particle* . . . would have. . . ." Besides these signals, the sentence explicitly asserts "~ p": "Bier could not read Chinese." In the rest of the paragraph, we find one implication after another all marked as counterfactual by the form *would have:* "would have discovered," "would have most influenced him," "would have been the fact," "would then have synthesized," and "would have overcome." *Would have, would have, would have*—and so, to the reader of English, did not. Which means that none of the statements 1 through 4 can be endorsed. One must check 5. None of the answers offered is appropriate because the story does not say that Bier in fact, did any of the things listed but only that he would have if he had been able to read Chinese.

When 55 Americans, both students and nonstudents, read the paragraph about Bier, 98% checked the fifth alternative and, in nontechnical terms, explained why. When, however, a Chinese translation was read by 120 native speakers of Chinese in Taiwan and Hong Kong, only 7% gave counterfactual interpretations. How did they explain their answers? A great many said that by the end of the story they had lost track of the fact that Bier could not read Chinese. About the same number said that they remembered Bier could not read Chinese, but when so many implications were spelled out they concluded that the author must intend them to be understood as true. "Otherwise, why write it?" The counterfactual realm does seem to be un-Chinese. Not in the sense that the Chinese are *unable* to think about contrary-to-fact matters and to draw out contrary-to-fact implications but rather in the sense that it is not a congenial, familiar way of thinking.

The Bier story quoted here (called "Version Two") does not in its Chinese version absolutely exclude conclusions 1 through 4. The story says of works of Chinese philosophy that "very few had been translated." Those very few translated works constitute a narrow but possible channel of communication from Chinese philosophy to a Bier who could not read Chinese. To be sure, the implications that follow all take the form *ru guo . . . jiu* ("if . . . then") and so build on a premise that has been said to be untrue, but since the Chinese verb is not marked for counterfactuality (as the English verb is), conclusions 1 through 4 could be taken as true in the Chinese story but not in the English story. Bloom's Version Two of the Bier story was intended to permit either interpretation in Chinese and so to expose a predilection for the factual over the counterfactual. However, Bloom also wrote a third version of the Bier story which might be said to "plug the leak" in Version Two and make more salient for Chinese readers the counterfactual logic. In Version Three, no works of Chinese philosophy had been translated. This story was read by 102 native speakers of Chinese in Hong Kong and Taiwan and by 52 native speakers of English. As Bloom had predicted, the more salient counterfactual logic made no difference to English-speaking subjects (96% counterfactual answers) but significantly increased the counterfactual responses of Chinese-speaking subjects (50%). There remained a large significant difference between the two groups.

There is a third piece of evidence using the Bier stories which Bloom finds most compelling of all. Some (21) of the Taiwanese who had marked the fifth alternative to Version Two of the Bier story only 6% of the time spoke English as well as Chinese and spoke it every day in their businesses. They were all nonstudents. Three months after the first reading, Bloom contacted them again and gave them Version Three in English. Of the 21 bilinguals who read in English this story of counterfactual implications, 86% rejected all of the implications as untrue and checked the fifth alternative. Apparently, it is possible for someone who thinks as a Chinese when using the Chinese language to think as a speaker of English when using that language. To be sure, the story in English was the leak-proof Version Three whereas the story in Chinese had been Version Two, but the 86% counterfactual responses to Version Three in English is significantly above the 55% obtained from a comparable group when Version Three was in Chinese.

Bloom's work on counterfactual reasoning fascinated me, and soon after reading about it I described it with great enthusiasm in a course at Harvard. I also tried the effect of Bloom's stories in Chinese with several local informants. One of my informants was Terry Kit-fong Au, an undergraduate concentrator in psychology, born in Hong Kong, whose first language is Chinese. Au made no mistakes herself and furthermore doubted that there really was a difference in the availability of counterfactual reasoning that depended on whether one was thinking in English or in Chinese. For her undergraduate honors thesis, she designed a set of experiments to be conducted with Hong Kong subjects bilingual in Chinese and English. Eventually, Au had 989 subjects, which probably sets a numerical record for an honors thesis; we think of it as a Chinese "n."

Au has written an article reporting all her results (1983) so I will be very selective here. Most of Bloom's work compares speakers of English in the United States with speakers of Chinese in either Hong Kong or Taiwan, and while there is no clear reason to expect culture to make a difference in comprehension of the Bier stories (all subjects lived in cities and were about equal in schooling), the fact remains that in these studies language and culture are confounded. The more powerful design using bilinguals in a single culture who receive the problem in English or in Chinese was used once, but the design was less than ideal. In Au's studies comparing problem solving in English and in Chinese, all subjects were bilinguals in the same culture: Anglo-Chinese secondary schools in Hong Kong. Subjects (aged 15 to 25) had studied English as a second language for about 12 years. They were always randomly assigned on an individual level to receive materials in Chinese or else in English.

The Bier story (both Version Two and Version Three) seemed to Au, as indeed it does to most people, convoluted in structure and esoteric in subject matter. She thought it possible that a more concrete and "lively" story that retained the counterfactual structure would not show so great an English language–Chinese language difference simply because the story as such would be more readily understood. She composed the following undeniably "good" tale, "Human Broth."

Once a Dutch explorer ventured into Central Africa and saw a tribe of natives gathered around a fire. Hoping to make some interesting discoveries, this Dutch explorer held his breath and observed the natives attentively from behind the bushes. He heard one of the natives shout in a language which he unfortunately did not know. He then saw the natives throw a dead human body into a big pot of boiling water. And when the "human broth" was done, the natives all hurried to drink some of it. Upon seeing this event, the explorer was absolutely astonished, and fled as soon as he could. If this explorer had been able to understand the language spoken by the natives and had not fled so quickly, he would have learnt that the dead native was actually a hero of the tribe, and was killed in an accident. The explorer would also have learnt that the natives drank the "broth" of their hero because they believed that only by doing so could they acquire the virtues of their hero. If this explorer had been able to understand the language spoken by the natives and had not fled so quickly, he would have learnt that the natives were very friendly, and were not cruel and savage as he thought.

Please indicate, by choosing *one or more* of the following answers, which thing or things about the natives the Dutch explorer knew according to the above paragraph:

1. The dead native was a hero of the tribe.
2. The dead native was killed in an accident.
3. The natives believed that they could acquire a dead hero's virtues only by boiling the dead hero's body in water and then drinking the "broth."
4. The natives were friendly and not cruel and savage as the Dutch explorer thought.
5. None of the above. (Please explain your opinion briefly.)

This story has exactly the same logical structure as Version Three of the Bier story. The English version reduces to: "A was not the case; if A had been the case, B would have been the case; C would have been the case. If A had been the case, D would have been the case." Premise A is explicitly negated and implications B, C, and D are stated but marked counterfactual in each instance by *would have*. The Chinese version of Human Broth has the same logical structure, but since the verb is not marked for counterfactuality, there are no repeated reminders that A is not the case. It reduces to: "A not being the case. If A being the case, then B will be the case; C will be the case. If A being the case, then D will be the case."

Some of Bloom's Chinese-speaking subjects told him they had accepted one or more implications as factual because by the time they got to the end of the story they had forgotten that premise A was not the case. Au noticed that this could hardly happen in the English story with the repeated *would haves*, but she also knew that English grammar permits the clauses containing *would have* to be deleted and so one could write "Human Broth" in a succinct form having the same logical structure but without the reminders of counterfactuality, which are absent from Chinese. To illustrate: ". . . he would have learnt that the dead native was actually a hero of the tribe, and was killed in an accident. The explorer would also have learnt that the natives drank the broth of their hero . . ." becomes, making permissible deletions: ". . . he would have learnt that the dead native was actually a hero of the tribe and was killed in an accident; that the natives drank the broth of their hero. . . ." Au, therefore, wrote an English version of "Human Broth" that kept the three implications but reduced the *would have* cues to a single instance, and this story also was given to randomly selected Hong Kong subjects. If the memory factor were the important one in Bloom's original Chinese-English contrast, then the one-cue story should be more difficult than the multiple-cue story. If the concreteness and clarity of the story were important, then all results with "Human Broth" would be better (more often counterfactual) than Bloom's results with Bier.

The results were surprising. Au had expected to find Bloom's Chinese-English difference much reduced with the human broth story using multiple *would have* cues and still further reduced using a single cue. She had not, however, expected what she found: no evidence of any difficulty with counterfactual reasoning in any version of the story. Scores were effectively perfect (the range was 96% to 100%) whether the story was in Chinese or in a redundant English with multiple cues or a succinct English with a single cue. It seemed, therefore, that a control Au had thought she could do without was, after all, essential: Version Three of the Bier story in Chinese and in English must be administered to subjects in her population to see whether the original Chinese-English difference would be repeated. The result was 93% counterfactual answers for the English version and 88% counterfactual answers for the Chinese version, a difference that does not even approach significance. In effect, no version of either counterfactual story offered any difficulty to these bilingual students. The research question became, what could account for the difficulty Bloom's Chinese-speaking subjects had had with the Chinese version of the Bier story?

In all of Au's samples, the largest difference had been between "Human Broth" in Chinese (100% correct) and Bier in Chinese (88% correct). Several Chinese bilinguals, including Au, thought that there was a difference in the quality of the language in the two stories. The Chinese of "Human Broth" impressed them as fully idiomatic whereas the Chinese of the Bier story seemed to them quite unidiomatic. Bloom's Chinese version of the Bier story was written by a Chinese research assistant under Bloom's guidance as to context. It appeared to be possible that if the Bier story were revised so as to make it fully idiomatic, the 12% difference between the two stories in Chinese would be reduced. The story was revised, and everything was run once more with new samples from Hong Kong secondary schools. Once again, "Human Broth" in Chinese elicited 100% correct responses and the revised fully idiomatic Bier story was only slightly below with 97%.

It seems likely that an unidiomatic translation had contributed to the seeming deficiency associated in Bloom's studies with the Chinese language. That cannot, however, have been the only factor because the overall rate of correct answers he obtained for this Chinese story was only 55%. There are many possibilities. Au's subjects wrote their answers at school with their teachers present and so may have tried harder than did Bloom's adults. Bloom did his studies between 1975 and 1977, whereas Au did hers in 1981—the westernization of Hong Kong Chinese in that interval may have made counterfactual thought congenial. The instructions in Chinese which preceded the Bier story seemed to Au as unidiomatic as the story itself and that may have confused or annoyed subjects. Au weighs all these possibilities and finds an ingenious way to provide evidence on the degree of westernization hypothesis.

The Hong Kong Chinese westernized to the 1975 to 1977 level, when Bloom did his study, are gone forever; adult Chinese who do not know any English are superabundant on the mainland but hard to find in Hong Kong. What could be found in 1981, however, were Hong Kong young people whose knowledge of English did not yet extend to the subjunctive counterfactual, and one could see whether such young people—monolingual with respect to the construction of interest—had more problems with counterfactual reasoning than the secondary school children. This time, subjects were 12 to 15 years old rather than 15 to 21. Their knowledge of the English subjunctive was tested at Time 1 by asking for a simple translation from Chinese to English: "Mrs. Wong does not know English. If Mrs. Wong knew English she *would* be able to read English." With a very liberal definition of the subjunctive that accepted *could, would, would have,* etc., only one student could be credited with knowledge of the subjunctive. At Time 2, one month later, the same students were given "Human Broth" in Chinese in a version developing just one counterfactual implication (not described here) which had also been given to secondary-school students. The secondary school students (presumed to know the English subjunctive) gave 99% correct counterfactual answers; the younger students (ignorant of the subjunctive on the evidence of the translation test) gave 98% correct counterfactual responses. Evidently, knowledge of the English counterfactual construction is not a necessary condition for correct counterfactual reasoning on story problems presented in Chinese.

The possibility that unidiomatic materials can introduce noise that causes the performance of one set of subjects but not the other to be unrepresentative of real logical competence inspired Au to a language and thought study originating on the Asian side of the Pacific. What if, she reasons, showing no impairment of counterfactual thought, a Chinese psychologist had undertaken a Chinese-English contrast using the Bier story?

Version Three of the Bier story, in the fully idiomatic form, was translated into English by two Chinese bilinguals who had studied English for about 12 years. The translations were judged to be similar in content to the original but less idiomatic. These two story problems (others also, for which see Au 1983) were administered to monolingual speakers of English, aged 15 to 18, in a public high school in the United States. To account for the unidiomatic English, subjects were told (truly) that some stories had been written by Hong Kong high school students.

The less idiomatic translation of the two used is quoted here just to show the kind of thing that can happen:

Bier was a German philosopher in the 18th century. To study about the theory of the Great Harmony and the laws of nature was his greatest interest. In those days, the communication between China and Europe had already developed to some extent. Chinese works could be found in Europe but the translations of them were still not available. If Bier had known about the technique to master the Chinese language, he would certainly discover the different attitudes between the Chinese philosophers and the European philosophers when describing the natural phenomena: the Chinese stressed the interrelationships among these aspects while the European ignored them and studied each aspect separately. Suppose Bier had learnt about Chinese philosophy, he would certainly develop his own theory, which included not only a thorough study about the nature of natural phenomena, but also a clear explanation of the relations among various natural aspects. Such theory not only patched up the disadvantages of the Western philosophy, but also influenced deeply and furthered the development of philosophy in Germany, France, and Holland toward science.

From the above article, what new influence had Bier brought to the West? Please choose *one or more* of the following answers:

1. Awakened the consciousness of the Western philosophers about the nature of natural phenomana.
2. Awakened the consciousness of the Western philosophers about the interrelationships among the natural phenomena.
3. Pushed the European philosophy a step towards science.
4. Pushed the Western philosophy a step towards Chinese philosophy.
5. None of the above. (Please explain your opinion briefly.)

Notice that the counterfactual starts out in nearly perfect form with "If Bier had known . . . he would certainly discover. . . ." However, the verbs in the last two sentences have shed *would have;* it is Bier "included" and "patched up" and "influenced." It is not surprising then that some of the English-speaking subjects thought some of the implications were factual.

Back in Hong Kong, our imaginary Chinese psycholinguist receives the result for the English language version of the Bier story which is 60% correct for the two translations combined, and he compares this outcome with the result obtained in China with the original: 97% counterfactual answers. The difference is highly significant. The conclusion is that the Chinese language facilitates thinking in the counterfactual mode whereas English makes it difficult.

I do not say, of course, that Bloom's original result can be explained by an unidiomatic translation (nor does Au), but her demonstration that an unidiomatic translation can produce results that might be interpreted as differences in cognitive competence is directly relevant to Whorf's (1956) original arguments in favor of linguistic relativity. The evidence he offered was very often no more than a juxtaposition of some English construction with a very literal translation from some American Indian language: Hopi, Zuni, Shawnee, Nootka, or Apache. For instance, where English makes a sequence of free forms to say "he invites people to a feast," the Nootka language of Vancouver Island makes affixations to a basic verb stem to yield something that might be literally translated as "boiled eaters go for [he] does." How very unlike our way of thinking, Whorf seems to say. As strange as the Apache way of saying "it is a dripping spring," which Whorf translates as "as water or springs whiteness moves downward." Critics of

Whorf's evidence (e.g., Brown 1958; Lenneberg, 1953) long ago made the point that nothing about Nootka cognition can be inferred on the basis of such translations alone; it is necessary to study directly relevant cognitive structures or processes in speakers of the languages contrasted. What the English and Chinese demonstration shows, in addition, is that if the cognitive research employs linguistic materials that are idiomatic in one language but not in the other, the results may still be misleading.

The comparative research on counterfactual reasoning started, as did the work on color names and color recognition, in a spirit of linguistic relativity and with evidence to sustain it, but it has come to a (not necessarily final) conclusion of cognitive universality. Counterfactual logical competence seems to be the same for speakers of English and speakers of Chinese once the noise of unidiomatic translation (and probably other situational factors) is removed. Differences of performance caused by problems of translation are not interesting, but I do not think that all differences of performance are as uninteresting as some of the literature on competence seems to suggest. It would, for instance, be very interesting if Bloom's initial observation were true, that counterfactual reasoning is somehow "un-Chinese"—recall what scholar informants told him and also his content analyses of a Taiwan newspaper over a three-week period. It would be interesting if counterfactual reasoning were un-Chinese, not as a logical competence but as a cultural tendency. It would be interesting, indeed, if the Taiwanese or citizens of Hong Kong or mainland China do not "go in for" counterfactual post mortems in the way that Americans do or if their social thought and scientific thought somehow manage without counterfactual reasoning as this present paper, which is filled with subjunctives, presumably could not. A cultural difference of this kind, essentially a frequency of performance difference, even if not linguistically caused, would still be important. I do not, however, think that Bloom's observations suffice to establish such a difference.

Now that so much has been clarified by the work of Bloom and Au, I have a hypothesis as to how the appearance of a cultural difference in counterfactual reasoning could have been produced. The Chinese counterfactual construction that first negates a premise ($\sim$ p) and then expresses a conditional (p $\supset$ q) is used only when it cannot be taken for granted that addressees know the premise to be false (e.g., when an unknown Mrs. Wong does not know English). Premises that are known to be counterfactual are not linguistically negated; e.g., "I being President, I will work hard for arms control." In English, however, the subjunctive is obligatory not only when a premise really needs to be negated but also in the very many cases where it does not. To be sure, not all speakers would say, "If I were President, I would . . ."; many, less schooled or less pedantic, would say, "If I was President, I would. . . ." But *were* is not the essential form; it is *would* or *could* or *would have* that invariably marks the counterfactual conditional, and we speakers of English use it even when the counterfactuality is obvious and the marking of the verb is not really necessary. One cannot say, "If I am President, then I will . . ." without it being understood that the presidency is a real possibility. This extended obligatory use of "If were (was) then would (could)" where Chinese uses only *ru guo* and *jiu* ("if . . . then") could easily give the impression that speakers of English very frequently think counterfactually whereas speakers of Chinese rarely do so. What the actual case may be has not been determined but, with so much ground cleared by Bloom and Au, is easily determinable.

Implicit Causality

My current research is on the psychological causality implicit in language, and the problem of language and thought has once again arisen. The discovery that certain English verbs carry a semantic feature of causal attribution that assigns greater causal weight to one argument of the verb than to the other was made by Garvey, Caramazza, and their associates (1974, 1976, 1977). These investigators have studied the role of implicit causality in sentence processing and in pronoun disambiguation. Brown and Fish (1983) have recently made a further discovery about implicit causality in English verbs: the division of causal weighting between verb arguments is predictable from facts of English morphology (the rules for word formation).

The first paper-and-pencil task used by Brown and Fish goes like this.

Ted likes Paul.

How likely is it that this is because:

A. Ted is the kind of person that likes people.

   Not likely 1 2 3 4 5 6 7 8 9 Definitely likely

B. Paul is the kind of person that people like.

   Not likely 1 2 3 4 5 6 7 8 9 Definitely likely

C. Some other reason.

   Not likely 1 2 3 4 5 6 7 8 9 Definitely likely

You are asked to rate each of these explanations on how likely it is to have caused the stated event. Do so by circling the appropriate numbers.

What varies from problem to problem is the verb. Interest centers on alternatives A and B, and the question is which argument of the predicate (Ted or Paul) is assigned the greater causal weight and whether there is any lawful consistency in the apportioning of causality between the two arguments. In their first study, Brown and Fish used 36 verbs, all transitive and all acceptable in the context Ted_____Paul or Sue_____Anne or, for that matter, A_____B. The list includes *help, harm, disobey, charm, attract, deceive, like, honor,* and *detest.*

All of the 36 verbs used form bases in English for derived adjectives: *help-helpful; compete-competitive; charm-charming; like-likable.* If we take the depicting sentence (e.g., *Ted helps Paul; Ted likes Paul*) and ask the causal question, "Why?", then acceptable minimal answers are provided by the respective derived adjectives—because *Ted is helpful* and because *Paul is likeable.* Between the two adjectives in this example there is an important difference; *helpful* is attributive to, or predicative of, *Ted,* the sentence subject, whereas *likable* is attributive to *Paul,* the sentence object. English seems not to have a dispositional adjective based on *help* attributive to the sentence object (the person helped); we have no form *helpable.* English seems also not to have an adjective based on *like* that is attributive to the subject (the person who likes; we have neither *likeful* nor *liking* as an adjective). Each of the 36 verbs, in short, has an adjective attributive to one argument of the verb but no adjective attributive in this way to the other argument. The argument for which an attributive adjective existed was in all cases the argument assigned the greater causal weight in the rating task and, as can be seen in table 9.1, the mean differences were significant for 30 of 36 verbs, often highly significant.

The 36 verbs of the first task were selected because they had only one derived adjective attributive to either the subject or object argument, and that derived form had to meet a frequency criterion of one-or-more occurrences per million in the Kučera and Francis (1967) computational analysis in English. The method of selection was to enter the Kučera and Francis alphabetical list at 36 random points and move through the list until finding a derived form of the targeted type; the verb base for the form was then added to the list. There was, of course, a reason for selecting twice as many cases (24) in which the derived form was attributive to the sentence subject as cases attributive to the sentence object, but the explanation must be deferred until a later point. It may, however, be useful to say here that the grammatical role of the verb arguments—subject or object—has nothing to do with the explanation of the result. The rating task for the 36 verbs was carried out by another 20 subjects with the depicting sentences in the passive voice (*Paul is helped by Ted; Paul is liked by Ted*) and, exactly as in table 9.1, the greater causal weight was assigned the argument having a derived adjective—whether subject or object.

Brown and Fish report results with the 36 verbs using four convergent procedures. Besides direct causal ratings in the active voice and in the passive voice, a questionnaire required judgments based on the Kelley (1967) ANOVA analysis of attribution. Finally, a free, causal-listing questionnaire offered the depicting sentence followed by the question "Why?"

Table 9.1   Causal Weightings for Two Classes of Verbs

Class A	Derived Adjective Attributive to Object	Subject Mean	Object Mean
apologize to	apologetic	5.65	3.2 **
cheat	cheating	7.7	4.4 ***
compete with	competitive	7.7	5.35***
criticize	critical	6.95	4.5 ***
defy	defiant	6.2	4.0 **
disobey	disobedient	5.6	5.15
dominate	dominant	7.55	6.7
flatter	flattering	7.4	6.1 **
harm	harmful	6.7	3.4 ***
help	helpful	7.6	5.15***
protect	protective	6.65	5.45*
slander	slanderous	6.9	3.75***
astonish	astonishing	6.65	3.8 ***
attract	attractive	6.85	3.95***
charm	charming	7.2	3.25***
deceive	deceptive	7.15	4.4 ***
delight	delightful	6.2	3.9 ***
exasperate	exasperating	6.5	4.4 ***
impress	impressive	7.3	4.1 ***
influence	influential	7.15	5.8
repel	repellent	5.7	5.05
scorn	scornful	6.05	4.7 *
shock	shocking	6.2	4.45**
trouble	troublesome	6.2	3.95***

Class B	Derived Adjective Attributive to Object	Subject Mean	Object Mean
abhor	abhorrent	4.05	5.5 *
admire	admirable	4.1	8.05***
despise	despicable	4.2	6.05**
detest	detestable	3.2	6.15***
dread	dreadful	3.8	6.15**
enjoy	enjoyable	5.8	6.75
esteem	estimable	4.2	7.2 ***
honor	honorable	4.05	7.0 **
like	likable	5.7	7.05**
loathe	loathsome	3.8	6.25***
notice	noticeable	5.3	7.2 ***
pity	pitiable	5.15	6.25

S>O or O>S $p \leq .05^*$ $p \leq .01^{**}$ $p \leq .001^{***}$

(*A likes B. Why?*), and instructions required the subject to say something explanatory in terms of either A or B but not both; the choice between A and B was taken to be the predicate argument assigned the greater weight. All four procedures yielded the same result: that argument of the verb for which there was a verb-based attributive adjective was assigned the greater causal weight.

Because certain facts about English morphology predict certain ways of thinking about causality in verbs, the results reported by Brown and Fish seem to be a Whorfian effect, a case of language affecting thought. The Whorfian argument would go like this. The English language, for whatever accidental reasons, has laid down adjectives based on verbs which are attributive to one or the other of two arguments, and wherever English has laid down an adjective, speakers of English assign the preponderant causal weight to the argument modified by the adjective. It is even possible to sketch a Whorfian processing model using the notion of priming within an associative network that includes both the verbs and their derived adjectives. It may be that when a particular verb (e.g., *help*) is activated by presentation of a sentence (e.g., *Ted helps Paul*), that activation flows to any adjective derived from the verb stored in long-term memory (e.g., *helpful*) and that the definition of the adjective (e.g., "the kind of person that helps people") stored with the adjective mediates the choice between alternative A, "Ted is the kind of person that helps people" and alternative B, "Paul is the kind of person that people help."

Brown and Fish, however, have argued that their effect probably is not a Whorfian one but is rather another instance of thought affecting language. The first part of their argument is a demonstration that the verb-based adjectives in question are not unsystematically or accidentally laid down but rather are laid down in a principled way. In order to state the principle, it is necessary to define a few terms.

The verbs involved belong to two distinct types: (1) state verbs, such as *like, charm, trouble,* and *notice,* name mental events that are conceived of as involuntary (according to various grammatical tests described by Miller and Johnson-Laird 1976; (2) action verbs, such as *help, harm, criticize,* and *cheat,* which name actions—in effect, behavior—and which are conceived of as voluntary.

The two arguments of state verbs are: (1) Stimulus—someone or something giving rise to a certain experience (e.g., *Paul* in *Ted likes Paul; Ted* in *Ted charms Paul*); (2) Experiencer—someone having a given experience (e.g., *Ted* in *Ted likes Paul; Paul* in *Ted charms Paul*).

The two arguments of action verbs are: (1) Agent—someone or something that instigates an action, usually animate, but not always (e.g., *Ted* in *Ted helps Paul*); (2) Patient—someone or something suffering a change of state (e.g., *Paul* in *Ted helps Paul*).

The principle that seems to have governed the derivation in English of adjectives from verbs naming person interaction is as follows: for action-verb bases, adjectives are derived that are attributive to the Agent, not the Patient. For state-verb bases, adjectives are derived for the Stimulus, not the Experiencer. This principle is followed by all 36 verbs used in the Brown and Fish experiments. In addition, these authors have shown (1983) that the principle is true very generally, though not exceptionlessly, of the total population of relevant English verbs.

In English, the Agents of the action verbs with which we are concerned (*help, criticize, flatter*, etc.) are, like the Agents of almost all action verbs, sentence subjects, and the Patients are sentence objects; these verbs constitute Brown and Fish's Class I. For the state verbs with which we are concerned, the Stimulus is sentence subject and the Experiencer sentence object with about half of all verbs (e.g., *charm, attract, repel*); these constitute Class II. For the remaining state verbs (about half of all of them) the Stimulus is sentence object and the Experiencer, subject (*like, detest, admire*); these constitute Class III. The results of table 9.1 are regrouped in table 9.2, in terms of Class I, Class II, and Class III. Now one can understand why, in table 9.1, there were 24 verbs with derived adjectives attributive to the subject and only 12 attributive to the object. The set of 24 (Class A in table 9.1) comprises Class I plus Class II, whereas the set of 12 (Class B in table 9.1) coincides exactly with Class III. In selecting a sample of verbs, the investigators picked the same number (12) from each of Classes I, II, and III.

The fact that verb-based adjectives are not unsystematically created but rather conform to a principle favoring Agent over Patient (action verbs) and Stimulus over Experiencer (state verbs) is the first step in the Brown and Fish argument that the implicit causality in verbs is a result of thought affecting language. The second step is recognition of the fact that a distinction between derivational adjectives that do and do not exist in English cannot, in fact, be made in linguistic terms; that is, in terms of a lexicon or grammar. The generative morphological system of English is not biased in favor of adjectives attributive to Agent and Stimulus and against adjectives attributive to Patient and Experiencer. All types are equally possible—gramatically. The suffixes *-ing* and *-able* are fully productive, and there is no linguistic reason (no rule of grammar) that prohibits the existence of *liking* as in a *liking person* or *helpable* in the sense of a person easy to help. As far as English grammar is concerned, adjectives attributive to Patient and Experiencer, such as *attractable, cheatable, charmable, detesting* (adj.), *loathing* (adj.), etc., are all "possible" words. Still, a distinction can be drawn between "existent" and "possible" words.

Perhaps the linguistic level involved is not morphological but lexical. Surely existent words are those one can find in the English lexicon, and

Table 9.2 Causal Weightings for Three Classes of Verbs

Class I: Agent-Patient Subject-Object	Subject Mean	Object Mean
apologize to	5.65	3.2 **
cheat	7.7	4.4 ***
compete with	7.7	5.35***
criticize	6.95	4.5 ***
defy	6.2	4.0 **
disobey	5.6	5.15
dominate	7.55	6.7
flatter	7.4	6.1 **
harm	6.7	3.4 ***
help	7.6	5.15***
protect	6.65	5.45*
slander	6.9	3.75***

Class II: Stimulus-Experiencer Subject-Object	Subject Mean	Object Mean
astonish	6.65	3.8 ***
attract	6.85	3.95***
charm	7.2	3.25***
deceive	7.15	4.4 ***
delight	6.2	3.9 ***
exasperate	6.5	4.4 ***
impress	7.3	4.1 ***
influence	7.15	5.8
repel	5.7	5.05
scorn	6.05	4.7 *
shock	6.2	4.45**
trouble	6.2	3.95***

Class III: Experiencer-Stimulus Subject-Object	Subject Mean	Object Mean
abhor	4.05	5.5 *
admire	4.1	8.05***
despise	4.2	6.05**
detest	3.2	6.15***
dread	3.8	6.15**
enjoy	5.8	6.75
esteem	4.2	7.2 ***
honor	4.05	7.0 **
like	5.7	7.05**
loathe	3.8	6.25***
notice	5.3	7.2 ***
pity	5.15	6.25

S>O or O>S $p \leq .05^{*}$ $p \leq .01^{**}$ $p \leq .001^{***}$

possible words are morphologically conceivable but not to be found in the lexicon. The problem is to locate that official Ultimate Lexicon. It cannot be the Oxford English Dictionary, which includes adjective entries most of us would not recognize as words: *amazable, amusable, depressible, fightable*, etc. In fact, there is no actual lexicon that makes the distinctions we feel between actual and possible words, and that fact is recognized in linguistic science (Aronoff 1976). Brown and Fish conclude that the distinction can be drawn only in terms of frequency. Of the four varieties of possible derivational adjectives, it is those attributive to Agent and Stimulus that satisfy a minimum frequency criterion (one or more per million words in the Kučera and Francis, 1967, word count). It was on the basis of this frequency criterion that words like *helpful, critical, charming,* and *noticeable* were defined as existent whereas their counterparts (*helpable, criticizeable, charmable,* and *noticing* (adj.)) were defined as possible but nonexistent. Frequencies are usage, and usage is the way a community deploys its language. This fact together with the principle governing adjective derivation in English suggested to Brown and Fish the following non-Whorfian explanation of their discoveries.

Perhaps human beings generally think about psychological causality in terms of two schemas. Interpersonal actions or voluntary behavior always involve both an Agent and a Patient; such behavior is always really an interaction, but humans may conceive of the causality as unequally apportioned between Agent and Patient, being greater for the Agent. Brown and Fish call this mode of thought the Agent-Patient Schema. Interpersonal experiences, or involuntary states, always involve a Stimulus and an Experiencer and so are really causal interactions, but humans may think of the Stimulus as carrying the greater causal weight. Brown and Fish call this mode of thought the Stimulus-Experiencer Schema.

The Agent-Patient Schema and the Stimulus-Experiencer Schema implicit in the psycholinguistic operations of native speakers of American English seem intuitively sound. Suppose that one of us likes and the other dislikes a particular singer. How would we discuss this disagreement, which is a disagreement about affect, an involuntary mental state. One might way: "But listen to this, the natural phrasing, the beautiful timbre." The other might say: "The vibrato is excessive and the pitch is not always well centered." In effect, we would discuss our difference in terms of properties of the stimulus. The attractiveness or not of the stimulus seems to us, as it does even more strongly to the child, to inhere in the external stimulus almost as surely as do its primary sensory qualities. We do not so easily and naturally think of the qualities as dependent on the Experiencer, and in discussing disagreements we will not often say: "The truth is that I am just the kind of person to whom that voice appeals and you are not." Our involuntary mental states seem to us to be elicited by external stimuli even though we, of course, know that causal interaction is always the true state of affairs. We seem to think of voluntary actions, of behavior, differently than we think of mental states. An act of cheating, helping, criticizing, or flattering seems to us to arise primarily from a disposition, residing like a coiled spring, in the Agent. The act is performed upon some Patient, but the role of the Patient is less critical than that of the Agent.

Brown and Fish hypothesize that the two schemas of psychological causality are cognitive universals. In positing universality, they definitely do not posit innateness but are able to show that the schemas might plausibly be induced from the observation of interpersonal behavior and states. The process of induction would be the same as that described by Kelley's (1967) ANOVA model of attribution. The full argument and evidence offered cannot be detailed here, but the gist is fairly simple. Consider first such actions as *help, harm, flatter,* and *slander.* For each of these predicates, two people are involved (Agent and Patient) and so generally two classes of person: the helpful and the helpable; the harmful and the harmable; the flattering and the flatterable; the slanderous and the slanderable. It seems reasonable to think that the size of these classes will not be equal. Just about anyone is susceptible to being helped, harmed, flattered, or slandered. There seems to be no particular prerequisite; it suffices to be human, and so the Patient classes are very large, approximately coincident with the number of humans in the world. Agent classes would seem to be smaller. Not everyone is disposed generally to help or to harm or to flatter or to slander. If Agent and Patient classes differ in size as described, it follows, from information theory, that there would seldom or never be any occasion to characterize a human being as *helpable, harmable, flatterable,* or *slanderable;* the predicate follows from their humanity and so is fully redundant. The case is otherwise with *helpful, harmful, flattering, slanderous.* In short, the Agent role is worth naming (existent words by a frequency criterion) because there is a disposition there to name but the Patient role is not worth naming because the disposition or susceptibility follows from the humanity of the instances. This situation is pictured in figure 9.3*a.*

The argument for Stimulus and Experiencer is the same. The capacity to be charmed or astonished or attracted or to take notice or like someone would seem to be very general in human beings, which means the related Experiencer classes must be very large. On the other hand, the capacities to charm, astonish, attract, be noticed, and liked seem less general. It follows that Stimulus dispositions would be more worth naming—there is something to talk about—than would Experiencer dispositions—there is no information to be conveyed. The situation is pictured in figure 9.3*b.*

Brown and Fish have made what seem to be plausible arguments for the view that implicit causality in English verbs results not from particular

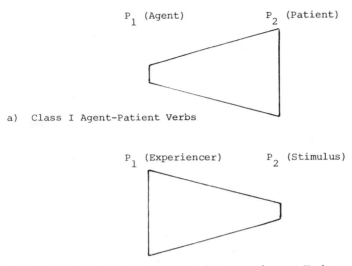

a)   Class I Agent-Patient Verbs

b)   Class II and Class III Stimulus-Experiencer Verbs

Fig. 9.3. Relative sizes of classes of persons to whom predicate arguments apply.

English adjectives, derived from verbs in a happenstance way, mediating causal ratings but rather from two universal schemas of thought affecting the derivation of adjectives as well as ratings for implicit causality. They have not, of course, established their case; far from it.

To conclude this essay I will report some new evidence bearing specifically on the universality of the Agent-Patient and Stimulus-Experiencer schemas, evidence arguing that the apportioning of causality by English-speaking subjects in a direct rating task (of the type "A____B. Why?") is not a function of the English language, not caused by rules of morphology, not a Whorfian result at all.

The report will be brief, leaving details and qualifications to be discussed, together with additional data now being collected, in research papers. We had our original paper-and-pencil task ("A likes B. How likely is it that this is because" etc.) translated into Chinese and into Japanese and administered to native speakers of these languages. In the Chinese language, there are no verb-based derived adjectives analogous to English *likable, helpful,* etc., and so there is no possibility that causal ratings could be mediated by such linguistic forms. In addition, of course, Chinese is not historically related to English, and so if results for speakers of Chinese are in conformity with the two schemas posited by Brown and Fish, we must score a point for universality. The Japanese language has some deriva-

Table 9.3 Causal Weightings for Three Classes of Chinese Verbs

Class I: Agent-Patient Subject-Object	Subject Mean	Object Mean
apologize to	3.47	3.42
cheat	5.25	4.20
compete with	(6.15)	(6.95)
criticize	5.90	4.60*
defy	5.42	3.47**
disobey	(5.80)	(5.85)
dominate	6.05	5.55
flatter	6.26	5.73
harm	5.20	4.55
help	7.85	4.30***
protect	6.45	4.80*
slander	6.57	3.52***

Class II: Stimulus-Experiencer Subject-Object	Subject Mean	Object Mean
astonish	(5.05)	(5.15)
attract	6.80	4.75***
charm	6.70	4.85**
deceive	5.90	5.35
delight	6.50	5.35
exasperate	5.30	4.75
impress	6.94	4.84***
influence	(6.36)	(7.36)
repel	(4.45)	(6.25)**
scorn	5.89	5.36
shock	4.60	4.30
trouble	5.05	4.94

Class III: Experiencer-Stimulus Subject-Object	Subject Mean	Object Mean
abhor	4.25	6.05**
admire	3.89	6.73***
despise	(6.11)	(4.61)*
detest	4.05	4.95
dread	3.95	5.20*
enjoy	5.20	5.45
esteem	4.55	6.95***
honor	4.50	7.25***
like	5.25	6.70*
loathe	4.40	6.25**
notice	5.95	6.75
pity	(6.80)	(4.25)**

S > O or O > S $p \leqslant .05$* $p \leqslant .01$** $p \leqslant .001$***
( ) Difference is in direction contrary to prediction

Table 9.4   Causal Weightings for Three Classes of Japanese Verbs

Class I: Agent-Patient Patient-Object	Subject Mean	Object Mean
apologize to	3.71	2.76
cheat	6.28	4.95*
compete with	5.47	5.09
criticize	(5.61)	(5.90)
defy	4.71	4.71
disobey	(4.47)	(5.38)
dominate	6.61	4.33**
flatter	7.0	4.90***
harm	5.28	3.47**
help	5.66	4.85
protect	5.71	4.76
slander	6.04	4.66*

Class II: Stimulus-Experiencer Subject-Object	Subject Mean	Object Mean
astonish	5.80	4.23*
attract	7.85	4.85***
charm	6.28	4.90*
deceive	5.47	5.14
delight	7.09	4.38***
exasperate	5.90	4.57*
impress	7.04	4.80***
influence	6.76	5.0*
repel	(4.04)	(5.14)
scorn	5.61	4.76
shock	5.04	3.14**
trouble	5.61	3.66**

Class III: Experiencer-Stimulus Subject-Object	Subject Mean	Object Mean
abhor	3.23	5.28**
admire	4.90	6.61*
despise	4.19	5.42
detest	3.71	4.52
dread	2.57	5.38***
enjoy	4.38	7.57***
esteem	4.04	7.52***
honor	3.85	6.95***
like	4.14	6.04**
loathe	3.14	5.04**
notice	(5.95)	(5.09)
pity	(5.04)	(5.61)

S>O or O>S $p \leq .05$* $p \leq .01$** $p \leq .001$***
( ) Difference is in direction contrary to prediction

tional morphology but nothing for the 36 verbs in question comparable to the English derived adjectives, no linguistic machinery that could account for results in line with the two schemas. Japanese also, of course, is unrelated to English and so constitutes another test of the hypothesized universality.

The results appear in tables 9.3 and 9.4, displayed in a way that makes them directly comparable with the results for English-speakers in table 9.2. The verbs in table 9.3 should be understood to be Chinese-equivalents and the verbs in table 9.4 Japanese equivalents of the English words listed. The results are not so unequivocal as those for English, but they do quite strongly favor the theory of the two schemas. For Chinese, the direction of the causal balance in 29 of 36 verbs is in accordance with hypothesis and 16 of the differences are significant at the .05 level or better. Of the seven verbs that went contrary to hypothesis, two did so in significant degree, but one of these, *repel,* has turned out to have been a mistranslation. For Japanese, the direction of the causal balance in 30 of 36 verbs is in accordance with hypothesis and 22 of the differences are significant at the .05 level or better. Of the five verbs that went contrary to hypothesis, none did so in significant degree. We conclude that these results favor the universality of the Agent-Patient and Stimulus-Experiencer cognitive schemas.

The translation into Chinese was initially done by Terry Kit-fong Au and then checked for idiomatic accuracy by her sister in Hong Kong. The Chinese paper-and-pencil instrument was administered in Hong Kong to Chinese-speaking, secondary school students in the classroom, entirely in Chinese. The translation into Japanese was made by Professor Minoru Fujii of Kansai University who was a Visiting Scholar at Harvard in 1982–1983 and administered by him to Japanese-speaking adults of his acquaintance who were in the Boston area that year.

None of our subjects (neither Chinese nor Japanese) was completely without knowledge of English. Indeed, it is difficult for us to gain access to native speakers of these languages who do not know any English because instruction in English is given to all public school students in both Hong Kong and Japan. However, the resultant knowledge of English is not very great. To obtain a rough index of relevant knowledge of English, our subjects were asked, once the task had been completed in the native language, to attempt to translate the Chinese or Japanese verbs of the paper-and-pencil instrument into English. No subject could translate any but a few very familiar verbs such as *like* and *help.* The number of verbs correctly translated was used as an index of individual knowledge of relevant English, and this index proved to be unrelated to the results obtained which argues that mediation by English (actually the derived adjectives would have to be known) is not likely to be responsible for the results obtained. Nevertheless, we have underway replications with other convergent tasks, other translators, and subjects more nearly monolingual. From the subtle and critical translation problems that arose in the work of Bloom and Au on counterfactuals, we take it for granted that we have still much to learn about the role of the two causality schemas in Chinese and Japanese. Why did some translated verbs yield results contrary to hypothesis—in a few cases, significantly so? Were the tasks fully equivalent psychologically? (For example, Au finds the English expression "kind of person that _____" difficult to render into a natural-sounding Chinese.) But the caveats must wait. At this point, the work on implicit causality suggests that thought shapes language rather than language, thought.

Conclusion

This review of theory and research on linguistic relativity has not been comprehensive. Rather, it has been three research stories, family stories, if I can say that without appearing to boast of accomplishments that are not mine. It has been the luck of one psycholinguistic family from the 1950s to the 1980s to venture forth expecting to find evidence favoring linguistic relativity only to come up against cognitive universality. Perhaps the fact that we did not expect what we found, at least we did not until the earlier experiences made us revise our expectations for the current venture, should count in favor of the credibility of the evidence against relativity. I think it should.

References

Aronoff, M. *Word formation: Linguistic inquiry monograph one.* Cambridge, MA.:MIT Press, 1976

Au, T. K.-f. Chinese and English counterfactuals: The Sapir-Whorf hypothesis revisited. *Cognition,* 1983, *15,* 155–187.

Berlin, B., & Kay, P. *Basic color terms: Their universality and evolution.* Berkeley and Los Angeles: University of California Press, 1969.

Bloom, A. H. *The linguistic shaping of thought: A study in the impact of language on thinking in China and the West.* Hillsdale, NJ: Lawrence Erlbaum Associates, 1981.

Bodine, A. Androcentrism in prescriptive grammar: Singular "they," sex-indefinite "he" and "he or she." *Language in Society,* 1975, *4,* 129–146.

Bornstein, M. H. The influence of visual perception on culture. *American Anthropologist,* 1975, *77,* 774–798.

Bornstein, M. H. Name codes and color memory. *American Journal of Psychology,* 1976, *89,* 269–279.

Bornstein, M. H., Kessen, W., & Weiskopf, S. Color vision and hue categorization in young human infants. *Journal of Experimental Psychology: Human Perception and Performance,* 1976, *2,* 115–129.

Brown, R. *Words and things.* New York: Free Press, 1958.

Brown, R., & Fish, D. The psychological causality implicit in language. *Cognition*. 1983, *14*, 237–273.

Brown, R. W., & Lenneberg, E. H. A study in language and cognition. *Journal of Abnormal and Social Psychology*, 1954, *49*, 454–462.

Caramazza, A., Grober, E., Garvey, C., & Yates, J. Comprehension of anaphoric pronouns. *Journal of Verbal Learning and Verbal Behavior*, 1977, *16*, 601–609.

DeValois, R. L., & DeValois, K. K. Neural coding of color. In E. C. Carterette & M. P. Friedman (Eds.), *Handbook of perception* (Vol. 5). New York: Academic Press, 1975.

Elman, B. Review of A. Bloom's *The linguistic shaping of thought: A study in the impact of language on thinking in China and the West. Journal of Asian Studies,* 1983, *42*, 611.

Friedl, E. Colors and culture change in Iran. *Language in Society*, 1979, *8*, 51–68.

Garvey, C., & Caramazza, A. Implicit causality in verbs. *Linguistic Inquiry*, 1974, *5*, 459–464.

Garvey, C., Caramazza, A., & Yates, J. Factors influencing assignment of pronoun antecedents. *Cognition*, 1976, *3*, 227–243.

Gleason, H. A. *An introduction to descriptive linguistics*. Rev. Ed. New York: Holt, Rinehart, and Winston, 1961.

Heider, E. R. Universals in color naming and memory. *Journal of Experimental Psychology*, 1972, *93*, 10–20.

Heider, E. R., & Olivier, D. C. The structure of the color space in naming and memory for two languages. *Cognitive Psychology*, 1972, *3*, 337–354.

Henley, N. M. *Body politics*. Englewood Cliffs, NJ: Prentice-Hall, 1977.

Kelley, H. H. Attribution theory in social psychology. *Nebraska Symposium on Motivation*, 1967, *15*, 192–238.

Kučera, H., & Francis, W. N. *Computational analysis of present-day American English*. Providence: Brown University Press, 1967.

Lakoff, R. Language and woman's place. *Language in Society*, 1973, *2*, 45–80.

Lantz, De Lee, & Stefflre, V. Language and cognition revisited. *Journal of Abnormal and Social Psychology*, 1964, 472–481.

Lenneberg, E. H. Cognition and ethnolinguistics. *Language,* 1953, *29*, 463–471.

MacKay, D. G. Psychology, prescriptive grammar, and the pronoun problem. *American Psychologist*, 1980, *35*, 444–449.

MacKay, D. G., & Fulkerson, D. On the comprehension and production of pronouns. *Journal of Verbal Learning and Verbal Behavior*, 1979, *18*, 661–673.

Miller, G. A., & Johnson-Laird, P. N. *Language and perception*. Cambridge, MA: Harvard University Press, 1976.

Orwell, G. *1984*. New York: Harcourt Brace, 1949 (Signet, 1955).

Sapir, E. In D. G. Mandelbaum (Ed.), *Selected writings of Edward Sapir*. Berkeley and Los Angeles: University of California Press, 1949.

Stefflre, V., Vales, V. C., & Morley, L. Language and cognition in Yucatan: A cross-cultural replication. *Journal of Personality and Social Psychology*, 1966, *4*, 112–115.

Whorf, B. L. In J. B. Carroll (Ed.), *Language, thought and reality: Selected writings of Benjamin Lee Whorf*. Cambridge, MA:MIT Press; New York: Wiley, 1956.

10. Dismembering Cognition
George A. Miller

William James first made America conscious of the new German science, but it was G. Stanley Hall, the sometime student of both William James and Wilhelm Wundt, who planted the new experimental psychology firmly on American soil. Hall founded the Psychological Laboratory at the Johns Hopkins University only four years after the science had officially been born in Leipzig at Wundt's Psychologisches Institut.

The new psychology quickly spread across the United States. By 1891, there were fifteen laboratories of experimental psychology; by 1900, twenty-seven (Ruckmich 1912). Throughout the rapid growth and diversification of psychology in the twentieth century, experimental psychology played a central role. Although it is now merely one among many branches of contemporary psychology, it still contributes importantly to the discipline's image of itself. Psychologists value their status as scientists, a claim that relies heavily on their willingness and ability to submit hypotheses to experimental test.

But experiments alone do not make a science; the purpose and meaning of experimentation must be provided by theory. Although theories come in all shapes and sizes, experimentalists generally favor those that reduce a large question to several smaller questions: the smaller the question, the better the chance of answering it experimentally.

This favoritism for analytic theories is not peculiar to experimental psychologists. All scientists share it. Analysis is the scientific reflex: when you want to understand something, take it apart. The implication for psychology, therefore, is that the first step toward a scientific understanding of the mind is to take it apart. But how should that step be taken? A history of psychology might be written around the ways that philosophers and psychologists have tried to analyze the mind. What are the conceptual elements, the atoms into which it should be analyzed? Faculties, ideas, images, beliefs, reflexes, functions, factors, and information processes have all enjoyed their day as conceptual atoms. Proponents of different elements have debated vigorously, but none has achieved more than a temporary ascendancy.

Why has analysis proved inconclusive in psychology? Have psychologists not yet done it correctly? Or should they not be doing it at all? A centennial observance is an appropriate time to consider such questions.

Perhaps because James was no experimentalist his devotion to analytic theories was something less than compulsive. Was he right when he wrote: "We really gain a more living understanding of the mind by keeping our attention as long as possible upon our entire conscious states as they are concretely given to us, than by the *postmortem* study of their comminuted 'elements.' This last is the study of artificial abstractions, not of natural things" (1892, iv). At the time he wrote, James was objecting to the analysis of subjective experience into elementary sensations and feelings, which were supposed to form compound ideas by association, but his complaint is easily generalized to subsequent attempts at analysis.

Or was James wrong? Perhaps the analytical experimentalists have been on the right track all along. Perhaps the mind is in fact an analyzable domain whose analysis no one has yet got the hang of.

It has been said that a successful analysis carves a topic at its joints. An unsuccessful analysis, on the other hand, is hardly an analysis at all. What should we call an attempted analysis that violates the natural joints, that leaves its object shattered in lumps? I propose to call it a dismemberment. And I shall argue that psychological theorists have persistently dismembered the mind in their attempts to analyze it.

It is relatively easy to recognize the mistakes of our predecessors. It is not as easy, lacking the perspective of history, to know whether we today are doing any better. I am keenly aware that I may be too close to current trends to see clearly what is wrong with them, but I do believe that we have made considerable progress. After a century of dismemberments, I believe we are beginning to understand how mental life can be described and explained scientifically.

Today we talk less of the analysis of mind—*cognition* is currently the fashionable term. I shall speak, therefore, of the dismemberment of cognition.

Disciplinary Dismemberment of Cognition

Consider first an example of dismemberment that is a consequence of the deplorable dissociation of our academic departments. Several disciplines currently covet cognition: psychologists take for granted that cognition is a "problem" defined for their experimental convenience, philosophers, who were there first, feel that psychologists are intruders who obscure rational argument by premature empiricism, computer scientists, who invent artifically intelligent systems, freely define cognition in their own likeness, linguists claim special cognitive intuitions about language as their intellectual birthright, social anthropologists speak as if their concern for culture gave them some special authority to study cognition, even neuroscientists now speak of cognitive brain processes. Moreover, each discipline has proceeded as though its own enterprise were the only one of consequence.

This state of affairs can be called the disciplinary dismemberment of cognition. No doubt it existed for many years before an interdisciplinary program sponsored by the Alfred P. Sloan Foundation brought it to everyone's attention.

In the late 1970s, the Sloan Foundation offered financial support for something that it proposed to call Cognitive Science. Since this attractive offer presupposed a unitary science of cognition, the interested parties were strongly motivated to stop ignoring one another.

Many interdisciplinary conferences followed. In 1978, at one of the more memborable meetings a group of distinguished supplicants was asked to summarize the state of cognitive science at that time, and thereupon the fable of the blind men and the elephant was reenacted. No one had a broad view of cognitive science. Everyone knew his or her own field and had heard of two or three interesting findings in other fields. After hours of discussion, experts in discipline X grew unwilling to make any judgments about discipline Y. In the end, they did what they were competent to do: each summarized his or her own field, and the editors patched a report together with bandaids (Keyser, Miller, and Walker 1978).

Perhaps the Sloan Foundation took the report as evidence that collaboration was desperately needed, for they went ahead. As a consequence of the foundation's initiative, many cognitive scientists are now much better acquainted than they were ten years ago. But many still speak of cognitive sciences in the plural. Some have even argued that the singular will always remain an impossible dream.

Take language, for example. Linguistics, psychology, and physiology each has its own approach and its own answers to questions about relations among the various cognitive systems involved in language (Osherson and Wasow 1976). A grammar may characterize the admissible sentences of a language, but it says little or nothing about the mental processes involved in producing or comprehending those sentences: a psychological description of the mental processes, in turn, says little or nothing about the neurophysiological mechanisms that realize them. According to Osherson and Wasow, pluralism is unavoidable: physiological mechanisms, psychological processes, and linguistic structures will never submit to a single analysis.

An alternative view is that a unitary science of cognition is not impossible, but merely premature. If physiology, psychology, and linguistics are all studying the same thing, they should eventually converge on a unitary theory of it. We cannot foresee how they will converge, any more than scientists in 1800 could have foreseen how chemistry and physics would come together. But to assume that pluralism is inescapable betrays a limited imagination.

Although cognitivists from different disciplines disagree about many things, there are a few matters on which all can unite. Everyone agrees that the right research strategy is to identify some subdomain that is well integrated yet interacts only loosely with everything else. As the number of interrelated variables that must be considered increases, the potential complexity of their combinations increases explosively. Unless the larger problem can be analyzed into independent, self-contained subproblems, understanding becomes difficult, if not impossible.

Unfortunately, in the study of cognition this analytic strategy has not yet led to a unique result. The subdomains have been different for each discipline. Whatever the future may hold, at present every science carves cognition differently.

It is not necessary to cross disciplinary boundaries in order to discover incompatible analyses: the difficulties can be illustrated without leaving the field of psychology. Let me remind you of analyses proposed by experimental psychologists and by psychometricians.

Experimental Dismemberment

Experimental psychologists have long been accustomed to analyzing cognition into processes: perception, attention, memory, imagination, thought, and judgment, each of which has, over the years, developed into a specialty in its own right, with its own problems, its own experimental methods, its own literature, and its own expert constituency.

Having grown up in this tradition, I am usually comfortable with it. But sometimes I think divide-and-conquer is carried too far. Whole books are written on perception (or even on some limited aspect of perception), with little concern for attention, memory, imagination, thought, or judgment; they are matched by whole books written on attention, with little concern for perception, memory, imagination, thought, or judgment; and so on for the other processes. In the universities, separate courses are taught in each specialty. A literal-minded student can take away a strangely fractionated conception of mental life.

One difficulty for this traditional analysis that has always been of great interest to me arises from our human propensity to talk. A cognitive psychologist can hardly ignore language, but is it just one more cognitive process, on a par with all the others? Or does it cut across the cognitive processes? Perception, attention, memory, imagination, thought, and judgment cannot all be held invariant while language is studied experimentally. An alternative view is that language is a unique arena in which the different roles of cognitive processes can be observed.

A more serious difficulty is that, even granted the traditional analysis into processes, nobody seems to know how to put them back together.

If one gives credence to the pretheoretical concept of a mental act, surely one would also grant that any interesting exemplar would comprise all these cognitive processes working together to accomplish some coherent result. The recognition of a man's face, to take an example at random, involves attending to him selectively, perceiving him clearly, remembering his appearance and judging that perception and memory match, then recalling his name. The complete mental act may even involve such noncognitive processes as feeling affection or dislike, or deciding whether to greet or to avoid him. What could it mean to abstract one of these processes and ignore all others?

Although cognitive processes are usually studied separately, I know of no principled argument that the different processes do not interact. Nor can processes be rendered inoperative: your memory cannot be eliminated while your perceptions are studied, or vice versa. Instead, it has been assumed that it is possible to study one cognitive process experimentally while all others are held constant. This kind of experimental manipulation of the variables affecting performance is appropriately called the experimental dismemberment of cognition.

From this point of view, processes are seen as more like attributes than like components of cognition. It is as though each process were a dimension of some hyperspace in which all mental acts can be located—a space in which every mental act has a value on every dimension. Experimental psychologists try to explore this space one dimension at a time.

When the experimental strategy is characterized in this way, it immediately becomes clear that the effects of variations in one dimension may differ widely depending on what values the other dimensions happen to have. That is to say, it immediately becomes clear that holding all other aspects constant is not good enough. Experimental dismemberment—the strategy of studying one cognitive process at a time—is a risky business, indeed. Yet studying everything at the same time is impossible.

A common response to this dilemma is denial. Since the difficulty surfaces only when you ask how all the elementary processes fit together in ordinary experience, the comfortable solution is not to ask. It is no accident, therefore, that experimental psychologists tend to share an occupational aversion to broad views of mental life. Given an interesting phenomenon, their reflex is not to ask how it fits into a larger system; their first impulse is to reduce it to something uninteresting.

Newell (1973) has taken experimental psychologists to task for the fragmented and noncumulative science that has resulted from their lack of interest in integrative theories. Although he recognizes that experimentation sometimes uncovers fascinating psychological phenomena, Newell feels that the list of fascinating phenomena simply grows longer and longer, without converging. It does not converge, he says, because experimental psychologists have not conceptualized what they are doing in terms of any general theory, but only in terms of binary oppositions: heredity versus environment, peripheral versus central, conscious versus unconscious, massed versus distributed, analogue versus digital, and so on.

Implicit in this approach, Newell suggests, is a view of science as a game of Twenty Questions played against Nature. One tries to frame general yes / no questions that can be attacked experimentally. Having settled one bit of information, another binary choice is formulated. "The policy appears optimal," he admits, "one never risks much, there is feedback from nature at every step, and progress is inevitable." But then he adds, "Unfortunately, the questions never seem to be really answered, the strategy does not seem to work" (290).

In their excellent textbook of cognitive psychology, Lachman, Lachman, and Butterfield (1979) accept Newell's description of the experimental study of cognition but disagree with his evaluation. The fragmentation is, they claim, "an unavoidable consequence of normal science." In their view, there has been a genuine cumulative advance in knowledge: "it results not from this particular characteristic of normal science, but despite it" (528).

Perhaps Lachman, Lachman, and Butterfield are right and all is well with cognitive psychology. Even so, Newell's critique merits attention: the fragmentation is real, and the rate at which the fascinating phenomena have been converging is painfully slow.

Factorial Dismemberment

Since I am not a psychometrician, I shall not linger over the factorial dismemberment of cognition, but psychometric factors do provide an interesting contrast to experimental processes. Whereas an experimentalist focuses on processes that are assumed to occur within a single mind, a psychometrician takes differences between people as the fundamental data.

Multiple factor analysis goes as follows: many mental tests are administered to many people; scores on all pairs of tests are correlated over individuals; the resulting matrix of correlation coefficients is analyzed to determine the space of lowest dimensionality in which the tests can be represented; the coordinates of that space are then rotated into some theoretically satisfying pattern. These coordinates are the factors; each test has a value, or loading, on every factor; factors are usually given names suggested by the nature of the tests that load heavily on them.

To cite a famous example, on the basis of his factor analytic studies Thurstone (1938) proposed, tentatively, that intelligence consists of seven factors, or primary mental abilities, as he called them: verbal comprehension, word fluency, number, reasoning, spatial visualization, perceptual speed, and memory. People were assumed to possess these primary abilities to different degrees; tests were assumed to demand them in different proportions.

The details of this analytical process do not concern me here. After the choice of tests and up until the naming of the factors I am willing to assume that everything is proper and straightforward. I even grant that the results have often been useful in practical applications. Where I find analysis slipping into dismemberment is in the claims that are often made for the psychological significance of the results.

The most obvious objection, and one that has been frequently voiced over the years, is that, despite the elegant use of matrix algebra, no psychological claims are put forward. If you ask, for example, *why* the loadings are whatever they are—*why* people who do well on test A also do well on test B, poorly on test C, and may do anything at all on test D—the answer comes from common sense, not from factor analysis.

The first to note this difficulty was Thurstone himself, and it is to his credit that he spoke of multiple factor analysis as an experimental method that could yield successive analyses until all theoretical questions were eventually answered. In fact, however, that was not what happened. Factor analysis was more often used for data reduction than for theory construction. The chance of accidentally discovering anything of fundamental importance under those circumstances was indeed slim. Guilford (1979) has commented that "the choice of variables to be analyzed together is all important to success . . . you *cannot* get out of a factor analysis what you *do not* put into it" (4).

I remind you of this situation in order to emphasize my point that cognitive processes and psychometric abilities have not converged. What would be most remarkable and important, of course, would be to find that the primary memory ability that Thurstone identified is indeed the same as the memory process that experimental psychologists study, or that his primary reasoning ability is the experimentalists' thought process, and so on. The terminology certainly promises a convergence, and some factor analysts have looked for it (Guilford 1979). But mental processes and individual differences are very different creatures, so different that it is not entirely clear what such analogies could mean, much less whether or not they hold.

Recently, Sternberg (1977) has tried to bring these two traditions together. By analyzing a task into components, which are assumed to give rise to mental processes, he hopes to provide the kind of psychological theory required to explain factors, which are assumed to give rise to individual differences. This program is undoubtedly interesting and, if it were to succeed, many of my misgivings about attempts to analyze cognition might be dismissed. But it is an ambitious program and, judging by peer commentary (Sternberg 1980), not yet widely accepted.

For my present purpose, however, I need not attempt to pass judgment on Sternberg's work, or on the work of others who pursue similar goals. It is enough to note the existence of active attempts to show how experimental observations of cognitive processes might be used to understand individual differences in performance. If the two methods of analysis yielded the same cognitive atoms, no such program would be required.

Thus, even within a single discipline it is possible to find attempts at cognitive analysis that are as different, and as difficult to reconcile, as are those between disciplines.

Some Ancient History

How did psychology get into this state? Let me share with you some opinions about the history of the experimental psychology of cognition.

I believe the story should begin with the folk model of the mind that is characteristic of Western civilization, the model that our ancestors unselfconsciously evolved long ago and passed on to us in the very languages we speak. According to D'Andrade (1983), this folk model includes perceptions, thoughts, feelings, desires, and intentions, each characterizable either as states or as processes, organized in constrained causal patterns, and used to relate a person's actions to the situations and circumstances in which they are observed. This folk model of the mind is shared implicitly by all adults: every socialized individual appreciates what mental states or processes will be attributed to any person who behaves in a particular manner in a particular context.

By claiming that the story should begin with this folk model I mean to suggest that the history of faculty psychology is best understood as a process of discovering and making explicit the presuppositions about mind already incorporated in common speech. Common speech attributes perceptions and thoughts to people; these attributions were taken as evidence for cognitive faculties. Common speech attributes desires and intentions to people; these were taken as evidence for conative faculties. Common speech attributes feelings to people; these were evidence for emotive faculties.

In the eighteenth century, several psychologically minded philosophers compiled lists of mental faculties. A student of Leibniz, Christian Wolff, opened the game by distinguishing a *facultas cognoscitiva* from a *facultas appetiva*, a faculty for knowing and a faculty for desiring. Other German writers added a faculty for affection, or feeling, in order to account for esthetic preferences. According to Hilgard (1980), "Finally, the man who put it all together was a self-taught philosopher and psychologist, Moses Mendelssohn (1729–1789). His *Letters on Sensations* (1755) contained the first clear statement of the threefold classification, that the fundamental faculties of the soul are understanding, feeling, and will"(111). A similar classification was proposed by Johann Nicholaus Tetens, sometimes called "the father of psychology" for his early use of introspective methods. But it was the prestige of Immanuel Kant that established the trichotomy. Kant's *Critique of Pure Reason* is a philosophical study of understanding, or cognition; his *Critique of Practical Reason* is a study of the will, or conation; his *Critique of Judgment* considers pleasure and pain, or emotion.

Late in the eighteenth century, the Scottish philosopher Thomas Reid began drawing up lists of mental faculties. The Scottish school of "common sense philosophy"—Reid, Dugald Stewart, Thomas Brown, and Sir William Hamilton—listed some thirty-seven powers and propensities of the mind. (Their list was adopted by Franz Joseph Gall for his phrenological speculations.) At first the Scots did not classify these faculties as cognitive, conative, or affective, but by Hamilton's time they, too, had adopted the tripartite theory.

Merely to speak of cognition, therefore, is to presuppose that some kind of analysis of mental life is possible. The next step was to analyze cognitive states and processes into perceptual and intellectual faculties; then to analyze perceptual faculties into the several sensory modalities and to analyze intellectual faculties into memory, imagination, attention, reason, and judgment.

These divisions are now chapter titles in our textbooks of cognitive psychology. Experimental psychologists have, in one way or another, extended this analytical program at least one more level and, in some places, two or three. If the intelligent layperson were to judge solely by topical headings—chapter titles, journal titles, convention program sessions, and the like—little evidence would suggest that modern psychologists have not been unswervingly loyal to the original program of faculty psychology.

Yet we know that has not been the case. By the late nineteenth century— by the time psychologists were ready to declare themselves experimental scientists independent of philosophy—faculty psychology had been generally discredited and discarded. Some historians have called Hamilton the last of the faculty psychologists. After him the emphasis shifted from lists of faculties to the association of ideas. Associationistic theory holds that both the composition and the succession of ideas can be explained with nothing more than a set of experiential atoms and the psychological laws whereby they become associated in compounds or chains.

For example, an association theorist does not require any special faculty of perception in order to explain why smell, touch, and sight are integrated in the experience of a rose; all that is needed is the co-occurrence of the smell, the touch, and the sight of similar roses in prior experience. Again, a faculty of memory is not needed to explain why a rose reminds you of someone; it is enough to say that the rose and the person are associated. And so on. The traditional faculties became unnecessary.

Why, then, has the old faculty terminology persisted? Why was it not replaced by a leaner, simpler language of association? Indeed, strenuous efforts toward that end were made by associationistic behaviorists. But it is difficult for the average person to understand what is being explained without translating the new language back into the more familiar, more comfortable folk model of the mind. Thus, the traditional concepts persist, but now as phenomena to be explained rather than as capacities to use in formulating explanations.

Recently there has been a revival of interest in mental faculties—or mental organs, as Chomsky (1980) has called them—but faculties with a special twist. The cognitive structures that seem to be required in order to account for human language appear so peculiar and unique that some theorists have proposed a special language-specific mode of perception, a language-specific memory, and language-specific forms of inference. Moreover, if language has its own perceptual, mnemonic, and inferential resources, why not assume similarly specialized support for other capacities: for number, vision, music, logic, spatial orientation, or whatever?

Such speculations led Fodor (1983) to distinguish a "vertical" from a "horizontal" conception of mental faculties. If, for example, you believe in one memory that serves all mental acts, you hold what Fodor calls a horizontal conception of the memory faculty; if you believe in many independent memories serving different activities, you hold the vertical conception. Franz Joseph Gall argued for vertical faculties; Fodor feels it is time psychologists took such arguments seriously.

A Parenthetical Word about Attribution

I have been careful to say that the folk model of the mind is attributed. Since psychologists have had much to say about attribution in other contexts, I must pause briefly to clarify my own use of the term.

The sense I intend here is closer to Premack's (Premack and Woodruff 1978) than to Kelley's (1967). An extensive and fascinating body of experimental research in social psychology has explored the evidential basis on which one person will attribute the behavior of another person to specific causes. Premack has a rather different idea in mind. His point is that it is extremely difficult to know whether some mental process has actually been instantiated, but if that mental process is attributed, or imputed, to another organism, there are observable consequences that an experimenter can work with.

A folk model is a theory (Churchland 1979). The convenience of being able to look at others through the lens of some theory of mind, even a vague or incorrect theory, can hardly be overestimated. If we could not deal with one another at the abstract level that theory allows, the resulting cognitive overload would surely bring all intelligent social interaction to a halt. Moreover, since everyone who shares the same cultural background believes roughly the same theory—makes similar abstractions, draws similar inferences—the theory acquires a kind of pragmatic social validity that is not easily distinguished from truth itself.

As to its truth, strong opinions are held on both sides. One view is that all folk models are false, that a science has not reached maturity until its lay antecedents have been disproved and discarded. The alternative opinion is that this particular folk model must be different. In a sense, a folk model of mind is a self-fulfilling prophecy: it must be right because it creates the very thing that it is a model of.

Whichever view proves correct, it is unlikely that this socially well-assimilated conceptual framework will be easily abandoned. Scientific psychology is unlikely to replace it, or even to differ from it in important respects, until psychologists become self-consciously aware of the presuppositions they inherit from their culture.

Perplexity is heightened when a variety of highly detailed hypotheses begin to pour in from computer science and artificial intelligence. Although often inspired by the same kind of common sense that I am calling the folk model of the mind, computerized versions of intelligent behavior raise issues that far outrun any layperson's intuitions. When asked, "Is this really the way people do it?" intuition is hard pressed to find a plausible answer.

It is much easier to attribute some state or process to a person than it is to prove that the attribution is correct. Any interesting cognitive mechanism that is known, say, to be a true description of some intelligent machine, might be harmlessly attributed to humans on a metaphorical, "as if" basis. Some psychologists are content to leave the matter there. But others insist that the attribution must be correct, because people really are computers.

If thought really is computation (and what else could it be?), then people really are computers of some kind. The difficult question is, *what* kind?

Since I believe we are at present far from any satisfactory account of what kind of universal Turing machine the human brain really is, I believe it is prudent to speak cautiously, to talk about attributing minds to men and machines, rather than about the mental states and processes that some psychologists confidently assert are veritably there, awaiting discovery and analysis. In my opinion, it is premature to assume that when God created Adam He programmed his nervous system in LISP. Whether drawn from common sense or computer simulation, attributions must be treated with great care.

To return now to my central theme: the presuppositions of common sense, the nature of scientific explanation, and three centuries of philosophical and psychological discussion agree that there exists something cognitive that can and should be analyzed scientifically. In the face of this impressive convergence, I have argued that the strategy of analysis, when applied to the human mind, has not yet yielded the kind of scientific results we have learned to expect from it in the natural sciences. Why this is the case, and whether after one hundred years the time has come to declare the whole analytic enterprise bankrupt, are questions I want to raise even though I know how difficult they are to answer.

My dissatisfaction is not some personal idiosyncracy. Many cognitive scientists have become critical of the traditional list of cognitive processes; their uneasiness is manifest in various ways, but perhaps most directly in proposals for alternative analyses. The quality of their restlessness can be illustrated by considering briefly three such proposals, all of which I consider to be symptoms of desperation.

Chronometric Dismemberment

The experimental psychology of cognition has made extensive and often ingenious use of chronometric methods. Whereas the measurement of choice reaction time was once a research specialty in itself, in recent years it has become a widely used methodological tool, useful in the analysis of a wide variety of mental phenomena (Posner 1978).

The rebirth of experimental interest in cognition during the 1950s and 1960s was stimulated in large measure by a series of brilliant studies using various chronometric techniques: Hyman (1953), Sperling (1960), Neisser (1963), Slobin (1966), Sternberg (1966), Posner and Mitchell (1967), Collins and Quillian (1969), Rubenstein, Garfield, and Millikan (1970), Meyer and Schvaneveldt (1971)—to name but a few of the older studies that stand out in my memory. Not only were reaction times used to estimate which of two cognitive processes is the more complex, but they also served to isolate independent mental subsystems. If some experimental manipulation increases or decreases the time required for one response while leaving the time required for another response unchanged, the two responses must result from the operation of (at least partially) independent subsystems.

One of the more optimistic rationalizations of this preoccupation with time has been offered by Blumenthal (1977), whose introductory textbook in cognitive psychology is written around his organization of the basic cognitive phenomena into temporal categories and temporal functions. He argues that experimental psychologists study mental processes, and that processes unfold in time. Therefore, chronometry is indispensable. He writes: "It appears that there is a general principle of temporal integration underlying mental processes. It is the transformation of sequences of events into simultaneities of perception, thought, or memory. The living organism's temporal integrations of the flux of events that occur in and around it generate consciousness" (188). Viewed in that light, measurement of the time required for various cognitive processes seems an unmixed blessing.

It is a plausible extrapolation of the assumptions implicit in much current research to categorize cognitive processes on the basis of their duration, putting together all those that take approximately the same time. Thus, Blumenthal distinguishes rapid attentional integrations (50–250 msec), preattentive buffer delays (0.5–2.0 sec), postattentive delay or short-term memory (5–20 sec), and longer temporal integrations. The result is a novel and interesting perspective on the experimental psychology of cognition, and one that is consistent with what many cognitive psychologists are actually doing. Still, Blumenthal's attempted analysis has won few adherents—it does not seem to be consistent with what most cognitive psychologists hope to accomplish.

Without questioning the importance or value of chronometric research, there is reason to suspect that some of its admirers have made a virtue of necessity. Many cognitive processes are so rapid and automatic that introspective reports are useless and so highly practiced and accurate that errors seldom occur. Given those conditions, reaction times are almost the only source of data left to an experimenter. Fortunately for the scientific health of the enterprise, it is truly remarkable how many ways of exploiting this source the experimentalists have thought of.

It is also worth noting that the flowering of mental chronometry coincided with the arrival of digital computers in psychological laboratories. Whereas the measurement of reaction times was formerly a tedious chore for the experimenter, it is now easily automated. Today, mental chronometery is tedious only for experimental subjects.

I have no quarrel with mental chronometry per se—I have on occasion committed a few chronometries myself—but one must always remember that a method, even a highly successful method, is not a theory. Mental chronometry can support a microgenetic analysis of processes into successive stages, but it does not provide theoretical alternatives to the processes themselves.

Perhaps mental chronometry has been too successful. The danger is that a highly successful method can tempt the unwary to assume either that theory is unnecessary or that, if enough facts are all piled up in one place, a theory explaining what they mean will eventually become self-evident. In either case, the result can be that the successful method is used to the exclusion of any other.

Relentless devotion to a single experimental technique has always spelled trouble in psychology, whether it was threshold measurement, conditioning, rote memorization, factor analysis, or projection tests. Each is a good technique in itself, but when it becomes the focus of an ever-narrowing pursuit of details that only insiders can appreciate, when the experimenter's operations receive more emphasis than the subject's, when the experimental results prove useless outside the laboratory, then its sterility becomes apparent and the next generation of psychologists move on to other things.

Such developments seem to be examples of what Koch (1981) has called the pathology of knowledge. His list of fourteen symptoms of this pathology includes: "tendency to make so restrictive a definition of the field as to render the study beside the point," "tendency to accept any 'finding' conforming to some treasured methodology," "tendency to buy into stable or fashionable profession-centered myths," and "a view of all aspects of the cognitive enterprise as so thoroughly rule-regulated as to make the role of the cognizer superfluous" (258–59)—all of which I believe I have seen recent signs of in cognitive psychology.

Perhaps the other symptoms are also developing—Koch finds them characteristic of every systematic position in psychology. But pathology is surely a matter of degree; in my opinion, cognitive psychology is still reasonably healthy. Those who put blind faith in chronometry are still in the minority. Many experimentalists, including many of those whose clever use of chronometry helped launch experimental psychology into the study of cognition, have now turned to other approaches to supplement their earlier work. Some have turned to developmental studies of cognition, some to social cognition, others to neuroscience.

I find this diversification highly encouraging. Many ways are available to study cognition. The greatest credibility should be given to those generalizations that are supported by results obtained from converging operations (Garner, Hake, and Eriksen 1956).

Computational Dismemberment

What would count as evidence in favor of cognitive analyzability? Since much cognitive theory is presently based, directly or indirectly, on the assumption that the human mind is an information processing system, the most persuasive argument for many psychologists would be to demonstrate a modular computational system—more precisely, an effective procedure that could provide a basis for writing modular computer programs—that would make it possible to predict with reasonable accuracy the outcome of a great variety of experiments on and observations of human cognition.

Much ingenuity has gone into the development of artificially intelligent systems in the past thirty years. The result, as far as cognitive analyzability is concerned, has been to contribute still another way to dismember cognition.

Computer scientists generally prefer to work with a complete system that is capable of performing some well-defined function or operation. In order to get such systems to perform intelligently, it has been necessary to limit them to very specific task domains: proving theorems, playing chess, answering questions about specific bodies of data, solving equations, or whatever. The current focus is on what are called expert systems—systems for medical diagnosis, chemical analysis, geological search, trouble shooting—impressive systems that are of obvious practical value but, if taken as the basic theoretical components of cognition, suggest a disturbingly heterogeneous kind of cognitive structure, as heterogeneous as the environmental situations in which intelligent systems have been able to function.

A modern computer is a general purpose device that can, in principle, compute any computable function. When the task is to simulate human intelligence, however, meticulous analysis of the task environment is required in order to determine the function to be computed. The artificial intelligence analysis, therefore, has seemed to reflect the structure of the environment far more than the structure of the mind. In this respect, computational psychology resembles associationistic psychology.

In the course of constructing intelligent systems, however, certain general problems of organization, search, analysis, and planning seem to recur repeatedly. Thus, Pylyshyn (1978) comments: "It may turn out . . . that one cannot understand perception, reasoning, and memory independently of one another—that the general laws of cognition are at the level of abstract information handling principles (representation and control). Intelligence may be a phenomenon that appears when a large system of specific mechanisms and a large body of knowledge are organized along the lines of these abstract principles" (94).

One of the most difficult problems, however, has been to provide computers with large bodies of organized knowledge. The experimental psychology of thinking and problem solving has repeatedly demonstrated the importance of background knowledge, of familiarity with the problem domain. Careful analysis of the ways sentences are used also indicates extensive reliance on background knowledge. No one doubts that such knowledge is a critical component of any intelligent human performance. But, so far, background knowledge limited to very specific task domains is all that has been realized. Thus, the modules into which cognition has been computationally dismembered have been task modules.

The computational psychology of cognition has been plagued by an odd mismatch between theory and observation. When programs are written to simulate the monologues of a problem solver who is engrossed in thought (Newell and Simon 1972), the fit to psychological data can be impressive. Programs have even had considerable success in predicting errors during the course of learning. Where programs are of the least value is in simulating response latencies and reaction times: the time it takes a person to make the response and the time it takes a computer to execute its program are not really comparable. Thus an incongruity: the experimental evidence is strongest just where theory is least trustworthy.

Perhaps it is unfair to accuse computational psychologists of dismembering cognition into environmentally determined tasks. It is not entirely clear whether or not the artificial intelligence approach to cognition necessarily leads to cognitive modules. The current limitation to specific task domains seems more a matter of convenience than of principle. Speak to most computer scientists about modules and they will think of self-contained program segments, not tasks, faculties, or processes.

Modular Dismemberment

Complex computer programs are almost necessarily written in modular units; it is the only practical way to keep track of what has been done and what remains to do. Perhaps the programmer's conception of a module could be adapted to psychological analysis. A first step in this direction would be to get as clear as possible on what a mental program would look like if you saw one. What criteria would a psychological process have to satisfy in order to justify calling it modular?

The question of modularity has been discussed at length in the recent literature of cognitive theory. I shall merely illustrate that debate by citing Pylyshyn (1980) and Fodor (1983), both of whom would probably want to be counted as supporters of some version of a modularity hypothesis.

As I have already indicated, experimental psychologists have argued only for a kind of weak decomposability, a claim that circumstances can be arranged in such a way that one process can be studied while others remain invariant. Apparently discouraged with this approach, Pylyshyn (1980) has called for strong decomposability, for modules that cannot interact. To say that it is possible for systems not to interact is very different from saying that their interaction is not possible.

Pylyshyn's concern is to find a principled boundary between the cognitive software (which should be explainable psychologically) and the intrinsically given hardware (which should be explainable biologically). The fixed, built-in components—the hardware—should, he suggests, demonstrate a property he refers to as "cognitive impenetrability." That is to say, its operation should always be the same, regardless of any extrinsic information that might be available about the organism's goals, beliefs, inferences, intentions, interpretations, and so on.

On Pylyshyn's analysis, most familiar candidates for primitive mental functions—association, reinforcement, generalization, perception, selective attention, memory, and imagery—fail the test of cognitive impenetrability. Most of those that do satisfy the test are peripheral—early stages of visual processing or late stages of motor response. This result leaves the theoretical cupboard rather bare, which may mean either that Pylyshyn's criterion is too rigorous or that the program of designing a computational system with human functional architecture will not be as easy as it once seemed. Or both.

Fodor (1983) relaxed Pylyshyn's criterion, renamed it "informational encapsulation," and made it one of nine properties characteristic of modular processes. By his definition, the only modules are "input systems"— roughly, sensory (pre-perceptual) systems plus language comprehension. The central processes, those processes most characteristic of human intelligence, are nonmodular: any information that the person happens to possess can be brought to bear on their outcomes.

Attempts to decompose the mind into the penetrable and the impenetrable, or into the unencapsulated and the encapsulated, can be viewed as attempts to capture, in a more rigorous form, those aspects of the conscious-unconscious distinction that are valuable for cognitive analysis. So conceived, they do seem to touch on matters of central importance for any science of mental life. Unfortunately, however, they do not yield components of any value for the analysis of those mental processes that most cognitive scientists find most interesting.

Fodor contends that "the limits of modularity are also the limits of what we are going to be able to understand about the mind" (1983, 126), and he criticizes attempts to simulate higher mental processes with computers because, he claims, they have treated these central cognitive processes as if they were modular: "Intellectual capacities were divided into what seem, in retrospect, to be quite arbitrary subdepartments (proving theorems of elementary logic; pushing blocks around; ordering hamburgers), and the attempted simulations proceeded by supplying machines with very large amounts of more or less disorganized, highly topic-specific facts and heuristics. The result was an account of central processes which failed to capture precisely what is most interesting about them: their wholism" (127). What emerged, he says, was a picture of the mind that looked "embarrassingly like a Sears catalogue."

Fodor's thesis is that, in the absence of informationally encapsulated modules, no science of cognition is possible. In Fodor's hands, therefore, the modularity hypothesis is transformed into an argument for the impossibility of cognitive science.

Fodor's claim is hardly compelling, however. To show that the mind cannot be analyzed into modules of the type Pylyshyn or Fodor have defined would not show that the mind could not be analyzed in some other way. But even someone who is inclined to grant Fodor's holistic conclusion need not abandon all hope for cognitive science. In a holistic system, anything can interact with anything else, and everything interacts with something else, but it does not follow that everything must interact with everything else.

Hypothesis for Some Future Historian

Seven different attempts to analyze cognition have now been considered. Fairer and better-informed summaries could certainly be written, but they would not change the basic criticism that has been brought against all of them. In each case it has been argued that, whatever other merits the program might have, the analysis of mind into natural and self-contained cognitive elements has been a failure. This critique could continue through more analyses, but if these seven have not made the point, piling up further examples is unlikely to make it, either.

Instead of pursuing other analyses, therefore, I shall assume that the point has been made: attempts at cognitive analysis have failed so far. The failure does not mean that analysis is impossible. It may simply be that we have not yet discovered how to do it, that in another one-hundred years our grandchildren will have located the joints that have so far eluded us. Although experimental psychology has not advanced as rapidly as Hall and his contemporaries expected it would, the situation I have described is certainly no reason to close it down now. But it does seem reason enough to question whether a head-on attack is the best possible approach.

What alternatives do we have? Let us step back into history for perspective on that question. The only defensible theory of history is the view that every moment of time is a new miracle. Nevertheless, the human mind cannot resist a search for pattern and meaning. On the assumption that meaning is where you find it, therefore, I want to offer a speculation to be evaluated by some future historian of psychology.

Successful analysis may be as much a consequence as a source of intellectual progress. Students are normally introduced to a science through a discussion of the basic elements whose properties and relations the science serves to explain, but that order may be simply an expository convenience. It does not necessarily reflect the order in which insight was actually achieved. Historians of science could probably provide examples where the recognition of basic elements preceded the formulation of good scientific theory, but there must also be examples where a good theory dictated what the elements should be. The historical question is no doubt subtle and complex, but any claim that analysis is necessarily the first step along the road to science strikes me as suspiciously oversimplified. Insight may come as often from synthetic as from analytic intentions.

A satisfactory analysis should be reversible: matter is analyzed into atoms, but atoms combine lawfully to form compounds; living things are analyzed into cells, but cells combine lawfully to form organs. Elements proposed for the analysis of cognition seldom meet this test: the parts may indeed be simpler than the whole, but laws governing the reconstruction of the whole from its parts are too often neglected, or left to that reliable standby, common sense.

The hypothesis that I hope some future historian will consider is that psychology's scientific progress has generally followed the rejection or abandonment of ill-advised attempts at analysis. Recovery from analytic pathology is a repeating theme in the history of psychology. First, a style of analysis is adopted and driven to the kind of systematic absurdity that Koch (1981) has characterized. Then, just as the whole enterprise is nearing collapse, it is saved and redirected, only to adopt a new style of analysis that is again driven to absurdity, and so on. Repeatedly, the science has been snatched from the brink of futility just in the nick of time. Moreover, it is instructive to observe how these rescues have been effected. Deliverance generally comes either in the form of a new application or a new theory, or both.

Hall had an aversion to theorizing, but he knew well the value of a practical problem: "Mere knowing disaggregates if divorced from practical life" (1898, 390). When the next experiment in any program of research comes to seem too trivial to justify the effort of doing it, a useful application can do wonders to revitalize and redirect the work. A healthy science must generate technology and meet human needs: psychology is no exception. Today, however, I am less interested in instances where help comes from outside the discipline and more interested in what we can do to save ourselves.

I would argue that on those rare occasions when the enterprise has been saved by theoretical insights, they have almost always been synthetic insights, proposals that broke out of the prevailing analytic categories and forced reconsideration of mental life in broader terms.

For example, when the mind had been parceled out into dozens of faculties, the theory of association—surely a synthetic cognitive hypothesis if there ever was one—proposed a general mechanism that cut across the independent faculties. Then when the search for the mental elements to be associated had worked itself into analytic pathology, the evolutionary approach of American functionalism and the field theories of Gestalt psychology, each in its own way, offered integrative alternatives that revitalized the science. And when the decomposition of behavior into reflexes became intolerable, the computer revolution with its emphasis on integrated systems arrived just in time to offer a broadening alternative.

Cognitive psychology is now thirty years into the computer age. Signs of analytic pathology are once again appearing, but if we are aware of history, we need not repeat its mistakes. Although my recipe for avoiding the dismemberment of cognition should be evident by now, I shall conclude by summarizing it:

Never relax the criteria of evidence that set experimental psychology apart, but avoid methodolotry. Put highest value on experiments that involve converging operations, and on results that can be confirmed and supplemented by other methods of investigation, by social, psychometric, comparative, developmental, or neurophysiological methods, or even by methods borrowed from other disciplines.

Specialization in scientific research is unavoidable, but avoid specious specialization. Cherish interesting hypotheses that ignore the usual boundaries between cognitive processes, and theories that envision integration as well as analysis.

Finally, nothing is more useful than a good theory, but avoid becoming lost in thought. Treasure the practical problem that tests the usefulness of your theory.

References

Blumenthal, A. L. *The process of cognition.* Englewood Cliffs, NJ: Prentice-Hall, 1977.

Chomsky, N. *Rules and representations.* New York: Columbia University Press, 1980.

Churchland, P. M. *Scientific realism and the plasticity of mind.* Cambridge: Cambridge University Press, 1979.

Collins, A. M., & Quillian, M. R. Retrieval time from semantic memory. *Journal of Verbal Learning and Verbal Behavior,* 1969, *8,* 240–247.

D'Andrade, R. *A folk model of the mind.* Unpublished manuscript, 1983.

Fodor, J. A. *The modularity of mind: An essay on faculty psychology.* Cambridge, MA: MIT Press, 1983.

Garner, W. R., Hake, H. W., & Eriksen, C. W. Operationism and the concept of perception. *Psychological Review,* 1956, *63,* 149–159.

Guilford, J. P. *Cognitive psychology with a frame of reference.* San Diego, CA: EdITS Publishers, 1979.

Hall, G. S. Some aspects of the early sense of self. *American Journal of Psychology,* 1898, *9,* 351–395.

Hilgard, E. R. The trilogy of mind: Cognition, affection, and conation. *Journal of the History of the Behavioral Sciences,* 1980, *16,* 107–117.

Hyman, R. Stimulus information as a determinant of reaction time. *Journal of Experimental Psychology,* 1953, *45,* 188–196.

James, W. *Psychology: Briefer course.* New York: Holt, 1892.

Kelley, H. H. Attribution theory in social psychology. In D. Levine (Ed.), *Nebraska symposium on motivation* (Vol. 15). Lincoln: University of Nebraska Press, 1967.

Keyser, S. J., Miller, G. A., & Walker, E. *Cognitive science: 1978.* Unpublished report to the Alfred P. Sloan Foundation, New York, 1 October 1978.

Koch, S. The nature and limits of psychological knowledge: Lessons of a century qua "science." *American Psychologist,* 1981, *36,* 257–269.

Lachman, R., Lachman, J. I., & Butterfield, E. C. *Cognitive psychology and information processing: An introduction.* Hillsdale, NJ: Lawrence Erlbaum Associates, 1979.

Meyer, D. E. & Schvaneveldt, R. W. Facilitation in recognizing pairs of words: Evidence of a dependence between retrieval operations. *Journal of Experimental Psychology,* 1971, *90,* 227–234.

Neisser, U. Decision time without reaction time: Experiments in visual scanning. *American Journal of Psychology,* 1963, *76,* 376–385.

Newell, A. You can't play 20 questions with nature and win. In W. G. Chase (Ed.). *Visual information processing.* New York: Academic Press, 1973.

Newell, A., & Simon, H. A. *Human problem solving.* Englewood Cliffs, NJ: Prentice-Hall, 1972.

Osherson, D. N., & Wasow, T. Task-specificity and species-specificity in the study of language: A methodological note. *Cognition,* 1976, *4,* 203–214.

Posner, M. I. *Chronometric explorations of mind.* Hillsdale, NJ: Lawrence Erlbaum Associates, 1978.

Posner, M. I., & Mitchell, R. F. Chronometric analysis of classification. *Psychological Review,* 1967, *74,* 392–409.

Premack, D., & Woodruff, G. Does the chimpanzee have a theory of mind? *Behavioral and Brain Sciences,* 1978, *1,* 515–526.

Pylyshyn, Z. W. Computational models and empirical constraints. *Behavioral and Brain Sciences,* 1978, *1,* 93–99.

Pylyshyn, Z. W. Computation and cognition: Issues in the foundation of cognitive science. *Behavioral and Brain Sciences,* 1980, *3,* 111–132.

Rubenstein, H., Garfield, L., & Millikan, M. A. Homographic entries in the internal lexicon. *Journal of Verbal Learning and Verbal Behavior,* 1970, *9,* 487–492.

Ruckmich, C. A. The history and status of psychology in the United States. *American Journal of Psychology,* 1912, *23,* 517–531.

Slobin, D. Grammatical transformations and sentence comprehension in childhood and adulthood. *Journal of Verbal Learning and Verbal Behavior,* 1966, *5,* 219–227.

Sperling, G. The information available in brief visual presentations. *Psychological Monographs,* 1960, *74,* whole no. 11.

Sternberg, R. J. *Intelligence, information processing, and analogical reasoning: The componential analysis of human abilities.* Hillsdale, NJ: Lawrence Erlbaum Associates, 1977.

Sternberg, R. J. Sketch of a componential subtheory of human intelligence (with commentary). *Behavioral and Brain Sciences,* 1980, *3,* 573–614.

Sternberg, S. High-speed scanning in human memory. *Science,* 1966, *153,* 652–654.

Thurstone, L. L. *Primary mental abilities.* Chicago: University of Chicago Press, 1938.

11. Social Behavioral Effects of a First Cesarean Delivery on Both Parents
Doris R. Entwisle

Prologue

When I started graduate school, I was interested in physiological psychology. My first research, supervised by Donald Lindsley, was an experiment on responses to physiological and psychological stress in behavior problem and normal children. Almost all my research since then has also focused on preadolescent children. Only a decade ago did I return to the topic of stress, however, and the context of my research is now different. Among other things, I am interested in the social determinants and consequences of the stress associated with major life transitions. So far, two transitions have occupied my attention.

One is a transition to which life-stage theorists have paid scant attention: children's entry into full-time schooling. With Karl Alexander, I have begun a long-range study tracking several hundred Baltimore school children from the time they begin first grade to the end of the summer after their second grade year. That research is not far enough along for me to be able to report any findings, and a prior large-scale study of a similar nature has already been fully reported (*Early Schooling* 1982).

The other is a transition to which theorists have paid a great deal of attention but which has been badly neglected by social scientists who do empirical research. It is the birth event and young parents' assumption of the parent role. The dearth of scientific research on the transition to parenthood has mirrored attitudes of the rest of society. Most couples manage to become parents, so the whole process appears ordinary. It does not excite scientific interest. But, to be fair, scientific neglect of these issues is also because of their complexity. Until the last decade or so, it has been virtually impossible to analyze interwoven sets of multivariate relationships over time. Whatever the case, the *Zeitgeist* now favors research of this kind, and about 10 years ago I became involved, with Susan Doering, in researching how families cope with a first birth (*The First Birth*

1981). The study I will report here carries that work further and evaluates the early postpartum effects for both parents of cesarean delivery of their first child.

The rate of cesarean delivery has gone up sharply in recent years, from 5.0% in 1968 to 12.8% in 1977, while over the same period the birth rate has declined 12% (Marieskind 1979, 1; Consensus Report 1981, 6). In fact, the cesarean rate in some areas of the country increased more than 300% in a dozen years (Consensus Report 1981, 127). The full extent of the increase in cesarean births is not known however, because in contrast with other operative procedures, no central clearinghouse tallies the number of obstetric operations in the United States.

Maternal mortality is estimated to be four (Consensus Report 1981, 268) to six (Minkoff and Schwartz 1980, 140) times as great for cesarean as compared to vaginal delivery and is probably underreported. The percentage of cesarean patients with some postpartum morbid event is at least 10 times greater (Minkoff and Schwartz 1980). The overall relative risks of cesarean delivery, however, especially those associated with sociopsychological status of mother, father, and infant, remain to be evaluated.

Effects of a cesarean birth on the psychological status of parents and on family relationships, although not well understood, are of keen interest because these effects, with cesarean deliveries becoming so numerous, are now being played out in a large proportion of young families. A stressful birth transition, for whatever reason, can have serious long-term consequences for families, especially in respect to child abuse and divorce (see, e.g., Leifer et al. 1972; Leiderman and Seashore 1975; Lynch 1975; Lynch and Roberts 1977). Still, despite the rapid increase in the number of cesarean births in the United States, so far there are only a few studies of its social-behavioral consequences. These studies, furthermore, are limited to mainly small samples of relatively high status families and are retrospective in nature.

This paper aims to fill in some of the gap in sociopsychological research on cesarean birth. It describes the experiences of both parents at the time of an unanticipated cesarean first birth. It then evaluates the early effects of the cesarean delivery on both parents' views of themselves and their spouses in comparison with a group of noncesarean parents. Methodologically, it extends previous work along three main lines: (1) it is prospective and takes into account parents' attitudes and situations before the birth event; (2) it examines various facets of the birth event, like the mother's state of awareness during the birth or the mother's early interaction with the baby, that may covary with cesarean delivery and therefore be confounded with effects of cesarean delivery; (3) it searches for differences between middle- and working-class couples in reactions to cesarean delivery. Stressful birth could have rather different consequences for people who are well positioned in society as compared to their less fortunate counterparts.

PRIOR RESEARCH

Although the Consensus Report (1981) called for "longitudinal development followup studies" (p. 20) and lamented the "many methodologic problems" (p. 434) in behavioral studies of cesarean delivery, it did not make clear the absolute necessity for information on couples' status during pregnancy in evaluating their reactions to delivery. Some variables predict, and may cause, cesarean delivery, e.g., age, health status in pregnancy, and possibly a number of sociopsychological factors (Glick, Salerno, and Royce 1965; McDonald 1968; Sherman 1971; Grossman et al. 1980a). Another class of variables, which are not likely to be direct causes of cesarean delivery, could nevertheless be correlated with postpartum behaviors of cesarean and other parents. In small samples of parents, some of whom experience cesarean delivery and are compared with others who do not, it is common for many hundreds of variables to be examined. On average, 5% of the variables assessing parents' status will differ between delivery groups if that significance level is used. But some of these "chance" significant variables could include variables that differentiated the two delivery groups before the birth. If so, clearly these prenatal differences should be acknowledged in assessing effects of the birth on postpartum parental behavior. Most previous behavioral studies of cesarean birth nevertheless enroll families at delivery and then attribute postnatal differences in parents' psychological status or in family functioning between cesarean and vaginally delivered couples entirely to mode of delivery. Any differences between delivery groups before the birth are ignored. Obviously, the differences afterward could well be continuations of differences that existed beforehand, and this danger is real in the typical small-sample study that examines large numbers of parental variables.

A few previous studies of social-behavioral effects of cesarean delivery have obtained data prepartum (Grossman, Eichler, and Winikoff 1980; Bradley, Ross, and Warnyca 1983; Williams et al., n.d.) but unfortunately the available information documenting prepartum differences between delivery groups beforehand was not used in assessing the net effects of delivery mode in these studies. Grossman et al. (1980a), for example, measured women's anxiety and religiosity during pregnancy, found them to be correlated, and also found that women who were more religious required fewer cesarean deliveries. They did not analyze these relationships to estimate how the association between anxiety and religiosity known to exist during pregnancy could affect conclusions about the occurrence of cesarean birth, however. In many instances, differences reported in the literature between cesarean and other women could reflect merely the continuing effects of factors that differed between the two before delivery.

Another weakness in the prior research on cesarean delivery is failure to evaluate the several factors that covary with delivery mode. Birth is not a simple unitary event. In addition to a surgical (cesarean) delivery, medication levels for cesarean mothers are almost always higher, father involvement during the labor and delivery is usually less, and parents' early experiences of seeing, holding, and feeding the infant are likely curtailed. Cesarean infants, for example, are usually placed immediately in intensive care nurseries and isolated from both parents, whereas other infants often interact with both parents from the moment of birth. The few studies that examine fathers' reactions to cesarean babies focus on father-infant interaction several months postpartum (Grossman et al. 1980b; Vietze et al. 1980; Pedersen et al. 1981). How the cesarean father reacts to the delivery itself and reacts to the infant over the early postnatal period are topics about which little is known. Similarly, from the research presently available one cannot tell whether it is the early isolation experienced by the cesarean infant or the maternal surgery that may account for later differences in maternal reactions to cesarean infants.

Still another weakness in prior research on social-behavioral effects of cesarean birth is its focus on mostly middle-class couples. A cesarean birth likely has different significance depending on the parents' socioeconomic status. Factors known to differ along social class lines include the following: reactions to stress (e.g., Kessler and Cleary 1980); parent-infant relations (Kilbride, Johnson, and Streissguth 1977; Moss and Jones 1977); spousal roles (Bott 1957); family role concepts (Bernstein 1971); family values (Kohn 1969); family functioning (Hess 1970); and views of motherhood (Hoffman 1978). All these factors could come into play in comparing parents' reactions to vaginal versus cesarean births.

The main social-behavioral effects of cesarean delivery, as so far uncovered, are: (1) some added maternal discomfort and difficulty in adapting soon after delivery; (2) superior father-infant relations later in the baby's first year; and (3) little or no effect on babies themselves. These major conclusions are documented extensively in the Consensus Report (1981) as previously mentioned. Details of this research and other relevant prior work on cesarean delivery can best be reported and interpreted along with our own findings, however.

The remainder of this chapter is organized as follows. After a brief description of the sample and study design, both parents' experience during the cesarean birth of a first child is described and compared with experience of parents whose first child is delivered vaginally. The chapter then analyzes how cesarean birth affects couples' views of their own and their spouse's effectiveness as parents, and their views of the baby in comparison with couples who experience vaginal births. All along, the methodological themes developed above inform the analysis and interpretation.

The Data

For reasons of space, the study design is described briefly. Full information on characteristics of the sample, interview content, and measurement of variables is given in Entwisle and Doering (1981).

The sample consists of 120 white Maryland women and 60 of their husbands, followed prospectively from the sixth month of pregnancy. Twenty of the women experienced cesarean delivery.

The sample is designed to be homogeneous in several respects. All couples were white. This was the couple's first birth.[1] At least 19 of the 20 cesarean deliveries were not anticipated by the couple. No mother had serious health problems in pregnancy such as diabetes or preeclampsia.

In other ways the sample is not homogeneous. Levels of medication ranged from general anesthesia to none whatever. Parents' early postpartum contact with infants ranged from none at all to parents being continuously together and with the infant from the moment of birth. Father's participation in the birth ranged from his being excluded to his being present for all of both labor and delivery. Effects of each of these delivery-related factors, insofar as possible, are assessed separately for cesarean and vaginally delivered couples.

Half of the couples were classified as "middle-class" and half as "working-class" according to the woman's father's occupation while the women were growing up (Siegel 1971). Women whose fathers were professionals, proprietors, managers, owners of small businesses, and the like are labeled middle-class. Women whose fathers were manual workers of relatively high-skill levels are labeled working class. This group is from a "stable working class" in that their fathers had considerable education, income, and skill.[2]

The women's average age is 24.7, somewhat higher than the mean age (22.4) for women having a first child in the United States in 1973 (U.S. Bureau of the Census 1975). The women averaged a little over two years younger than their husbands. Couples had been married a little over two and a half years before conception. All but four of the pregnancies were definitely or "mostly" planned.

The women gave birth at sixteen different hospitals in the central Maryland area except for five who had planned home deliveries. Sixty-five different obstetricians, 3 midwives, 12 residents, and 1 father carried out the deliveries.

The 120 women were interviewed face-to-face in their homes by female interviewers twice in the last trimester of pregnancy and a third time two to three weeks after delivery. A short telephone interview was conducted with the women when the baby was about six months old. Sixty of the women's husbands were interviewed at home by male interviewers, separately from their wives, early in the last month of their wives' pregnancies. Of these 60 men, 57 were reinterviewed about four to eight weeks postpartum.

All interviews took three to three and a half hours and were taped. The interviews were transcribed from tapes and reviewed before coding. Coders, blind to delivery status, achieved agreement in 85% of judgments or better in rating variables used in the analyses to be presented here. (The study design, interviews, and scheduling are fully described in Entwisle and Doering 1981.)

Differences between delivery groups that existed before the birth are discussed in the appendix. Ratings on a number of variables assessed late in pregnancy did differ at or beyond the 5% level, but the number of such variables is consistent with sampling fluctuations. Where pertinent, these preexisting differences between delivery groups are taken into account in evaluating effects of delivery mode.

Results

This portion of the chapter has two major sections. First are descriptions of what may be some critical details of cesarean parents' experience during the birth and shortly after which have not previously been systematically catalogued. Second are evaluations of how cesarean delivery impacted the emergent parent role, as defined by changes in each parents' attitudes toward the self, spouse, and infant.

THE BIRTH EVENT

Labor. Of the 20 cesarean women, 2 missed the first stage of labor, and all missed the second stage. For the 18 cesarean women who did experience labor, its average duration was 12.0 hours (S.D. = 9.20 hours). For the vaginally delivered women, the first stage of labor lasted 13.5 hours (S.D. = 10.64 hours). The proportion of fathers present for labor is about the same for both delivery groups (89% of the cesarean fathers and 85% of other fathers). For the 17 women whose husbands were entirely absent from first-stage labor,[3] cesarean delivery was somewhat less likely than it was for the 101 women whose husbands were present (.118 versus .158), a difference in incidence that is not significant.[4]

Often, failure to progress in labor is cited as a reason for cesarean delivery. Since the father's presence and his support may improve the laboring woman's ability to continue (Sosa et al. 1980), the incidence of cesarean delivery in this sample was tallied in light of the woman's perceptions of her husband during labor and of his helpfulness then. Cesarean wives reported their husbands had significantly less positive feelings about being present during labor than the other wives reported their husbands had (2.87 vs. 3.79, t = 2.19, p <.03, where 1 = very negative, to 6 = enthusiastic). Compared to the other women, the cesarean women also reported that their husbands helped them less in labor (borderline significant, scored on a scale where 1 = was there but did nothing to help, to 6 = did everything possible to help [3.31 vs. 4.04, t = 1.91, p = .06]). In addition, the cesarean women were also significantly less enthusiastic about having their husbands present during labor than the other women were, although still positive (4.31 vs. 4.87, t = 2.16, p <.05, where 4 = mild positive and 5 = solid positive).

Of the 57 men interviewed, only 5 were cesarean husbands who were present during labor. Their reports of their feelings during labor agreed with their wives'. They felt less positive about being there than other fathers did (3.00 vs. 4.21, t = 1.95, p <.06, where 3 = neutral, 4 = mild positive, and 5 = solid positive).

One explanation for the cesarean husbands' more negative perception of labor could be that they did not want to be there or their wives did not want them there. But the evidence is contrary. When questioned one month before the birth about whether they wished to be in the labor room, cesarean fathers were just as favorable as other fathers (1.43 vs. 1.34 with 1 = very much, 2 = generally favorable, difference not significant). Cesarean fathers' and other fathers' perceptions one month prepartum about their wives' wishes for them to be present in labor also agreed (1.29 vs. 1.23, respectively, with 1 = wife very much wanted, and 2 = wife generally favorable toward). In terms of the woman's expressed desire in the ninth month of pregnancy to have a companion in labor and for the husband to be that companion, the two delivery groups were also virtually identical (90% of cesarean and 89% of other women wanted the husband as a companion in labor). It seems unlikely, therefore, that the differences in fathers' reactions to labor are attributable to prepartum differences in either spouse's wishes for the husband to be present.

Another explanation for the cesarean fathers more negative reactions during labor might be that the wife's labor was more difficult than that of the other women,[5] or even just more difficult or longer than cesarean mothers or fathers expected. Again, however, the evidence is contrary. The cesarean group found the first stage of labor a little more painful than expected (.26 units), but other women's expectations were further off the mark (.57 units). The cesarean women also did not underestimate the length of first-stage labor any more than the other women did (t = .61, p = .55).

Cesarean fathers' negative reactions to labor also cannot be attributed to more unrealistic expectations about labor on their parts compared to other fathers. Comparing the pain wives experienced with what the fathers expected beforehand,[6] cesarean fathers scored somewhat lower than other fathers but not significantly so (2.16 vs. 2.82, t = 1.29, p = .20. Like their wives, men in both delivery groups underestimated the length of first-stage labor, but estimates were about equally far off.

In sum, cesarean wives' reactions to their husbands' presence during labor were more negative than other women's reactions, and cesarean husbands who were queried directly were less positive about being present for labor than were other husbands, but these differences cannot be ascribed to longer or more severe first-stage labor for the cesarean women or to less desire in advance for the father to be present for labor. Possible explanations for the cesarean fathers' reactions during labor will be presented later.

Mother's delivery experience. The 20 cesarean women, as would be expected, reported significantly more medication than did the other women (table 11.1). For example, 10 cesarean but only 2 other women were unconscious at delivery.[7] The cesarean women also scored lower than the other women did on a scale designed to measure the subjective quality of their birth experience (table 11.1).[8]

Father's participation in delivery. Of the 20 cesarean fathers, 15 were absent at delivery,[9] 11 by choice and 4 against their will. For the five cesarean couples where fathers were present for delivery, wives were asked what their husbands had done to help. One reported that her husband did nothing to help, three at first reported the husband did nothing to help but in response to probes then reported some help. The remaining woman believed her husband helped just by being there.

Considering all couples with husbands present for delivery, there was no significant difference in the wives' desire to have the husband present whether or not the delivery was cesarean. However, the cesarean women felt that their husbands were slightly negative about being there, whereas the vaginally delivered women felt their husbands were "solid positive" about being there. This difference between delivery groups is highly significant (table 11.2).

All women whose husbands were excluded against their wishes were on average somewhat negative about the husband's absence from delivery, but cesarean mothers were a little less disappointed than other mothers

Table 11.1 Woman's Average Level of Awareness and Perceived Quality of Birth Experience

| | Middle-class | | | | | | |
| | Cesarean Delivery | | | Vaginal Delivery | | | |
	N	Mean	SD	N	Mean	SD	t-value
Level of awareness[a]	10	1.60	0.97	50	4.12	1.87	4.13**
Quality of birth experience[b] (Range = 5 to 30)	10	13.20	2.90	50	19.11	5.32	3.40**

| | Working-class | | | | | | |
| | Cesarean Delivery | | | Vaginal Delivery | | | |
	N	Mean	SD	N	Mean	SD	t-value
Level of awareness[a]	10	2.20	1.32	50	4.46	2.02	3.38**
Quality of birth experience[b] (Range = 5 to 30)	10	12.37	4.71	50	19.76	5.60	3.90**

[a]1 = unconscious (asleep); 2, 3 = confused, numb; 4 = awake but numb; 5 = whiffs of gas; 6 = pudendal block only; 7 = local infiltration only; 8 = awake and feeling everything.

[b]The woman's birth experience is rated on a scale that is the sum of scores on five items. Respondents, after describing the birth in detail, were asked, "How did you feel?" for the moment right after the baby was born or for the first conscious moment in the case of those who were unconscious at birth of the baby. Both physical and emotional responses were sought. Then emotions and physical feelings (items 1 and 2) were separately coded on scales from 1 to 6 and 1 to 5, respectively. Women gave similar information about their emotional and physical feelings in recovery, and these responses (item 3 and item 4) were coded on scales from 1 to 6 and 1 to 5, respectively. At another point in the interview respondents were asked, "Many women feel, right after the birth, that they never want to go through all that again; did you have any feelings like that, right after?" Answers to the fifth item were scored from 1 (yes, never again go through birth) to 8 (no, can't wait to have another). The alpha reliability of this scale is .734.

**Significant at or beyond 1% level.

were (table 11.2). Cesarean husbands who were excluded against their will were not as negative (borderline) about being excluded as were other fathers. When husbands chose to be absent, cesarean wives were also less negative (borderline) about their husbands' lack of participation than were other wives.

The cesarean women's subjective birth experience, in contrast to that of other women, was of slightly lower (not significant) quality if the husband was present. There is negligible correlation (.087, not significant) between husband's participation in delivery and cesarean women's birth experi-

Table 11.2   Wife's Feelings about Husband's Participation during Delivery

| | Wife's Own Feelings about Husband's Participation (or Lack of Same) in Delivery (2 = negative; 3 = neutral; 4 = mild positive; 5 = solid positive) | | | | | | |
| | Cesarean Delivery | | | Vaginal Delivery | | | |
	N	Mean	SD	N	Mean	SD	t-value
Husband present	5	4.60	0.89	74	4.89	0.85	0.74
Husband absent against will	4	2.25	1.23	4	1.75	0.96	0.63
Husband absent by choice	11	3.18	0.75	22	2.50	1.14	1.79†

| | Wife's Perception of Husband's Feelings (or Lack of Same) in Delivery (2 = negative; 3 = neutral; 4 = mild positive; 5 = solid positive) | | | | | | |
| | Cesarean Delivery | | | Vaginal Delivery | | | |
	N	Mean	SD	N	Mean	SD	t-value
Husband present	5	2.80	0.84	73	4.95	0.97	4.82*
Husband absent against will	4	2.50	1.00	4	1.50	0.58	1.75†
Husband absent by choice	10	3.20	1.13	22	2.55	1.18	1.47

*a*See note 9 for definition of husband's participation in delivery.
†Significant between 5% and 10% level.
*Significant at or beyond 5% level.

ence. The same correlation for the vaginally delivered women is large and positive (.526, p < .01).

This set of findings about mothers' and fathers' reactions to husbands' participation in cesarean delivery suggests that, unlike husband participation for vaginally delivered mothers, the degree of husband participation is not very important for the cesarean mother and is negative for the father. Taking these findings as a guide, husbands who wish to be present for delivery probably should be present, whether the delivery is cesarean or vaginal. However, since cesarean women were less distressed by the husband's absence than were other women, and since husbands who chose to be absent from a cesarean delivery did not actually disappoint their wives, encouraging reluctant fathers to be present for cesarean delivery on grounds of improving the woman's birth experience does not seem justified.

The Consensus Report (1981, 431) says that "recently the opinion was reaffirmed" that the presence of the father or other support person may be psychologically helpful to the (cesarean) mother. The reference to our study (Doering and Entwisle 1977) cited in the Consensus Report in support of father's presence in delivery misinterprets our earlier work—we did not earlier make a separate and detailed study of cesarean women's birth experience as affected by the father's participation, although we did report the positive effects of father participation for women with vaginal deliveries (Doering, Entwisle, and Quinlan 1980; Entwisle and Doering 1981, 116). The limited information about father participation in cesarean delivery analyzed and presented here for the first time suggests instead that father participation at cesarean delivery was not associated with the quality of cesarean women's birth experience, although women were positive about the father being there if he chose to be.

Effects of father presence are also not entirely clear according to other reports. Nolan (1979) and Gainer and Van Bonn (1977) found that cesarean mothers were consistently more satisfied with delivery if the father had been present, although the women's greater satisfaction attained statistical significance only when the woman received some teaching on the third postpartum day. Marut and Mercer (1979) found a borderline positive effect of having a support person (usually the father) for primiparious cesarean women but do not comment on the issue of father's desire to be present, which our analysis indicates is a critical variable to take into account.

An unsettled but important question is whether the cesarean women's generally negative recollections of their husbands' feelings during labor and their own relatively less favorable perceptions of their husbands during labor could have contributed to the need for cesarean delivery in the present sample. This is not likely for several reasons.

First, there is the question of whether any psychological distance separating cesarean husbands and wives during labor actually antedated the onset of labor. Such prepartum rifts in spousal relations could have a number of serious consequences, possibly including cesarean delivery. This conjecture was checked in several ways by examining variables measured before the birth that reflected marital closeness. No differences in marital quality between cesarean and other couples were found.[10]

Second, men's recollection of their feelings as obtained in interviews a few weeks after delivery may not be especially accurate. If the men had been questioned about their feelings at the time labor was in progress, findings might have been different. Possibly since cesarean men had more negative delivery experience than other men did, these feelings could have "spread backward" in time to color the men's recollections of their experiences during the period of labor as well. Labor was unsuccessful, so in fathers' eyes it might be thought unnecessary.

Third, fathers may have developed negative feelings gradually over the course of the labor as disturbing events began to occur. If the woman was sent for X rays, if dilation was not progressing and the like, the deteriorating picture would become apparent to the father. If so, the father's negative emotions during labor could be a consequence rather than a cause of cesarean delivery. This explanation seems the most likely of all the possibilities.

There is one other study of fathers' reactions during labor in relation to cesarean delivery. Klein and Gist (1982) investigated how father support in labor affected cesarean delivery by observing six cesarean couples for an hour in midlabor before the women received any medication and then comparing the cesarean couples with 34 vaginally delivered couples. They found no difference between delivery groups in the husband's psychological support (conversing, touching) but cesarean husbands provided significantly less instrumental support (proffering a comfort item, modeling breathing). In their sample, there was a significant negative correlation between the amount of father instrumental support and the number of complications in labor and delivery.

Clearly, our sample of five cesarean fathers and Klein and Gist's sample of six such fathers are not adequate to address issues of how father support may affect delivery complications, but there may be some connection between the two.

Recovery. The cesarean women took longer to recover from the birth than the other women did. They were hospitalized for five or more days compared to less than three days for the other women. Significant differences in physical condition after delivery included: length of delay in first meal after the birth, sleeping pills taken in hospital, pain killers taken in hospital, delay in walking after the birth, delay in bladder and bowel function. (See Entwisle and Doering 1981, 110, for details.)

Earlier we noted more infant crying and more severe postpartum depressions[11] reported by cesarean mothers in comparison with other mothers (Entwisle and Doering 1981, 134). Further study reveals that these differences are significant only for women of one social class or the other—more infant crying reported by middle-class cesarean women, more serious depressions reported by working-class cesarean women.

In this sample the origins of these effects are obscure. Infant crying and maternal depression could not be predicted by any variables measured in pregnancy or by infant's sex. There are no significant zero-order correlations between amount of infant crying or the severity of depression and any measure of worry or anxiety measured prepartum, whether of husband or wife, although the literature points to this kind of association. For example, Tod (1964) found anxiety level in pregnancy associated with postpartum depression. So did Grossman et al. (1980a, 80).[12] Pitt (1968), on the other hand, who questioned a random sample of 305 English women in the seventh month of pregnancy and again six to eight weeks after delivery, did not find that depressives were significantly more anxious in pregnancy than controls.[13] (See Entwisle 1982 for details.)

In the present sample, crying and depression seem best classified as among the "incidental" negative accompaniments of cesarean delivery, such as women's longer hospital stays. Since the amount of reported crying or depression failed to predict later parenting behaviors or parental role concepts either in the first few weeks after delivery or at one year postpartum (with the single exception that women who reported more depression took longer to "feel like a mother"), these variables are omitted from further consideration.

Mother's early contact with the infant. In approximately the middle of the interview two to three weeks postpartum, after describing the onset of labor, the trip to the hospital, and the birth in great detail, the women were asked a series of questions[14] about (1) the number of minutes they had spent with the child in the first postpartum hour; (2) the number of hours they had spent with the infant within the first 12 hours; and (3) the number of hours per day they had spent with infants over the second and third postpartum days (table 11.3). They were also asked in detail about their early feeding experiences with their babies and their use of rooming-in.[15]

The cesarean women did not see, hold, or feed their babies as soon as the other women in this sample did (table 11.3). There are differences by mode of delivery in the average number of minutes women reported spending with their babies during the first postpartum hour (0.85 vs. 9.69 minutes for cesarean and other women, $t = 2.95$, $p < .01$), during the first 12 hours after delivery (6 minutes vs. 72 minutes, $t = 2.02$, $p < .05$), and over the first three days (average of 4.8 hours vs. 7.7 hours, $t = 1.84$, $p < .07$). One clear consequence of cesarean delivery for this sample is thus a difference in the time when mothers and their infants began to interact and in the extent of that interaction.

Since delivery mode and the amount of early maternal-infant contact are confounded in this sample and since the first postpartum hour is a time that some theorists (e.g., Klaus, Kennell) believe is especially important for later mother-infant relations, I tried to assess the consequences of the cesarean delivery independent of the lessened maternal-infant contact. Analyses to be presented later suggest that the cesarean middle-class women were less responsive to their infants two to three weeks after delivery

Table 11.3 Mother's Early Interaction with Her Infant

| | Middle-class | | | | | | | Working-class | | | | | | |
| | Caesarean Delivery | | | Vaginal Delivery | | | t-value | Caesarean Delivery | | | Vaginal Delivery | | | t-value |
	N	Mean	SD	N	Mean	SD		N	Mean	SD	N	Mean	SD	
Contact														
(1) minutes within first hour	10	0.20	0.60	50	11.10	13.90	2.45*	10	1.50	4.70	50	8.32	12.60	1.68†
(2) average hours within first 12 hours	10	0.16	0.41	50	1.01	1.91	1.40	10	0.53	0.09	50	1.40	2.90	1.48
(3) average hours over first 3 days	10	4.50	3.10	49	7.44	6.55	1.38	10	5.10	4.36	50	8.12	7.15	1.28
When first saw baby	10	2.70	1.25	50	3.92	0.44	5.50**	10	2.70	1.49	50	3.88	0.48	4.63**
2 = in recovery; 3 = in delivery but not immediately; 4 = as born or immediately after														
When first held baby	10	3.10	1.66	50	5.54	1.83	3.90**	10	2.70	1.34	50	5.22	1.73	4.34**
3 = 13–24 hrs. later; 4 = 7–12 hrs. later; 5 = 1–6 hrs. later; 6 = in recovery or hall														
How long first held baby	10	4.00	2.82	49	2.82	1.50	2.23*	10	4.20	1.32	49	3.20	1.57	1.87†
2 = 5–10 min.; 3 = 11–15 min.; 4 = 16–30 min.														

Variable	N	M	SD	N	M	SD	t	N	M	SD	N	M	SD	t
When first fed baby 2 = 25–48 hrs.; 3 = 13–24 hrs.; 4 = 7–12 hrs.	10	2.50	0.97	50	3.88	1.55	2.71**	10	2.20	0.63	50	3.70	1.53	3.03**
Number of feedings first day Actual number	10	1.00	0.94	50	2.82	2.02	2.78**	10	0.80	1.14	50	2.60	1.88	2.90**
Number of feedings second day Actual number	10	3.20	2.30	50	4.74	2.01	2.16**	10	3.10	2.51	49	4.84	1.90	2.49*
How felt about baby on first view 2 = mildly negative; 3 = neutral; 4 = mildly positive	10	2.40	0.97	49	3.88	1.27	3.47**	10	3.50	1.08	47	3.91	1.21	1.00
How felt about baby when first held it 2 = mildly negative; 3 = neutral; 4 = mildly positive	10	2.80	0.92	47	4.09	1.16	3.29**	10	3.90	1.29	47	4.55	1.08	1.68†
How felt about holding baby first time 2 = mildly negative; 3 = neutral; 4 = mildly positive	10	2.60	1.51	50	4.08	1.38	3.05**	10	4.80	1.03	47	4.13	1.45	1.39
How felt about caring for newborn 3 = strongly ambivalent; 4 = mildly ambivalent	10	3.10	0.50	50	4.24	0.20	2.33*	10	4.20	0.51	50	4.40	1.28	0.43
Early maternal responsiveness (See note 17)	10	7.70	3.02	50	10.28	3.10	2.41**	10	8.80	2.97	50	10.00	3.23	1.08

†t-test significant between 5% and 10% level.
*t-test significant between 1% and 5% level.
**t-test significant at or beyond 1% level.

but this reaction appears to stem more from reduced contact with their infants than from delivery mode per se.

Mother's early attitude toward the baby. For a series of questions about emotions[16] on first seeing or holding the baby right after the birth, mothers of the two delivery groups differed, and there is an interaction by social class (table 11.3). The middle-class cesarean women reported more negative feelings about the baby on first seeing it, less desire to hold the baby for the first time, and significantly more negative attitudes about caring for a newborn than other middle-class women. These effects are weaker or reversed for the working-class women (table 11.3), a finding in agreement with Blumberg's research (1980). She found among mostly low-status mothers of at-risk infants a modest correlation (r = .25, p <.05) between cesarean delivery and mothers' positive perception of their newborns.

The middle-class cesarean women in this sample also scored signficantly lower on a scale of reported maternal responsiveness[17] than did other middle-class women (8.25 vs. 10.14, t = 2.47, p <.02). This difference, however, must be weighed in light of the middle-class cesarean mothers relatively lower ratings of the coming baby compared to other middle-class women when all were six to seven months pregnant (see appendix) as well as reduced maternal-infant contact mentioned above. Analyses of these issues will be undertaken in a later section.

Father's birth experience. In this sample, 7 cesarean fathers were among the 57 fathers who were interviewed on both occasions. The 13 other cesarean fathers were not interviewed directly but were described by their wives. To my knowledge, no other research evaluating effects of cesarean delivery takes into account fathers' prenatal status or examines caretaking behavior of fathers in the very early weeks.

Elsewhere a model to explain the quality of men's birth experience[18] suggests it responded directly to the extent of the man's participation in delivery and to the quality of the wife's birth experience (Entwisle and Doering 1981, 121ff.). It is not surprising that cesarean fathers reported more negative birth experience than did other fathers, in part because we know cesarean women rated their birth experience more negatively than the other women did. The 7 cesarean fathers' average birth experience score is 7.4 (S.D. 2.57), compared to 11.9 (S.D. 3.61) for the 50 other fathers. Of the cesarean fathers interviewed, four were absent from delivery by choice and their average birth experience score was 8.8. The two who were present for delivery scored 6.0, and the other father, absent against his will, scored 5.0.

To measure the contribution of delivery mode to the quality of the father's birth experience, a multiple regression model, which explains

52.2% of the variance, included preparation and father participation in delivery. Cesarean delivery has a borderline negative effect on men's birth experience (standardized coefficient of $-.183$, 1.79 times its standard error). In this model, as in a similar model omitting delivery mode (Entwisle and Doering 1981, 120ff.), whether men attended preparation classes had negligible effects, but father participation in delivery had strong and significant positive effects (standardized coefficient of .594). This analysis cannot speak to whether some of the negative effect of cesarean delivery on father's birth experience might be mitigated if fathers were allowed to participate more actively in delivery, but the earlier tally of the average birth experience of cesarean fathers who were absent from delivery compared to those who were present suggests not.

Father's early contact with the infant. Most fathers of vaginally delivered infants held their babies within the first six hours or less on average. The seven interviewed fathers of cesarean babies reported seeing the baby in the recovery room or as it was being taken to the nursery, but only one cesarean father held his infant within the first 12 hours. The fact that only 5 of the 20 fathers (25%) of cesarean infants were present for delivery, compared to over 70% of other fathers, probably causes some but not all of the differences in early father-infant contact.

Father's early attitude toward the baby. Cesarean delivery apparently did not affect the father's early interactions with the infant. Average scores on reported paternal responsiveness[19] for cesarean and other fathers four to eight weeks after delivery did not differ significantly. Also, delivery groups did not differ with respect to the father's involvement in child care,[20] whether reported by him or by his wife (Reilly 1981). Furthermore, multiple regression models did not indicate that delivery mode affected paternal responsiveness or the father's early involvement in child care as reported by the wife[21] at two to three weeks postpartum.[22]

CHANGE IN PARENTS' ATTITUDES TOWARD SELF, SPOUSE, AND INFANT

We now move from the description of parents' experiences to analysis of change in role perceptions. Semantic differential ratings are used to measure parents' evaluations of the self, spouse, and infant. Using 20 bipolar adjectives, the parents rated themselves in the parental role both before and after the birth. For example, the women rated "Self as Mother" and "Husband as Father," while the men rated "Self as Father" and "Wife as Mother." The ratings were factor analyzed using standard procedures and then screened to locate a "potency" factor in order to assess parents' judged role effectiveness as a parent. (See Smith 1968 and Franks and

Marolla 1976 for prior research using Osgood's semantic differential to measure judgments of role competence.) The final set of items was selected according to whether loadings were consistently large in analyses of ratings of the same concept procured over all interviews.[23]

Six semantic differential items identified a potency factor in women's perceptions of "Myself as Mother." These were "powerful-helpless," "strong-weak," "capable-fumbling," "fast-slow," "wise-foolish," and "complete-incomplete." The same six items, but taken from the men's interviews, were used to scale the men's perceptions of "Wife as Mother."

Similar procedures yielded four items that identified the men's perception of "Self as Father." These were "powerful-helpless," "brave-scared," "strong-weak," and "capable-fumbling." These same four items, but taken from the women's interviews, were used to measure women's perceptions of "Husband as Father." Thus, there are judgments of the wife's effectiveness as a mother by her and by her husband before and after the birth. There are also judgments of the husband's effectiveness as a father by him and by his wife at both times.

Both before and after the delivery, men and women also rated "My Baby" on the 20 bipolar adjectives. Factor analysis pointed to two items that reflected perception of the infant ("sad-happy," "angry-peaceful"). Scores on these items were summed to provide separate measures, one as assessed by the father and another as assessed by the mother. Factor analysis of the infant ratings also pointed to an overall evaluation scale composed of the two items mentioned above plus three others ("healthy-sick," "kind-cruel," "good-bad"). A more general indicator of the parent's rating of the baby was obtained by summing these five items.

Table 11.4 gives the average semantic differential ratings for the various role concepts. None of the variables derived from the semantic differential ratings (self as parent, spouse as parent, the baby's score) differed between parents of the two social classes at any one point in time.

The cesarean women's average ratings did not differ from other women's ratings either before the birth or after except that the middle-class cesarean women had significantly more negative views of the baby both before the birth and after than did the other middle-class women. (The infant adjustment ratings contain two items. Both are included in the five items forming "My Baby," so these two measures overlap.)

The women's concepts of themselves as mothers dropped significantly from before the birth to afterward. This drop holds for both classes of women and both delivery groups (borderline for cesarean mothers). Women's ratings of the baby also dropped, but did so significantly only for the vaginal-delivery groups. The cesarean women lowered their ratings of the baby somewhat but not as much as the other women and not significantly. The women's ratings of their husbands as fathers also dropped from

Table 11.4 Summary of Average Values of Parents' Semantic Differential Ratings of Self as Parent, Spouse as Parent, and Infant

		Women				Men	
		Prepartum		Postpartum		Prepartum	Postpartum
		Middle-Class	Working-Class	Middle-Class	Working-Class		
Self as	CSECT	34.50	34.00	30.80 +	30.30†	23.00	21.29
parent	OTHER	33.60	34.55	32.40*	31.96*	22.58	21.20*
Spouse as	CSECT	23.90	22.89	23.50	22.80	29.43	34.14
parent	OTHER	24.74	24.06	23.08*	22.74*	33.94	35.10
My baby	CSECT	28.30	31.50	27.05	29.80	30.71	31.57
	OTHER	32.08	31.82	30.17*	29.68*	31.23	29.10*
Infant	CSECT	10.90	12.20	9.90	11.80	12.00	12.29
adjust-ment	OTHER	12.57	12.38	11.70*	11.68*	12.26	11.26*

†Difference from mean of same concept at previous time significant between 5% and 10% levels.
*Difference significant at or beyond 5% level from mean of same concept at previous time for pairwise present cases.

before the birth to after but again the drops were smaller and not significant for the cesarean group. One effect of cesarean delivery for mothers is apparently to insulate their views of the husband and infant against the erosion in views of these other family members that characterizes the vaginally delivered women.

Table 11.4 also tallies ratings given by the men. On average, like the mothers, the fathers' views of themselves as parents dropped. Although the drop for the cesarean fathers (-1.71) exceeds that for other fathers (-1.38), only the latter is significant because of the small sample size. Also, like the cesarean mothers, the cesarean fathers' views of themselves after the birth did not differ significantly from other fathers'. But men's views of their wives as mothers improved over the perinatal period, and the cesarean men's ratings of their wives went up considerably more than those of other men (4.71 units compared to 1.16 units), although the improvement in fathers' ratings is not statistically significant. In addition, while noncesarean fathers' ratings of the infant decreased significantly on either the five-item or the two-item scale, there are nonsignificant increases in cesarean fathers' ratings of the infant.

Cesarean fathers' relatively higher ratings of the baby compared to other fathers is also substantiated in a separate analysis of fathers' relative rankings of the infant as compared with self, wife, etc. (ranking from 1 to

8). The cesarean fathers' average rankings of the baby fell .57 points from before the birth to after, but the rankings of other fathers fell 1.20 points, a differential change that is significant (t ; 2.04, p <.04). (The cesarean fathers ranked the coming baby higher than other fathers did before the birth and the comparison here takes account of that preexisting difference.)

Changes in judgments of effectiveness of self as parent are negative for both women and men irrespective of delivery mode. Cesarean delivery appears to defend both parents' ratings of the baby and cesarean mothers' ratings of fathers from the erosion seen for other parents over the perinatal period, however. All men's views of their wives improved, but the cesarean men's ratings increased more markedly. The consequences of cesarean delivery in terms of these surface manifestations are thus positive compared to experience of couples with vaginal births. Models in the rest of this section attempt to infer the degree to which these changes in parents' views can be attributed to cesarean delivery per se.

Rationale for the model explaining change in parents' judgments of role competence. To describe women's transition to parenthood, Reilly (1981) proposed the model in figure 11.1, with women's evaluations of themselves in the maternal role explained in terms of the infant's perceived adjustment, the husband's involvement in child care, the circumstances of delivery (husband participation, cesarean delivery) and the woman's status in pregnancy (woman's evluation of self as mother before the birth, prior experience caring for young babies.)

Reilly's original model included three equations (Reilly 1981; Entwisle 1982; Reilly, Entwisle, and Doering 1984) with infant rating and husband involvement in child care as well as the wife's evaluation of herself in the maternal role taken as outcomes. This three-equation structural model was supplemented by a measurement model. It turned out that when the joint measurement and structural models were estimated by LISREL (Jöreskog and Sörbom 1978) the maximum likelihood estimates of structural parameters were close to estimates of the same three-equation model using ordinary least squares and assuming perfect measurement (Reilly 1981; Entwisle 1982). Also, in a separate sensitivity analysis, potential bias from possible correlation between disturbance terms of role concepts measured at successive times appears negligible (Reilly 1981). Estimates of a "stacked" model (LISREL IV), however, revealed structural differences in the model's fit for women of the two social classes. Put another way, Reilly's model fit well according to chi-square tests of goodness of fit when estimated separately for each social class group but the fit was significantly reduced when data were pooled (stacked model).

Here I will follow Reilly's lead and estimate parameters separately for parents of the two social classes, but I will simplify Reilly's model in two ways: (1) I will focus mainly on the third equation in the model, the equation that explains parent's role concepts; and (2) I will estimate the paremeters by ordinary least squares and assume no measurement error. This strategy, which is justified by the prior research cited earlier, greatly simplifies the presentation.

I will explain the several varieties of parents' role evaluations (self as mother, self as father, spouse as mother, spouse as father) in terms of the same constructs except that the variables in each version of the model, such as "previous baby care experience," will relate to the woman's previous experience if she is the evaluator, or to the man's previous experience if he is the evaluator. In other words, the same constructs and structure characterize every version of the model to explain parents' role concepts, but for any particular role construct, the data are derived from interviews with the wife or husband, as appropriate. In each version of this model, the aim is to explain what causes change in the parent's evaluation of self or spouse in the parent role a few weeks after delivery ("self as mother" and "husband as father" by women, and "self as father" and "wife as mother" by men).

A brief justification for assumptions in the model follows (fig. 11.1).

Two constructs involving other family members are assumed to affect the parent's evaluations: the parent's evaluation of the infant, measured as described in the previous section, and the parent's assessment of husband

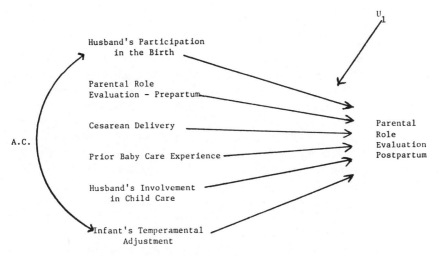

Fig. 11.1.   Model of development of parental role evaluations from prenatal period through first few weeks after birth. A.C., there are covariances among all of the exogenous constructs.

involvement in child care (defined in notes 20 and 21). A "difficult" infant would be expected to depress either parent's feelings of competence. Children who are intense, negative, and withdrawing in their reactions place different caregiving demands on their parents than do children who are less intense, and more positive and adaptable (Thomas and Chess 1977). Children with such temperamental differences are also differentially perceived by their caregivers (Bates 1980; Thomas, Chess, and Korn 1982).

The degree of the husband's involvement in child care, being discretionary for these couples (all husbands worked and all wives had resigned from the labor force, at least temporarily) could signify for the wife the value the husband placed on parenting activities and so affect her self-image as a parent. If the husband is active, for example, this may define child care as a highly valued activity and so the wife may see her motherly role as more important. Accordingly, the husband's contribution will have positive effects on her self-image.

For the man's self-image as a parent or for the woman's image of her husband as a father, the husband's involvement in child care is a measure of the "voluntary" investment of the father. One would expect that fathers investing more time in child care would see themselves more favorably as parents and that their wives would also see them favorably as parents.

For men's ratings of their wives as mothers, husband involvement in child care could have positive or negative effects. If husbands value the sharing of infant care, wives who allow them to participate may get higher ratings (the baby is not the wife's "property"). Or the reverse could hold: husbands may take a more active role in child care if they see the wife as inept.

There are three other sets of exogenous predictors. The first set, concepts of self as parent and spouse as parent measured before the birth, permit us to measure stability or its lack in these concepts over the birth transition. For example, if a parent "expects" to be competent (or the reverse), this may be a self-fulfilling prophecy. Also, if parents expect the spouse to be competent, they may take actions that cause this to happen. The woman may offer to teach the husband how to bathe the baby, for instance. Measuring the level of these concepts before the birth also permits assessing the contributions of other variables to change in those concepts net of their original level.

The second set of exogenous predictors reflects couples' previous child care experience.[24] Mothers and fathers with more experience with very young infants may feel more competent. Additionally, a parent with more experience may assess the spouse's role performance more severely.

The third set of exogenous predictors involves events during the birth: father participation (see note 9 for definition) and delivery mode. The husband's degree of participation during the birth could affect both his and his wife's views of him as a parent. Men who participate may be regarded as better fathers. Also, men's participation in delivery could affect views of the wife's parental competence in that women who encourage their husbands to take an active part in the birth may be seen by their husbands and by themselves as more competent mothers.

Cesarean delivery might depress ratings of women's role competence in the eyes of both parents because of the women's need to recover after a relatively more difficult birth. Cesarean delivery might affect fathers' role competence because cesarean fathers, while their wives were recovering, might become more involved with the infant than other fathers.

The same structural model (fig. 11.1) will be estimated to explain changes in couples' views of themselves as parents and views of their spouses as parents over the perinatal period. This model includes parents' prepartum ratings of the same role concept as well as several other variables besides cesarean delivery that could affect these role concepts. The aim is to explain how cesarean delivery may lead to change in couples' assessments of themselves as parents over the perinatal period, allowing for effects of the other variables in the model.

As noted, there are no differences in role concepts between social class groups at any one point in time. There are also no differences associated with social class in any of the other variables that appear in the model with the exception that the working-class women had more previous baby care experience. In other words, father's participation in delivery, the incidence of cesarean delivery, father's invovement in child care, and the men's previous baby care experience did not differ in average levels between these middle- and working-class parents.

Woman's judgments of their own role effectiveness. When the model in figure 11.1 is estimated to explain woman's judgments of their effectiveness as mothers soon after the birth, cesarean delivery does not appear important (table 11.5). It does not explain any significant portion of the decrease in women's perceptions of their effectiveness in the maternal role when their previous experience with newborns, husbands' participation in delivery, husbands' early involvement in child care, and ratings of the infant are taken into account, although coefficients for women in both classes are negative ($-.018$, $-.183$). Probably all women find child care harder than they expected, but cesarean delivery itself does not contribute significantly to this. A further observation is that middle-class women's views of themselves in the parent role remained stable from before to after the birth whereas working-class women's views did not. (Unstandardized coefficients are .605, which is significant, and .075, which is not signifi-

Table 11.5 Least Squares Estimates for Predicting Parental Role Competence (Standard Errors in Parentheses)

	Mother's Role Competence							
	Estimated by Women				Estimated by Men			
	Middle-Class (N = 56)		Working-Class (N = 55)		Middle-Class (N = 26)		Working-Class (N = 29)	
	Metric Coefficients	Standardized Coefficients	Metric Coefficients	Standardized Coefficients	Metric Coefficients	Standardized Coefficients	Metric Coefficients	Standardized Coefficients
Mother as parent, before the birth	.605*[a] (.142)	.538[a]	.075[a] (.204)	.057[a]	.114 (.133)	.174	-.054 (.114)	-.088
Previous baby care experience	.594 (.618)	.103	-.174 (.748)	-.031	1.243 (1.294)	.207	.884 (2.001)	.079
Husband participation in birth	.105 (.086)	.141	-.067 (.104)	-.085	.189†[b] (.114)	.374[b]	-.129[b] (.118)	-.220[b]
Husband involvement in child care	.012 (.137)	.009	-.198 (.147)	-.180	.314† (.174)	.348	-.072 (.204)	-.061
Infant adjustment	.518† (.343)	.200	1.247* (.476)	.406	.602* (.277)	.412	1.121* (.432)	.492
Delivery mode	-.239 (1.603)	-.018	-2.600 (1.905)	-.103	1.378[b] (2.073)	.134[b]	-4.240†[b] (2.153)	-.378[b]
Constant term	2.459		18.427		14.862		25.980	
R²	50.0%		23.2%		40.2%		37.5%	

Father's Role Competence

	Estimated by Women				Estimated by Men			
	Middle-Class (N = 56)		Working-Class (N = 55)		Middle-Class (N = 26)		Working-Class (N = 29)	
	Metric Coefficients	Standardized Coefficients	Metric Coefficients	Standardized Coefficients	Metric Coefficients	Standardized Coefficients	Metric Coefficients	Standardized Coefficients
Father as parent before the birth	.696* (.158)	.553	.540* (.144)	.465	.530* (.154)	.567	.215 (.164)	.229
Previous baby care experience	−.076 (.384)	−.020	−.154 (.480)	−.038	−1.374 (.924)	−.246	.500 (1.456)	.056
Husband participation in birth	.184*^{a} (.059)	.383^a	.004^a (.067)	.007^a	.037 (.082)	.080	−.136† (.084)	−.290
Husband involvement in child care	.185* (.086)	.219	.188* (.094)	.237	−.022^a (.127)	−.027^a	.497*^{a} (.148)	.535^a
Infant adjustment	.287 (.216)	.173	.361 (.280)	.164	.566* (.204)	.416	.399 (.334)	.221
Delivery mode	2.514*^{b} (.976)	.301^b	−.230^b (1.230)	−.023^b	1.293 (1.572)	.135	−1.131 (1.505)	−.127
Constant term	−3.203		4.188		4.513		10.669	
R²	51.7%		38.3%		63.2%		47.5%	

*Significant at or beyond 5% level.
†Significant at 5.01 to 10% level.
^{a}Significantly different between social class groups at or beyond 5% level.
^{b}Significantly different between social class groups at 5.01 to 10% level.

cant, respectively. These coefficients differ significantly between the social class groups.) See Reilly (1981), Entwisle (1982), Entwisle and Doering (in preparation), and Reilly, Entwisle, and Doering (1984) for further details.

Women's views of their husbands' role effectiveness. Although vaginally delivered women's ratings of their husbands as fathers declined significantly (in table 11.4: -1.66 units for middle-class and -1.32 units for working-class) ratings of fathers by cesarean women did not decline significantly (-0.40 units for middle-class and -0.09 units for working-class). When the model in figure 11.1 was used to explain change in women's judgments of their husband's role effectiveness (table 11.5), cesarean delivery (standardized coefficient of .301) and husband's participation in delivery[25] (standardized coefficient of .383) both had significant positive effects on middle-class women's views, but had little effect for the working-class women (standardized coefficient of $-.023$ for cesarean delivery, .007 for husband participation). The differences are large enough to be significant across social class groups (beyond the 5% level for husband's participation; beyond the 10% level for cesarean birth). Delivery variables thus appear to have some effects on middle-class but not working-class women's ratings of their husbands as fathers.

Husband involvement in child care is a significant factor conditioning women's ratings of the husband as father for both social class groups. A further analysis suggests that an interaction between the baby's sex and cesarean delivery may explain part of this effect,[26] but the sample is too small to pursue this matter further.

Men's judgments of their own role effectiveness. When the model given in figure 11.1 is estimated to explain men's judgments of their effectiveness as fathers soon after the birth, cesarean delivery does not appear important. The coefficients for men of the two social class groups differ in sign but neither is significantly different from zero (table 11.5). Thus, cesarean delivery does not explain any significant portion of the decrease in men's perceptions of their effectiveness in the paternal role when their previous experience with newborns, participation in delivery, involvement in child care, and ratings of the infant are taken into account.

The overall pattern in how variables in this model contribute to explaining change in the father's judgments of his own role effectiveness does look different between social class groups, however, especially in regard to the effect of the man's interaction with the baby. The middle-class men, like their wives, take some responsibility for the infant's perceived adjustment. The coefficient for the working-class men is not significant. Furthermore, while the working-class father rated himself in terms of changing diapers and the like, the middle-class father did not. See Entwisle and Doering (in preparation) for further discussion of social class differences in men's transition to parenthood.

Husband's evaluation of wife as mother. The same model, when estimated to explain change in men's evaluations of their wives in the maternal role, suggests that cesarean delivery has a borderline negative effect on change in working-class men's judgments of their wives' maternal effectiveness (metric coefficient of -4.240) but a positive and nonsignificant effect on change in middle-class men's judgments (metric coefficient of 1.378). These two coefficients are (borderline) significantly different. The other variable associated with delivery, husband participation in the birth, is borderline significant and positive for the middle-class men, but nonsignificant and negative for the working-class men. These coefficients are also (borderline) significantly different between men of the two social class groups. A strong effect of cesarean delivery upon working-class husbands was apparently for them to perceive that it interfered with their wives' ability to mother, but the middle-class husbands did not share this perception.

The picture as a whole suggests that when middle-class fathers are more active, whether in delivery or in child care, they view the mother as more competent, whereas the working-class fathers' views are, if anything, negatively affected by such activity (both coefficients are small but negative). The working-class fathers who are more involved with the infant may actually see the infant more negatively. See Entwisle (1982) and Entwisle and Doering (in preparation) for further details.

Women's rating of infant adjustment. The women's perceptions of their infants' adjustment were generally lower after the birth than the women had estimated they would be beforehand. A model to explain change in the mother's rating of the infant attributable to cesarean delivery is the second equation in Reilly's more general model that explains change over the birth transition (see Reilly 1981). This model takes into account the mother's previous experience with infants under six weeks of age, the woman's evaluation of her competence in the maternal role as obtained prepartum, the woman's rating of the coming infant's adjustment before it was born, and the mother's evaluation of the husband's participation in child care in the first two to three weeks after delivery. It omits father participation in delivery, however, because there is no obvious reason why father participation should directly affect the mother's judgments of infant adjustment.

Estimates of this equation (table 11.6) suggest that the influence of cesarean delivery on changes in the mother's rating of infant adjustment is different for women of the two classes. Unstandardized parameters are

Table 11.6   Least Squares Estimates for Predicting Mother's Rating of Infant Adjustment, 2 to 3 Weeks Postpartum

	Dependent Variable, Mother's Rating of Infant Adjustment 2 to 3 Weeks Postpartum			
	Middle-Class (N = 56)		Working-Class (N = 55)	
	Metric Coefficients	Standardized Coefficients	Metric Coefficients	Standardized Coefficients
Mother's previous experience	−.264 (.248)	−.118	.157 (.225)	.085
Cesarean delivery (CSECT)	−1.536*a (.600)	−.305*a	.150a (.558)	.032a
Mother's rating of self as parent, before the birth	.230 (.047)	.529*	.214 (.055)	.504*
Mother's rating of infant adjustment, prepartum	.243 (.146)	.198	.099 (.136)	.095
Husband involvement in child care	−.071 (.054)	−.142	.042 (.044)	.116
Constant term	1.986		2.364	
R²		43.7%		33.9%

*Significant at or beyond 5% level.
aSignificantly different between social class groups at or beyond 5% level.

−1.536 for middle-class and +.150 for working-class women and these coefficients differ significantly. For the middle-class women, cesarean delivery has a negative effect on the mother's ratings (which were more negative to start with than those of other middle-class women[27] but for working-class women the coefficient is positive and not significant.

This analysis especially points up the need for information secured before the birth, because the impact of cesarean delivery on the middle-class mother's perception of infant adjustment would be judged to be considerably more negative than it actually is without knowledge of her ratings of the baby-to-come.

Maternal responsiveness. The mother's reported responsiveness to the baby, as mentioned earlier, is significantly lower for the cesarean middle-class women than for other middle-class women. Early maternal responsiveness could be affected indirectly by the negative impact of cesarean delivery on the middle-class women's ratings of the infant noted above, as well as directly by cesarean delivery. In the analysis that follows, I first included the postpartum perception of infant adjustment to determine whether or not there is a separate indirect effect of delivery mode on early maternal responsiveness mediated through this variable. When this indirect effect proved negligible, I then estimated a second model omitting this variable. A critical feature of both models is their inclusion of a measure of the amount of contact between mother and infant immediately after the birth. As noted, the amount of early contact between mother and child is sharply reduced for cesarean women and this fact in itself could account for some portion of the effects of cesarean delivery.

The first model, which included a measure of women's preparation level (attending childbirth preparation classes and the like), delivery mode, the number of minutes the mother reported she was with the baby in the first hour after delivery, and the mother's postnatal rating of the baby, did not explain significant variance for the working-class group ($F_{4,55} = 1.99$, p $> .05$). It did account for significant variance (20.4%) for the middle-class women. For them, the findings are as follows. Only minutes of first-hour contact between mother and child are significant (standardized coefficient of .338, 2.43 times its standard error). The influence of cesarean delivery is negative but small and not significant (standardized coefficient of $-.143$). Perceived infant adjustment affects maternal responsiveness in a positive fashion but the effect is small and not significant (standardized coefficient of .162). For the middle-class women, cesarean delivery thus appears to influence maternal responsiveness very little, either directly or indirectly through perceived infant adjustment when the amount of early contact between mother and child is taken into account. The amount of early contact is an important influence itself, however.

The second model, which omits infant adjustment, explains significant variance for the women of both social classes. It points in a similar direction, with a borderline negative effect of cesarean delivery on maternal responsiveness for the middle-class women together with a strong and significant effect of contact (standardized coefficient of .316). Neither delivery mode nor contact has significant effects for the working-class women. Since maternal-infant contact is fully significant and delivery mode is not in the first model and since delivery mode is only borderline significant in the second model but contact retains its strong effect, it appears that the reduced maternal-infant contact that accompanies cesarean delivery is a more likely explanation of the reduced responsiveness of the middle-class cesarean mothers in this sample than is the surgery itself. The two variables are confounded, but the amount of maternal-infant contact appears prepotent for the maternal responsiveness of the middle-class women.

The analysis of women's ratings of the baby in the preceding section together with the analysis of maternal responsiveness in this section suggest that the negative change in the cesarean middle-class woman's rating of her baby is a separate effect from her relatively lower responsiveness. Change in the infant rating appears to stem from cesarean delivery per se, whereas diminished responsiveness appears to stem from lack of early maternal-infant contact. Contact does not predict ratings of the infant, and delivery mode does not predict responsiveness when the postpartum infant rating is taken into account. In addition, the infant rating does not affect responsiveness. In both models, however, significant effects are found only for the middle-class women. The working-class women are unresponsive to delivery variables in either model.

The issues involving early maternal-infant contact are much too complex and controversial to address here (see Richards 1979). Nevertheless, the separate components of cesarean delivery apparently had distinctive effects for women in this sample in the early postpartum.

Why would findings associated with delivery mode differ across social class groups? A full discussion of this question will be postponed, but the transition to motherhood occurred more quickly for the working-class women than it did for the middle-class women (Reilly 1981; Reilly, Entwisle, and Doering, in preparation). Perhaps the relatively greater responsiveness of the middle-class women who experienced more first-hour contact is explained by their being stimulated to make the transition to motherood sooner than their counterparts with less contact.

Husband's evaluation of infant. No models I have yet been able to devise explain the changes in husbands' ratings of the infant from before the delivery to afterward.

The father's more inclusive rating ("My Baby"), like the father's rating of infant adjustment which overlaps it, is strongly correlated with his estimate of his wife's effectiveness as a mother. For middle-class fathers this correlation is .742; for working-class fathers it is .744. The partial correlation between this more comprehensive measure of father's rating of the baby and cesarean delivery, controlling on the husband's rating of his wife's effectiveness as a mother, is virtually zero for the middle-class husbands ($-.059$). For working-class husbands, the same partial correlation is large, positive (.473), and significant beyond the 5% level ($t_{25} = 2.69$). Cesarean delivery appears to have a positive effect on the working-class father's overall evaluation of the baby, net of the (negative) association between delivery mode and his evaluation of his wife as mother.

Cesarean delivery thus seems to significantly enhance the rating of the baby in the eyes of the working-class father but not the middle-class father, an important qualification in interpreting the means of table 11.4. The average rating assigned babies by fathers four to eight weeks after deliery increased for the cesarean men (1.33 units and .50 units for middle- and working-class, respectively) but decreased for other men (-3.20 and $-.92$ units for middle- and working-class, respectively) compared to ratings assigned before delivery.

There is no previous research to my knowledge on how, or whether, cesarean delivery affects the father's view of the mother or the mother's view of the father in the early postpartum, but there are positive effects of cesarean delivery on father's parenting reported later in the first year of the child's life (Vietze et al. 1980; Pedersen et al. 1981). Effects of cesarean delivery on fathers in the early postpartum have not previously been evaluated. With 57 fathers it is difficult to study these complex effects, but the analyses summarized in this paper and other analyses of this sample reported elsewhere suggest that cesarean delivery has little direct effect on the men. It did not affect men's reported parenting activities, their paternal responsiveness, their early child care activities, or their ratings of themselves as fathers. It did affect the working-class father's, but not middle-class father's, views of other actors in the system, however, in that it affected the rating the working-class father gave the baby and his rating of his wife's competence as a mother. See Entwisle and Doering (1981, in preparation) for further details.

Discussion

The limitations of this research deserve emphasis. It uses a nonprobability sample of volunteer white couples interviewed between 1973 and 1976. To my knowledge, the sample size exceeds that of similar studies, but the sample (120 women, 60 of their husbands, with 20 couples experiencing cesarean delivery) is small by statistical standards. Also, although couples looked fairly typical compared to national samples of young adults interviewed at around the same time, they may not be.

Another limitation is that all data are drawn from in-depth interviews of the parents. No medical records were consulted. No direct observations of parent-infant or spousal behaviors were made. No measurements were made directly of infants. For most of the key topics covered in this paper— couples' views of their own experiences, couple's attitudes toward themselves and each other, and perceptions of the self or spouse as parents— verbal reports are the best available information. But information for other variables, like parents' responsiveness to the infant or child care activities, is limited to verbal reports of these behaviors.

A major strength of this study is its prospective longitudinal nature. No one knew at the outset which couples or how many would experience cesarean births. Other advantages are homogeneity of the sample (all first births in healthy white women with unanticipated cesarean delivery), the ability to examine various facets of the birth event (father participation in delivery, early parental-infant contact, and mother's awareness at delivery), and the stratification of the sample by social class.

Another strength of this study is the detail provided about couples' experiences during the birth and shortly afterward in light of their attitudes and intentions. Effects of father absence in delivery depended, as one would expect, on whether his absence was voluntary or involuntary. The focus on change in couples' evaluations of themselves and their spouses in their parental roles proved to be productive, especially in terms of their changing views of the spouse in relation to cesarean delivery.

The changed views of the spouse attributable to cesarean delivery may explain the longer term effects of cesarean delivery noted for fathers (Grossman et al. 1980a; Pedersen et al. 1981) and for mothers (Reilly, Entwisle, and Doering, in preparation). Cesarean mothers at one year postpartum rated themselves significantly higher as mothers than did other women. And favorable parental self-concepts are apparently important for the infant's well-being. Heinicke et al. (1983) found that significant predictors of the 12-month infant's endurance in the Bayley test situation included the mother's prebirth confidence in visualizing herself as a mother, and Shereshefsky and Yarrow (1973) report that the mother's ability to visualize herself clearly as a mother when only three months pregnant correlated with her infant's alertness at six months.

In the remainder of this discussion I will summarize the key findings and then try to interpret them in light of two themes, methodological issues and the issue of social class differences.

KEY FINDINGS

Cesarean husbands' more negative attitudes during labor. Most variables measured before the birth do not differ between delivery groups (see appendix). The few that do differ do not seem to predict delivery mode. An exception, however, is that the perception of husband's attitude toward labor is more negative for cesarean as compared to other women in this sample. The cesarean women thought their husbands were less enthusiastic about being with them during labor than other women thought their husbands were, and the cesarean women also said they themselves were less enthusiastic about their husbands' presence. Perceptions of husbands agreed. (Spouses were interviewed at separate times and by different interviewers.) There was also a perception of cesarean women (borderline) that their husbands helped less in labor than other women perceived their husbands to have helped. The cesarean husbands who were interviewed did not share this impression, but Klein and Gist (1982) did observe fewer physical acts of help by cesarean husbands in their sample.

No obvious explanation could be found for the cesarean husbands' more negative attitude during labor, either in terms of couples' prior views of each other or the quality of the labor. The lessened social support of cesarean husbands of their laboring wives is actually in a direction contrary to the more favorable division of household tasks reported by the cesarean couples in this sample during the pregnancy and contrary to a difference favoring marital communication in the cesarean group (see appendix).

One possible explanation is that recollections of events in labor are colored by the character of the subsequent delivery. A conclusion that is attractive—but which exceeds the evidence—is that less husband support in labor is not an antecedent but a consequence of cesarean delivery: as surgical delivery impends, the husbands find it hard to continue in their support roles.

Although one cannot rule out lessened husband support during labor as a "cause" of cesarean delivery, in this sample it seems unlikely. The only way to settle the issue decisively is to observe couples during labor, a difficult task when unanticipated cesarean delivery is the focus.

Couples' negative delivery experiences. Cesarean women in this sample reported more negative birth experiences than the vaginally delivered women, in agreement with previous research. But evidence on this point is not as solid as one might expect. Other research lacks a vaginally delivered comparison group (Affonso and Stichler 1980), lacks sufficient documentation (Grossman et al. 1980a), or reports only a relatively few borderline significant differences out of many possibilities examined (Marut and Mercer 1979).

In this sample there is a (borderline) negative effect of cesarean delivery on the quality of the father's perceived birth experience. There are no known drawbacks to fathers being present for cesarean delivery (Nolan, Gainer, and Van Bonn, cited in Consensus Report, 438–39), but cesarean fathers in other studies also report negative birth experiences (Pedersen et al. 1981).

No effects of father participation. Proportionately more cesarean than other husbands in this sample either chose to be absent or were excluded from delivery, so the data on effects of father participation in cesarean delivery are limited. But the birth experience of both cesarean parents is actually a little better (not significantly) when fathers are absent. The cesarean women reacted less favorably to having their husbands present in delivery than the other women did. Affonso and Stichler (1980) likewise found that only 14% of their sample of cesarean women were angry with or depressed by their husbands' absence from delivery. Marut and Mercer (1979), on the other hand, found a borderline significant improvement in cesarean women's birth experience when a "support person"—husband or significant other—was present.

More generally, father participation in delivery definitely improves the quality of vaginally delivered women's perceived birth experience and that of their spouses (Norr et al. 1977; Doering, Entwisle, and Quinlan 1980; Entwisle and Doering 1981) but its influence seems limited to that. Our data do not show effects of father participation on the later parenting of either spouse (Entwisle and Doering 1981; Entwisle 1982) or on the woman's transition into the maternal role (Reilly, Entwisle, and Doering, in preparation). There is also the possibility of a negative effect of father's birth participation on the transition of working-class fathers into the paternal role (Entwisle 1982). All told, in this sample there are no apparent benefits from fathers' participation in cesarean delivery for either spouse.

Cesarean fathers not more involved in early child care. In the early postpartum, there is no evidence in this sample that cesarean fathers of either social class group are more involved in child care or more responsive to their infants than other fathers. This finding is at variance with findings about father caretaking over the longer term. In this sample there was more involvement of (only) working-class cesarean fathers in child care at one year postpartum (Reilly 1981) and both Pedersen et al. (1981) and Vietze et al. (1980) found more participation by cesarean fathers than other fathers at 5 or at 6 and 12 months, respectively.

The present analysis identifies several mechanisms that could explain the increased involvement of cesarean fathers in child care later on: the more positive spousal relations in the working-class cesarean couples, the middle-class cesarean women's more positive views of husband as father, or the apparently lessened disappointment of cesarean couples compared to other couples when the actual baby is compared to the anticipated baby. Apparently, the social meaning of the cesarean birth for the new parents rather than the stressful nature of the event itself or the early physical debilitation it causes the mother are the causes of most effects of cesarean delivery for both spouses.

Parents' role evaluations. Except for the decline in the working-class father's view of the mother's effectiveness in her parent role (which apparently has positive longer term consequences as noted above), cesarean delivery either does not affect parents' role evaluations or affects them positively. Women's estimates of their own effectiveness in the maternal role went down after delivery but cesarean delivery did not additionally depress these ratings. The wife's view of the husband as father is (borderline) affected positively for cesarean middle-class women. The husband's view of himself in the father role also generally went down but did not go down much for cesarean fathers net of other variables.

Perhaps the most striking effects of delivery mode are on the parents' views of the baby. For working-class fathers, cesarean delivery raised ratings of the baby; for middle-class mothers, cesarean delivery depressed ratings of the baby.

Separate effects of contact and delivery mode on maternal-infant relations. Previous research regarding effects of cesarean delivery on early maternal-infant relations is limited and findings are mixed. On the negative side, Pedersen et al. (1981) reported that cesarean mothers had more problems in the initial adaptation period and that at five months postpartum they had less reciprocal positive affect with the child than other mothers did. On the positive side, Field and Widmayer (1980) found that cesarean mothers rated their infants more optimally on temperament at both four and eight months than did other mothers; and Vietze et al. (1980) noted cesarean mothers showed more touching and holding of their infants than other mothers at 12 months. Croghan, Connors, and Franz (1980) found cesarean mothers are more responsive to their infants, but all their cesarean mothers were having repeat elective cesareans and experienced no labor. A number of other investigators report minimal differences in maternal attachment between cesarean and other women (Joy cited in Consensus Report 1981, 438; Bradley, Ross, and Warnyca 1983; and Williams et al., n.d.)

The present research differs from previous research in that prenatal differences are controlled for, effects of early contact between mother and child are evaluated along with delivery mode, and social class is taken into account. Given these constraints, cesarean delivery depresses middle-class women's ratings of the baby compared to other middle-class women, and there is borderline indication that reduced first-hour contact between mother and child depresses the maternal responsiveness of all middle-class women. There appear to be two distinct aspects of the middle-class cesarean mother's response, one involving her attitude toward the baby and the other involving her reported responsiveness. Attitude responds to delivery mode and responsiveness responds to early maternal-infant contact. If early maternal-infant contact were not included as a predictor variable in models evaluating effects of cesarean delivery, the delivery itself would be implicated as the cause of lessened maternal responsiveness since cesarean women generally had much less early contact with their infants. In other research, these separate aspects of cesarean delivery are not evaluated.

The conclusions here about effects of early contact gain some credibility in that they agree almost exactly with those from an experiment in which McClellan and Cabianca (1980) randomly assigned 20 cesarean mothers for "extra" contact and 20 other cesarean mothers for "brief contact" (five minutes' visual contact in the first six hours). Mothers' perceptions of infants at one month did not respond to the extra contact condition (although they did so in the first or second day) but more maternal caretaking behavior was seen in the first or second postpartum day and again at one month for the extra-contact cesarean mothers. The educational level of the women in this experiment (14.0 years) suggests they are middle-class like ours. The findings from this experiment that extra contact affects responsiveness more than maternal perceptions agree nicely with our findings which are based upon nonexperimental data.

METHODOLOGICAL ISSUES

At the beginning, I stated that the prospective nature of this research and other aspects of its design could be important in understanding effects of cesarean delivery. Is this true and, if so, in what respects?

Possible causes of delivery mode. First, it is possible that some of the social behavioral indices measured before the birth differ between couples who will experience a cesarean birth and those who will experience a vaginal birth. In other words, some of the social-behavioral differences between cesarean and other couples observed during the pregnancy could actually be causes of cesarean delivery. If so, it would be important to see whether this is true.

This hypothesis is examined in two ways in the appendix. First, social-behavioral variables that distinguished between delivery groups before the birth were identified. Out of several hundred variables examined, the number that did differ significantly between delivery groups before the birth is about at chance level. This in no way proves, of course, that one or more of these variables did not "cause" cesarean delivery. On the other hand, the dearth of variables distinguishing between the two groups beforehand and the nature of these variables supports the presumption that prepartum variables were not causally related to delivery mode.

A second strategy for searching out possible causes of cesarean delivery involved testing a logistic regression model. One set of variables caught my attention. Cesarean mothers-to-be were planning fewer children, were not mentioning closeness as a reason for breastfeeding, were annoyed by fetal movements, and differed in other respects (see table 11.A) that suggested a kind of psychological negativism toward the fetus. Such negativism might, one way or another, lead to difficulties at delivery. The analysis in the appendix indicates, however, that the joint predictive power of this set of variables (although most are discriminants individually) is not impressive.

It is impossible to rule out other clusters of variables as potential causes of cesarean delivery, of course, but no other obvious ones appeared.

Some variables previously found to be correlated with delivery complications were not diagnostic in this sample. In contrast with reports by Davids and DeVault (1962) and Grossman et al. (1980a), neither women's prepartum anxiety level nor worries in pregnancy was significantly associated with cesarean delivery in the present sample. Also, religiosity and the quality of the marital relationship did not differ by delivery mode, contrary to findings of Grossman et el. (1980a, 66–67). They found that religiosity was negatively correlated with occurrence of cesarean delivery and that marital adjustment correlated with maternal adaptation to labor and delivery. An assessment of quality of marriage from variables measured prepartum in the present sample showed, if anything, the reverse. Apart from middle-class cesarean women's somewhat less favorable ranking of the husband at the six-months-pregnant interview, a ranking that became more favorable by the ninth month, other indicators suggested possibly better marital relations in the cesarean group (better husband wife communication, more egalitarian division of household labor).

It is possible that the significant "negative" variables reported heretofore are manifestations of sampling fluctuation. Grimm and Venet (1966) did not find relationships between emotional and/or attitudinal characteristics in pregnancy and the mother's physical condition at delivery, nor did Klein and Gist (1982) find differences between cesarean and other couples on prenatal measures of a number of sociopsychological variables, including the emotional support provided by the husband during pregnancy.

Whether some psychological or social variables cause cesarean delivery is not an issue lightly put aside, however, even though the data assembled here suggest not. More research is needed where data are procured before the birth, as well as from direct observation of couples during the birth event.

The need for baseline data. Although prepartum measures do not point to causal mechanisms, obviously baseline data secured before the birth are essential if we wish to evaluate the magnitude of cesarean delivery effects on parental role conceptions. The actual findings with regard to changes in parents' role conceptions differ quite a bit from what would be concluded by looking at only the postpartum differences between delivery groups in table 11.4. For example, the fathers' "My Baby" evaluations would not be judged significantly different between delivery groups if only the postnatal ratings were available, whereas delivery groups are (borderline) different when prenatal to postnatal differences are tested, and an interaction emerges between delivery groups and class. Additionally, the decrease in middle-class cesarean mothers' infant ratings would be overestimated, and the increases in their ratings of husbands as fathers would be missed without knowledge of the parallel ratings they assigned before the delivery.

Even more important in my view is the ability to assess changes in parents' relative position in the distribution from before the birth to after. Without prepartum measures, one could not establish the important finding that both working-class parents' views of themselves were unstable over the period of the birth while those of the middle-class parents were highly stable. This knowledge sheds considerable light on social class differences in response to cesarean delivery (to be discussed later).

Other methodological issues. The several facets of the cesarean birth event appear to have distinct effects. The analysis here suggests: the level of awareness (medication) of cesarean mothers did not seem to be critical in accounting for the outcomes considered in this paper; father's presence in labor and delivery probably took on a different meaning in a cesarean as compared to a vaginal delivery, and father's absence in cesarean delivery did not have negative effects; denial of contact between mother and infant, especially in the first hour after birth, accounted for some negative effects that could easily be confounded with cesarean delivery effects. Since all these aspects of a cesarean delivery (medication level, father participation, infant contact) in principle at least can be manipulated, there are a number of obvious policy recommendations. Anyone would agree that medication should be minimal, consistent with surgical requirements. Fathers should participate if they wish. Most important, since separation of cesarean mothers and infants is often "routine" and not really necessary, early separation should be avoided except when mandatory. It appears here to have negative consequences for some mothers, and on the basis of other work, it could have negative consequences for infants (see, e.g., Ringler et al. 1978).

Evaluation of mothers' reactions and fathers' reactions separately and evaluation of their changing views of each other is another kind of methodological issue. The interpersonal nature of the birth event is an important aspect of these parents' cesarean delivery experience. The early effects of cesarean birth on fathers in this analysis appear to be more striking than those upon mothers, and other investigators draw similar conclusions about effects of cesarean delivery seen over the longer term. Also, cesarean delivery appears to alter both parents' attitudes toward the infant. To limit research only to cesarean mothers would hamper the understanding of subsequent family or couple behaviors, because effects of cesarean delivery on fathers may overshadow effects on mothers.

The distinctiveness of the various aspects of cesarean delivery may be even more important in sorting out longer term effects of the procedure. Elsewhere (Entwisle 1982), I show that lower amounts of early maternal-infant contact in the first hour after birth predict the mothers' use of negative sanctions (spanking, slapping) before infants are one year old, while cesarean delivery net of first-hour contact is not a predictor of the mother's later use of negative sanctions. Thus, unless the two aspects of the birth event are looked at separately, it would be easy—and likely—to conclude that such outcomes were prompted by the delivery itself rather than its incidental accompaniments.

SOCIAL CLASS

Differential effects of cesarean delivery along social class lines are provocative but hard to explain. Why would differences appear in one social class group and not the other? One explanation is sampling fluctuation. The samples upon which these analyses are based are exceedingly small. This explanation loses appeal, however, in light of other facts. The cesarean middle-class mothers responded more negatively to the infant in ways other than those listed here, with (borderline) less breastfeeding (Entwisle, Doering, and Reilly 1982) and more reported infant crying (Entwisle 1982). The cesarean working-class mothers did not differ from other working-class mothers in these ways.

One possible line of explanation for social class differences in response to cesarean delivery is based on the ideas that role negotiation and breadth of a role are associated with social class. Kohn's (1969) and Bernstein's (1971) theories, among others, suggest that middle-class people are more self-directed and define roles in less stereotyped ways than persons lower in social class. They exercise more options in determining their roles. Steffensmeier (1982) documents that lesser educated parents have clearer role conceptions of parenthood than do more highly educated parents. If so, while the arrival of an infant could prompt the working-class parents to step into a new but well-defined role for which there are clear prescriptions, the same event may not have clear implications for the middle-class parents. Middle-class men and women may fashion their parental self-concepts more individualistically and innovatively. The data here bear out these ideas in that the role concepts of both middle-class parents remained stable over the perinatal period, possibly showing that these parents did not abandon their previously held ideas of themselves and that they did proceed slowly in defining their new role in order to define it in ways they would find personally most congenial, while the role concepts of the working-class parents were very unstable over the perinatal period. For them, the outlines of the new role appeared abruptly, so the new role was not integrated with the old role.

Reilly's (1981) further work with this sample is consistent with this line of thinking because he finds that the middle-class women, by the end of the first year, had changed their role concepts and were at that time responsive to infant ratings even though they had not been in the early postpartum. The middle-class women appeared to take longer to make the same role transition that the working-class women made almost immediately. Other evidence consistent with these ideas is that marital quarreling increased only for the middle-class couples over the first year (Entwisle 1982). Perhaps the middle-class women began paying more attention to the baby and less to the husband as the baby was being slowly integrated into the middle-class family, so friction erupted. In the working-class family, where both parents quickly stepped into a stereotypical role, the baby was perhaps integrated quickly and so did not precipitate quarrels later on.

From this point of view, middle-class parents' role concerns in the period right after delivery may be in a refractory state, insulated against effects of cesarean delivery as well as most other influences. During this refractory period, the middle-class parents are trying out new strategies, taking time to develop an individualistic style. Because their parent role remains insulated in its prepartum state while they do the psychic work required to move into parenthood, their role concerns do not respond to current events. Other data also support this interpretation. We found (Entwisle and Doering 1981) that the two middle-class parents seemed to parent independently, in that early parenting of middle-class fathers did not respond to the early parenting of middle-class mothers. By contrast, the working-class father modeled his parenting after that of the working-class mother in the early postpartum, so whatever affected her in that period, including cesarean delivery, could be transmitted to him. Since the working-class mother leads the way in child care activities, her physical state could affect the father's activities. One source of difference between classes in reaction to cesarean delivery, therefore, could stem from class differences in how parents adopt the new role, especially the speed and completeness with which they do it.

A related line of explanation hinges on how the event is perceived. Besides being more receptive to delivery mode effects, as argued above, working-class persons, especially fathers, may perceive cesarean delivery as a significant and challenging event. Although men of both classes had somewhat more education on average than their wives, the education gap was considerably larger between the middle-class cesarean parents than it was between the working-class cesarean parents. The middle-class men, who were of considerable education, were perhaps more knowledgeable about health and surgery than their wives and matter-of-fact in their thinking about cesarean delivery. The working-class men, on the other hand, may have seen cesarean birth as mysterious and threatening. Evidence for this, besides the different educational patterns within couples, is the strong difference by social class in men's perception of the effect of cesarean delivery on the mother's functioning, with working-class fathers seeing negative effects for mothers. Other evidence is that the working-class cesarean couples waited the longest of any group after the birth to resume intercourse. The working-class men may have been readier to place their wives in a sick role after a cesarean delivery than were the middle-class men.

The working-class father's view of the mother as significantly impaired, together with other data suggesting that working-class cesarean fathers gave more help at home in the first two weeks after delivery (Entwisle 1982), point in the same direction. The working-class father responded strongly to the fact of cesarean delivery, and this, coupled with the more receptive state of both working-class parents' self-concepts to outside influences over the early postpartum, could account for the differences by social class in these families' early response to a cesarean birth. Parents' early self-concepts or attitudes toward the spouse have not been evaluated in prior research. It is possible that parents' attitudinal changes as found in this sample soon after delivery cause the paternal-infant behavioral differences so generally observed later on.

MORE GENERAL IMPLICATIONS

The birth event has a number of stressful components for parents, some physical, some psychic. A cesarean delivery would be expected to exacerbate some of these forms of stress, especially the physical and psychic stress right at delivery. In addition, the mother's relatively longer recovery period after a cesarean delivery might make it harder for her to attend to the needs of the neonate, and her extended recovery might impose "extra" burdens of child care on her husband. For these reasons, before there were any data, most people expected social behavioral effects of cesarean delivery to be negative. The added stress of cesarean delivery was suspected of leading to behavioral dysfunctions or disability and perhaps of impeding early family functioning. The analyses presented in this paper, however, like other prior research on behavioral effects of cesarean delivery, point to mainly positive effects for parents. Effects for infants have not been investigated with the present sample, but existing research does not suggest negative social behavioral effects of cesarean delivery for them either (Croghan, Connors, and Franz 1980; Field and Widmayer 1980; Gewirtz,

Hollenbeck, and Sebris 1980; Grossman et al. 1980a; Sullivan, Horowitz, and Byrne 1980; Vietze et al. 1980).

Other kinds of sociopsychological "morbidity" that were anticipated are absent also. For example, contrary to speculation, couples who failed to achieve a vaginal delivery with both parents present did not rate themselves as "failures." Some cesarean women whose husbands were absent rated their husbands-as-fathers higher. Cesarean delivery did not add to the decrease in mothers' feelings of self-competence that generally follow a first birth. Cesarean fathers who were not present for delivery did not feel especially deprived—the majority chose not to be present. Nor did cesarean wives find it hard to forgive husbands for their absence. So although father participation in delivery and the mother's state of full awareness were clearly positive factors in the birth experience of vaginally delivered women in this sample, the special circumstance of unanticipated cesarean delivery changed couples' expectations and responses to delivery. Father absence was seen in a different light by the cesarean couples.

There is evidence of negative effects of cesarean delivery in the first few weeks after delivery, especially for the middle-class mothers, but overall there appear to be more positive than negative effects even in the short term. Working-class fathers placed a higher value on their infants than other fathers placed upon their infants. Such an increase in "attributed value" could eventually benefit parent-infant relations. The working-class father also interpreted cesarean delivery as an impediment to his wife's mothering. This may explain both the fact that his wife depended on him more for help in the first two weeks at home and also the longer term positive effects of cesarean delivery on husband's child care observed by Reilly (1981) in this sample, and by Grossman et al. (1980a). Pedersen et al. (1981). and Vietze et al. (1980) in other samples. The working-class marriage could become closer and better integrated as a consequence of the cesarean husband's concern for his wife. Consistent with this idea, Grossman et al. (1980a, 179) reported that a man's relationship to his wife concerning parental issues was better if there were complications in labor and delivery.

Stress involves two key notions: predictability and control (Janis 1958; Lazarus 1966). If a person knows what will happen and how to cope, stress is reduced. Couples underoing unanticipated cesarean delivery, like those in this sample, may feel relatively powerless because the event is a surprise, and they have had no specific preparation to teach them how to deal with major surgery.[28] These cesarean wives were not helped by ordinary childbirth preparation classes, and their husbands apparently were not helped either. But the stress of a cesarean delivery apparently challenged these parents, and because the families were able to cope, it had mostly positive consequences.

There is an unfortunate tendency for researchers not to search for positive consequences of stress. Many studies focus on particular stressful life events and then search only for negative consequences. But, as here, consequences can also be positive. Also, intervening states need to be examined (Gersten et al. 1977; Turner and Noh 1982). It seems likely that many of the positive consequences of cesarean delivery reported in this paper and elsewhere are actually outcomes of psychological states intervening after the event and before the behavioral "consequences." A stressful delivery had no special effects on fathers' reported behaviors in the early postpartum weeks but it did change fathers' views of mothers and infants. Over the long run, these changed views apparently led to measurable behavioral differences in that cesarean fathers were more active participants in child care at one year than were other fathers.

Cesarean birth or other complications, under conditions like those prevailing for this sample, probably represents a degree of stress that is challenging to couples, not debilitating. This was a first birth for these couples. Spouses were still in a honeymoon phase, ready to offer psychological support to each other. These were two-parent, relatively affluent families without other children to supervise. In short, the families in this sample likely had the necessary resources to cope with a cesarean birth. Other families might not, so the rosy picture seen here cannot necessarily be generalized to other kinds of families. I suspect even the distinction of an anticipated cesarean versus an unplanned one may be important. Meeting an unexpected crisis may cause couples to mobilize psychic resources in ways they would not mobilize them for an expected event. The fact that behavioral effects are mainly positive is both fortunate and fortuitous. As cesarean operations become more numerous, positive effects may diminish. Whatever the case, continuing research is needed to monitor the social-behavioral consequences of changes in birth management.

Appendix 11.A   Evaluation of Prenatal Status by Delivery Groups

To determine whether the 20 women who would undergo unanticipated cesarean delivery differed in prebirth sociopsychological status from the 100 women who would undergo vaginal delivery, 98 variables derived from two prenatal interviews with the women and 34 variables derived from a single prenatal interview with 60 of their husbands were screened. In addition, several sets of semantic differential ratings of the baby by both parents, obtained before the birth, were screened. For the women, t-tests were run for the entire sample and then run separately for each social class group. (In each social class group there were 10 cesarean deliveries out of 60.) For the men, t-tests were run only for the sample pooled by social class (7 cesarean fathers versus 53 fathers of vaginally delivered infants).

WIFE'S REPORT TWO TO THREE MONTHS PREPARTUM

Of 51 variables screened from the women's six-months-pregnant interview, the two delivery groups are closely matched on all but five. The cesarean wives are close in average age to the others (25.1 versus 24.6 years), as are cesarean husbands (27.6 versus 26.8 years). There are no differences in wife's educational background (both groups average slightly above 14 years of education), in religiosity, or in wife's job prestige. Time of stopping work is almost identical—between the fifth and sixth month of pregnancy for both delivery groups. Exposure to childbirth preparation classes was very similar (scored as 4.55 versus 4.68 for cesarean and vaginal groups, measured on a scale from 1 to 7).[29] Fathers were equally willing to participate in the research—30% of cesarean fathers refused versus 27% of other fathers.

There is no evidence to support differences in anxiety level before the birth. Two to three months prepartum the amount of current general worrying was equal as judged from women's answers to the following question: "Toward the end of pregnancy many women find that they tend to worry about things more than usual. How is it with you? Do you find that you worry—a lot more than usual, a little more than usual, worry the same as usual, worry less than usual." Answers were assigned scores from 1 to 4, respectively. Both groups worried very slightly more than usual. There was no difference in how much the women worried specifically about what would happen in labor and delivery (asked separately from other worry items) with five alternatives (constantly, often, sometimes, seldom, never, assigned scores from 1 to 5, respectively). Both groups averaged between "sometimes" and "seldom." The total number of worries (24 specific worries were inquired about, including gaining too much weight, disagreements with the doctor, that having sex might hurt the baby, losing the baby, and so on) did not differ.[30] The average scores on a set of 21 items drawn from the Taylor anxiety scale[31] were comparable.

Wives' menstrual histories were also on a par. There were no differences in reported menstrual regularity or in the total number of menstrual symptoms reported when 10 specific symptoms were inquired about, such as headache, cramps, backache, and so on.

Difficulties associated with the pregnancy were also comparable across delivery groups. The total number of first or second trimester symptoms[32] reported (out of 19 inquired about for each trimester, including fatigue, dizzy spells, nausea, etc.) was very similar. The total number of pregnancy problems reported in response to two separate questions ("What have you found to be most upsetting about being pregnant?" "What do you find to be the biggest problem about being pregnant?") was approximately the same for both groups. Average weight before pregnancy (119.7 versus

120.7 for cesarean and other women, respectively) did not differ nor did average weight gain (26.4 versus 27.1 lbs., respectively).

There were no average differences between delivery groups in the wife's perception of the husband's first reaction to news of the pregnancy, of the husband's interest in the pregnancy, of the husband's interest in attending preparation classes, or of the husband's interest in fetal movements. There was a borderline difference in a score evaluating the division of household labor, using a scale adapted from Blood and Wolfe (1960).[33] Cesarean mothers-to-be reported slightly more household help from husbands than other mothers reported in the six- to seven-months-pregnant interview (9.40 versus 10.98, t = 1.80, p < .08), a picture consistent with husbands' reports (see below). All in all, quality of marriage did not appear to differ across delivery groups, nor did women's attitudes toward their husbands differ, as judged from the variables discussed above and a number of others.

As noted, five variables differed significantly between the two delivery groups on t-test. (1) According to wives' perception of husbands, there was better husband-wife communication in the cesarean group (an average score of 3.90 versus 3.15, where 3 = some problems and 4 = milder problems, t = 2.52, p < .02). (2) Although there were no significant differences in age or in the degree to which women reported this pregnancy to be planned, there was a difference in years married before this conception, with cesarean women married about seven months longer (t = 2.55, p < .02). (3) There is also a difference in when women experienced a first conception (which may or may not be this one) with the cesarean group married about six months longer (t = 2.92, p < .01). (4) There was a significant difference in the women's attitudes toward fetal movements (3.65 for cesareans versus 4.37 for others, where 3 = ambivalent and 4 = neutral, t = 2.02, p < .05). (5) The reasons women gave for selecting whichever feeding mode they chose, differed (0.35 for cesareans versus 0.61 for others, where 0 = closeness not mentioned, and 1 = closeness mentioned as a reason, or said "closeness was equivalent for bottle and breast," t = 2.17, p < .04).

WIFE'S REPORT ONE MONTH PREPARTUM

Of the 47 variables from the interview in the ninth month of pregnancy that were screened, only two differed at or beyond the 5% level.

As pregnancy neared its end, there continued to be no difference between delivery groups in variables related to anxiety—the amount the women worried, the total number of worries, worry about childbirth, or Taylor anxiety scores. There was no significant difference in the total number of drugs taken during pregnancy, number of pregnancy problems reported, the number of third trimester symptoms reported, or subjective reports on health during the pregnancy (both groups saw themselves on average as "healthy as usual").

The two significant differences out of 47 were: (1) expectation for pain in the second stage of labor without the "usual" drugs was a little higher for cesarean women (3.84 versus 3.20, t = 2.11, p < .04, where 3 = moderate amount of pain and 4 = bad pain most of the time). (2) in the ninth month of pregnancy, the cesarean women worried a little more about losing the baby (0.84 versus 0.49, t = 2.25, p < .03, where 0 = not at all and 1 = a little).

A few other borderline differences appeared. One was in expectation for pain in the first stage of labor assuming the "usual" drugs were given (3.26 for cesarean versus 2.95 for others, t = 1.95, p ≅ .05, where 2 = occasional slight pain, 3 = moderate pain, and 4 = bad pain most of the time). Another was that cesarean women on average planned fewer children (2.0 versus 2.5, t = 1.76, p = .08). The cesarean women (who produced three times as many boys as girls) expressed a preference for a girl in the nine-months-pregnant interview (3.42 versus 2.77, t = 1.89, p = .06, where 2 = leaning toward boy, 3 = really doesn't care, 4 = leaning toward girl), although the two delivery groups did not differ on this item in the six-months-pregnant interview. However, this prepartum difference did not lead to significant differences between delivery groups in disappointment about the baby's sex as expressed later, because in the interview two to three weeks postpartum, 10% of women with vaginal deliveries expressed disappointment, 28% were neutral, and the remainder (62%) were pleased or very pleased with their baby's sex. Of the 19 cesarean women who responded to this question, 4 (21%) expressed disappointment, 6 (31%) were neutral, and 9 (48%) were pleased or very pleased.

HUSBAND'S REPORT ONE MONTH POSTPARTUM

Of the 20 cesarean fathers, seven were among the 60 fathers interviewed before delivery. The seven cesarean fathers-to-be were compared with the 53 other fathers on 34 variables derived from the husband's interview held about one month prepartum. These variables included demographics, religiosity, division of labor around the house, interest in the pregnancy, and the like. Spouses' reports agreed on average. For example, the men's average scores on division of household labor were 8.71 versus 10.30 (t = 1.18, p = .24) for cesarean and other fathers-to-be, values a little more favorable to themselves than those obtained from the women but not significantly different between delivery groups.

As was true for the women, very few differences across delivery groups emerged for the men. Cesarean fathers-to-be reported themselves to be happier (1.57 versus 1.96, t = 2.68, p = .01, where 1 = always happy and 2 = usually happy). They reported fewer spare-time activities with their wives (an average of 0.86 versus 1.70 activities, t = 2.35, p < .03), and they ranked the baby significantly higher in relation to spouse, work, etc., than did other fathers (1.86 versus 2.58, t = 2.78, p < .01, with ranks assigned from 1 to 8). They reported more worrying (1.67 versus 2.24, t = 2.16, p < .04, where 1 = a lot and 2 = a little). Surprisingly, despite wives' positive views of their own health, cesarean husbands saw their wives as less healthy than other husbands did (2.86 versus 2.06, t = 3.60, p < .01, where 3 = less healthy and 2 = as healthy as usual) and with more pregnancy symptoms (22.86 versus 15.02, t = 3.14, p < .01).

Of the six prenatal differences found for the men, two are in a positive direction (cesarean fathers being happier and ranking the baby higher). There is thus a "net" excess of two negative variables out of 34 variables examined for the men, which turns out to be 5.7%, close to the 5% significance level chosen.

CLASS-SPECIFIC PRENATAL DIFFERENCES

The same variables tested for the entire sample of women were compared again within each social class group. All five of the significant differences found in the women's first prepartum interview tended to fade. Three of the variables that were significantly different for the group as a whole in the six-months-pregnant interview were significant only within one class group. The differences in time of this conception or of first conception held up only for the working-class women. The attitude-toward-fetal-movement difference held up only for middle-class women. The other two variables (couple communication and closeness as a reason for breastfeeding) were not significantly different within either class group.

The two differences found in the women's nine-months-pregnant interview also became less convincing when the sample was stratified by class. Worry about losing the baby is borderline significant for the middle-class and not significant for the working-class. The expectation of pain in the second stage of labor does not differ significantly between delivery groups for either class. In addition, the borderline difference in mothers' sex preference for the baby in the ninth-month interview is found only for the middle-class women.

A few variables were significantly different for one class or the other when they had not been found significantly different in the sample as a whole. Middle-class cesarean women reported painful sex more often than other middle-class women (1.60 versus 1.21, t = 2.57, p < .01 where 1 = no pain experienced and 2 = some pain); husband's age was greater for the working-class cesarean group (28.50 versus 25.58, t = 2.17, p < .04) despite the close match for the total sample; there was a more favorable division of labor among the working-class cesarean husbands and wives compared to other working-class couples (8.20 versus 11.04, t = 2.46, p < .02 where lower scores indicate more husband help); the middle-class cesarean women ranked their husbands relatively lower (1.90 versus 1.49, with ranks assigned from 1 to 8, t = 2.03, p < .05); working-class cesarean women used a few more drugs in the third trimester (2.00 versus 1.46, where 1 = none and 2 = one drug [not nose drops, aspirin, antibiotics, or vitamins], t = 2.02, p < .05). All in all, of 196 comparisons (98 variables × 2) made within the two social class groups, 10 turned out to be significant beyond the 5% level, compared to an expectation of 9.8.

SEMANTIC DIFFERENTIAL RATINGS

Along with ratings of several other role concepts, both parents rated their coming baby on a set of 20 semantic differential scales at each prepartum interview.[34] Although four significant differences between delivery groups appeared in the 20 ratings given by women in the six-months-pregnant interview (cesarean mothers-to-be saw the baby as less healthy, less happy, less active, and less kind than the other mothers did), in the women's second prepartum interview when they gave 40 ratings—20 for "My baby if girl" and 20 for "My baby if boy"—no significant differences between delivery groups appeared on any rating. Neither did significant differences appear between cesarean husbands' and other husbands' 20 semantic differential ratings of the baby-to-come. Altogether, out of 80 parents' ratings of the baby-to-come, four differed significantly between delivery groups at or beyond the 5% level, exactly what chance would predict. Furthermore, the four differences in mothers' ratings that appeared in the women's sixth-month interview failed to reappear in the ninth-month interview.

SUMMARY

Of 98 sociopsychological variables measured prenatally for women, 7 differed beyond the 5% level compared to an expectation of 4.8. When these seven variables were tested within social class strata, all seven failed to achieve significance in one or both groups. The total number of comparisons (10) that did achieve significance in the separate social class analysis was almost exactly at chance expectation (9.8).

Of the 6 variables found to differ for the men, out of 34 variables tested, 2 were in a positive direction, leaving a net of 2 variables in a negative direction for the cesarean group. This pattern is not one of a convincing excess of negative indicators for the cesarean men.

Of 60 semantic differential ratings of the baby-to-be made by the women, four differed beyond the 5% level in the first interview, and none differed in the second. Of 20 ratings of the baby-to-be made by the men, none differed. The total number of comparisons involving semantic differential ratings of the baby achieving significance (4 out of 80) is exactly what chance would predict.

CAN PRENATAL DIFFERENCES PREDICT CESAREAN DELIVERY IN THIS SAMPLE?

According to analyses summarized above, the number of significant differences between cesarean couples and others in the prepartum period did not seem excessive, especially with some like marital communication and division of household labor being in a positive direction. On the other hand, some variables that did differ in the total sample suggested a possible pattern of negativeness toward or rejection of the fetus. These variables were: (1) the number of years married before first conception; (2) number of years married before conceiving this child; (3) "closeness" mentioned as a reason for choice of feeding mode; (4) number of children planned, including adoption (borderline); (5) attitude toward the fetal movements; and (6) whether the woman worried about losing the baby.

These six variables suggested a possible common factor related to rejection of the fetus. Postponement of pregnancy, which can be ruled out in this sample as a "physiological" factor,[35] could represent a psychological factor—taking contraceptive action, being subfertile because of unconscious negativism toward becoming pregnant, and the like.

Although a comprehensive review of the role of emotional factors in obstetric complications sees "no conclusive evidence of causal relationships" between emotional factors and such complications (McDonald 1968, 222), the earlier findings of associations between anxiety level and complications and other related findings are not easily dismissed. Blau et al. (1963), for example, found that, for 30 women who would deliver prematurely for no obvious medical reason as compared with 30 matched control women who delivered at term, the premature group showed more negative attitudes toward the pregnancy as well as other psychological differences when retrospective information was secured. Because prospective data on the psychological status of cesarean mothers are not common and also because the methodology for answering causal questions rigorously has not, to my knowledge, previously been employed in this area of research, I tested the success of two models in predicting delivery mode on the basis of the women's psychological status in pregnancy. Each model used the six sociopsychological variables listed earlier, plus two others that were closely related conceptually (how much the woman looked forward to childbirth and how the woman felt about "having a baby growing inside"), to predict whether or not a cesarean delivery would occur. Simply put, even though the number of significant differences between delivery groups does not seem excessive in relation to the number of variables that was screened, the question now to be examined is whether a set of these variables that suggest rejection of the fetus can predict delivery mode.

THE LOGIT MODEL

To model a discrete outcome (whether or not cesarean delivery was carried out) with individual level data, I first used a logistic model. Such a model endeavors to predict P_i (the operation outcome) using the equation below:

$$P_i = \frac{1}{1 + e^{-\Sigma X_{ij} B_j}}$$

The X_{ij} and B_j terms in this equation are analogous to independent variables and regression coefficients, respectively, in an ordinary least squares analysis, with X_{ij} being scores on the variables in the cluster.

In estimating this logit model the independent variables were the six significantly different variables listed earlier, plus the two others of the same nature that were not significant (how much the woman looked forward to childbirth and how the woman felt about "having a baby growing inside"). The results of the logit analysis are listed in table 11.A.

No one of the single coefficients achieves significance (no t-test of any individual parameter achieved significance), and the overall predictive power of the equation based on all eight variables is unimpressive. The difference in chi-square values measuring the improvement in fit using these eight variables compared to fitting only the mean is 13.176 with 8 d.f., not large enough to be significant at the 5% level. Therefore, even though most of these variables when tested one at a time differ significantly (beyond the 5% level) between the 20 pregnant women who would undergo cesarean delivery and the 100 other women who would not, the joint predictive power of this set of negative psychological variables does not achieve significance.

DISCRIMINANT FUNCTION MODEL

Essentially the same conclusion was borne out by a discriminant function analysis. In this model, a linear function was derived that is the optimally weighted sum of the same eight variables in terms of predicting the dichotomous outcome (operation versus no operation). Predictive power is assessed by means of a canonical correlation, which turned out to

Table 11.A Parameters Estimated in Logit Model to Explain Delivery
Outcome

Variable[a]	Coefficient	Standard Error
When first conception	.571	.508
Attitude toward fetal movements	−.184	.215
Feeding for reasons of closeness	−1.008	.676
Years married before this conception	−.044	.055
Worry about losing the baby	.419	.525
Look forward to childbirth	.242	.302
Number of children planned	−.900	.570
How feel about baby growing inside	.126	.278

[a]Questions and coding information available from author on request.

be 0.336. The variance explained by the function formed from the 8 variables is $(.336)^2$ or 11.29%, and the associated test statistic (Wilks' lambda $= .88$) corresponds to a X^2 of 11.51 with a probability level of .174. This analysis agrees with the logit analysis reported above and indicates again that the eight variables do not appear to form a pattern or cluster together.

SUMMARY

In this sample of couples, the significantly different psychological or social factors measured before delivery do not appear to "cause" cesarean birth. Further, the variables other research suggests as causal (marital quality, religiosity, anxiety levels) were screened and did not seem to distinguish between the two delivery groups in this sample before delivery occurred. This of course in no way rules out other factors not measured that would prove predictive.

Estimation of the models to predict delivery mode bears directly on the structure of analyses evaluating delivery mode effects. Since the models do not predict the birth event, the influence of the set of prenatal factors that did differ significantly beforehand is not mediated through the birth event. Thus, influence of factors that differed between delivery groups prepartum on behavioral events postpartum can be taken to be direct rather than indirect. In evaluating effects postpartum, one equation rather than two is thus the necessary minimum number. Variables that do differ prepartum must, of course, be included in any equation if those variables bear on outcome variables measured after the birth. For example, when relative rankings of the husband by middle-class women are analyzed, it is important to control on their rankings of the husband in the six-months-pregnant interview, because the cesarean women's rankings were significantly lower than other middle-class women's rankings were at that time. Without such control, any later differences in husband ranking favoring vaginally delivered women could reflect merely persistence of effects present before delivery rather than effects of delivery mode. In fact, failure to control on prepartum differences between delivery groups flaws other research on behavioral effects of cesarean delivery to date.

Acknowledgments

This work was supported mainly by NICHD Grant HD13103, "Cesarean Section: Social and Psychological Factors." The analyses are based on data collected collaboratively with Susan Doering.

Notes

1. One woman at age 16 had given up a baby for adoption. She did not take care of the child and had never seen it except for a glimpse through glass after it was born.

2. Census categories 0, 1, and 2 were always designated as "middle," while categories 4 and above were always designated as "working." Census category 3 was sometimes designated as middle, sometimes working. For example, door-to-door salesmen with less than a high school education were designated as working, while salesmen for a trucking firm or buyers for a family-owned store with a year or two of college were designated as middle.

3. Of the 19 husbands absent from labor (including those 2 whose wives did not experience it), 2 were among the 7 cesarean fathers interviewed postpartum.

4. In the remainder of this chapter, *significant* means "at or beyond the 5% level" or "2 or more times the parameter's standard error." "Borderline significant" means "at or beyond the 10% level" or "1.50 through 1.99 times the parameter's standard error." All t-tests are two-tailed unless specifically identified as one-tailed.

5. Men were asked: "How much pain would you say that your wife, personally, felt in the first part of labor, the opening up part. Did she feel no pain at all, occasional slight pain, moderate amount of pain, bad pain most of the time, terrible pain (agony)?" Answers were coded on a scale from 1 to 5. Fathers who were not present were asked to guess from what the wife said or indicated about her experience.

6. The men were asked: "Think back how painful you expected your wife's labor to be [*pause*] then tell me, was her labor a lot more painful than you'd expected, somewhat more painful, just as painful as expected, somewhat less painful than expected, a lot less painful than expected?" Answers were scored from 1 to 5.

7. The questions to evaluate the woman's level of awareness are:

Were you awake or asleep when the baby was born?

_____ asleep

_____ awake [get R's interpretation]

Were you glad or sorry that you were _____(above response)_____?

Why? [details]

[if awake] Were you awake with drugs that numb the sensations
of birth or awake and able to feel everything?

_____ numb

_____ feeling everything

Were you glad or sorry that you were _____(above response)_____?

Why? [details]

[if any drugs] What drugs were you given? [describe briefly]

[check:] Local for the episiotomy?

Anything to speed up your labor? Make your pains harder?

Anything to calm you down? To relax you?

Anything to make you sleep?

Did you have an I.V.?

Why? What was in it?

Did you have the fetal monitor?

Belts around your stomach to measure the contractions and the baby's
heartbeat?

Why?

Did you have any complications or was it a normal labor?

_____ normal

_____ complications

[if complications] What were they?

What happened? Why does that happen?

What was done about it?

Is it serious when that happens?

etc.

[get details: Dr.'s definition of what happened, why & how
serious. R's definition of what happened, why & how
serious. What was done about it & why.]

Other information on awareness was provided by the respondent's description
of her experience in the delivery room. See footnote a, table 11.1, for coding of
women's awareness level.

8. See footnote b, table 11.1, for definition of quality of women's birth
experience.

9. This scale is the sum of six scores measuring the degree of husband's participation during labor and delivery, as estimated by his wife.

The first item is how the wife thought her husband felt during labor, whether he
was with her for all of it, part of it, or none of it. The second item involved the wife's
perception of how her husband felt during delivery, whether or not he was present.
The third item asked women how they felt about their husbands being or not being
with them during labor. The fourth item asked women how they felt about their

husbands being or not being with them during delivery. Answers to each of these four questions were scored from 1 (very negative) to 6 (enthusiastic).

For the fifth item, respondents were asked what their hsubands did that helped most during labor. After that action was described, they were asked what else their husbands had done that helped and were pressed until they could not think of anything else. These discussion-type answers were coded as follows: 0 = husband wasn't there; 1 = there, but did nothing; 2 = nothing, but turned out to be something; 3 = just being there; 4 = being there, plus specific help; 5 = several helpful activities; 6 = really helpful, constantly busy.

For the sixth item, respondents were asked about husband's help during delivery in the same manner as for labor. The coding was similar to that for the fifth item, running from husband not there to really helpful.

The alpha reliability for this scale is .842. The correlation between the measure of this variable based on wives' replies and a measure based on husbands' replies for couples where both responded is .832, and equals the reliability of the scale.

10. (1) As shown in the appendix, the middle-class cesarean wife's ranking of the husband in the sixth and seventh month of pregnancy compared to seven other topics such as self, baby, and parents, was significantly lower than other middle-class women's rankings (average ranks of 1.90 vs. 1.49, $t = 2.03$, $p < .05$). However, by the ninth month, the relative ranking of the husband by the cesarean middle-class mothers-to-be had decreased considerably (to 1.50) while the other middle-class mothers' ranking had increased only slightly (1.55), so the difference vanished. Within the working-class group, the relative ranking of the husband did not differ between cesarean and other women at the sixth to seventh month interview, and changes between then and the ninth-month interview were small. The wife's perception of the husband's relative ranking of her compared to seven other topics, asked only in the nine-month interview, was also close for cesarean and other wives (1.58 vs. 1.49, respectively).

(2) In their interviews when six months pregnant and nine months pregnant, women assigned 20 semantic differential ratings to several concepts related to the husband. (a) Average differences in the women's semantic differential ratings of "My Husband" between the six-months- and nine-months-pregnant interviews revealed that ratings tended to improve more than decline for the cesarean mothers (12 improved versus 10 improving for others) and in no instance (0 out of 20 comparisons) did the average change in ratings differ significantly between delivery groups. (b) In the sixth-month interview, the women gave separate semantic differential ratings of "My Husband" and "Ideal Man." The cesarean women saw their husbands more favorably than their ideal men in 11 of 20 ratings, whereas the other women saw their husbands more favorably in only 5 ratings. However, none of the 20 discrepancies is significantly different between delivery groups. (c) In semantic differential ratings of "My Husband as Father" compared to ratings of "Ideal Father" in the ninth-month interview, both delivery groups saw their husbands not quite as favorably as Ideal Father (15 of 20 comparisons favored "Ideal") but in no instance were the discrepancies significantly different between delivery groups.

11. The sequence of questions on depression asked in the interview two to three weeks after delivery is as follows:

Since the baby's birth, have you experienced a day or two where you felt very emotional and became upset over every little thing?
[*if no*] Have you had any crying spells since the baby's birth?
_____ no   _____ yes
Any moods of depression or fearfulness?
_____ no   _____ yes
[*if yes to either of above, go on*]
[*if yes*] When did that occur? _____
So you were _____ still in the hospital
                _____ at home by then
How long did the feelings last? _____ [*hours? days?*]
Describe how you felt then? [*details*]
[*probe*] Did you cry a lot?
          What seemed to set you off? [*examples*]
          Did you feel like you just couldn't cope?
          With what?
How did you get over these feelings?
[*probe*] What helped?
          Who helped?

12. Since Grossman et al. (1980a) note that women more depressed in the first trimester were also more depressed at two months postpartum, their simple association between prepartum anxiety and postpartum depression is not conclusive.

13. Postpartum depression is often attributed to hormonal factors, but this theory can be questioned on grounds of "postpartum equivalent" reactions after adoption of a child (Breen 1975, 39).

14. The questions on postpartum contact are:
          When was the first time you saw the baby? _____ [*o'clock*] _____ [*day*]
          Where were you? _____
          What did the baby look like? [*full description*]
          [*probes*] What was its color?
                    Did it have hair?
                    Did it look like anybody in particular?
                    Was it messy?
                    What was it doing?
                      Activity?
                      Crying or quiet?
                    How did you feel about the baby at that moment? [*details*]
          Could you hold or touch the baby right then? _____ no _____ yes
          [*if no*] Why not?
                    How did you feel about that?
                    [*if wanted to*] Why couldn't you?
                    Did you ask if you could?
                    Why / why not?
          When was the first time you *were* allowed to hold the baby?
                    _____ [*o'clock*]   _____ [*day*]
          [*go on to ques under "if yes" for this holding*]
          [*if yes*] How did you feel about holding the baby?

Was it kind of awkward at first?
What did the baby look like? [*full description*]
[*use relevant probes above*]
What was it doing? [*details*]
What did you do with it? [*details. close out*]
Did you unwrap it? _____ no
_____ yes [*get description*]
[*if no*] Why not? Did you want to?
Did you talk to it? What did you say?
How did you feel about the baby the first time
you held it?
[*details*]
How long did you hold it? _____
Was that amount of time _____ just right?
_____ too short?
_____ too long?
Why was the baby taken away then?

15. These questions are available from the author on request.

16. Mother's attitude was assessed from several long-answer questions in the interview two to three weeks postpartum and coded into four variables (baby's initial appearance, how the woman felt on first view, how she felt when she first held the baby, how she felt about holding the baby). The text of these questions is available on request.

17. This scale is a weighted sum of scores for three questions. The first question was: "Are you feeding the baby on demand or on a schedule? [*if demand*] About how often does he / she want to eat? [*Describe if necessary. Get yesterday's pattern in detail.*] How soon will you try to get the baby on a schedule? How will you get him / her on a schedule? [*if schedule*] What is the schedule? How closely do you stick to it? What do you do to help him / her wait if he / she wakes up and cries early? Do you wake him / her if he / she sleeps through a feeding time?" Answers to this question was scored 1 = rigid schedule, 2 = semischedule, 3 = demand. Scoring was based on the interviewer's observation as well. For example, some women responded "demand" but it was clear they waited to feed the baby even though the baby rooted vigorously and showed other clear signs of hunger. (2) After being asked how much the "baby cries these days," women were asked "What do you do when it cries?" followed by probes. Answers were scored: 1 = let cry first response; 2 = other things but let baby cry regularly; 3 = other things but let baby cry occasionally; 4 = somewhat solicitous, let cry not mentioned; 5 = very solicitous, does everything can think of. (3) This question followed (2) above. "How do you feel when it starts crying again? [*details*] What else do you feel?" Answers were scored: 1 = no concern, negative emotions toward baby; 2 = neutral, doesn't bother her; 3 = some concern for baby, some netural or negative feelings; 4 = mild concern for baby; 5 = overriding concern for baby. To form the scale, the first item was weighted by 2. The alpha reliability of this scale is .705.

18. Men's birth experience is the sum of three variables: how the father summed up the whole labor and delivery experience scored from 1 (very negative) to 6

(extremely positive); a rating of the quality of that experience scored from 0 (just glad it was over) to 6 (giving birth with a very active role for both parents); a measure of the father's emotions at the birth rated from 1 (very negative) to 6 (a peak experience). The alpha reliability of this scale is .656.

19. The scale to measure early paternal responsiveness is the weighted sum of four variables.

The first variable is the coded answer to the following: When was the first time you were allowed to hold the baby [_____ o'clock; _____ day]; how did you feel about holding the baby? scored from 1 = definitely negative to 6 = overjoyed (average = mild positive).

The other three variables were coded from answers to a series of questions. After being asked "How much does the baby cry these days?" the next question was "What do you do when it cries? [details, probes] Do you ever pick it up? Do you prefer to hold it when it's quiet?"

The second variable is a measure of the father's actions when the baby cries (1 = let cry or call wife to get baby; 2 = other things first, but lets the baby cry regularly; 3 = other things first, but lets the baby cry occasionally; 4 = somewhat solicitous—let cry not mentioned; 5 = very solicitous, does everything can think of).

The third variable is a measure of the father's feelings when the baby cries (1 = negative emotions toward the baby, no concern for baby; 2 = neutral, doesn't bother father, accepts that crying is what babies do; 3 = some concern, but some netural or negative feelings; 4 = mild concern for baby; 5 = overriding concern for baby).

The fourth variable (weighted by a factor of 3) is another measure of the father's actions, whether the father picks up the baby when it cries (1 = not mentioned or tells wife to pick it up; 2 = picks up if wife asks or if wife is busy; 3 = picks up on his own).

The alpha reliability of this scale is .640.

20. The husband's involvement in child care was measured by the sum of three items asked him directly concerning his bathing the baby (1 = no; 2 = helped; 3 = bathed baby alone), the number of diapers per day the husband had changed since the baby came home from the hospital, how much he had held the baby in the preceding 24 hours (from 0 = did not hold at all, to 6 = held four hours or more). The correlation between this score and the score derived from wives' answers to five questions, including three on the same topics, is .325. The husbands were interviewed four to eight weeks after delivery, the wives two to three weeks after, so there could be differences caused by timing.

21. For women these questions were: how often he fed the baby, how often he diapered the baby, how long he held the baby on the day preceding his interview, how he showed his interest in the baby, and whether or not he ever bathed the baby. Scores on average were close across class groups (9.44 versus 10.02 for middle- and working-class respectively). See Reilly (1981) for further details. The correlation between this score and the wife's assessment of division of labor in the six-months-pregnant interview is .257 (p < .01). Fathers of sons score slightly higher (not significantly) on involvement in child care (10.17 versus 9.25, t = 1.14, p = .26).

22. The correlation between father participation in delivery and child care scores for cesarean families is −.351 (not large enough to be significant with 18 d.f.) while that for the vaginally delivered is .101 (not significant).

23. Full details are given on construction of these scales in Entwisle 1982.

24. The measure of women's previous experience caring for newborns is derived from a single question asked in the ninth month of pregnancy about experience taking care of infants under six weeks of age (1 = none; 2 = some experience, not full charge; 3 = full charge). For men, a similar question concerning experience was asked in the prepartum interview (1 = no experience; 2 = a little experience; 3 = a lot of experience).

25. Other evidence along the same lines is the correlation between husband participation in delivery and increases in middle-class women's relative rankings of their husbands (compared to seven other topics such as self, baby, etc.) from before the birth to after (r = .412, p < .01). This relation is not found for lower-class women (r = .027, p = 0.42).

26. A t-test of change in vaginally delivered mother's rating of husband as father from before the birth to afterward shows that ratings of girls' fathers fell 1.86 units, ratings of boys' fathers fell 0.64 units (t = 1.94, p < .06).

27. In a closely related analysis, based on maximum likelihood estimation of a similar equation, which in addition took husband participation in delivery and measurement error into account, the difference between women of the two classes in effect of cesarean delivery upon women's rating of the infant was evaluated by a simultaneous analysis of groups. The effect of cesarean delivery upon women in this analysis also differed across classes (p < .01), and metric coefficients in this analysis are a little larger (−2.013 and 0.173 for the effect of cesarean delivery on women's ratings of the infant for middle and working-class, respectively). See Reilly 1981.

Estimating another equation involving all the predictors of table 11.6 and minutes of first-hour contact between mother and infant revealed that first-hour contact was not efficacious. For the middle-class women, the significant effect of cesarean delivery remained and the standardized coefficient of first-hour contact is only −.007.

28. There is evidence that if a person knows that major surgery will ensue, the person may do "the work of worrying" in advance, as well as be taught ways to reduce discomfort or to maintain feelings of control (Janis 1958; Egbert et al. 1964; Andrew 1970). Women undergoing emergency cesarean sections not only lack opportunity for mental rehearsal but are usually unaware of techniques to reduce discomfort after surgical procedures.

To my knowledge, there has not yet been a careful evaluation of the benefits of advance preparation of cesarean women which is geared to their special needs, although such classes have been given for some time and are evaluated positively in anecdotal terms (Hayes 1978). Data based on clinical impressions for 21 cesarean mothers who attended two cesarean support groups (Lipson and Tilden 1980) suggest that women who were prepared for cesarean birth apparently had a better birth experience and fared better emotionally afterward. Since there are no comparison groups (either cesarean women who did not attend classes or vaginally delivered women), this evidence is equivocal, however.

29. This scale, described in detail in Entwisle and Doering (1981, 62), takes into account the type of class attended, outside reading materials, and whether or not class attendance was regular.

30. The worry items are listed in Entwisle and Doering (1981, 56).

31. The items, taken from Taylor (1953) are available from the author on request.

32. See Entwisle and Doering (1981, 52) for the complete list.

33. See Entwisle and Doering (1981, 34ff.) for full details. Total scores range from 0 (all household work done by husband) to 18 (all household work done by wife).

34. The same 20 adjectives were used to rate every semantic differential concept. The adjectives were: healthy-sick; happy-sad; powerful-helpless; active-passive; large-small; brave-scared; calm-excitable; strong-weak; clean-dirty; sensitive-insensitive; nice-looking–ugly; feminine-masculine; capable-fumbling; fast-slow; kind-cruel; peaceful-angry; wise-foolish; hard-soft; good-bad; and complete-incomplete. The positive pole is listed first.

35. The two variables related to conception difficulties (number of years married before first conception and number of years married before conceiving this child) could be indicators of reproductive system problems. If women were "late" in conceiving because of previous miscarriages, infertility, and the like, a possible physiological link might exist between these problems and the need for cesarean delivery. A case-by-case check of the 25 women in this sample who reported longer than a six-month interval between the time they started to try to conceive and time of conception revealed that only 3 of these 25 women experienced cesarean delivery. In other words, of the vaginally delivered women, 22% (22 out of 100) experienced such problems compared to 15% (3 out of 20) of the cesarean women. This comparison makes it seem unlikely that postponement of conception by cesarean women was for medical reasons.

References

Affonso, D., & Stichler, J. Cesarean birth: Women's reactions. *American Journal of Nursing,* 1980, *80,* 468–470.

Andrew, J. M. Recovery from surgery with and without preparatory instruction for three coping styles. *Journal of Personality and Social Psychology,* 1970, *15,* 223–226.

Bates, J. E. The concept of difficult temperament. *Merrill-Palmer Quarterly,* 1980, *26,* 299–319.

Bernstein, B. *Class, codes and control.* London: Routledge & Kegan Paul, 1971.

Blau, A., Slaff, B., Easton, K., Welkowitz, J., Springarn, J., & Cohen, J. The psychogenic etiology of premature births: A preliminary report. *Psychosomatic Medicine,* 1963, *5,* 201–211.

Blood, R. D., & Wolfe, D. M. *Husbands and wives.* Glencoe, IL: Free Press, 1960.

Blumberg, N. L. Effects of neonatal risk, maternal attitude, and cognitive style on early postpartum adjustment. *Journal of Abnormal Psychology,* 1980, *89,* 139–150.

Bott, E. *Family and social network.* London: Tavistock, 1957.

Bradley, C. F., Ross, S. E., & Warnyca, J. A prospective study of mothers' attitudes and feelings following Cesarean and vaginal births. *Births,* 1983, *10,* 79–83.

Breen, D. *The birth of a first child.* London: Tavistock, 1975.

Consensus Development Conference. *Cesarean childbirth,* NIH Publication No. 82-2067, 1981.

Croghan, N., Connors, K., & Franz, W. *Vaginal vs. C-section delivery: Effects on neonatal behavior and mother-infant interaction.* Paper presented at the International Conference on Infant Studies, New Haven, 1980.

Davids, A., & DeVault, S. Maternal anxiety during pregnancy and childbirth abnormalities. *Psychosomatic Medicine,* 1962, *23,* 93.

Doering, S. G., & Entwisle, D. R. *The first birth.* Mimeo. Johns Hopkins University, Department of Social Relations, 1977.

Doering, S. G., Entwisle, D. R., & Quinlan, D. Modeling the quality of women's birth experience. *Journal of Health and Social Behavior,* 1980, *21,* 12–21.

Egbert, L. D., Battit, G. E., Welch, C. E., & Bartlett, M. K. Reduction of postoperative pain by encouragement and instruction of patients. *New England Journal of Medicine,* 1964, *270,* 825–829.

Entwisle, D. R. *Cesarean Sections: Social and Psychological Factors.* Final report, Grant HD13103, Johns Hopkins University, 1982.

Entwisle, D. R., & Doering, S. G. *The first birth: A family turning point.* Baltimore: Johns Hopkins University Press, 1981.

Entwisle, D. R., & Doering, S. G. The emergent father role. In preparation.

Entwisle, D. R., Doering, S. G., & Reilley, T. W. Sociopsychological determinants of women's breastfeeding behavior: A replication and extension. *American Journal of Orthopsychiatry,* 1982, *52,* 244–260.

Entwisle, D. R., & Hayduk, L. A. *Early Schooling: Cognitive and Affective Outcomes.* Baltimore: Johns Hopkins University Press, 1982.

Field, T. M., & Widmayer, S. M. Development follow-up of infants delivered by Cesarean section and general anesthesia. *Infant Behavior and Development,* 1980, *3,* 253–264.

Franks, D. D., & Marolla, J. Efficacious action and social approval as interacting dimensions of self-esteem: A tentative formulation throughout construct validation. *Sociometry,* 1976, *39,* 324–341.

Gainer, M., & Van Bonn, P. (1977). Cited in Consensus Development Conference, *Cesarean childbirth.* NIH Publication No. 82-2667, 1981, p. 438.

Gersten, J. C., Langner, T. S., Eisenberg, J. G., & Simcha-Fagan, O. An evaluation of the etiologic role of stressful life-change events in psychological disorders. *Journal of Health and Social Behavior,* 1977, *18,* 228–244.

Gewirtz, J., Hollenbeck, A., & Sebris, S. L. *Cesarean section and vaginally-delivered infants and their parents compared during the first postpartum month.* Paper presented at the International Conference on Infant Studies, New Haven, 1980. Cited in NICHD Report 1981, 448.

Glick, I., Salerno, L., & Royce, J. Psychophysiological factors in the etiology of pre-eclampsia. *Archives of General Psychiatry,* 1965, *12,* 260–266.

Grimm, E. R., & Venet, W. R. The relationship of emotional adjustment and attitudes to the course and outcome of pregnancy. *Psychosomatic Medicine,* 1966, *28,* 34–49.

Grossman, F. K., Eichler, L. S., & Winikoff, S. A. *Pregnancy, birth and parenthood.* San Francisco: Jossey-Bass, 1980a.

Grossman, F. K., Winikoff, S. A., & Eichler, L. S. *Psychological sequelae of Cesarean delivery.* Paper presented at the International Conference on Infant Studies, New Haven, 1980b.

Hayes, B. A survey of Cesarean childbirth education classes and a hospital parent education program for repeat Cesarean delivery. *Birth and the Family Journal,* 1978, 5, 95–101.

Heinicke, C. M., Diskin, S. D., Ramsey-Klee, D. M., & Given, K. Pre-birth parent characteristics and family development in the first year of life. *Child Development,* 1983, 54, 194–208.

Hess, R. D. Class and ethnic influence upon socialization. In P. H. Mussen (Ed.), *Carmichael's manual of child psychology.* New York: Wiley, 1970, pp. 457–557.

Hoffman, L. W. Effects of the first child on the woman's role. In W. B. Miller & L. F. Newman (Eds.), *The first child and family formation.* Chapel Hill, NC: Carolina Population Center, 1978, pp. 340–367.

Janis, I. L. *Psychological stress.* New York: Wiley, 1958.

Jöreskog, K. C., & Sörbom, D. LISREL: Version IV. Chicago: International Educational Resources, 1978.

Kessler, R. C., & Cleary, P. D. Social class and psychological distress. *American Sociological Review,* 1980, 45, 463–478.

Kilbride, H. W., Johnson, D. L., & Streissguth, A. P. Social class, birth order, and newborn experience. *Child Development,* 1977, 48, 1686–1688.

Klein, R. P., & Gist, N. F. *Antecedents of unanticipated Cesarean deliveries.* Paper presented at the Southeastern Conference on Human Development, Baltimore, 1982.

Kohn, M. L. *Class and conformity.* Homewood, IL: Dorsey, 1969.

Lazarus, R. S. *Psychological stress and the coping process.* New York: McGraw-Hill, 1966.

Leiderman, P. H., & Seashore, M. J. Mother-infant separation: Some delayed consequences. In M. A. Hofer (Ed.), *Parent-infant interaction.* Amsterdam: Elsevier, 1975, pp. 213–231.

Leifer, A. D., Leiderman, P. H., Barnett, C. R., & Williams, J. F. Effects of mother-infant separation on maternal attachment behavior. *Child Development,* 1972, 43, 1203–1218.

Lipson, J. G., & Tilden, V. P. Psychological integration of the Cesarean birth experience. *American Journal of Orthopsychiatry,* 1980, 50, 598–609.

Lynch, M. A. Ill-health and child abuse. *Lancet,* 1975, 2, 317–319.

Lynch, M. A., & Roberts, J. Predicting child abuse: Signs of bonding failure in the maternity hospital. *British Medical Journal,* 1977, 1, 624–626.

Marieskind, H. I. *An evaluation of Cesarean section in the United States.* Final Report to Dept. HEW, Seattle, Washington, 1979.

Marut, J. S., & Mercer, R. T. Comparison of primparas's perceptions of vaginal and Cesarean births. *Nursing Research,* 1979, 28, 260–266.

McClellan, M. S., & Cabianca, W. A. Effects of early mother-infant contact following Cesarean birth. *Obstetrics and Gynecology,* 1980, 56, 52–55.

McDonald, R. L. The role of emotional factors in obstetric complications: A review. *Psychosomatic Medicine*, 1968, *30*, 222–237.

Minkoff, H. L., & Schwartz, R. H. The rising Cesarean section rate: Can it safely be reversed? *Obstetrics and Gynecology*, 1980, *56*, 135–143.

Moss, H. A., & Jones, S. J. Relations between maternal attitudes and maternal behavior as a function of social class. In P. Leiderman, S. Tulkin, & H. Rosenfeld (Eds.), *Culture and infancy*. New York: Academic Press, 1977, pp. 439–467.

Nolan, G. H. (1979). Cited in Consensus Development Conference, *Cesarean childbirth*. NIH Publication No. 82-2067, 1981, p. 439.

Norr, K. L., Block, C. R., Charles, A., Meyering, S., & Meyers, E. Explaining pain and enjoyment in childbirth. *Journal of Health and Social Behavior*, 1977, *18*, 260–275.

Pedersen, F. A., Zaslow, M. J., Cain, R. L., & Anderson, B. J. Cesarean childbirth: Psychological implications for mothers and fathers. *Infant Mental Health Journal*, 1981, *2*, 257–263.

Pitt, B. "Atypical" depression following childbirth. *British Journal of Psychiatry*, 1968, *114*, 1325–1335.

Reilly, T. W. *Modeling the development of women's self-evaluations in parental role*. Unpublished doctoral dissertation, Johns Hopkins University, 1981.

Reilly, T. W., Entwisle, D. R., & Doering, S. G. Socialization into parenthood: A longitudinal study of the development of self evaluations. In preparation.

Richards, M. P. M. Effects on development of medical interventions and the separation of newborns from their parents. In D. Shaffer and J. Dunn (Eds.), *The first year of life*. New York: Wiley, 1979, pp. 37–54.

Ringler, N. M., Trause, M. A., Klaus, M., & Kennell, J. The effects of extra postpartum contact and maternal speech patterns on children's IQ, speech, and language comprehension at five. *Child Development*, 1978, *49*, 862–865.

Shereshefsky, P. M., & Yarrow, L. J. *Psychological aspects of a first pregnancy and early postnatal adaptation*. New York: Raven Press, 1973.

Sherman, J. *On the psychology of women*. Springfield, IL: Charles C Thomas, 1971.

Siegel, P. M. *Prestige in the American occupational structure*. Unpublished doctoral dissertation, University of Chicago, 1971.

Smith, M. B. Competence and socialization. In J. A. Clausen (Ed.), *Socialization and society*. Boston: Little, Brown & Co., 1968, pp. 270–320.

Sosa, R., Kennell, J., Klaus, M., Robertson, S., & Urrutia, J. The effect of a supportive companion on perinatal problems, length of labor and mother-infant interaction. *New England Journal of Medicine*, 1980, *303*, 597–600.

Steffensmeier, R. H. A role model of the transition to parenthood. *Journal of Marriage and the Family*, 1982, *44*, 319–334.

Sullivan, J. W., Horowitz, F. D., & Byrne, J. M. (1980). Cited in Consensus Development, Cesarean childbirth. NIH Publication No. 82-2067, 1981, p. 459.

Taylor, J. A. A personality scale of manifest anxiety. *Journal of Abnormal and Social Psychology*, 1953, *48*, 285–290.

Thomas, A., & Chess, S. *Temperament and development*. New York: Bruner / Mazel, 1977.

Thomas, A., Chess, S., & Korn, S. J. The reality of difficult temperament. *Merrill-Palmer Quarterly, 1982, 28,* 1–20.

Tod, E. D. M. Puerperal depression: A prospective epidemiological study. *Lancet,* 1964, *2,* 264.

Turner, R. J., & Noh, S. *Psychological distress in women: A longitudinal analysis of the role of stressors, self esteem, personal control and social support.* Paper presented at the National Conference on Social Stress, University of New Hampshire, 1982.

U.S. Bureau of the Census. *Current population reports.* Series P-25, no. 613, November 1975. Washington, DC: U.S. Government Printing Office.

Vietze, P. M., MacTurk, R. H., McCarthy, M. E., Klein, R. P., & Yarrow, L. J. *Impact of mode of delivery on father- and mother-infant interaction at 6 and 12 months.* Paper presented at the Second International Conference on Infant Studies, New Haven, 1980.

Williams, T. M., Davidson, S. M., Joy, L. A., & Painter, S. (n.d.). *Parent-Infant program.* Final Report, University of British Columbia, School of Nursing.

PART IV

The Future

12. The Journey Is Everything: General-Experimental Psychology in the United States after a Hundred Years
William Bevan

We shall not cease from exploration
And the end of all our exploring
Will be to arrive where we started
And know the place for the first time.

T. S. Eliot, *Little Gidding*

This is an exercise in style.
The pluperfect tense
Of countries imperfective.

Czeslaw Milosz,
Bells in Winter

The Fifth Business

Those among the readers of this essay who know me will have probably guessed that this is yet another nonlinear composition, and, of course, they will have been right. It does not begin with alpha and proceed through a rational sequence of events to omega. Rather, I have tried to reconstruct the web of complex interrelationships—some based in fact, others largely conjectural—that I think are important to an understanding of what general-experimental psychology is like one hundred years after its emergence as a separate field and how it got to be what, in fact, it is at present.

It was once a frequent practice in drama and opera companies to refer to the performer who was neither Hero nor Heroine, Confidante nor Villain, but whose responsibility it was to reveal the dénouement, as the Fifth Business. I suppose you might call my role in this chapter that of the Fifth Business. When invited to prepare a manuscript, I asked what might be appropriate for me to do. The gracious reply was that I might "try something statesmanlike." Such advice to a person like me is dangerous. I immediately declared that my essay would be a kind of timely integration; something that represented the history and sociology of academic psychology, the politics of science, science-government relations, and the current issues that will define the future of the research enterprise in the universities. That is a tall order, indeed, and I must say immediately that I am not so arrogant as to think I can deliver on my declared intention in any significant way nor so foolish as to think I can deceive the reader into thinking that I have. Scholarship in psychology has become so complex and so thoroughly specialized in so short a time that I am no longer qualified by direct knowledge or experience to deal in detail at the technical level with the substance of its now broad array of primary research journals. Rather, it seemed to me better that I view current psychological scholarship collectively and in an at-arms-length fashion and ask what it tells us about the nature of pscyhological science and where it is going. In attempting to do so, I must also make clear that I hold no credentials as historian or sociologist or, for that matter, as philosopher of science, and the circumstances surrounding the preparation of my manuscript were such that I found myself confined to readily available bibliographic sources. Often, data essential to the illumination of basic historical or sociological questions appeared not to exist in the literature, and I therefore frequently have had to make what I hope are responsible educated guesses.

When I describe the subject of my concern as general-experimental psychology, I imply those topics and that perspective that have characterized the so-called basic offerings of academic psychology departments from their inception, that is, the part of their programs that they conceive of as the classical science or classical science derivatives as contrasted with the more recent practice-related aspects of psychology, what some like to think of as the basic discipline as contrasted with the applications of psychology. Thus, I have given no attention to those topics and that perspective that are identified with the preparation of students for professional practice, that is, for the delivery of psychological services to the community at large. It is a fuzzy business. There are no simple criteria that allow for the clear separation of one part of psychology from the other, except on paper. I hope that you will recognize that I am aware of that fact but that you will allow me the definition I have chosen for the sake of the present discussion. If I were to use labels to identify the domain to which I refer, I would use words and phrases like sensory processes, perception, learning, cognitive processes, motivation, emotion, experimental study, intellectual content, empirical theory, the general case, etc., etc., etc., as the King of Siam would say.

Dominating my view of general-experimental psychology is the belief that it at present faces a critical period in its development as a coherent body of knowledge, a fact that is not readily recognized by psychologists because of the current immense popularity of the discipline as a whole and because of the exciting developments—brilliant individual advances, both technological and intellectual—of recent decades. Particularly ironic to me is the possibility that the source of psychology's increasing promise as a science may at the same time also be the source of its undoing. For the crisis that I perceive is less a matter of shortfalls in substance and more a matter of flawed intellectual character, less a matter of the logic of inquiry and more a matter of the social strategies that we use to advance our science. Our problem at base lies not so much in our vision of a science of psychology as in the sociology, the psychology, and the economics of the academic enterprise in 1984. If you have read Robert Nisbet's excellent book, *The Degradation of the Academic Dogma,* written more than a decade ago (1971) but still frighteningly on target, then you will know where I am coming from.

Some among my readers may be offended by what I say—after all, if I stomp about on sacred ground, I must expect to draw the lightning. More are likely to think me unduly pessimistic. Curiously, I do not perceive myself as pessimistic at all. I hold on to a kind of stubborn optimism about the ability of things to shape up. The basic social and intellectual character of psychology is such that the best of psychology can survive with its identity intact. But at the same time, I strongly believe that it is urgent that the social and scientific insights of psychologists not be 20 / 20 hindsight. If psychology is to be what it believes itself to be—and better than it is—it has to be willing to look increasingly at itself squarely and in focus.

While my preoccupations in these remarks center about academic psychology, my experience in the broader academic community leads me to believe that the same sermon can be preached for other disciplines as well, for the thing all academic disciplines have in common is the fact that they exist in the same institutional climate.

THE WINDMILLS OF THE SCIENTIFIC MIND

One further comment—broadly methodological—before I turn to the primary focus of my remarks. Why the nonlinear strategy? Again, those who know me are likely to reply, "Because that's the way his mind works," and I will be forced to agree. But I think that the reason is more profound than that. After years of intellectual resistance, I find myself facing the reality that psychology is a nonlinear discipline.

From our beginning as a separate field we have incorporated into our catechism the simple linear model of classical physical science. Antecedents give rise to consequents that, in turn, become antecedents in a progressive unfolding of events, and science, we proclaim, reveals the ultimate nature of reality by exploring those relationships in reverse. But one hundred or more years of this strategy have not yielded a confident picture of the ultimate character of psychological reality and I am increasingly uncertain that it ever will. Rather, we may have to content ourselves with a model that is far more complex than we are used to and which allows significant links to emerge at different locations in our multidimensional space in much the same way that pieces are placed in a three-dimensional jigsaw puzzle. Thus, I am increasingly drawn to Koch's (for me) still disturbing view (1976, 1981) that psychology is not a simple coherent discipline but a collectivity of studies of varied cast. Looked at in sociological terms, the character of psychology is seen in the rapid proliferation of rather narrowly focused and increasingly insular intellectual communities. It is tempting to view these communities as a socially evolved division of labor, but I am inclined to think that they are more than that. Rather, they are, I suspect, the reflection of—to borrow Koch's language—"the multiply determined, cognitively ambiguous, contextually environed, evanescent, labile nature of psychological events." Having lived my psychological youth in the forties and fifties in what soon must be a land that never was, I can sometimes feel A. E. Housman's lament (Ellmann and O'Clair 1973, 99) in my aging bones.

That is the land of lost content,
　I see it shining plain,
The happy highways where I went
　And cannot come again.

Coupled to the dominating simple linear model of reality has been the dogma of the scientific method. From our earliest days as students, my generation of psychologists were indoctrinated—and, in turn, I suspect many of us regrettably have indoctrinated our students—in the absolute nature of our methodological canons. Scientific knowledge possesses, we were taught, a hierarchical cognitive structure. First there are facts, and scientists must have available in their ken the full repertoire of such information as is relevant to the problem that they propose to solve. Then there are the hypotheses that scientists create to make sense of the existing facts and to aid in establishing new facts. These hypotheses, in turn, must be tested by experiment, and the alternating procedures of formulating and testing hypotheses constitutes the backbone of the scientific method in its highest form. When the relationship between antecedents and consequents has been confirmed a sufficient number of times, it takes on the character of a law, and facts and laws are bound together, in turn, by deeper-level explanatory theories. The cognitive structure of a science is supposed to be flexible. Laws may be modified in the face of new facts, and theories may be displaced by better, more comprehensive explanatory schemata. This science-making is held to be a public activity, and scientists are expected to share fully in such information and insights as each individual member of the scientific community may possess toward the end of advancing the community's collective knowledge and understanding. The quality of each contribution is assessed through the various mechanisms of peer review and through empirical confirmation by replication.

This dogma of the scientific method is a simplified, idealized conception of how science-making takes place. It is also a thoroughly rationalized version of the process. It overlooks the fact that scientists are like other human beings and that the scientific community has its fair share of the inflexible along with the flexible, of the prejudiced along with the open-minded, of the plodding along with the brilliantly insightful, of the self-centered along with the altruistic, of the primarily career-oriented along with the intellectually committed, and of the dishonest along with the honest. And competition and secretiveness—if not born then enhanced by the traditional emphasis on individual scholarly attainment within the academic community, the pressures resulting from selective tenure and promotion policies, and the prevailing project method of funding research used by extramural granting agencies—are far more common within the present-day scientific community than are cooperation and genuine collaboration. (The reader will find a thoughtful and balanced overview of the problem of competition and secrecy in science in Bok [1983, chap. 8].)

The quality of the science that we have available to us at any particular time is as much a reflection of these personal qualities of the science-maker as it is of the procedural formalities through which that science was made. Scientific theory does not always succumb to the onslaught of new facts. Scientists do not always grant the significance nor draw on the repertoire of already existing fact in the way that the idealized method assumes. The replication of experiments—in psychology, at least—is so rare as to be the exception rather than the rule. And outright dishonesty in science appears, in my personal view, often enough at present to threaten the credibility of our entire enterprise. Certainly logical thought and objectivity are important instruments in the advancement of scientific knowledge, but to believe that they are the only factors at work is to be co-opted by a myth.

EVERY WRITER TELLS A STORY

Indeed, the logical structure of scientific knowledge is itself imposed as much by the hindsight of the observer as by the properties of nature observed, and a persuasive case can be made that it, at least in part, grows out of the processes that shape the narrative through which scientific outcomes must inevitably be reported and their cumulative nature summarized. "Science flies," as Broad and Wade observe, "on the wings of rhetoric as well as reason" (1982, 142). Indeed, the conventions of scientific report-writing rigidly require that every aspect of an experimental study be described as if it conformed to the idealized method. Thus, the false leads, the intuitive gropings, the fortunate and the unfortunate guesses, the tinkering with procedure, the artful shaping that are part of every experiment, successful or otherwise, go unmentioned. So, too, do the assumptions and perspectives—the biases if you will—that are dictated by the experimenter's world view and location in time and place. Indeed, I venture to claim that there has never been a scientist who, in reporting the outcomes of his or her work, has not first selected and arranged the elements of his or her story to make a persuasive case for the study being reported. The preparation of the scientific report is as much an exercise of intellect as the planning of the experiment, and it is shaped as much by our ingrained arts of persuasion as it is by the tenets of our ideology. If, then, we view science as a social enterprise carried out by agents more alike than different from the rest of the human race and if we similarly admit the essential place of narrative in the communication of ideas, we will also then perceive science to share more in common with other forms of scholarship than our ideological tradition has allowed.

I shall say no more at the moment about the things that motivate and shape the outlook of individual scientists. However, a few more words about the importance of narrative form to all scholarship are in order. (Let me say, parenthetically, that I am certainly not up to a technical discussion of literary form as it relates to knowledge. To those who are interested in such questions I would simply say that there is now a growing literature on this topic and for starters I would refer you to a little book recently edited by Canary and Kozicki [1981], *The Writing of History,* especially the essays by Hayden White and by Louis Mink.) Narrative form is a primary cognitive instrument for making comprehensible an ensemble of human events, regardless of its setting. How a narrative is constructed will directly influence what is conveyed and how, a fact that certainly bears on the issue of the nature of knowledge, regardless of its setting—in science, in the humanistic fields, or in the arts. The form of narrative used will reflect the intellectual requirements of the field of scholarship in which the writer works but it will also impose requirements of its own.

The central requirement is, of course, coherence, and narratives are constructed toward this end. Aristotle in his *Poetics* commented that every story has a beginning, a middle, and an end, an observation that makes clear not only the role of the narrative in giving shape to data but also the requirement that a narrative must have a unity of its own. When the role of narrative form is recognized, a number of methodological issues arise. How, for example, does narrative structure determine what is and what is not relevant to it? And what criteria determine the coherence of narratives? Beyond the level of mere chronology is the achievement of understanding dependent upon chronologies being related through some larger theme about movement and direction? How can narratives be related to each other? Can they be combined? In what sense are narratives true or false? There are other questions as well.

The cognitive function of narrative form consists of more than relating a series of events. It brings together an ensemble of interrelationships of many different kinds as a unitary whole. And whether in science or elsewhere, the data simply in and of themselves do not determine what the ultimate construction will be. Moreover, there are no rules as such for the construction of a narrative. Thus, the final resolution of the matter must depend upon the imagination, sensibility, and sensitivity of the individual scholar. In including these brief comments about the role of narrative construction in shaping scholarship, I am not denigrating the scientific ideal of objectivity. But I am saying that this ideal is probably best thought of as a retrospective virtue. I am also saying that it is probably unwise to perpetuate the dogma that science-making is uniquely different in kind from other exercises of the human intellect.

Academic Psychology Today

What now may I say in general about the character of current academic psychology? If I can trust my experience in reviewing and editing manuscripts, my net impression is not encouraging. A disturbingly large proportion of the manuscripts I have read over the years were trivial, some were even contrived. The intellectual processes behind them lacked clarity and crispness and the motivation behind them I can only guess at. Indeed, I believe that, over all, as the psychological literature has proliferated, its average quality has deteriorated. But, again, perhaps I am indulging in the sentimentality of my September years.

The character of the literature of academic psychology is, for the major part, strongly empirical. The largest number of papers in most of our journals stick close to the level of the data and use the practical, work-a-day logic of the scientific practitioner. Few are explicitly concerned with fundamental, metaphysical issues. Most are narrowly focused—I do not use this phrase pejoratively—in the sense that they deal with a rather circumscribed, rather specifically focused question or set of questions. The mood, I think it is safe to say, is one of no-frills empiricism. There is no longer much talk of grand explanatory schemes or of world views, although if one knows the authors and the broader context of their work one will sense where they are coming from.

When one looks beyond the world of individual studies, one sees that general-experimental psychology in the United States in the 1980s has two major preoccupations: neuroscience and cognitive science. In this it extends a dual intellectual tradition that has been part of American psychology since its inception, for American psychology at its intellectual foundations remains a nineteenth-century enterprise, as Daniel Robinson makes clear both in *An Intellectual History of Psychology* (1976) and in his more recent *Toward a Science of Human Nature* (1982). The language has changed, the methodology is more sophisticated and refined, but the seminal problems remain the same in their general formulation.

HOW ACADEMIC PSYCHOLOGY HAS EVOLVED

Psychologists in significant numbers have only recently discovered Thomas Kuhn (1962), and it has become increasingly fashionable to equate scientific progress with the occurrence of paradigm shifts. Thus, one is prompted to ask if and when such shifts have, in fact, occurred in psychology. The paradigm, according to this perspective, is the basis of the research tradition. It is the frame of reference within which the aspects of nature that interest scientists at a particular time are viewed. It identifies the problems that serve that interest and indicates which of them are solvable. Kuhn refers to work within this context as "normal science." When the scientist doing normal science confronts only insoluble problems, progress ceases and the science enters a period of crisis. However, if a new way of conceptualizing the relevant aspects of nature emerges, opening up a path to solutions, then a new paradigm is said to have replaced the old; that is, a paradigm shift is said to have occurred.

Paradigm shifts, according to Kuhn, do not occur through the extension of logic. They are, he believes, the product of nonrational processes, something tantamount to a conversion experience, and, therefore, they cannot be programmed or forced to occur. The new paradigm continues to dominate until it in turn is replaced by a newer paradigm. When that happens another scientific revolution is said to have occurred. Thus, in Kuhn's formulation, contrary to the traditional view, the advancement of science is not the result of a cumulative process but of a succession of world views, each replacing its predecessor. Thus, new knowledge is always revealed in the context of some paradigm.

It has been frequently suggested in recent years that a paradigm shift has occurred in psychology in the past decade or two. Cognitive science is now viewed by many as having replaced behaviorism as the prevailing paradigm. Others are more cautious in their optimism. We are, they say, in what Koch (e.g., 1969), George Mandler (personal communications 1982, 1983) and others (e.g., Giorgi 1970) have called a preparadigmatic period, with a paradigm in vague outline at the end of the tunnel (Mandler). I am buoyed by their implied evolutional perspective and truly wish I could share it. But I do not think there yet have been true Kuhnian-type paradigm shifts in our field. Certainly we have experienced nothing that compares to the experience of physicists after the advent of General Relativity Theory or to that of geneticists after the emergence of molecular biology. Moreover, the mentalism that is supposed to have displaced behaviorism is really nothing new. Even when behaviorism in its most radical and advanced forms was at its apogee, there were sizable numbers of closet mentalists within the psychological community. I know, because I was one of them. With my basic temperament as a given and my early education in the tradition of Chicago Functionalism and graduate study with students of William McDougall and the Berlin Gestaltists, I have always been most comfortable in doing my thinking within a broadly sentential framework even when convention required that I communicate its outcomes in what were the dominant behavioristic idioms of the day. (On this general point, see, e.g., Samelson 1981.) At the same time, I share Robinson's (1979) concern that a productive mentalism for the 1980s and beyond must avoid both the limitations of the traditional form and what he calls the new computerism (Robinson, personal communication 1983). He is right when he says that, given our weakness for science as instrumentation, we need beware lest we think that there is a machine in the ghost. Meanwhile, we can, I think, all take heart from the increased recognition that the proper terrain for psychological inquiry lies inside rather than around the organism. It is nice to be able at long last to come in out of the intellectual cold.

My skepticism about paradigm shifts derives from a conviction shared with others that American psychology has lacked any real intellectual continuity in its first hundred years. There has been fad and fashion but no enduring, overarching, genuine intellectual structure. Individual psychologists have enjoyed important insights and have contributed significant knowledge to our storehouse of information during the past century, but none of this has in any ultimate sense required agreement concerning an authoritative body of theoretical concepts or even concerning what shall be our legitimate intellectual ambitions. Until it does so, we shall still be what Toulmin (1972) calls a "would-be discipline," immune from worry about such things as paradigms and paradigm shifts. What about the paradigm at the end of tunnel? As I said, I find Mandler's evolutional perspective buoying, but, at the same time, I recognize that by invoking Toulmin's concept of the "would-be discipline" I have placed us outside the country of paradigms and, therefore, paradigm shifts. Moreover, since paradigm shifts, are, by nature, unpredictable, they are infinitely difficult to anticipate at the end of the tunnel or anywhere else.

Finally, our condition as a "would-be discipline" is, I believe, as much a reflection of our national character as it is of the maturity of our science. Henry May, the distinguished intellectual historian, has described what he calls The Other American Tradition (1983). The impression that Americans most want to convey is characterized by adjectives like cheerful, self-confident, well-intentioned, progressive, and optimistic. But there is another tradition that is marked by inner struggle, alienation, and self-doubt, and it is seen most clearly, May says, in the American intellectual community. Its origins are several but, most of all, it derives, May thinks, from the Puritan spirit—the constant struggle for spiritual worthiness—that is our legacy. Articulate beliefs change with the passage of time. Emotional attitudes endure much longer. The American Protestant tradition was an inevitable part of American psychology a hundred years ago, and despite the secularization of American society, its ethnic diversification, and the radical social changes that have taken place, particularly during the last several decades, that tradition is still very much a part of us. Thus, I believe that we are now experiencing one of those recurrent waves of national soul searching that seem necessary for our balance, and what has begun to happen to you and to me and to our field is part of it.

The World in 1983

It is usual for me in pieces of this genre to include something about the kind of world we inhabit. I do so because I think it important that we not forget that science, above all else, is a social enterprise that both shapes and is shaped by forces and settings that also define the broader society. Moreover, all institutions—and most especially intellectual institutions—have to be reborn from time to time as the price of survival. I shall spare you the grim details and say only that we live in a period of instability, disruption, and violence. Great and justifiable anxiety has been evidenced in recent years concerning such matters as the depletion of natural resources, the explosive growth of population, the waning of economic productivity, and nuclear annihilation. Let me now add to this list the decline in the certainties that used to define the relations among members of the human species, both individual and collective; the weakening of formalities; and the deterioration in respect for the rule-of-law—indeed, the crisis in the nature of the law itself (Levi 1970). I hope I do not trivialize when I say that what has been lost is what, in the context of the small world of the individual, the nineteenth-century English called gentlemanliness—a kind of moral sensibility, a kind of natural decorum of the spirit, that meant behaving well and fairly, respecting limits and order and displaying scrupulosity and restraint. Now at—should I melodramatically say—the advent of 1984, we find that the globe has shrunk, political power has been concentrated in such fashion, and political and economic arrangements have taken on such character that the threat of violent social change is always dangerously at hand.

DOING SCIENCE IN 1983

It has been traditional to think of the intellectual character of American psychology in terms of the ideas of individual psychologists—Wundt, Titchener, James, Dewey, Freud, Köhler, Lashley, Hull, and Skinner—and the response of individual minds, yours and mine, to them. But in the world that I have described, no intellectual institution, and least of all the behavioral sciences, can afford not to understand better than we at present do the extent to which its directions and substantive character are determined by forces outside itself. Let me mention politics by way of example. "In our age," George Orwell observed in his 1946 essay on politics and the English language, "there is no such thing as 'keeping out of politics.' All issues are political issues, and politics itself is a mass of lies, evasions, folly, hatred, and schizophrenia." Because of the constraints of time, I shall limit myself to a few examples of the impact of politics on psychology, and describe these in only superficial fashion.

First, the economics of research funding in this country over the last thirty years has had a profound effect on the kind of science that has been conducted. The federal government is by far the largest sponsor of research, and this is especially the case where the so-called soft sciences are concerned. Moreover, the influence on the science that is conducted is greatest when constraints in funding, such as those that mark the present, are most severe. The federal budget process, in its several complex aspects, determines what areas and kinds of research will be funded and therefore done. The project method of funding and the politics of the peer review process determine not only the areas but the problems deemed important to be investigated and ultimately the kinds of experiments to be conducted.

Second, political ideology increasingly influences what questions may be posed, what strategies may be used to confront them, and what answers will be acceptable. The recent agitated concern over mental tests, both within the general public and within our profession itself, reflects the influence of the egalitarian philosophy that increasingly dominates public policy decisions in this country. Lest you mistake where my own biases lie, let me indicate that it is a philosophy to which I am inclined to subscribe. But I also understand the outcome when the values that underlie a broadly accepted philosophy conflict with those that govern a more narrowly circumscribed domain.

Third, special-interest politics is taking its toll of our science. A good case in point is the increasing harassment that researchers using animals are receiving from the antivivisection movement. Neal Miller (1983), in an invited address at the 1983 annual APA meeting, made clear the ultimately irrational grounds underlying these attacks. At the same time, he also made clear their effectiveness. One illustration will suffice. With the news that a small number of deeply anesthetized dogs and pigs were being sacrificed as part of a program to find ways of more effectively treating combat soldiers wounded by the new high-velocity weapons, a major campaign of protests was organized. False and misleading information was circulated. A barrage of phone calls was mounted. Legislators were persuaded to write letters to the secretary of defense. Against the judgment of his science advisor, the secretary ordered the work stopped, stating, according to the *Washington Post* of July 28, 1983, that no dogs would be sacrificed "as long as Casper Weinberger is Secretary of Defense." This while some 65 million animals a year are sacrificed for pure sport with little more than a few local protests from the antivivisectionists. (For a brief but fascinating exploration of the question of animal rights see Morrow 1983.)

PSYCHOLOGY MISDIRECTED

In his 1981 book, *Psychology Misdirected,* Seymour Sarason argues that American psychology has developed as a study of the individual organism while ignoring the characteristics of the world order in which that individual organism functions. This asocial psychology of the individual, he says, has kept psychologists unaware of the influence of their own views upon their psychology and the psychology itself painfully irrelevant to the real world. This situation, in turn, Sarason insists, has resulted in widespread dissatisfaction among psychologists about the adequacy—or even the potential adequacy—of their field and their consequent alienation from it. For the dissatisfied, psychology simply cannot work. In order for it to work and for the alienated to overcome their alienation, psychologists, he says, must give full attention to the social order—its history, its structure, and its multiplicity of world views—as the one inevitable context within which organisms must be understood. This attention to social and cultural context includes a better understanding of the place of psychology itself within the social order and makes social and intellectual history an essential basis for psychology. Such a broadening of psychology, he insists, will not make psychology history but will drastically shape how psychologists perceive and conceptualize their own subject matter. Two outcomes will be (a) a greater emphasis on understanding and less on numbers for numbers sake and (b) a transcendence of what he has called the "cult of standardization," that is, the compulsion toward contrived, unrepresentative situations as standard observational settings for all individuals and all circumstances. A new psychology, if it emerges, will not result, Sarason insists, simply from more of the same but because of broadened perspectives concerning what constitutes an adequate research strategy.

PSYCHOLOGISTS IN 1983

In its earliest years, the American psychological community was all academic, all white, and almost exclusively male and Protestant. Most were middle class or upper middle class with family backgrounds involving more than the usual amount of formal education and most were well off or at least sufficiently well off to study abroad, although there were some who came from more modest economic backgrounds. The community's leadership was young and included a large proportion educated for the clergy or with strong personal ties to organized religion (Kessen, personal communication 1983). For most, psychology was a high calling, what G. Stanley Hall called a sacred quest. Psychologists were then, of course, all generalists who were expected to have acquainted themselves with the significant literature, both current and past, relevant to psychology, not only that in English but also that in French and German.

Today the American psychological community is thousands of times larger than it was at its inception. I was not able to locate data to indicate the number of persons embracing the psychological label in the earliest years, but when the American Psychological Association was organized in 1892, there were thirty-one members present for the organizational meeting (Hildreth, personal communication 1983). By 1900, there were 127 members. By the mid 1940s, there were more than 4000. Today, the Association's membership has reached more than 60,000, and Rosenzweig (1982) reports Stapp's estimate that the entire community consists of some number between 70,000 and 120,000, depending on how one defines a psychologist. About half are academics and half are engaged in other settings. While the community is still predominately white, it has taken on a greater ethnic and other diversity. About 32% are women and 3.4% are black, Hispanic, Asian, and American Indian (Stapp, personal communication 1983). Psychologists today come typically from middle- and lower middle-class backgrounds, are of more limited financial means, with the costs of their education having been met by an elaborate system of fellowships, scholarships, and work-study awards. (A good overview of the growth of American psychology following World War II can be found in Gilgen 1982, chap. 2.)

The leadership is older. While again, there appear to be few reliable statistics on the membership at large, Hilgard (1978, 13) reports a clear trend upward in the average age of APA presidents. In the first decade of the Association's life, the average age of presidents was approximately thirty-seven and a half years. In the ninth and most recent decade, it is slightly over fifty-nine, reflecting, Hilgard (1978) says, the longer time required to become prominent in a large organization.

It is a commonly held view among those who are profession-watchers in psychology that the average level of creativity and acumen among psychologists today is below that of one hundred years ago. While one must be exceedingly cautious in registering impressions and in imputing causes, I venture to suggest that, if such is the case, it is in part at least a reflection of our rapid growth and size. While we still attract our fair share of exceedingly able young persons, the sheer number being educated as psychologists and the variation in quality among educational institutions now offering the doctorate has meant, I suspect, an overall drop in average intellectual quality. Psychologists during my professional life time have not seen themselves as members of a well-defined social establishment, but their conduct overall does not depart drastically from conventional standards as far as the major goals of society are concerned. Meanwhile, psychologists are more politically active today than they ever have been before, although academic psychologists have been slow to take up this mode of behavior.

If I were required to describe in a simple declarative sentence the greatest transformation that has taken place in psychology during the past century, I would answer that the gentleman scholar has given way over the years to the professional. What were once activities pursued primarily to satisfy intellectual curiosity or otherwise to meet some similar personal emotional need have long since become the basic means of providing the academic psychologist's livelihood. In others words, the pursuit of knowledge has become the means to something else rather than being an end in itself. (For an elaboration of the general case see Persons 1973 and Bledstein 1976.)

PROFESSIONALISM IN THE AMERICAN ACADEMY

The "professional outlook," to use Higham's phrase (1979), has had a profound effect upon scholarship, including scholarship in psychology. The academic generalist has been replaced by the specialist. Indeed, the generalist has virtually become extinct. The key to advancement to higher rank, to better salaries, to more prestigious honors, and to greater influence in the academic community is to become a leading expert on some highly specialized area of knowledge and / or a recognized master of some complex, state-of-the-art technical skill.

The notion of specialization among academics in and of itself should not be disconcerting. One is hard pressed to see the differentiation that lies behind it as something other than the normal consequence of social evolution in an intellectual enterprise. This is what Spencer (1961) argued a hundred years ago and the argument is still powerfully attractive. What *is* disturbing to see is that the specialization, which has so thoroughly transformed American intellectual institutions and so completely shaped the role models of American scholars, has become corrosive. It has proved to be self-limiting, as Toulmin (1972) noted more than a decade ago. With it has come a reluctance at communication outside increasingly narrowly defined circles, a turning inward of scholarly preoccupation, an insensitivity to history, and an ascendance of method and technique over ideas. Differentiation has given rise to separation; specialization has degenerated into exclusiveness; and a narrow view is a badge of honor. Thus, Koch, in discussing fragmentation in psychology with his special linguistic flair, has characterized our field as a congeries of weird insularities and has pointed out that this condition as a source of concern is nothing new. Grace Adams, for example, dealt with it in her book, *Psychology: Science or Superstition,* in 1931, and Higham (1979) reports that John Stuart Mill and Thomas Huxley, both vigorous nineteenth-century champions of science, were early on concerned over the narrowness of mind that they could see accompanying the rapid growth of the research enterprise.

A variety of reasons has been advanced to explain both specialization and fragmentation. Higham (1979) characterizes specialization as a process that makes possible a greater division of intellectual labor. Discussing psychology, Tyler (1981) sees both specialization and fragmentation as the inevitable result of psychology's rapid growth. James Grier Miller (personal communication 1983) sees them to be in part at least the consequence of information input overload, while Toulmin (1978) attributes them to the positivistic philosophy that has prompted the view among American psychologists that the more narrowly and sharply defined a question is, the more scientific it is. Koch (1971), again in the case of psychology, simply denies on apriori, historical, and empirical grounds that it ever has been or ever can be a coherent discipline. My own view is perhaps too cynical to be valid, although I have come by it honestly as part of my experience as dean, provost, and now foundation officer. I would distinguish between the differentiation of knowledge and the fragmentation of the intellectual enterpise. Differentiation is the result of intellectual evolution, and specialization, as has been suggested, is our strategy for responding to it.

Fragmentation, I am convinced, is attributable to the sociology of the university and the politics of the extramural funding process. These reflect chiefly, I believe, the political philosophy of modernity, the cult of unbridled individualism that dominates all of our society but that exists in its most extreme form in our colleges and universities. (For a good general discussion of modernism see Will 1983, 28–46.) The problem within the academy at present is that it is overpopulated by dedicated operators masquerading as dedicated scholars. Maybe it always has been thus. At any rate, even if fragmentation had had other origins, it has been facilitated by the increasing competition for status within university and college faculties and by the project method of federal funding. This latter has meant an inevitable politicization of American science as scientists and their institutions became heavily dependent upon government and upon the prejudices—no matter how well-intentioned—of a government bureaucracy. Publications have become the coin of the realm. Today, one does not write so much to communicate ideas as to add gloss to one's curriculum vitae, to obtain salary increases, and to gain promotion, attention, and status among one's peers. I do not mean to imply that self-serving motives are anything new or that they are the only engines that drive the scholar. But for the last 30 years they have been increasingly the dominant ones. Henry Gleitman put the matter eloquently in a recent letter to me.

I think that of late (say, since the end of World War II), things have become more ominous. I don't care that half or three quarters of our graduate students no longer know anything about the field as a whole. But is there anyone who does . . . ? In the old days, there was an audience for those—relatively few—people who had something to say, in literature, in philosophy, in the sciences. I suspect that much of our progress in all areas is made by a relatively few people. And that is what the academy supplied. "Men-of-letters" . . . who might add to knowledge but who didn't feel they had to, for they were high-level, educated *consumers* [italics added] of knowledge. But not now. For the academic system—with competitive research grants, peer review, publish-or-perish and all the rest of it—has destroyed the audience. Our fellow academicians may be a potential audience, but they have neither the time nor the inclination to act as one. Their only chance of staying in the theater hall (getting their first job, getting tenure), the price of admission, is to get up on stage as well and be an actor. As a result, the stage is crowded, we are all up there acting, orating, and there is no one in the auditorium seats listening. Even my most scholarly colleagues only read what they must to help them in their own work. The audience has left its seats, and has moved out on the stage. As a result, there are fewer and fewer of us—in all fields—who know anything except our own little parts. . . .

You might say, that specialization of this kind is inevitable when knowledge accumulates. This happened when biochemistry split off from chemistry; or biophysics and so on; and after all, all science was once housed within the halls of philosophy. One could argue that psychology will soon split up: one branch going into neuroscience, another into what is now called "cognitive science"; still another joining up with, say, sociology and so on. Perhaps. But what will become of "Psychology" itself? As the various branches of science split off from philosophy to strike off on their own, philosophy remained. It continued to formulate the problems, to state the issues, to develop the speculations that were not yet ready to become the subject-matter of a separate science. I believe that no matter how highly developed neuroscience, or computer science, etc. ever becomes, there will always be a need for a central discipline that continues questioning and keeps alive the initial questions about the nature of the human mind and the human passions that underlie the entire enterprise from its inception millennia ago.

SLOPPINESS, FUDGING, AND DOWNRIGHT DECEIT

The most distressing outcome of what Gleitman describes as the rush for a place on stage has been the apparently rapid explosion of shoddy work and downright fraud in science. You see notice of it in growing numbers of newspaper and magazine accounts, an extremely careful sociological study of the phenomenon (Zuckerman 1977), and two more recent books (Broad and Wade 1982; Kilbourne and Kilbourne 1983). Moreover, one does not need a learned dissertation to recognize the declining character of morality in the everyday transactions of life and in the furtive quality of our organized thinking about morality (see, for example, Quinton's Lionel Trilling Seminars [1983]). Fraud in science is nothing new. Broad and Wade trace it back to Ptolemy and implicate such science greats as Galileo, Newton, Dalton, Mendel, and Millikan. Nor has psychology been free of its share. Samelson (1980) has raised doubt about Watson's study of Little Albert. Pavlov's successful Lamarckian experiments were the work of a laboratory assistant and had to be retracted (Broad and Wade 1982, 182–83). Gould claims that Goddard used retouched photographs to give the Kallikaks their look of pathology (Gould 1981, 27, 177). And within the last few years we have all been brought up short by what appears to have been the most colossal case of systematic deception of all among psychologists. I refer, of course, to the case of Cyril Burt. (For a careful summary, see Hearnshaw 1979.)

The scientific community, when confronted by such cases of fraud, has steadfastly assumed that they are relatively infrequent anomalies. This complacent attitude is based on the assumption that the self-correcting mechanisms of science, peer review and replication, will detect fraud when it occurs. That simply is not the case. None of the cases in the spate of recently revealed fraud were detected in this fashion. Indeed, there is the growing suspicion that peers no longer take time for careful review—as Gleitman says, there are too many preoccupied with starring in their own act. And no one bothers to replicate. There is no pay-off in it. Moreover, to write off cases of fraud as occasional anomalies is to miss the point. Every case of fraud that occurs is a serious threat to the institution of science and the confidence that society at large places in it.

What can be done about this regrettable situation? This occasion does not allow the time needed to respond in a responsible fashion. Let me simply say that if we take the time to investigate its causes, I strongly suspect that we will find that chief among them are the excessive competition and secrecy that today mark the academy in this country.

Moreover, there can be no cure save through removing the circumstances that give rise to fraud and cause its risk of detection to be low. One, of course, can treat the symptoms. One might, as Broad and Wade suggest, try closing down the manuscript factories run by demanding P.I.'s and their attendant fringe of vanity presses—although there is little likelihood of successfully doing so. One might raise research standards across the board. One might set higher criteria for admission to the field. One might indoctrinate the young scientist in the significance of absolute honesty to the survival of the enterprise. One might be more conscientious in peer review. One might institutionalize replication, if only as part of the training of students. Or one might seek to reason beyond the behaviors to the root causes.

Whatever our strategy, we must, above all, it seems to me, attempt to return balance to the system. That is, we must recognize that the house of science is a complex community with many different responsibilities to be discharged, and accordingly provide attractive incentives for activities other than the lemminglike rush toward a research reputation. I have no illusions about how difficult this would be to accomplish. However, as long as scholars are required to raise a significant portion of their annual institutional salaries through hustling grants and contracts and as long as the job security of the young among us depends less on the competence with which they discharge their responsibilities as educators and more on the frantic race toward stardom, there will be unhealthy competition and secrecy and with them fraud and other unhappy practices.

IS THERE LIFE FOR PSYCHOLOGY AFTER FRAGMENTATION?

What of fragmentation? Is there anything we can do about it? I am not certain that there is. Both Tyler (1981) and Neisser (1981) suggest the importance of new models. The former gives special attention to Probabilistic Functionalism, Contextualism, and General Systems Theory as perspectives that free us from the tyranny of the machine model. The latter similarly stresses the importance of new and fundamentally biological metaphors. I share their bias. However, as we outgrow the machine, we must be wary of what John Ruskin once called "rogue words," other concepts that tend to deceive through their ability to appeal to our need to simplify and integrate. Still, as Sir Hubert Read (1967), the noted British art and literary historian, pointed out some years ago, the world moves ahead through the strength of a few simple ideas and, as Toulmin (1972) contends, the abandonment of the great philosophical themes that once were the preoccupation of scientists—Max Born's "iridescent fancies of metaphysics"—is indeed denying us the benefit of clarifying and innovating new insights.

Meanwhile, my own anxiety derives in part from the force of Koch's contention that psychology is a collection of apples and oranges, a few of which may qualify as science while the greater number clearly better fit other intellectual molds. If this is the case, and I am increasingly inclined to admit that it may be, then we have no unifying assumptions relating either to substance or to method. Koch (1980) seems content to accept these specialized "language communities" with the hope that the future will yield broader, more flexible, and more revealing perspectives than we now enjoy. He has pleaded for a more humane philosophy that will make us at once both accepting of our lot and more excited by the adventure that can lie ahead. Granting the reasonableness of Koch's position, I nevertheless believe with Gleitman (personal communication 1983) that "there is still need for a central disclipine that continues questioning and keeps alive the initial questions about the nature of the human mind and the human passions that underlie the entire enterprise from its inception millennia ago."

I would suggest two remedial strategies worthy of serious attention, one relating to the individual scholar, the other to the institutional structure of our enterprise. David Daiches (1963), the distinguished British humanist, some twenty years ago made much of our need to search for linkages between Koch's language communities. He warned that this would be the most demanding intellectual task that we could face and stressed his view that already-existing fields can be used as "bridge subjects." These bridge subjects, he contended, should be the growth points in university curricula today. Such a commitment would, of course, require that at least some subset of the scholarly community be trained in more than one of Koch's languages.

In an earlier paper (Bevan 1980), I made much of the need for a radical change in our style of graduate education and proposed a flexible integration of the historical strengths of liberal education and the professional school. Along with this must go postdoctoral education that broadens perspectives and skills rather than narrows them. This means creating more generalists and institutionalizing a rewarding career alternative for them. This is easier said than done, for one cannot simply train two classes of people, specialists and generalists. To attempt to do so is to overlook one very important fact, namely, that the complex nature of any field of modern scholarship precludes effective general education that is not at the same time education in depth. Somehow we have to devise ways of creating individuals who, in the face of this bewildering circumstance, are capable of performing both roles, and this is as much a matter of style and perspective as it is of substance. A. T. Poffenberger used to advise his

Columbia graduate students to read broadly but "to get in a rut experimentally." He argued that the probability of contributing significantly to any one field is small but that by thinking about psychology in the broadest possible terms one might preserve one's perspective (Liebowitz, personal communication 1984). Similarly, I believe that the history, philosophy, and sociology of science and of our particular science are especially important "bridge subjects," although they are given scant attention in the typical graduate curriculum of today.

Finally, I believe that we must also go beyond the level of the individual to that of the institution if we are to expect any sort of success. Higham (1979) has made clear that specialization has not only profoundly affected the character of American intellectual life but has restructured the institutions that serve American education and scholarship as well. The university department, for example, is a reflection of the narrowing focus of scholarship that was already apparent in the nineteenth century. Without present space to specify details let me simply say that it is now time to take a fresh look at the whole network of institutions and connections that constitute the academy and link it to the larger society.

Whatever the answer to our future, to seek to understand a continuously evolving social enterprise like psychology in the 1980s, to plot its complexity in such a way as to seek a way out of labyrinths rather than into them will require a kind of faith, hard work, and staying power that I hope we psychologists are all capable of. Moreover, as I have suggested earlier, I firmly belief that the problem is more than one of individual scholarly habits and the modes of their institutionalization. It is at root a matter of the motivation and values of the individual scholarly practitioner and the collectivity of which he or she is a part. The integrity of the university lies in the idea of community. Fragmentation is both the result and the cause of our loss of community. Within the past roughly thirty-five years, we have seen the university drifting toward near anarchism, the philosophy that any form of institutional governance, no matter what, interferes unjustly with individual liberty and therefore need not be accepted. Thus, I believe, with Nisbet (1971, 215), that community cannot be restored until the university is able to create again some system of authority such as it had down until the end of the fifties. For, as Nisbet makes clear in his splendid book, the distinctiveness of the university as an institution has never lain in what it has taught and studied, but rather it rests in its unique structure of authority, legitimated by the tradition of reason and knowledge, that has functioned effectively, generation after generation.

I have proposed an explanation that is situational in character for what I view to be the excessive specialization of current scholarship and its untoward consequences. I have focused on the climate of the modern university and on the project method of funding research as the chief determinants of much that I regard to be unhealthy about the present research enterprise. But there is another perspective. Increasingly often these days I note reference to the zoological metaphor applied by Sir Isiah Berlin (1953) in his now famous essay on Tolstoy's view of history. Drawing his inspiration from an ancient Greek fragment, Berlin describes humankind as consisting of two varieties of person: those who know many things, the foxes; and those who know one big thing, the hedgehogs. The foxes have a wide and versatile knowledge at the level of individual events; the hedgehog insists on making order out of diversity, on imposing a world view upon first-hand experience. Richard Rovere, discussing his own temperament in his last book of essays (1984), diagnoses himself as a fox. Jerome Bruner (1983) in his recent autobiography does likewise. The latter talks of having a syntagmatic rather than a paradigmatic mind. In reflecting on Paul Lazersfeld's scholarly career, Johada recently (1979) described him as a fox forced by circumstances to behave like a hedgehog.

The Berlin typology as it now stands implies several things. First, that class differences are constitutional—that is, biological, for foxes and hedgehogs are different species. And second, that they differ in multiply significant ways: one type pursues many ends, the other is guided by a single organizing principle; one deals with events at their surface, the other looks for the underyling unifying theme; one seeks the significant universals, for the other, this matters less. Indeed, the dichotomy, one versus many, is confounded by the difference, greater versus lesser, and my personal experience within the scientific community leads me to conclude that the critical distinction is, in fact, one versus many. The style of researching that I see most often involves beating a single problem to death, with little thought to its significance. I once had a colleague who devoted his entire research career to the study of transfer of training through rotating a finger maze through various degrees of arc on the test trial. Sociologists of science have recently turned their attention to the sociological outcomes of adopting one rather than the other style of problem choice. Gieryn (1979), for example, reports that hedgehogs are, on the average, better recognized than foxes, while Cozzens (1983) suggests that foxes are more likely to have a wider set of contacts in multiple research networks.

Freeman Dyson has recently introduced a different nomenclature for the Berlin types (Miller 1984), one with which I feel far more comfortable. He calls them diversifiers and unifiers and says science needs both. By labeling them as he does, he sidesteps the question of their origin and at the same time prompts a whole series of fascinating questions. Why, for example, do diversifiers dominate present-day science? Is there a relationship between the prevalence of diversifiers and the persistence of normative science? Am I right in my guess about the impact of the sociology of the university and the politics of the funding process upon the character of present-day science? Whatever the case, I suspect that when we know more than we now do about the sociology of the research enterprise we will likely find that foxes and hedgehogs are made not born.

Psychology Yesterday, Today, and Tomorrow

My agenda for this chapter includes one further item requiring comment. Knowing what psychology has been over the course of the last century, can we anticipate what it will be like in the years ahead? Certainly not over the next one hundred. Indeed, I am neither so bold nor so innocent as to think seriously that I can reliably predict the future even to the turn of the century, some seventeen years away. I think Popper (1962, 1–8) is basically right in his attitude toward what he calls historicism, namely, the assumption that the future follows from the past as a matter of historical necessity. I am skeptical that one can make long-range predictions where the long course of history is concerned. The great value that does derive from a knowledge and understanding of history lies rather in its benefits to other aspects of scholarship.

In organizing myself to do my best in speculating about the next five to ten years, I have had access to a number of reports in addition to my own various acquaintenceships within psychology. There have been, for example, the recent volumes of the *Annual Review of Psychology,* in which the opening chapter of each volume has been especially helpful; the National Research Council's 1982 overview of behavioral and social science research (Adams, Smelser, and Treiman 1982); the Institute of Medicine's study of health and behavior (Hamburg, Elliott, and Parron 1982); and the not-yet-released report to the director of the National Institute of Mental Health concerning behavioral science research in mental health (Behavioral Science Research Review Panel 1983). All were helpful, but I came away from my reading of them feeling that some at least were designed as much to persuade and to advocate as to take stock.

Three works, on the other hand, have caught me up short. In one, a paper by R. M. Cooper (1982) in *Canadian Psychology,* the author, a physiological psychologist, frankly declares psychology a failure and predicts that such biological science as takes place within it can not expect to flourish. Cooper's disaffection results from his conviction that psychology fails both the methodological standards and the standards for achievement in the physical and biological sciences and from the real tensions between both the methods and the perspective of experimental psychology and present-day neurobiology. In the second paper, also by a Canadian, the author, this time a clinical psychologist, echoes Cooper's conclusion but for different reasons (Conway 1984). Conway's concern results, in contrast to Cooper's, both from his judgment that too much of what passes for psychological research is, for the clinician's purpose, simple-minded, superficial, and irrelevant and from his conviction that the positivism that typically underlies it is overly narrow and confining. Psychology as a discipline, he feels, is not enough like the arts and humanities to be of value to clinical practice. In the third publication, the first of the five-year overviews of American science mandated by the National Science and Technology Policy, Organization, and Priorities Act of 1976 (National Research Council 1979), psychology is conspicuous by its absence. In a book of 544 pages, the word *psychology* appears neither in the table of contents nor in the index. In only two places is anything covered with which we psychologists can identify as a field. There are about twenty pages on the neurosciences in a chapter on the life sciences and ten pages on the biobehavioral sciences and mental illness in a chapter on health.

Since the 1960s, general-experimental psychology has been dominated, as I have indicated, by psychobiology on the one hand and by the psychology of cognition on the other. Within each, the domain is marked by rather narrowly focused special interests. Otherwise, psychology, over all, is characterized by a strong preoccupation with application. Psychologists being people and people being what they are, I cannot see this recipe changing radically or rapidly for the field as a whole in the immediate future. Viewed in the broader context, it tells us several things about how social dynamics affect institutional outcome. First, psychology, like every other intellectual enterprise of which I am aware, reflects the societal themes and pressures of our time. For example, both the relative vigor of different areas of specialization and the present broad emphasis on application strongly reflect the priorities and the philosophy of the major sponsors of research. Second, psychology cannot subsist independent of any of a wide variety of other fields—computer science, a number of the branches of biology (the neurosciences, biochemistry, pharmacology, evolutionary theory, embryology, perhaps even immunology), linguistics, economics, sociology, policy studies, history, and, of course, philosophy in its various manifestations. This interdependence displays itself not only in the nature of psychology's intellectual content but in the character of its successful application as well. Human-factors psychology, for example, provides ready illustrations of the latter. Third, psychology's dependence upon external developments may be too great for its own good as the enterprise we now know. The ascendance of biopsychology provides convenient evidence for the last proposition, for its impressive development over the last decade or two has been attributable in no small measure to what has happened in a number of the biomedical sciences, not the least of which have been the developments in neurochemistry and neuropharmacology and the arrival of the newer noninvasive clinical and research technologies like computer-assisted tomography, positron emission tomography, and nuclear magnetic resonance.

Guion (personal communication 1983) and Amsel (personal communication 1983) are correct in their observations that what may be residual as present-day academic psychology is more like the psychology of a hundred years ago than like the psychology of, say, fifty years ago. Academic psychology has not only fragmented, but much that would otherwise be academic psychology has been incorporated into a variety of new disciplines or quasidisciplines. What is left of general-experimental psychology, Amsel has observed, is just about what it began with. It has come full circle. But there are differences. Sokal (personal communication 1983) has emphasized the cultural relativism that now prominently marks psychology as a whole and that has come to influence the scientific aspects of psychology as well, and Buxton (personal communication 1983) points out quite clearly how American academic psychology over the years has thoroughly acquired an evolutionary perspective, that is, the broad conviction that human beings are part of the biological scheme of things, developing and functioning in adaptive fashion. Thus, we should not be surprised that developmental psychology may become increasingly the glue that holds together what used to go under the label of general-experimental psychology. Developmental psychology can provide the context for acquiring basic data and at the same time is capable of generating essential political and economic support in a way that other areas of psychology at present can attract only with difficulty.

That psychology as an intellectual and social entity will hold together for the future is a matter of doubt in the minds of many with whom I have raised the question of fragmentation and its alternatives. The dominant view is that at least as far as the tradition of general-experimental psychology is concerned, its course has bifurcated and will run now in divergent directions, ultimately trickling down to nothing as psychologists take up membership in other disciplines. If, however, you allow me Gleitman's hunch that psychology is not headed for total disintegration, then there is an alternative way of looking at things that is more hopeful.

OF FOXES AND HEDGEHOGS

You will recall that on an earlier page I expressed my personal reservation about the ultimate usefulness to psychology of the attractive Kuhnian model. A more congenial strategy, I believe, is to conceptualize the evolution of ideas that shape our intellectual history in terms of multiple oscillating trends—principally two, the cognitive and the mechanistic—each of which perhaps possesses a different periodicity. These concurrent trends wax and wane in the extent to which each can command our thinking at any particular moment in time. The cognitive and the mechanistic explanatory strategies have together been part of our history for a very long time, and if one looks at them in narrow cross-section at just the right moment in time the impression given can, of course, be that of the paradigm shift. If one accepts this perspective, then one's overriding challenge becomes one of discovering how to bring them into phase in order to achieve what Posner (personal communication 1984) calls "a developmental portrait of how a maturing nervous system is socialized to support particular forms of cognition." When one looks to the physical sciences for intellectual strategies, it is important to remember that there is no rule against employing alternative strategies to deal with different settings. For example, we remember from our high-school introduction to physical optics that the properties of light may be treated alternatively in either undulate or corpuscular terms, depending on the scientific purpose to be served.

Some years ago, while browsing in a second-hand book store, I came upon a little book on the history of science that continues to console me as I view the course of intellectual development in our science. The title of the book is *The Path of Science*, the author is C. E. K. Mees, and the central thesis is that the fundamental questions of a science always remain the same and that in attempting to answer them, scientists, with each successive attempt, are brought full circle but at a higher conceptual level and with a greater treasury of data. This course of conceptual development may thus be graphically described as a helix. If we are in fact back to where we were, we are there at a far more insightful level. We at present know a great deal more than our intellectual ancestors did about the nature of sensory and perceptual events, about language, and about the way the brain and nervous system work, among other things. As we confront the fact of functional interdependence, we shall begin again to ask questions concerning motivation, learning, and emotion. Indeed, there are indications that we are, in fact, beginning to do so. Interest in social cognition is growing; so is interest in what is now being called "hot cognition." And, prompted by a general concern for the effectiveness of the public schools, questions concerning learning are again receiving attention from experimental psychologists, albeit now in quite a different way.

PARADIGMS REVISITED

Work during the last decade and a half by philosophers of science other than Kuhn is raising serious questions about how faithfully the Kuhnian paradigm fits the history of science. Chief among its difficulties have been the assumptions that paradigms are incommensurable and monopolistic, i.e., the view that (a) paradigm shifts represent discontinuities between incomparable explanatory frameworks and that (b) when a given explanatory framework is in force, it brooks no exception. Nearer to the actual state of affairs, as I have suggested, is the fact that multiple competing orientations can exist side-by-side; that, indeed, competing views can emerge from within the same conceptual tradition; that elements of competing conceptual traditions can, over time, even be melded; and that transitions may have a more continuous quality than the Kuhnian perspective has allowed. An alternative perspective that seeks to deal with the historical realities more adequately has been presented by Lakatos (cf., eg., 1978) and refined by Laudan (cf., eg., 1981). Gholson and Barker (1985), in a philosophical analysis that covers a significant sample of the major episodes in the history of general-experimental psychology between the thirties and the present, make a convincing case for the promise of this post-Kuhnian approach. Time precludes a discussion of their argument but I commend their paper to you.

PSYCHOLOGY AND THE UNIFIED WELTBILD

This chapter makes no pretense to scholarship. It is rather the rambling—although I would vigorously insist not random—thoughts born of a forty-year fascination with what psychology purports to be and a growing uneasiness concerning what it may become. I do not believe that salvation lies with the blinkered empiricism that has marked the last roughly thirty years any more than it did with the self-conscious preoccupation during the previous thirty with theories that were, in point of fact, no theories in the physical scientist's sense at all. However, I would argue that whatever our destiny, we will be in better shape along the way if we incorporate into our ways of thinking greater attention to our intellectual and social history and to the contribution such considerations can make to the quality and depth of our understanding. I remind you of my opening comment. Much of what I have said you may have perceived as doomsaying. But underneath the gloom there has been, as I also insisted, a stubborn optimism for, in my view, psychologists and other high-wire artists have no alternative but to be optimists.

Moreover, if we look in the right places, we must surely find genuine grounds for hope. Two, indeed, lie, I believe, right under our noses. By the mid 1970s, physical and biological scientists had begun to shift from narrow disciplinary concerns to interests shared across disciplines. At the present time, a new conceptualization of the scientist's role—a change from arm's-length observer of nature to shaper of natural events—has begun to emerge and with this latter circumstance we have begun to see a blurring of the institutional lines between pure and applied science and between understanding and practice. We have also begun to see the drive toward understanding being tempered by a commitment to ethical concerns. What took place in the physical and biological sciences in the decade of the seventies we can begin to claim for the behavioral sciences in the eighties. The new nomenclature with which we are all becoming familiar demonstrates the change: health psychology, psycholinguistics, psychobiology, behavioral neuroscience, behavioral neuroendocrinology, psychoneuroimmunology, human engineering, industrial-organizational psychology, humanistic psychology—again, etc., etc., etc.

Psychology may very well be entering what Toulmin (1982) and others have called the postmodern period, and one consideration that prompts my own optimism is Toulmin's contention that this transition, and the broader, more flexible perspective that results from it, can stimulate a return to the great cosmological questions that have fascinated our more imaginative and adventuresome minds in the past. But, if Toulmin is right, it will be cosmology with a difference, for it will, as he says, incorporate human agents into the natural world and put back together the whole that science, over the past three hundred years, has rent asunder. It will be a cosmology in which *order* and *design* as characterizing nouns will be joined by *evolution* and *adaptation* and in which psychology must therefore inevitably assume a significant role. My growing discontent with psychology over the past several decades stems, as you now know, from my perception that too many psychologists hug the intellectual shoreline and are content to paddle quietly on their own small ponds. We live in a coherent world, though one of never ending complexity. The big questions about it will never be answered if scholars simply attend to the comfortable little questions, no matter how important this latter exercise might in itself be. The deepest intellectual aim of fundamental scholarship in any science still remains that of seeking, to borrow Holton's language, a "logically unified and parsimoniously constructed system of thought" (Holton 1981, 23). Robert Browning, the great nineteenth-century poet laureate, once described his interests as lying on the "dangerous edge of things." His phrase is an apt one. Living at the dangerous edge of things is what psychologists should be doing as they enter the new postmodern world.

The Journey Is Everything

I had first planned to title these observations "Is There Life for Psychology after Fragmentation?" to reflect my apprehension about the unfortunate side of our professionalization. But this struck me as a bit flip for my role as statesman and I began searching for something rather more dignified, something like "Professionalism, Intellectual Structure, and the Character of Scholarship in Psychology after 100 Years." Midway through this search I read a poem by my Duke colleague, essayist Helen Bevington, and changed my mind. The poem is titled "The Journey Is Everything" (Bevington 1983, 3) and the first two triplets run as follows:

Montaigne believed the journey, in itself,
Was the idea. Yet from this moving plane
I look down on the dazzle of the world,

Conscious of his words but wondering
When, when shall I be there, at journey's end?
The journey, said Montaigne, *is everything.*

In finding meaning in this final assertion, I insist that I am not adopting an Alex Guinness, stiff-upper-lip kind of stoicism. Quite the contrary, I am emphasizing that, whatever one's concerns for outcomes may be, there are compensating delights in the pursuit of psychology itself that, after all is said and done, make anyone's lifetime commitment to it worthwhile. Sometime ago, I had occasion to read Whitehead's 1925 lecture on the then state of cosmology. One paragraph in particular has stuck with me, for it recites eloquently what must be the credo of every dweller in that quotidian world devoted to impossible ambitions and elemental questions.

> There is no parting from your own shadow. To experience this faith is to know that in being ourselves we are more than ourselves: to know that our experience, dim and fragmentary as it is, yet sounds the utmost depths of reality: to know the detached details merely in order to be themselves demand that they should find themselves in a system of things: to know that this sytem includes the harmony of logical rationality, and the harmony of aesthetic achievement: to know that, while the harmony of logic lies upon the universe as an iron necessity, the aesthetic harmony stands before it as a living ideal molding the general flux in its broken progress toward fairer, subtler issues. (Whitehead 1925, 23–24)

In a scene late in the recent successful Broadway play, *Agnes of God,* the mother superior of the convent where Agnes lives, struggling to protect the emotionally disturbed young novice, debates with the psychiatrist appointed by the court to evaluate her. At issue is whether parthenogenesis could have occured in Agnes's case. The nun says, "You'll never find the answer to everything, Doctor. One and one is two, yes, but that leads to four and then to eight and soon to infinity. The wonder of science is not in the answers it provides but in the questions it uncovers. For every miracle it finally explains, ten thousand more miracles come into being" (Pielmeier 1982, 62).

When we look at psychology and at ourselves as psychologists in 1983, we most certainly recognize that as we have advanced our academic enterprise we have also accelerated specialization and fostered a technological frame of mind at the expense of one that is broadly historical and philosophical. We have in point of fact denigrated the currency of general ideas. If then this constitutes, as I have suggested, an unhealthy imbalance, it cannot be rectified by recognition of that fact alone but only by a fierce and constant will to locate our specialized knowledge and insight, whatever it may be, within some significantly broader philosophical, historical, and— may I add?—moral perspective. Meanwhile, the journey *is* indeed everything!

Acknowledgments

I stand greatly in debt to the persons whose names follow. As I found myself long past the 1983 summer solstice and still not yet in high gear in the preparation of this chapter, I felt greatly in need of checking my own thoughts, their being selected and prepared for the present recipe, with those of others. Accordingly, I prepared a series of discussion questions that I felt cut to the heart of my intended manuscript and submitted them to a number of colleagues that I had reason to believe had, of late, been thinking of such matters. Their responses were gratifying: thoughtful, careful, displaying immense scholarship, infinitely patient, and mercifully prompt. They have had a strong influence on what I have written and each will recognize his or her contribution in the ideas that I have selected for inclusion, in the general tone of my observations, and even in my phraseology.

I take this opportunity to express my deeply felt thanks to Abram Amsel, Ludy T. Benjamin, Lyle E. Bourne, Jr., Claude E. Buxton, Charles N. Cofer, Rochel Gelman, Henry Gleitman, Robert M. Guion, Eliot Hearst, Lloyd G. Humphreys, William Kessen, Herschel W. Leibowitz, George Mandler, James Grier Miller, Carl Pfaffmann, Michael T. Posner, Charles E. Rice, Arthur J. Riopelle, Daniel N. Robinson, Sandra Scarr, Michael M. Sokal, and Delos D. Wickens.

Following oral presentation of the initial draft, I sent copies to another sample of colleagues requesting comments. I greatly appreciate the thoughtful observations of the following persons: Abram Amsel, Mortimer H. Appley, Lyle E. Bourne, Jr., Roger Brown, Alphonse Chapanis, John B. Conway, W. D. Davies, Doris R. Entwisle, Henry Gleitman, Bert F. Green, Ernest R. Hilgard, Stewart H. Hulse, Herschel W. Leibowitz, James Grier Miller, Michael T. Posner, A. Kenneth Pye, Charles E. Rice, Daniel N. Robinson, Seymour B. Sarason, Jan D. Sinnott, Michael M. Sokal, Richard F. Thompson, Richard D. Walk, and Hilda Wing.

References

Adams, G. *Psychology: Science or superstition?* New York: Covici-Friede, 1931.

Adams, R. M., Smelser, N. J., & Treiman, D. J. (Eds.). *Behavioral and social science research: A national resource.* Washington, DC: National Academy Press, 1982.

Aristotle. *On the art of poetry.* Translated by I. Bywater. Oxford: Oxford University Press, 1920, pp. 39–41, 79–81.

Behavioral Sciences Research Review Panel. *Behavioral sciences research in mental health. An assessment of the state of the science and recommendations for research directions.* Rockville, MD: National Institute of Mental Health, June 1983.

Berlin, I. *The hedgehog and the fox.* New York: Simon & Schuster, 1953.

Bevan, W. Graduate education for the earthquake generation. *Human Development,* 1980, *23,* 126–136.

Bevington, H. *The journey is everything.* Durham, NC: Duke University Press, 1983.

Bledstein, B. *The culture of professionalism.* New York: Norton, 1976.

Bok, S. *Secrets. On the ethics of concealment and revelation.* New York: Pantheon Books, 1983.

Broad, W., & Wade, N. *Betrayers of the truth. Fraud and deceit in the halls of science.* New York: Simon & Schuster, 1982.

Bruner, J. *In search of mind: Essays in autobiography.* New York: Harper & Row, 1983.

Canary, R. H., & Kozicki, H. (Eds.). *The writing of history.* Madison: University of Wisconsin Press, 1981.

Conway, J. B. A place for discontent and tensions in psychology. *Canadian Psychology,* 1984, *25,* 96–104.

Cooper, R. M. The passing of psychology. *Canadian Psychology,* 1982, *23,* 264–267.

Cozzens, S. E. The internal structure of problem sets: A closer look. *4S Review,* 1983, *1,* 4, 41–42.

Daiches, D. The university curriculum and the idea of the unity of knowledge. *Advancement of Science,* July 1963, 128–132.

Eliot, T. S. *The complete poems and plays, 1909–1950.* New York: Harcourt Brace Jovanovich, 1971.

Ellmann, R., & O'Clair, R. (Eds.). *The Norton anthology of modern poetry.* New York: Norton, 1973.

Gholson, B., & Barker, P. Kuhn, Lakatos, and Laudan: Applications in history of physics and psychology. *American Psychologist,* 1985, *40,* 755–769.

Gieryn, T. F. *Hedgehogs and foxes: Style of problem choice in science.* Paper presented at the Meeting of the Midwest Sociological Society, Minneapolis, April 1979.

Gilgen, A. R. *American psychology since World War II: A profile of the discipline.* Westport, CT: Greenwood Press, 1982.

Giorgi, A. *Psychology as a human science: A phenomenologically based approach.* London: Harper, 1970.

Gould, S. J. *The mismeasure of man.* New York: Norton, 1981.

Hamburg, D. A., Elliott, G. R., & Parron, D. L. (Eds.). *Health and behavior: Frontiers of research in the biobehavioral sciences.* Washington, DC: National Academy Press, 1982.

Hearnshaw, L. S. *Cyril Burt, psychologist.* Ithaca, NY: Cornell University Press, 1979.

Higham, J. The matrix of specialization. In A. Oleson & J. Voss (Eds.), *The organization of knowledge in modern America, 1860–1920.* Baltimore: Johns Hopkins University Press, 1979.

Hilgard, E. R. (Ed.). *American psychology in historical perspective.* Washington, DC: American Psychological Association, 1978.

Holton, G. Thematic presuppositions and the direction of scientific advance. In Heath, A. F. *Scientific Explanation.* Oxford: Clarendon Press, 1981, 1–27.

Housman, A. E. Into my heart an air that kills. In R. Ellmann and R. O'Clair (Eds.), *The Norton anthology of modern poetry.* New York: W. W. Norton & Co., 1973, 99.

Johada, M. Hedgehog or fox? In R. K. Merton, J. S. Coleman, and P. H. Rossi (Eds.), *Qualitative and quantitative social research.* Papers in honor of Paul F. Lazersfeld. New York: Free Press, 1979, 3–9.

Kilbourne, B. K., & Kilbourne, M. T. *The dark side of science.* San Francisco: Pacific Division, American Association for the Advancement of Science, 1983.

Koch, S. Psychology cannot be a coherent science. *Psychology Today,* 1969, *3*(4), 14, 64–66.

Koch, S. A possible psychology for a possible postpositivist world. *Psychology in a postpositivist world—three perspectives.* Symposium conducted at the meeting of the American Psychological Association Montreal, September 5, 1980.

Koch, S. Reflections on the state of psychology. *Social Research,* 1971, *38,* 669–709.

Koch, S. Language communities, search cells, and the psychological studies. In W. J. Arnold (Ed.), *Nebraska Symposium on Motivation* (Vol. 23), 1975. Lincoln: University of Nebraska Press, 1976.

Koch, S. The nature and limits of psychological knowledge: Lessons of a century qua "science." *American Psychologist,* 1981, *36,* 257–269.

Kuhn, T. *The structure of scientific revolutions.* Chicago: University of Chicago Press, 1962.

Lakatos, I. *The methodology of scientific research programs.* Cambridge: Cambridge University Press, 1978.

Laudan, L. *Science and hypothesis.* Boston: Reidel, 1981.

Levi, E. H. The crisis in the nature of the law. *The Record of the Association of the Bar,* City of New York, March 1970, 3–23.

May, H. F. The other American tradition. In H. F. May (Ed.), *Ideas, faiths, and feelings: Essays on American intellectual and religious history, 1952–1982.* New York: Oxford University Press, 1983, 52–64.

Mees, C. E. K. *The path of science.* New York: John Wiley & Sons, 1946.

Miller, J. Realist and visionary: Physicist Dyson preaches a logical sermon of hope. *Newsweek,* April 16, 1984, 84–85.

Miller, N. E. *Value and ethics of research on animals.* Invited address presented at the convention of the American Psychological Association, Anaheim, CA, August 29, 1983.

Milosz, C. *Bells in winter.* New York: Ecco Press, 1978.

Mink, L. O. Narrative form as a cognitive instrument. In R. H. Canary & H. Kozicki (Eds.), *The writing of history.* Madison: University of Wisconsin Press, 1981, 129–150.

Morrow, L. Thinking animal thoughts. *Time,* October 3, 1983, 50–51.

National Research Council. *Science and technology. A five-year outlook.* San Francisco: W. H. Freeman & Co., 1979.

Neisser, U. *Psychology and society.* The Miller Lecture presented at the University of Illinois, October 20, 1981.

Nisbet, R. *The degradation of the academic dogma: The university in America, 1945–1970.* New York: Basic Books, 1971.

Orwell, G. Politics and the English language. In G. Orwell (Ed.), *A collection of essays.* New York: Harcourt Brace Jovanovich, 1946, 156–171.

Persons, S. *The decline of American gentility.* New York: Columbia University Press, 1973.

Pielmeier, J. *Agnes of God.* New York: Samuel French, 1982.

Popper, K. R. *The open society and its enemies* (Vol. 1). Chicago: University of Chicago Press, 1962.

Quinton, A. Character and culture. *New Republic,* October 17, 1983, 26–30.

Read, H. Whatever happened to the simplicities. *Saturday Review,* February 18, 1967, 21–23, 48–49.

Robinson, D. N. *An intellectual history of psychology.* New York: Macmillan, 1976.

Robinson, D. N. *Systems of modern psychology.* New York: Columbia University Press, 1979.

Robinson, D. N. *Toward a science of human nature.* New York: Columbia University Press, 1982.

Rosenzweig, M. R. Trends in development and status of psychology: An international perspective. *International Journal of Psychology,* 1982, *17,* 117–140.

Rovere, Richard. *Final report.* New York: Doubleday, 1984.

Samelson, F. J. B. G. D. Watson's little Albert, Cyril Burt's twins, and the need for a critical science. *American Psychologist,* 1980, *35,* 619–625.

Samelson, F. Struggle for scientific authority: The reception of Watson's behaviorism, 1913–1920. *Journal of the History of the Behavioral Sciences,* 1981, *17,* 399–425.

Sarason, S. *Psychology misdirected.* New York: Free Press, 1981.

Spencer, H. *The story of sociology.* Ann Arbor: University of Michigan Press, 1961.

Toulmin, S. E. *And shall we have science forever and ever?* Invited lecture, 139th meeting of the American Association for the Advancement of Science, Washington, D.C., December 30, 1972.

Toulmin, S. *Human understanding.* Princeton, NJ: Princeton University Press, 1972.

Toulmin, S. The Mozart of psychology. *New York Review of Books,* September 28, 1978, 51–57.

Toulmin, S. *The return to cosmology.* Berkeley and Los Angeles: University of California Press, 1982.

Tyler, L. More stately mansions: Psychology extends its boundaries. *Annual Review of Psychology,* 1981, *32,* 1–20.

White, H. The historical text as literary artifact. In R. H. Canary & H. Kozicki

(Eds.), *The writing of history.* Madison: University of Wisconson Press, 1981, 41–62.

Whitehead, A. N. *Science and the modern world.* New York: Macmillan, 1925.

Will, G. F. *Statecraft as soulcraft.* New York: Simon & Schuster, 1983.

Zuckerman, H. Deviant behavior and social control in science. In E. Sagarin (Ed.), *Deviance and social change.* New York: Sage, 1977, 87–138.

G. Stanley Hall Centennial Contributors

Anonymous
AT&T
Baenninger, Ronald
Banks, William
Becker, Jim
Berninger, Ginger
Blumberg, Herbert
Bohannon, Wayne
Bond, Lloyd
Bosley, John
Carlson, Virgil
Cheek, Jonathan
Collyer, Stanley
Cramer, Elliott
Exxon Education Foundation
Friedberg, Sidney
Gage, Rusty
Gilmore, Grover
Gordon, Barry
Gottfredson, Stephen
Green, Bert F.
Grill, Donna
Haier, Richard
Hall, Warren
Hamill, Bruce
Handel, Stephen
Hock, Howard
Horowitz, Leonard
Hulse, Stewart H.

Imai, Shiro
Jacewitz, Marion
Kingsbury, Nancy
Kolsrud, Gretchen
Krueger, Gerald
Kurtines, William
Lawrence Erlbaum Associates, Inc.
Leuba, Harald
Lipsey, Mark
Macht, Martin
McGraw-Hill Book Company
Monrad, Diane
Murphy, Robert
Osler, Sonia
Pedersen, Patricia
Rotberg, Iris
Santee, Jeff
Scarpa, Lorraine
Sen, Tapas
Snodgrass, Stephen
Stanley, Julian
Sweet, Alex
Teitelbaum, Philip
Van Hemel, Paul
Van Hemel, Susan
Walker, John
Wall, Sally
Wing, Hilda
Yates, Jack B.

Name Index

Subject Index